Communicating Early English Manuscripts

In an obvious way, manuscripts communicate. This is the first book to focus on the communicative aspects of English manuscripts from the fourteenth to the nineteenth centuries. It investigates how the authors and scribes of these manuscripts communicated with their audiences, how the characters depicted in these manuscripts communicate with each other, and how the manuscripts communicate with scholars and audiences in the twenty-first century. It covers a wide variety of genres, such as stories, scientific writing, witchcraft records, personal letters, war correspondence, courtroom records and plays. The volume demonstrates how these handwritten texts can be used to analyse the history of language as communication between individuals and groups, and discusses the challenges these documents present to present-day scholars. It is unique in bringing together studies by distinguished international experts examining primary handwritten sources from the perspectives of several fields, including historical pragmatics, historical sociolinguistics, corpus linguistics and literary scholarship.

PÄIVI PAHTA is Professor of English Philology in the School of Modern Languages and Translation Studies at the University of Tampere.

ANDREAS H. JUCKER is Professor of English Linguistics at the University of Zurich.

STUDIES IN ENGLISH LANGUAGE

General editor
Merja Kytö (Uppsala University)

Editorial Board
Bas Aarts (University College London),
John Algeo (University of Georgia),
Susan Fitzmaurice (University of Sheffield),
Christian Mair (University of Freiburg),
Charles F. Meyer (University of Massachusetts)

The aim of this series is to provide a framework for original studies of English, both present-day and past. All books are based securely on empirical research, and represent theoretical and descriptive contributions to our knowledge of national and international varieties of English, both written and spoken. The series covers a broad range of topics and approaches, including syntax, phonology, grammar, vocabulary, discourse, pragmatics and sociolinguistics, and is aimed at an international readership.

Already published in this series:

Christain Mair: *Infinitival Complement Clauses in English: A Study of Syntax in Discourse*
Charles F. Meyer: *Apposition in Contemporary English*
Jan Firbas: *Functional Sentence Perspective in Written and Spoken Communication*
Izchak M. Schlesinger: *Cognitive Space and Linguistic Case*
Katie Wales: *Personal Pronouns in Present-Day English*
Laura Wright: *The Development of Standard English, 1300–1800: Theories, Descriptions, Conflicts*
Charles F. Meyer: *English Corpus Linguistics: Theory and Practice*
Stephen J. Nagle and Sara L. Sanders (eds.): *English in the Southern United States*
Anne Curzan: *Gender Shifts in the History of English*
Kingsley Bolton: *Chinese Englishes*
Irma Taavitsainen and Päivi Pahta (eds.): *Medical and Scientific Writing in Late Medieval English*
Elizabeth Gordon, Lyle Campbell, Jennifer Hay, Margaret Maclagan, Andrea Sudbury and Peter Trudgill: *New Zealand English: Its Origins and Evolution*
Raymond Hickey (ed.): *Legacies of Colonial English*
Merja Kytö, Mats Rydén and Erik Smitterberg (eds.): *Nineteenth Century English: Stability and Change*

John Algeo: *British or American English? A Handbook of Word and Grammar Patterns*
Christian Mair: *Twentieth-Century English: History, Variation and Standardization*
Evelien Keizer: *The English Noun Phrase: The Nature of Linguistic Categorization*
Raymond Hickey: *Irish English: History and Present-Day Forms*
Günter Rohdenburg and Julia Schlüter (eds.): *One Language, Two Grammars? Differences between British and American English*
Laurel J. Brinton: *The Comment Clause in English*
Lieselotte Anderwald: *The Morphology of English Dialects: Verb Formation in Non-standard English*
Geoffrey Leech, Marianne Hundt, Christian Mair and Nicholas Smith: *Change in Contemporary English: A Grammatical Study*
Jonathan Culpeper and Merja Kytö: *Early Modern English Dialogues: Spoken Interaction as Writing*
Daniel Schreier, Peter Trudgill, Edgar Schneider and Jeffrey Williams: *The Lesser-Known Varieties of English: An Introduction*
Hilde Hasselgård: *Adjunct Adverbials in English*
Raymond Hickey: *Eighteenth-Century English: Ideology and Change*
Charles Boberg: *The English Language in Canada: Status, History and Comparative Analysis*
Thomas Hoffmann: *Preposition Placement in English: A Usage-based Approach*
Claudia Claridge: *Hyperbole in English: A Corpus-based Study of Exaggeration*

Communicating Early English Manuscripts

Edited by
PÄIVI PAHTA
University of Tampere

and

ANDREAS H. JUCKER
University of Zurich

CAMBRIDGE UNIVERSITY PRESS

CAMBRIDGE UNIVERSITY PRESS
Cambridge, New York, Melbourne, Madrid, Cape Town, Singapore,
São Paulo, Delhi, Dubai, Tokyo, Mexico City

Cambridge University Press
The Edinburgh Building, Cambridge CB2 8RU, UK

Published in the United States of America by Cambridge University Press,
New York

www.cambridge.org
Information on this title: www.cambridge.org/9780521193290

© Cambridge University Press 2011

This publication is in copyright. Subject to statutory exception
and to the provisions of relevant collective licensing agreements,
no reproduction of any part may take place without the written
permission of Cambridge University Press.

First published 2011

Printed in the United Kingdom at the University Press, Cambridge

A catalogue record for this publication is available from the British Library

Library of Congress Cataloguing in Publication data
Communicating early English manuscripts / edited by Päivi Pahta, Andreas H. Jucker.
   p.   cm. – (Studies in English language)
Includes bibliographical references and index.
ISBN 978-0-521-19329-0
1. Manuscripts, English – History   2. Manuscripts, English (Middle) – History.
3. Manuscripts, Medieval – England.   4. Authors and readers – England – History.
5. Transmission of texts – England – History.   6. English literature – Middle
English, 1100–1500 – History and criticism.   7. English literature – Early modern,
1500–1700 – History and criticism.   8. English letters – History and criticism.
9. English language – History.   10. Written communication – England – History.
I. Pahta, Päivi.   II. Jucker, Andreas H.   III. Title.   IV. Series.
Z106.5.G7C66   2011
091.09 – dc22   2010041663

ISBN 978-0-521-19329-0 Hardback

Cambridge University Press has no responsibility for the persistence or
accuracy of URLs for external or third-party internet websites referred to in
this publication, and does not guarantee that any content on such websites is,
or will remain, accurate or appropriate.

Contents

List of illustrations	page x
List of tables	xii
List of abbreviations	xiii
Notes on contributors	xiv
Preface	xxi

Introduction

1 Communicating manuscripts: authors, scribes, readers, listeners and communicating characters   3
   ANDREAS H. JUCKER AND PÄIVI PAHTA

Part I
Authors, scribes and their audiences

2 Commonplace-book communication: role shifts and text functions in Robert Reynes's notes contained in MS Tanner 407   13
   THOMAS KOHNEN

3 Textuality in late medieval England: two case studies   25
   GABRIELLA DEL LUNGO CAMICIOTTI

4 The significance of now-dispersed Bute 13: a mixed-language scientific manuscript   38
   PATRICIA DEERY KURTZ AND LINDA EHRSAM VOIGTS

5 Communicating attitudes and values through language choices: diatopic and diastratic variation in *Mary Magdalene* in MS Digby 133   55
   MAURIZIO GOTTI AND STEFANIA MACI

6 Constructing the audiences of the Old Bailey Trials 1674–1834   69
   ELIZABETH CLOSS TRAUGOTT

Part II
Communicating through handwritten correspondence

7 A defiant gentleman or 'the strengest thiefe of Wales': reinterpreting the politics in a medieval correspondence 83
MERJA STENROOS AND MARTTI MÄKINEN

8 Sociopragmatic aspects of person reference in Nathaniel Bacon's letters 102
MINNA PALANDER-COLLIN AND MINNA NEVALA

9 Poetic collaboration and competition in the late seventeenth century: George Stepney's letters to Jacob Tonson and Matthew Prior 118
SUSAN FITZMAURICE

10 Handwritten communication in nineteenth-century business correspondence 133
MARINA DOSSENA

Part III
From manuscript to print

11 The relationship between MS Hunter 409 and the 1532 edition of Chaucer's works edited by William Thynne 149
GRAHAM D. CAIE

12 The development of play-texts: from manuscript to print 162
JONATHAN CULPEPER AND JANE DEMMEN

13 Communicating Galen's *Methodus medendi* in Middle and Early Modern English 178
PÄIVI PAHTA, TURO HILTUNEN, VILLE MARTTILA, MAURA RATIA, CARLA SUHR AND JUKKA TYRKKÖ

14 Prepositional modifiers in early English medical prose: a study *on* their historical development *in* noun phrases 197
DOUGLAS BIBER, BETHANY GRAY, ALPO HONKAPOHJA AND PÄIVI PAHTA

15 The pragmatics of punctuation in Older Scots 212
JEREMY SMITH AND CHRISTIAN KAY

Part IV
Manuscripts and their communicating characters

16 Greetings and farewells in Chaucer's *Canterbury Tales*   229
    ANDREAS H. JUCKER

17 Attitudes of the accused in the Salem Witchcraft Trials   241
    LEENA KAHLAS-TARKKA AND MATTI RISSANEN

    Bibliography   259
    Index of manuscripts   283
    Index   284

List of illustrations

Plates

1. Sixteenth-century English translation of Johannes Schöner, 'Instructio intelligendae Ephemeridos', *Opusculum astrologicum*. Lawrence J. Schoenberg Collection, MS ljs 188, f. 1r. Reproduced with permission of Lawrence J. Schoenberg. *page* 40
2. Johannes Schöner, 'Instructio intelligendae Ephemeridos', *Opusculum astrologicum*, Nuremberg, 1539. A3r. Reproduced with permission of the Linda Hall Library of Science, Engineering & Technology, Kansas City, Missouri. 46
3. Fifteenth-century English translation of Bartholomaeus Mariensüss, commentary on the *Ephemerides* of Regiomontanus. Lawrence J. Schoenberg Collection, MS ljs 191, f.18v. Reproduced with permission of Lawrence J. Schoenberg. 48
4. Text in Bank of Scotland letter book no. NRAS945/1/146/44. Reproduced courtesy of Lloyds Banking Group plc Archives. 138
5. Glasgow University Library, MS Hunter 409 (V,3.7), f 115r. By permission of Glasgow University Library. 153
6. Glasgow University Library, MS Hunter 409 (V.3.7), f. 17v. By permission of Glasgow University Library. 154
7. Glasgow University Library, MS Hunter 409 (V.3.7), f. 145r. By permission of Glasgow University Library. 156

Figures

2.1 Patterns of role shift in text communication in Robert Reynes's commonplace book 17
13.1 Total word counts of the three English versions of *Methodus medendi*, Book 3 184
13.2 Word counts for the ten chapter equivalents in the three English versions of *Methodus medendi*, Book 3 185
13.3 Average sentence lengths in the three English versions of *Methodus medendi*, Book 3, and reference corpora 187

13.4	Average sentence lengths for the ten chapter equivalents in the three English versions of *Methodus medendi*, Book 3	187
14.1	Noun post-modifier types in medical prose, across periods	199
14.2	*In* as noun modifier versus other functions, across periods	203
14.3	*On* as noun modifier versus other functions, across periods	204
14.4	*In* as noun modifier: concrete versus abstract meanings	205
14.5.	*On* as noun modifier: concrete versus abstract meanings	205

List of tables

5.1	Breakdown of Southern ending *-en* in *Mary Magdalene*	page 63
5.2	Breakdown of plural present indicative forms in *Mary Magdalene*	65
7.1	A comparison of distinctive dialectal forms in the three letters	90
12.1	The present-day plays: five comedies, 1974–1984	169
12.2	The early modern plays: five comedies, 1594–1607	169
12.3	The present-day plays: number of words, turns and average number of words per turn	170
12.4	The early modern plays: number of words, turns and average number of words per turn	171
12.5	The present-day plays: number of words and standardised type-token ratios	172
12.6	The early modern plays: number of words and standardised type-token ratios	172
12.7	The present-day plays: number of terms of address, turns and average number of terms of address per turn	175
12.8	The early modern plays: number of terms of address, turns and average number of terms of address per turn	175
13.1	The most common reporting verbs in the three English versions of *Methodus medendi*, Book 3	188
13.2	Summary of terms used for describing and characterising wounds in the three English versions of *Methodus medendi*, Book 3	191
13.3	*Souded* and *soudyng(e)* in MS Sloane 6 with parallels in Gale's and English's versions of *Methodus medendi*, Book 3	194
16.1	Recurring elements in greetings and farewells in Chaucer's *Canterbury Tales*	234
16.2	Nominal terms of address in greetings and farewells in Chaucer's *Canterbury Tales*	237
17.1	Examination records including direct speech of the defendants in the Salem Witchcraft Trials	244

List of abbreviations

19CSC	*Corpus of Nineteenth-century Scottish Correspondence*
ARCHER	*A Representative Corpus of Historical English Registers*
CED	*A Corpus of English Dialogues, 1560–1760*
EEBO	Early English Books Online
EETS	Early English Text Society
EMEMT	Corpus of *Early Modern English Medical Texts*
f., ff.	folio, folios
FTA	face-threatening act
LALME	*A Linguistic Atlas of Late Mediaeval English*
ME	Middle English
MED	*Middle English Dictionary*
MEMT	Corpus of *Middle English Medical Texts*
MF	Maitland Folio Manuscript
MS	manuscript
NLS	National Library of Scotland
ODNB	*Oxford Dictionary of National Biography*
OE	Old English
OED	*Oxford English Dictionary*
PDE	Present-day English
PP	prepositional phrase
r	recto
RV	reporting verb
STS	Scottish Text Society
UCREL	University Centre for Computer Corpus Research on Language, Lancaster
v	verso

Notes on contributors

DOUGLAS BIBER is Regents' Professor of English (Applied Linguistics) at Northern Arizona University. His research efforts have focused on corpus linguistics, English grammar and register variation (in English and cross-linguistic; synchronic and diachronic). He has written thirteen books and monographs, including *Variation across Speech and Writing* (1988), *Dimensions of Register Variation (1995)*, *Corpus Linguistics*, with S. Conrad and R. Reppen (1998), *Register, Genre and Style*, with S. Conrad (2009) all published by Cambridge University Press; also *University Language* (2006), *Discourse on the Move*, with U. Connor and T. A. Upton (2007) and the co-authored *Longman Grammar of Spoken and Written English* (1999).

GRAHAM D. CAIE is Vice-Principal and Clerk of Senate at the University of Glasgow. He has also held the Chair of English Language at Glasgow since 1990 and written a number of books and articles on Old and Middle English language and literature.

JONATHAN CULPEPER is Senior Lecturer in the Department of Linguistics and English Language at Lancaster University, UK. His work spans pragmatics, stylistics and the history of English, and his major publications include *History of English* (2005, second edition), *Cognitive Stylistics* (co-edited with Elena Semino, 2002), *Exploring the Language of Drama* (co-edited with Mick Short and Peter Verdonk, 1998) and *Language and Characterisation in Plays and Other Texts* (2001). He has recently completed *Early Modern English Dialogues: Spoken Interaction as Writing* (co-authored with Merja Kytö, Cambridge University Press).

GABRIELLA DEL LUNGO CAMICIOTTI is Professor of English at the Department of Linguistics of the University of Florence, Italy. Her main research interest focuses on the pragmatic and discursive analysis of both narrative and academic/professional texts from a diachronic perspective from the Middle Ages to the nineteenth century. She has published many studies dealing with the stylistic aspects of Middle English texts with special reference to women's mystic discourse and saints' lives. She has published articles and co-edited volumes on corpus-based studies of varieties of specialised discourse. She is currently researching letter writing in the history of English.

JANE DEMMEN is a research student at Lancaster University with interests in historical pragmatics, stylistics and sociolinguistics. She has conducted several corpus-based studies of Early Modern English texts, and is currently undertaking a comparison of the language in Shakespeare's plays, other contemporary drama and speech-like genres. Previously, she has investigated the different stylistic effects created by recurrent word combinations in the dialogue of male and female characters in Shakespeare's plays, and she has also conducted a sociolinguistic analysis of the distribution of talk in Early Modern English language teaching text dialogues.

MARINA DOSSENA is Professor of English Language, and Head of the Department of Comparative Languages, Literatures and Cultures at the University of Bergamo. Her research interests focus on the features and origins of British varieties of English and the history of specialised discourse. Recent publications include *Diachronic Perspectives on Domain-Specific English* (co-edited with Irma Taavitsainen, 2006), *Studies in Late Modern English Correspondence: Methodology and Data* (co-edited with Ingrid Tieken-Boon van Ostade, 2008) and *Studies in English and European Historical Dialectology* (co-edited with Roger Lass, 2009). She is also the author of the monograph *Scotticisms in Grammar and Vocabulary* (2005) and is currently compiling a corpus of nineteenth-century Scottish correspondence.

SUSAN FITZMAURICE is Professor of English Language at the University of Sheffield. She has published extensively on the language of letters and essays in early eighteenth-century English, most recently in *Eighteenth-Century English: Ideology and Change* (edited by Raymond Hickey, Cambridge University Press, 2010) and in the *Journal of Historical Pragmatics* (2009). She is also co-editor with Donka Minkova of *Studies in the History of the English Language IV: Empirical and Analytical Advances in the Study of English Language Change* (2008).

MAURIZIO GOTTI is Professor of English Language and Translation at the University of Bergamo. His main research areas are English syntax (*English Diachronic Syntax*, editor, 1993; *Variation in Central Modals*, co-author, 2002), English lexicology and lexicography (*The Language of Thieves and Vagabonds*, 1999) and the features and origins of specialised discourse, both in a synchronic and diachronic perspective (*Robert Boyle and the Language of Science*, 1996; *Investigating Specialized Discourse*, 2005 and 2008). He is a member of the Editorial Boards of national and international journals, and edits the Linguistic Insights series for Peter Lang.

Notes on contributors

BETHANY GRAY is a PhD candidate in Applied Linguistics at Northern Arizona University. Her research investigates register variation using corpus linguistics methodologies, with a focus on documenting variation across written academic registers and disciplines. She has published in the *Journal of English for Academic Purposes*.

TURO HILTUNEN, MA, is a postgraduate researcher and member of the Scientific Thought-styles project at the Research Unit for Variation, Contacts and Change in English, University of Helsinki. His research interests include corpus linguistics, English for academic purposes, the history of scientific and medical writing and historical pragmatics. He is currently writing his PhD on disciplinary differences in Present-day English academic writing.

ALPO HONKAPOHJA is currently working on his PhD thesis, a digital edition of a fifteenth-century medical manuscript, at the Research Unit for Variation, Contacts and Change in English, University of Helsinki. Previously, he worked as a research assistant in the *Middle English Medical Texts* corpus project. He is also a member of the Digital Editions for Corpus Linguistics project and has published on digital editing with Samuli Kaislaniemi and Ville Marttila.

ANDREAS H. JUCKER is Professor of English Linguistics at the University of Zurich, where he is also Vice Dean for Resources of the Faculty of Arts. His current research interests include historical pragmatics, speech-act theory, politeness theory and the grammar and history of English. His recent publications include *Diachronic Perspectives on Address Term Systems* (2003), *Speech Acts in the History of English* (2008), both co-edited with Irma Taavitsainen, *Early Modern English News Discourse* (2009) and *Corpora: Pragmatics and Discourse* (2009) co-edited with Daniel Schreier and Marianne Hundt. He is the editor of the *Journal of Historical Pragmatics* (with Irma Taavitsainen) and series editor (together with Wolfram Bublitz and Klaus P. Schneider) of a nine-volume *Handbook of Pragmatics*.

LEENA KAHLAS-TARKKA is University Lecturer of English Philology, and Senior Researcher at the Research Unit for Variation, Contacts and Change in English at the University of Helsinki. Her main areas of interest are diachronic syntax and, more widely, medieval English language and literature. She has published a monograph on the syntax and semantics of Old and Early Middle English pronouns, and articles on various aspects of historical English. She has recently contributed to the volume *Records of the Salem Witch-Hunt* (Cambridge University Press, 2009) as an associate editor.

CHRISTIAN KAY is Professor Emerita of English Language at the University of Glasgow and one of the editors of the *Historical Thesaurus of the Oxford English Dictionary* (2009). She founded the *Scottish Corpus of Texts and*

Speech (SCOTS) and is a member of the team producing its successor, the *Corpus of Modern Scottish Writing 1700–1945*. She is Convener of Scottish Language Dictionaries, which has responsibility for developing academic dictionaries of Scots, is co-author of *A Thesaurus of Old English* (2000), has co-edited volumes of papers and has written articles reflecting her interests in historical semantics and lexicography.

THOMAS KOHNEN is Professor of English Language and Medieval Studies at the University of Cologne. His major fields of study include historical pragmatics and historical text linguistics, corpus linguistics (both synchronic and diachronic), historical syntax, speech-act theory, orality and literacy, and the history of English grammar.

PATRICIA DEERY KURTZ teaches Latin and Advanced Placement English at Liberty High School, and medieval literature at William Jewell College in Liberty, Missouri. Her research interests include Francis Douce and both Latin and Middle English saints' lives. She published with Linda Ehrsam Voigts *Scientific and Medical Writings in Old and Middle English: An Electronic Reference* (CD-ROM 2000), a database of information on more than 8,000 texts. A second edition of this research tool, eVK2, is now hosted by the University of Missouri at Kansas City and available through a link at the Medieval Academy of America website, http://medievalacademy.org.

STEFANIA MARIA MACI is Researcher of English Language and Translation at the University of Bergamo. She is currently involved in national and international research projects on academic English and legal discourse genres. Her research is focused on the analysis of English language in academic contexts, with particular regard to the analysis of English and identity in national and professional contexts. She is carrying out research concerning the genres of arbitration and medical English discourse. In addition, her research interests are related to the history of the English language in specialised and religious discourse. She has recently published a monograph on *The Linguistic Design of* Mary Magdalene (2008).

MARTTI MÄKINEN is University Lecturer at Hanken School of Economics, Helsinki. His research interests include corpus linguistics, manuscript and genre studies and historical linguistics. His dissertation was on the medieval English herbal genre (University of Helsinki). He was one of the compilers of the corpus of *Middle English Medical Texts* (2005), and currently he is a co-compiler of *The Middle English Grammar Corpus* (University of Stavanger, www.uis.no/research/culture/the_middle_english_grammar_project).

VILLE MARTTILA, MA, is a postgraduate researcher at the University of Helsinki, currently working on his PhD thesis on medieval culinary recipes and their pragmatic features. He is a member of the Scientific Thought-styles project at the Research Unit for Variation, Contacts and Change in English,

xviii Notes on contributors

and of the Digital Editions for Corpus Linguistics project. His research interests include manuscript studies, digital editing, historical pragmatics and the historical development of the recipe genre.

MINNA NEVALA is a researcher at the Research Unit for Variation, Contacts and Change in English, University of Helsinki. Her current project involves referential terms in Early and Late Modern English. She is the author of *Address in Early English Correspondence: Its Forms and Socio-Pragmatic Functions* (2004). She is also one of the compilers of the *Corpus of Early English Correspondence*.

PÄIVI PAHTA is Professor of English Philology at the School of Modern Languages and Translation Studies, University of Tampere. Her research interests include manuscript studies, historical (corpus) linguistics, history of scientific writing, language contact and multilingualism. Her main publications include *Medieval Embryology in the Vernacular* (1998), *Medical and Scientific Writing in Late Medieval English* (co-edited with Irma Taavitsainen, Cambridge University Press, 2004), the corpus of *Middle English Medical Texts* (with Irma Taavitsainen and Martti Mäkinen, 2005), *Medical Writing in Early Modern English* (co-edited with Irma Taavitsainen, Cambridge University Press, 2011) and *Social Roles and Language Practices in Late Modern English* (co-edited with Minna Nevala, Arja Nurmi and Minna Palander-Collin, 2010).

MINNA PALANDER-COLLIN is Professor at the Department of English and Senior Researcher at the Research Unit for Variation, Contacts and Change in English, University of Helsinki. Her main research interests include historical sociolinguistics, historical pragmatics and corpus linguistics. She has published several articles on these topics and co-edited with Arja Nurmi and Minna Nevala *The Language of Daily Life in England (1400–1800)* (2009). She is also one of the compilers of the *Corpus of Early English Correspondence*.

MAURA RATIA, MA, is a PhD student and member of the Scientific Thought-styles project at the Research Unit for Variation, Contacts and Change in English, University of Helsinki, working on argumentative strategies in the Early Modern Tobacco Controversy in a multidisciplinary frame, combining the study of language and medical history. For her thesis, she has compiled a corpus of tobacco texts of different genres.

MATTI RISSANEN is Professor Emeritus of English Philology at the University of Helsinki. His main field of interest is corpus-based analysis of the history of English syntax and lexis, from Old to Late Modern English, with a special focus on grammaticalisation. He is one of the associate editors of *Records of the Salem Witch-Hunt* (Cambridge University Press, 2009).

JEREMY SMITH is Professor of English Philology, Department of English Language, University of Glasgow. His fields of study include English historical linguistics (including Scots) and early English literature. Publications include *An Historical Study of English: Function, Form and Change* (1996), *An Introduction to Middle English* (with Simon Horobin, 2002), *Essentials of Early English* (2005, second edition), *Sound Change and the History of English* (2007) and *Old English: A Linguistic Introduction* (Cambridge University Press, 2009). He is co-worker on the Stavanger-Glasgow Middle English Grammar Project and co-investigator on the Glasgow *Corpus of Modern Scottish Writing 1700–1945*.

MERJA STENROOS is Professor in English Linguistics at the University of Stavanger. She is project leader of the Stavanger team of the Middle English Grammar Project, and co-compiler of the *Middle English Grammar Corpus* (University of Stavanger). Her research interests include Middle English dialectology, historical linguistics and the study of orthography/writing systems.

CARLA SUHR holds an MA in History and in English Philology. She is Assistant at the Department of English, University of Helsinki, and a member of the Scientific Thought-styles project at the Research Unit for Variation, Contacts and Change in English. She is preparing her PhD dissertation on the evolution of Early Modern English witchcraft pamphlets.

ELIZABETH CLOSS TRAUGOTT is Professor Emerita of Linguistics and English at Stanford University. Her main research has been in historical syntax, semantics and pragmatics. She currently focuses on ways to bring the theories of grammaticalisation and construction grammar to bear on accounts of micro-changes. Recent publications include *Grammaticalization* (with Paul Hopper, Cambridge University Press, 1993; revised edition, 2003), *Regularity in Semantic Change* (with Richard Dasher, Cambridge University Press, 2002) and *Lexicalization and Language Change* (with Laurel Brinton, Cambridge University Press, 2005). She has been a Guggenheim Fellow, a Fellow at the Center for Advanced Study in the Behavioral Sciences, and is a Corresponding Fellow of the British Academy.

JUKKA TYRKKÖ, MA, is a postgraduate researcher and member of the Scientific Thought-styles project at the Research Unit for Variation, Contacts and Change in English, University of Helsinki. His forthcoming PhD thesis studies coherence in hypertext narratives. In addition to textual coherence and text linguistics, his research interests include the history of scientific writing, historical corpus linguistics and the history of the book, with a particular focus on early lexicography.

LINDA EHRSAM VOIGTS is Curators' Professor of English Emerita at the University of Missouri-Kansas City. She published with Patricia Deery

Kurtz *Scientific and Medical Writings in Old and Middle English: An Electronic Reference* (CD-ROM, 2000). A second edition, eVK2, is now hosted by the University of Missouri at Kansas City and can be searched on-line using a link at http://medievalacademy.org. This link also allows searching of eTK, an electronic version prepared by Voigts of Lynn Thorndike and Pearl Kibre, *A Catalogue of Incipits of Mediaeval Scientific Writings in Latin* (1963). Her publications include studies and editions of late medieval scientific and medical texts in Middle English and Latin.

Preface

This book deals with the communicating power of early English manuscripts. It seeks to shed light on how handwritten texts from the (late) medieval and (early) modern periods can be used to analyse the history of language as communication between individuals and groups, and to discuss the challenges these documents present to present-day scholars. As such, it is a bold attempt to combine manuscript studies and pragmatics. In an obvious way, manuscripts communicate. They are communicative means of interaction between an author and his or her audience, they tell their communicative histories to the scholar investigating them and they often relate communicative interactions between actual or fictional characters depicted within them. On all these levels, manuscripts provide ample opportunities for pragmatic analysis and this is exactly what the chapters in this book set out to do. They offer case studies that focus on one or the other of these communicative layers in early English manuscripts.

For the two editors, this book is our first collaboration, but we share a long and rewarding history of regular and intensive scholarly cooperation, albeit on independent projects, with Irma Taavitsainen. For both of us, Irma has been and still is the most important professional colleague with whom we cooperate on an almost daily basis. And it is for this reason that – on the occasion of her forthcoming birthday – we dedicate this book to her. But the book is not meant as a *festschrift* in the traditional sense. We knew that if we wanted to honour Irma with a book it would have to be a topically coherent volume of the highest possible standard and this is what we have endeavoured to achieve in order to pay respect to Irma's groundbreaking work on early English manuscripts, as an editor of such manuscripts, as a corpus compiler of medieval and early modern texts and as a historical pragmaticist interested in the communication of and within such manuscripts.

The jacket illustration of this book shows a leaf from a British Library manuscript, Harley 2320, f. 31, containing a passage from a Middle English astrological text called *Storia lune*. It is an extract of a text Irma edited in 1987. She also studied it in her doctoral research and the folio is reproduced in her PhD thesis, *Middle English Lunaries: A Study of a Genre*, published in the Mémoires de la Société Néophilologique in 1988. We thank the British

Library for permission to reproduce the folio here and the Research Unit for Variation, Contacts and Change in English (VARIENG) at the University of Helsinki for financial support in acquiring it.

We thank the contributors for their exemplary cooperation in the preparation of this volume, Danielle Hickey for her care in preparing the manuscript for print, Helen Barton and Merja Kytö for their encouragement and for recommending the book for publication in the series *Studies in English Language*, and the Cambridge University Press Syndicate for accepting it.

Together with all the contributors we present this book to Irma with our heartfelt thanks for her outstanding contributions to the fields of manuscript studies and historical pragmatics; for her cooperation on so many different projects; for her patience and enthusiasm; for sharing her scholarly insights with us; and above all for her friendship.

Andreas H. Jucker and Päivi Pahta
Zurich and Tampere, January 2010

Introduction

1 Communicating manuscripts

Authors, scribes, readers, listeners and communicating characters

ANDREAS H. JUCKER AND PÄIVI PAHTA

Before the advent of printing, written texts existed only in the form of manuscripts, produced by hand (Lat. *manu scriptum*) on parchment prepared of animal skin, on papyrus or, later, on paper. Each manuscript was unique, and even if several different manuscripts purportedly contain the same text, they rarely present exact copies of the original or of each other (see Burrow 1986, Parkes 1991). Each manuscript, perhaps even more than any printed text, has a communicative story to tell. And thus a medieval manuscript is not only the material evidence of a historical communicative act that took place many centuries ago but it also communicates to the modern scholar by revealing some of its communicative history. In addition to the communication of the manuscript and through the manuscript, there is often communication in the manuscript. The manuscript texts depict actual or fictional worlds with actual or fictional characters engaged in communication with each other. This volume provides a range of case studies that deal with these different levels of communication of manuscripts and in manuscripts, and the title of this volume is intended to capture all these communicative layers.

Manuscripts are the material evidence of communication between the author and the reader of the manuscript and as such they deserve our scholarly attention. The simple dyad of author and reader, however, is often complicated by the intervention of a scribe who copied a text authored by somebody else or who took down the text in dictation (see Parkes 1991, Beal and Edwards 2005). Different versions of the text can vary, for instance, in their substance, with passages of varying length omitted or added, by mistake or by intention. They can also display variation in the linguistic representation of the text, manifesting different dialectal or idiolectal features of the scribes who copied them (see e.g. Introduction to McIntosh *et al.* 1986). At the very least, their *mise-en-page*, the layout, the style of handwriting and the decorations usually vary. As a result, it may not always be easy to determine the difference between an author who creates something entirely new and a scribe who just copies. Furthermore, in an age when literacy was rare, the recipients of the communicative message may have either read the text themselves or it may have been read out to them. A pragmatic analysis that wants to investigate the communicative history of a manuscript or a range of manuscripts must spell out in detail the roles of all the participants in the communicative situation created by the manuscript or, where sociohistorical facts are lacking, at least consider the possible alternative scenarios.

With the introduction of printing in the fifteenth century, it became possible to produce large numbers of identical texts (see e.g. Blake 1989, Hellinga and Trapp 1999). Texts became increasingly fixed. By committing texts to print, authors gained greater control over their texts. They no longer had to rely on scribes to copy their texts more or less faithfully. However, the process that turns a handwritten manuscript into a printed text is by no means straightforward. A handwritten text and a printed text are not the same thing. And, therefore, the process itself deserves a pragmatic analysis. What happens to a text and its communicative context if it is committed to print?

The introduction of printing did not immediately cause all handwritten manuscripts to be phased out. For many purposes, people still wrote by hand, and even today – in spite of the large range of printed and electronic text types including email messages and short text messages sent via mobile phone – handwriting still has its place. Manuscripts are still produced, either as drafts for texts that are to be turned into printed texts or as unique communicative events, as, for instance, in the form of letters.

In addition, many manuscripts contain accounts of communicative situations outside of the manuscript. They may depict fictional worlds with fictional characters that interact in many ways or they may depict actual conversations of actual people as, for instance, in diaries, in court records or in witness depositions. Fictional communication was long seen as unsuitable for pragmatic analysis because it is unclear how it compares to actual communication. But in historical pragmatics it has now been accepted that fictional communication is interesting in itself (see Jacobs and Jucker 1995; Taavitsainen and Fitzmaurice 2007; Taavitsainen and Jucker 2010). It is not to be taken as a poor substitute for the real thing, but provides a communicative world with its own values that can be compared to other equally contextualised communicative worlds. When we analyse the greeting routines used by the characters in Chaucer's *Canterbury Tales*, there is no claim that this is how Chaucer's contemporaries greeted each other. But there is a claim that such an analysis of fictional data is of sufficient interest in itself. Our philological interest in Chaucer's language is no longer restricted to matters of phonology, morphology and perhaps syntax, but we also want to learn something about the communicative world that he depicted in his writings.

Court records and witness depositions purport to report actual conversations by actual interactants. But, in these cases, we also have to remember that the conversational behaviour of the interactants is contextualised. The speech patterns recounted in court records cannot be taken as straightforward evidence for how people interacted outside of the courtroom. When we study courtroom interaction, we learn something about courtroom interaction, which is again of sufficient interest in itself. A defendant will have spoken very differently in the courtroom when questioned by the judge than at home when talking to his or her family.

Last, but not least, manuscripts also communicate to the modern scholar. They reveal their textual histories and allow the researcher glimpses and insights into a communicative world that lives on in these artefacts (see Renevey and Caie 2008). Even if this kind of communication is not dyadic – the scholar cannot talk back to the manuscript – it is an important aspect captured in the title of this book. In this volume, we deal with early English manuscripts that tell us their communicative stories. The individual chapters differ in the way in which they take up these communicative stories. While some focus on the material histories of individual manuscripts and thus provide the groundwork for a more pragmatic analysis of the communicative situation for which the manuscript was originally produced, others focus directly on the pragmatics of the communicative situation or on the pragmatics of the conversations depicted within the manuscripts.

Thus, while most research on early English manuscripts has tended to be philological in nature, producing text editions of previously unprinted texts, focusing on the origin and transmission of texts or their specific linguistic characteristics, or examining manuscript codices in the frame of book history, the starting point in this book is very different, as it foregrounds the documents as pieces of communication. The types of communication analysed in the book vary from texts documenting language use in public or formal registers, e.g. in business letters, to more private contexts of discourse, e.g. in private letters. In addition to letters, a wide range of genres is addressed in the chapters, including literary texts of both poetry and prose, play-texts, religious writings, trial records and scientific treatises. The chapters also represent a range of theoretical and methodological approaches to the analysis of language and texts, including historical pragmatics, historical sociolinguistics, variation analysis, genre and register analysis, text and discourse studies, corpus linguistics, text editing and codicology. Finally, the chapters draw their data from manuscripts that extend over a long time-span – well into the modern period. Thus, the volume addresses handwritten sources both from the height of the English manuscript era and from the period of early printing; manuscript material of the latter, in particular, has often been neglected in historical language studies, as the focus of research has been on printed texts.

The sixteen chapters of this book fall into four parts. The first part containing five chapters is devoted to authors, scribes and their audiences. Four of these analyse specific manuscripts and the ways in which their authors and scribes communicated with their audiences through various linguistic and textual practices, while one chapter examines the interaction between authors and audiences in a diachronic frame in a dataset extending over a longer period of time.

Thomas Kohnen opens this section with a study of commonplace books, that is to say, compilations of texts and text extracts, such as medical recipes, letters, proverbs, prayers, obituaries and so on. He carries out a pragmatic analysis of the text genres and communicative context of one particular fifteenth-century commonplace book, the notes by Robert Reynes, which are contained in MS Tanner 407. Reynes was a churchwarden who communicated with a large range of people, and Kohnen provides a classification of the texts that Reynes included in his collection and the different role-relationships of the original senders and addressees of these texts. Reynes included in his collection texts that he wrote to a range of addressees as well as texts that he received.

The chapter by *Gabriella Del Lungo Camiciotti* is a case study of medieval textuality as represented in two works from different genres, both surviving in unique fifteenth-century manuscript copies: *The Book of Margery Kempe* (a life story of a pious lay woman, dictated by Kempe herself and written by two scribes) and the *Legends of Holy Women* (a collection of saints' lives by Osbern Bokenham mainly based on the Latin *Legenda Aurea*). The texts use different rhetorical strategies for creating interpersonality and audience involvement. These differences arise from a number of factors related to the production circumstances of the texts, different genre conventions and the envisaged author–audience relationship. The findings illustrate that the shift from an oral-based textual culture (texts meant for oral performance) to a literacy-based one (silent reading) is more complex than customarily realised and pre-dates the technological innovation of printing, to which this shift is often assigned.

Patricia Deery Kurtz and *Linda Ehrsam Voigts* focus in their chapter on the significance of MS Bute 13, a mixed-language paper manuscript that in the sixteenth century brought together a range of important astronomical and astrological treatises in Middle English, Early Modern English and Latin. In the 1980s, the codex was dismembered into four parts that are now dispersed. Kurtz and Voigts provide a detailed reconstruction of the original manuscript, showing that its compiler had the conscious aim to communicate a comprehensive body of knowledge required for astrological calculation and its uses. Although the manuscript contains some important unique vernacular treatises bearing witness to the vernacularisation of contemporary science, the value of the codex as a whole, with its complementary English and Latin texts, is even greater for our understanding of the communication of early scientific knowledge than the sum of its individual parts.

Maurizio Gotti and *Stefania Maci* provide a detailed analysis of the text of *Mary Magdalene*, a Middle English play preserved in a Bodleian Library manuscript, Digby 133. The manuscript contains several other texts as well, all of them probably written in the sixteenth or early seventeenth century. They focus, in particular, on what until now has been described as scribal inconsistency or carelessness. Their close analysis reveals that the use of a variety of morphological and syntactic features is far from arbitrary and, in fact, communicates specific social attitudes and moral values to the reader. Morpho-syntactically innovative features, for instance, are used to identify evil characters, while pious characters use more conservative linguistic forms in line with local usage. These variations are, therefore, interpreted as effective stylistic means that communicate specific messages to the readers and reinforce the religious and social identities of the characters of the play.

Elizabeth Closs Traugott investigates the communicative context of a very different type of text, the proceedings of the trials carried out at the Old Bailey in the years 1674–1834, contained in the *Old Bailey Corpus*. In the beginning, these printed texts were produced from originally handwritten proceedings as a commercial enterprise and were somewhat sensational in order to attract a readership. In later years, the printed versions were required to be approved by the Mayor of London and to be fair and accurate reports of the proceedings. Traugott shows how the authors of these texts interacted with their audiences. While in the early years they actively constructed an audience with a view to moral improvement, later they turned to a more objective tone.

The second part of this book contains four chapters on handwritten correspondence. In this case, the data continue several centuries into the era of print and demonstrate the importance of handwritten documents into the nineteenth century.

In the first chapter of this part, *Merja Stenroos* and *Martti Mäkinen* study three letters connected to the late stages of the Welsh Uprising in the early fifteenth century. The letters were written by representatives of opposing sides of the uprising, and one is addressed to the Prince of Wales. Stenroos and Mäkinen locate these letters within their social and historical context and then provide a detailed analysis on the three levels of the scribal text itself, its pragmatic impact in terms of politeness and impoliteness, and its significance for an understanding of the historical events surrounding these letters.

Minna Palander-Collin and *Minna Nevala* study sixteenth-century letters by Nathaniel Bacon (1546?–1622), a 'county magnate' and local politician. These letters were written to a wide range of addressees, including family members, servants, local yeomen, noblemen and other gentlemen. Dealing with family matters, with the management of estates and with county administration, they contain many references to people, and these referring expressions reflect the sociohistorical context. They indicate a person's social rank and gender and very often also his or her relation to the writer of the letter, and thus they place the person referred to within a societal and hierarchical framework. But the referring expressions also have a place in creating and maintaining certain text types and genres, and they are used to express the writer's interactional persona and his local communicative needs.

The chapter by *Susan Fitzmaurice* is devoted to two letters written by the diplomat and poet George Stepney. One of these letters, written on 24 February 1695, was addressed to his publisher Jacob Tonson; the other, written on 2 April 1695, to his friend Matthew Prior. In the first, Stepney makes some suggestions for revisions to one of his poems and asks Tonson to circulate it among some friends for their comments and suggestions, while in the second he discusses and criticises a poem written by the addressee of the letter, Matthew Prior. These letters serve as examples of the communication between literary collaborators. They highlight the interactive and sociable nature of literary production in the late seventeenth century among the members of a social network.

The final chapter in this section, by *Marina Dossena*, is devoted to handwritten business communication in the late nineteenth century, that is, at a time when, due to new technology, typed and printed messages were already beginning to spread. The analysis shows the importance of the physical appearance of the letter with neat and error-free handwriting, a generous spread of the text with empty lines between the main elements of the letter, printed letter heads and so on. On this basis, Dossena argues that politeness and face considerations went beyond the linguistic choices. These elements were designed to show due respect to the recipient of the letter. The Victorian times imposed what she calls a 'dress-code' on the genre of business communication and insisted on a high level of decorum.

The third part of this volume contains five chapters that focus on the transition from manuscript to print. The studies highlight and compare communicative features of writings in the two media from various angles. Some studies investigate specific manuscript copies of individual texts and how they were treated when they were committed to print. Others take a more general perspective, comparing and contrasting textual and discoursal features of texts originally composed in manuscript and printed forms.

In the opening chapter of this part, *Graham D. Caie* examines a literary text, the *Romaunt of the Rose*, a work frequently attributed to Geoffrey Chaucer. Caie analyses the relationship of the single extant Middle English manuscript copy of the text, held in Glasgow University Library, MS Hunter 409, and an early printed version of the text, included in the first printed edition of the collected works of Chaucer, by William Thynne in 1532. The study illustrates how a detailed linguistic analysis can be combined with a careful examination of physical manuscript evidence to establish a link between the handwritten and printed versions of the same text. In this case, for example, marks left in the margins of the manuscript by the printer preparing the edition, indicating textual problems in the manuscript or providing instructions on the layout of the printed text, show how Thynne used the Hunter manuscript in communicating the *Romaunt of the Rose* in print.

Jonathan Culpeper and *Jane Demmen* study the development of play-texts from manuscript to print. The chapter focuses on five plays written and performed in the time of Shakespeare, but the diachronic perspective is actually much longer, as the authors compare the dialogue of earlier plays, shaped by particular manuscript practices, with the dialogue of present-day plays, shaped by the context of printing. The corpus-based comparative analysis of early modern and present-day play-texts shows interesting differences in the dialogue that can be explained by the different media, including differences in the length of turns, level of lexical richness and the frequency of address terms.

The chapter by *Päivi Pahta, Turo Hiltunen, Ville Marttila, Maura Ratia, Carla Suhr* and *Jukka Tyrkkö* investigates medical communication in three early English versions of *Methodus medendi*, an ancient text by Galen, a Greek physician who remained the ultimate authority on Western medicine until the seventeenth century. The earliest version examined here, a unique copy of the text in a British Library manuscript, Sloane 6, is the first and only substantial medieval English translation of the authentic writings of this great ancient physician. In the analysis, the authors compare some textual and linguistic features of the three versions to illustrate variation and change in the communication of the same medical information to English readers over two centuries, a period that was characterised not only by the change in the medium of communication but also by major sociocultural and domain-specific changes affecting the construction and transmission of scientific knowledge.

Douglas Biber, Bethany Gray, Alpo Honkapohja and *Päivi Pahta* trace the origins and early history of a key characteristic of present-day academic writing, i.e. the heavy reliance on non-clausal modification in the noun phrase. They analyse the frequencies and meanings of *in* and *on* prepositional phrases as noun modifiers in specialised treatises in two medical corpora, *Middle English Medical Texts*, containing writings that circulated in manuscript sources, and *Early Modern English Medical Texts*, consisting of early printed texts. The study shows that the use of *in/on* prepositional phrases in noun modification can be traced back to medical communication in treatises of the manuscript era; however, it is only in the early printed treatises that the phrases begin to develop extended abstract meanings that dominate in present-day written academic communication.

In the last chapter of this part, *Jeremy Smith* and *Christian Kay* provide a critical examination of the process of editing manuscript texts. They problematise a range of contextual factors that affect the communication of early handwritten texts to modern readers in print. Their main focus is the key role of the 'third participant' in the communicative situation, i.e. the scribe or editor who mediates between the creator and the reader of the text. Their case in point is the complex editorial history of a short Older Scots poem, William Dunbar's *Discretioun in Taking*, extant in three early modern manuscripts. The analysis of the original manuscript texts and the various published editions of the poem shows that editors have brought their own time- and taste-driven interpretations of the poem to bear on their task, often without explicitly informing their readers about their choices. The study is an important reminder of the fact that editing is a transformative process, which can impede as well as aid communication and, by definition, always transmits an 'edited truth' of the original manuscript text.

The last part contains two chapters on communication as depicted in early English manuscripts. The papers look at conversations between characters in fictional writing and at conversations between the individuals involved in a trial.

The chapter by *Andreas H. Jucker* studies conversational behaviour as depicted in Geoffrey Chaucer's *Canterbury Tales*. The *Canterbury Tales* provides a rich source of fictional characters both in the frame story and in the stories told by the individual pilgrims. Jucker provides an analysis of two particularly interesting speech acts: greetings and farewells. These speech acts, which open and close spoken interaction, show considerable variability and creativity, and very little formulaicity. Several elements, such as well-wishing, identifying the addressee or interjections, can be identified. They occur frequently with greetings and farewells but none of these elements seems to be obligatory.

Leena Kahlas-Tarkka and *Matti Rissanen* also look at the communication between characters depicted in manuscripts, but in this case the characters are actual historical people and the recorded conversations are purported to have taken place in reality. Kahlas-Tarkka and Rissanen investigate the newly re-edited records of the Salem Witchcraft Trials that took place in colonial Massachusetts in the years 1692–3. They focus on the discourse strategies chosen by the defendants, who found themselves in an extreme and life-threatening situation in which the choice of the wrong strategy could lead to a death sentence. Their survival very much depended on whether they chose a simple and factual, an unsociable and aggressive, or a sarcastic and derisive strategy.

This book, then, illustrates a number of ways in which written materials from early periods can provide insights into the history of human interaction and its development across time. In the early days of pragmatics, pragmaticists focused exclusively on oral communication, but in recent years written communication has increasingly become the focus of attention for many pragmaticists. In fact, the inception of historical pragmatics as a field of study in the 1990s relied exactly on the acceptance of written material as legitimate data for pragmatics. The chapters in this book take this endeavour an important step beyond the mere acceptance of early written material for pragmatic analysis. They study the mediality and the communicative histories of these early texts themselves and thus provide fresh insights into the communication of, through and in early English manuscripts.

Part I

Authors, scribes and their audiences

2 Commonplace-book communication

Role shifts and text functions in Robert Reynes's notes contained in MS Tanner 407

THOMAS KOHNEN

1. Introduction

In the field of historical pragmatics, not much research has been devoted to the study of the different ways in which people in the Middle Ages used manuscripts to communicate with each other and how certain types of manuscripts enabled various kinds of communication. In this regard, commonplace books form one of the most interesting kinds of handwritten texts in late medieval England. Late medieval commonplace books are mostly idiosyncratic compilations of texts or text extracts that were considered important for further reference or worth being especially remembered. As individual collections, commonplace books may not only reveal remarkable details about the tastes, interests and concerns of their compilers; they also present a multifunctional reservoir of texts that reflect how the compilers communicated within their social network.

Although there is some substantial philological research on commonplace books (see, for example, Robbins 1955 and Rigg 1968), they have never been studied from the perspective of linguistic communication and historical pragmatics. This will be done in the present contribution. The chapter investigates the shifting patterns of communication and text functions that late medieval commonplace books reflect. Here, the focus will be on one specific commonplace book, the notes by Robert Reynes, which are contained in Bodleian Library, MS Tanner 407 (see Louis 1980).

The chapter falls into five sections: after this introduction, section 2 will give a short overview of the background of commonplace books in late medieval England, and of the data used in this study. The third section will then analyse shifts in the typical roles of text communication associated with the use of the commonplace book, that is, shifts across the roles of text sender and text receiver. Section 4 will focus on the functional changes of the texts that these role shifts entail. The functional changes will be classified as 'constative' and 'performative' uses of texts. In the conclusion, I will discuss the results of the analysis against the background of historical pragmatics and historical corpus linguistics and questions associated with text use.

2. Commonplace books: background and data

As stated in the introduction, commonplace books are particular collections of texts that were compiled for future reference or further use. Commonplace books contain a wide range of genres such as medical recipes, letters, proverbs, obituaries, chronicle entries, legal texts, prognostications, poems, etc., which may be arranged in a purely additive or in a more coherent order. In the philological literature, commonplace books were, at first, defined rather loosely as covering any collection of texts contained in a manuscript (see, for example, Hammond 1927: 192). Later scholars advocate a more restricted definition; for example, Rigg (1968: 24) says that commonplace books are 'collections of miscellaneous material assembled simply for the interest and amusement of the compiler'. Referring to Rigg's definition, Louis (1980: 101) adds the term 'use' in order to do justice to the great variability of text entries found in commonplace books. The term 'use' also highlights the multifunctional nature of commonplace books and the entries contained in them.

As Louis (1980: 101) points out, a definition of commonplace books along these lines may distinguish them quite clearly from collections in which one particular type of text prevails (for example, prayer collections) and from those miscellanies that were produced in *scriptoria* and which do not reflect the specific interests of the compiler to such an extent. The medieval commonplace book must also be distinguished from the early modern and later concepts of a commonplace book. Early modern commonplace books typically contain passages from various, mostly literate, authors and are organised according to rather strict subject headings (see, for example, Milton's commonplace book; Wolfe 1953).

Medieval English commonplace books are often associated with the rising middle classes of the late fifteenth century and evolving literacy. The compilers were often individuals with widespread interests, who could read and write well enough, but who could not afford to buy a large number of expensive volumes. However, as Louis (1980: 102) points out, different individual settings must be distinguished for the compilation of commonplace books. Commonplace books stemming from middle-class London citizens seem to be different from those evolving from religious institutions or those compiled in a more rural, manorial environment. The present commonplace book belongs to the latter category and clearly reflects less ambitious literary and intellectual aspirations.

Descriptions of various commonplace books are given, for example, in Dyboski (1908), Robbins (1955) and Rigg (1968). These authors place special emphasis on the entries that were considered 'literary items' and it was mostly these extracts that were edited and printed. Such a view of commonplace books does not do justice to the variability of their contents nor to their special multifunctional nature. Only when we include all items contained in them, do commonplace books show details about the tastes, interests and concerns of their compilers and reveal their potential as multifunctional text reservoirs that reflect how the compilers communicated within their social network. As far as I know, there are no linguistic analyses of commonplace books in the field of historical pragmatics or historical text linguistics that focus on this special multifunctional nature and the multilayered communication practices associated with them.

Now to my data, the commonplace book of Robert Reynes of Acle. The edition by Cameron Louis (1980) includes all entries contained in the Tanner MS and therefore lends itself to an exemplary historical pragmatic analysis of commonplace books. The work stems from the last third of the fifteenth century and was written in the small community of Acle, which is near Norwich in Norfolk. There is strong evidence that Robert Reynes was the scribe of the manuscript (see Louis 1980: 6–11).

Who was Robert Reynes? Louis (1980: 27–35) refers to a limited number of known biographical facts that relate to his position in the community of Acle: we know that Reynes was a church reeve, that is, a churchwarden. Churchwardens were responsible for the practical, mostly monetary affairs of the (local) church, for example, managing aspects of the parish income (collections, property endowments, etc.) or certain expenditures (overseeing repairs, buying vestments and equipment, etc.) (Britnell 2006: 170). Although their influence seems to have been limited to the local church, Duffy points out that 'the wardens would accumulate a host of other communal responsibilities, both religious and secular' (2006: 305) and that they became 'men with extensive and ever-increasing responsibilities' (1992: 132). Thus, it could be that Reynes's position entailed a greater responsibility and even the more prestigious position of reeve of the local manor, which belonged to Tintern Abbey. This would make Reynes responsible for many aspects of manorial activities. Reynes may, in fact, have been an important officer at the local manor.

We also know that Reynes was alderman of the guild of St Edmund and that he had another position in one of the St Anne guilds. This would further corroborate our picture of Reynes's prominent position in the local community. Duffy says that membership of the guilds 'might... be a source of prestige and power' (1992: 151) and that 'guild office was one of the recognised ways of establishing or consolidating one's weight in the community' (2006: 307). Louis (1980: 32) in fact points out that the position of alderman was fairly distinguished, and Reynes might have served some of the functions of a modern-day mayor.

So, all in all, it seems likely that Reynes occupied a fairly prestigious and responsible position in a rural community. But his education and training does not seem to have been as advanced as that of a late fifteenth-century London citizen. Reynes was clearly literate and could act as a scribe. He may, however, have only attended what Nicholas Orme (1973) has called 'business school'; these were institutions specialised in dictation, accountancy and drafting of deeds and charters.

What are the contents of Reynes's commonplace book? As might be expected, it contains a large variety of different genres from different spheres of life. Texts are in both English and Latin. A first group comprises texts that can be associated with Reynes's professional career, that is, with his position as an officer at the manor. These are mainly texts that belong to the administrative domain. They include, for example, records of the oaths of homage and fealty that the inhabitants of the manor would swear before their lord, regulations of the assize of bread and ale and of the standard weights and measures, the duties to be read to the constables and the watch, forms of swearing in and charging jurors in the courts, and so on. We also find some itineraries of business travels Reynes seems to have made.

A second group of texts comprises those that belonged to Reynes's everyday life and the private sphere. They are mostly instructional or documentary texts: weather prognostications, recipes and charms, instructions for divination, family notices and records (obituaries), mnemonic lists and tables (e.g. on the sacraments of the church). There are also entries that show an interest in geography and world history.

A third division of texts comprises verse texts. These texts include a number of short poems that contain complaints about the state of the world or advice concerning old age, daily life, death or the Last Judgement. A significant proportion of the verse texts include long poems and dramatic works that were obviously intended for public recitation or performance in connection with the St Anne's guild; for example, the *Life of St Anne* and a poem on the miracles of the virgin.

In general, the nature, combination and arrangement of the entries indicate that Reynes did not intend his notes for private relaxation and diversion but rather for more practical use in his professional life (see Louis 1980: 114). In this regard, Reynes's notes nicely illustrate that the communicative practices associated with commonplace books cannot be restricted to the personal sphere or private reading. Rather, they reflect fairly complex settings and comprise various functions. The next two sections will deal with these settings and functions.

3. Role shifts in text communication

Commonplace books can be seen as multifunctional text reservoirs. The texts collected there were supposed to be re-used and probably were re-used in different settings and constellations. This further use of the texts involves, among other things, a shift in what Egon Werlich (1976: 212) has called the roles of the communicants in discourse, that is, a shift involving the different manifestations of the sender role and the receiver role in text interaction. The typical roles that can be found in connection with commonplace-book

1. **receiver**	→ copyist / sender →	**receiver** (compiler / other members of the community)
2. **composer** / sender	→	**receiver** (compiler / other members of the community)
3. **receiver**	→ copyist / sender →	receiver → **sender** (compiler / other members of the community)
4. **receiver**	→ copyist / sender →	receiver → **scribe**

Figure 2.1 Patterns of role shift in text communication in Robert Reynes's commonplace book

communication are the role of the text receiver and the role of the text sender, which may or may not be combined with the roles of the text composer and the text copyist or scribe. By role shift I mean that the compiler of the commonplace book may appear in different communicant roles or that other text users may assume the roles one would usually associate with the compiler.

There are at least four basic patterns of shift that can be observed in the present commonplace book (see figure 2.1). I will first give a short overview of the patterns and then provide some illustration.

The first pattern is what I call the 'receiver–receiver pattern'. The compiler reads a text that for some reason interests him. He then enters the text in his manuscript; that is, he acts as a text receiver and as a copyist. The point of the copying is, of course, that the compiler wants to use the entry at a later date; that is, in copying the text he also acts as text sender for those occasions when he will act again as text receiver. The future receiver may be the compiler or some person in the community who is literate and has access to the commonplace book.

The second pattern is the 'composer–receiver pattern'. Here, the compiler is the author of the text that he enters into his commonplace book. That is, the compiler acts as text composer and text sender. These texts, of course, are written down for later reference. The future receiver may again be the compiler or other literate people in his community who have access to the commonplace book. The first two patterns comprise the typical re-uses associated with commonplace books. Texts or text excerpts are copied or composed for later reference. The third and fourth patterns build on either the first or the second one, adding an additional function.

The third pattern, which I call the 'receiver–sender pattern', is similar to the first pattern, with the addition that the compiler or some other member of the community re-uses the text as a text sender. For example, the compiler may copy some instructions, which he may not only re-read later himself but actually issue as text sender to give orders to other people.

In the fourth pattern, which I call the 'receiver–scribe pattern', the compiler copies administrative texts that he obviously intends to re-use in other contexts as model texts when acting as a professional scribe for other people in his community. Here, the compiler would act as a scribe, combining old sections of the text with some new entries, the actual text senders being other people from his community.

Among the four patterns found in Robert Reynes's commonplace book the receiver–receiver pattern is probably the most frequent. We may assume that most of the texts were copied because the compiler wanted to re-read them and have them at his disposal at a later stage. Here, Reynes was either a text receiver in the sense that he merely read the texts as documents for the sake of personal interest, or he was a text receiver in the sense that he actually used the text, for example, by following the instructions contained in it. A documentation function would probably apply to such texts as directions for blood letting or instructions for divination by the finger nails, using a child. It is rather unlikely that Reynes would have actually 'tested' the texts by following their instructions. In other cases, the compiler would have followed the directions or prognostications, for example, the directions for finding 'changes in the moon', that is, the conjunctions of sun and moon (see example (1) below), or the prognostications according to the Dominical letter, which included forecasts about weather, harvests and cattle (see example (2) below).

(1) To knowe on what day chaunge of the mone [conjunction of sun and moon] schal be, first **loke** in þe kalender wher ʒour prime [new moon] is, and **rekenny** iii dayes afore ʒour prime. And on þat thred [third] day schall ʒe haue your chaunge. But **take** noʒt ʒour prime day for on [one] of þe iii dayes, but **late** [let] it be vnrekenyd. (Louis 1980: 152–3)

(2) A: Qwanne [when] the Dominicall lettyr ffallyth vpon the A, than **schall be** a warme wynter and a peryyng [windy] somer, corne in the felde, but resonable frute in the same wyse, been in the same wyse also, pestelencez of ʒonge [young] pepyll and deth of bestys, but most of neet [cattle], gret aplynge [conflict] and fytyng of pelouris [robbers], and newe tydynggis of kynggis etc. (Louis 1980: 312)

In a similar way, Reynes may have followed the injunctions contained in the short exhortative poems he had noted down, as in example (3).

(3) Man, **take** hed what þu [you] arte [are]:
But wormys mete [meat], þu wost [know] wel þis.
What þat erthe hat taken hys parte,
Hevyn or helle wyl haue his.
ʒif [if] þu do weel, þu gost to blys,

> Yf þu do euyl, to þi foo [foe].
> **Loue** þi Lord and **thynk** on this,
> Or **wyte** [blame] **þiself þin** owyn wo. (Louis 1980: 188–9)

In many cases it is fairly difficult to decide whether a text would also include other members of the community as text receivers. This is likely with texts involving Reynes's professional activities. On the one hand, these entries were necessary for Reynes in connection with his position as a reeve; on the other hand, such texts would certainly have been important as documentation of relevant communal data for the other members of the rural community. Among them we find, for example, the entry specifying the forms for swearing homage and fealty to the landlord (see example (4) below), or lists of the fields of the manor, with the size of each and their value per acre per year, and also lists specifying land divisions.

(4) Whan a freman schall do his homage to his chef lord þat he halt [hold property by tenure] of his chef tenement, ... he schall this seyn: 'I become 3our man fro þis day forward and feyth bere [show faith] to 3ow for þat tenement' (Louis 1980: 145)

The composer–receiver pattern involves all the items that the compiler wrote down, not using extant texts or models. Apart from family notices and records (specifying, for example, deaths and marriages), typical examples are itineraries of business travels and lists of sights in London, which Reynes may not have copied from another source but recorded from his own travelling experience (see example (5) below). There are also notes on taxes, specifying when and by whom they were collected, and lists of people who had paid tax.

(5) Bysshoppesgate, Ledyn Halle, Chepe (þer arn the cundytes [conduits]; abowte the Gret Cundyte ben [are] ix cundytes rennyng), Newgate, Ludgate, Tempyl Barr, Fflet Strete, Charyng Cros, London Ston, London Brygge, Seynt Mary Ouerey [Southwark Cathedral] ... Seynte Bryde (these ben good paryssh [parish churches]), Tower Hyll, Smythfeld (þer ben þe iustys [tournaments] kept), Ffryday Strete, Stokkys [Stocks market] (þer the bocherys and fysshemen standen), Holburn, Colman Hegg, Strande. (Louis 1980: 238–9)

In the receiver–sender pattern, the compiler acted not only as a future receiver but also as a future sender. This seems to be a necessary conclusion from the content of some of the entries and what we know about Reynes's professional activities. I will give four examples.

A most plausible case is the entry specifying the duties that were to be read to the constables and the watch (see example (6) below). Here, it was absolutely important for the – mostly illiterate – members of the population who would act as constables and watches that somebody read out to them the specific regulations (see also Louis 1980: 376–7). It is most likely that the compiler (or some other official connected with him and using the book) had to do this.

(6) Charge to the Constabelis. ȝe schul first pryncypaly **take hede** þat þe pees [peace] be kepte in ȝour towne. And if ony man dystruble [disturb] or breke þe pees, ȝe schall arest hym and **brynge** hym to þe Kyngis preson as wel be day as nyght; item alle nyght-walkerys withowte cause resonable and ryetous persones, and **brynge** hem [them] to þe Kyngis preson. And alle comon tenys pleyeris [tennis players], hasardoures [gamblers], vacabundys, dyes [dice] pleyeris and tho [those] persones þat vse suspecyous placis, **take** hem and **bryng** hem to þe Kyngis preson. (Louis 1980: 154–5)

The same may apply to the regulations connected with the *Assize of Bread and Ale* (see example (7) below). These were ordinances regulating the weights and measures and the price of these articles. Reynes copied the law (which was in Latin) and added an English translation of some of the more relevant points with regard to price charges and punishments. He probably did so because as an auditor of the assize he would be entitled to enforce the law (see Louis 1980: 350). In this context, he may have read out part of the texts or he may have memorised and applied them.

(7) Assyse of Ale. **It is to wete** [be known] þat whan a quarter of whete is solde for iii s. or for xl d., and barly for xx d. or for ii s., and otys [oats] for xvi d., þan may well the breweres selle in citie and burgh ii galounys of good and conable [proper] ale to drynk for i d. . . . And **wyll ȝe wete** in kepyng the assyse of ale abouseyd alle costages [expenditures] and repryses [expenses] of brewars accounted and alowed well and largely, þei may in a quarter of malt bruyng [brewing] gete iiii d. . . . Item, **wyte ȝe** þat þe brewster [brewer] shall not encrese or dysencrese [reduce] þe assyse of ale (Louis 1980: 137–8)

Another possibility for re-using some texts as sender can be found in the context of family and religious instruction. Here, the lists of the *Ten Commandments*, the seven deadly sins, the seven virtues and other items were probably first noted down for the sake of documentation but later used for catechising, with the children of the family being addressees (see example (8)).

(8) Decem Precepta. The ffirste is: **Wurchep** [worship] God aboue alle thyng. The secunde is: **Take** not His name in idylnesse. The iii^{de} is: **Halwe** [hallow] treuly **thy** holyday. The iiii^{de} is: **Wurchep þi** ffader and moder bodely and gostly. The v^{te} is: **Sle** no man with **thy** toung. (Louis 1980: 243–4)[1]

---

[1] It goes without saying that this is a very idiosyncratic version of the *Ten Commandments*. On this see Louis (1980: 445).

Fourthly, the poems compiled for one of the St Anne's guilds, in particular the *Life of St Anne*, were probably intended for public recitation at a feast with poetic and musical entertainment. There is some external evidence for this and some evidence in the poem that points to this application ('this guild', 'this time of year', etc.; see Louis 1980: 414–15). Here, the compiler or some other person from the community may have recited the poems; see example (9).

(9) Souereynys and serys, ȝyf it be ȝour wylle
 To here and to lere [learn] of thyng that is good,
 Ffro tryflys and talys kepe ȝour tonggis style,
 And here ȝe this matere with a mylde mood. (Louis 1980: 196)

The last pattern, the receiver–scribe pattern, can be seen in a number of family documents and formulae from original Latin documents that Reynes copied in order to use them later as formulae for contracts and similar pieces (see Louis 1980: 503–4).

4. Change of text functions: 'constative' and 'performative' uses of texts

The patterns of shift in text communication I have just illustrated trigger important changes in the functions of the texts involved. The major changes are those which I would like to call the 'locking up' and 'unlocking' of the primary text function or, following Austin (1962), the 'constative' and 'performative' uses of texts.

When texts are entered in the commonplace book, they often undergo a functional restriction as documents. As was mentioned above, we may assume that Reynes entered many texts in his commonplace book first of all for the sake of documentation. For example, he may never have actually used the instructions for blood letting or divination but just wanted to record them as interesting items of information. When texts are entered merely as documents, the primary text function (which may, for example, be directive or commissive) is restricted or 'locked up' as a mere record or documentation of that function. This use of a text can also be called 'constative'. In his pioneering work on speech-act theory, John L. Austin (1962) introduced the distinction between constative and performative utterances. Whereas constative utterances only report states of affairs, which may be true or false, performative utterances 'do' things and may be felicitous or infelicitous. The transformation of a text with its primary function into a record can be called a constative use of the text because the performative nature of the text (for example, its directive or commissive function) is reduced to a mere documentation of it, which may be true or false.[2]

The constative use of a text is sometimes made explicit. For example, the entry specifying the forms for swearing homage and fealty to the landlord is embedded in a descriptive text, showing that the commissive function of the formula is not employed in a performative setting (*Whan a freman schall do his homage to his chef lord þat he halt of his chef tenement, . . . he schall this seyn*; see example (4) above).[3] We do not know whether it was the compiler who added this introductory section or whether the item was already a document when it was copied. It may also be possible that many items in Reynes's commonplace book were entered already as 'locked documents' and never went beyond that state.

The other major change of text function can be called the 'unlocking' of the primary text function or the 'performative' use of a text. This use of the text can be called performative because here the primary function of the text (for example, its directive or commissive purpose) is 'unlocked' and performed. The performative use of texts may happen on the part of the receiver or on the part of the sender. It is quite likely that Reynes actually used some of the prognostications and instructions contained in the texts he copied. Once the prognostications were unlocked or performed, Reynes, as text receiver, would act as the addressee of representative speech acts (see Searle 1976) relating to future states of affairs (see *schall be* in example (2) above). In the directions for finding changes in the moon, he would act as the addressee of the directive speech acts that can be found in the several imperatives (see *loke, rekenny, take* and *late* in example (1) above), and he would, of course, be the referent of the second-person pronoun (3e). The same would apply to the imperatives and personal pronouns in the moral injunctions contained in the short poems (see example (3) above).

The performative use of a text is not restricted to the role of the text receiver. A text user may also unlock the primary text function when he re-uses the text as a text sender, that is, when the receiver–sender pattern applies. This change is particularly conspicuous in the case of documents that are used as instructional texts. As was shown above, the compiler or some other person not only re-reads the instructions but passes them on to give orders to other people.

In the regulations connected with the *Assize of Bread and Ale* (see example (7) above) the three different text functions (the constative use as a document, the performative use as instruction addressed to Reynes, and the performative use as instruction issued by Reynes) are nicely reflected by the reference of

---

[2] Austin gave up the distinction between constative and performative utterances later in his book (1962) because constative utterances also entail a performative element. But this hardly seems to reduce the relevance of the terms for the present analysis.

[3] Although the term *schall* clearly implies a deontic modality, the combination of subordinate temporal clause plus main clause has a descriptive nature.

the address terms and the functions of the imperatives (*wyll ȝe wete, wyte ȝe* in example (7) above). Initially, as a document, the address terms refer to all people to whom the law may apply. On this level, Reynes may consult the entry in order to know about a law in which some people are requested to be aware of certain facts. Once unlocked by Reynes in the performative use as a text receiver, the personal pronouns and imperatives refer to him, because due to his position in the community he must know about the particular law. Lastly, when unlocked by Reynes in the performative use as a text sender, the text will refer to the brewers of the local community who have to follow the regulations (for example, *not encrese or dysencrese þe assyse of ale*).

In the case of the duties to be read to the constables and the watch (see example (6) above) the unlocking or performative use is shown by the fact that the referents of the address terms are specified with regard to the situation of application, that is, the respective people to whom the regulations are read out. A similar thing will happen in the list of the *Ten Commandments* (see example (8) above). Here, the text changes from a pure list, with enumerations using ordinal numbers, to a text of religious instruction, where the imperatives and modal expressions are directed, for example, at the children of the household.

5. Conclusion

This short study of Robert Reynes's notes contained in MS Tanner 407 has shown that late medieval commonplace books can be seen as multifunctional text reservoirs whose use involves role shifts in text communication and changes of text function. Since this investigation has focused only on one commonplace book, this section should start with some qualifications. The conclusions drawn from this study must be seen as provisional and further investigations are needed to confirm the patterns suggested here and to add more hard and fast external evidence on the further uses of the texts. It would be particularly interesting to find traces of scribal intervention, which might provide more definitive clues to the further use of texts, for example, changes or additions to the texts the compiler has made. Unfortunately, it seems that many of the more attractive, that is 'non-literary', commonplace books still await editing and publication.

Studies on late medieval commonplace books are not only attractive because they close a gap in the linguistic description of an important genre (or rather compilation type) in the history of the English language. They may also open up some new perspectives for the fields of historical pragmatics and historical corpus linguistics. Although it is the aim of historical pragmatics to study 'the patterns of intentional human interaction of earlier periods and their historical developments' (Jucker 2008a: 895) and although the main emphasis in historical pragmatics has been on language use in texts and discourse, the varying uses of texts and the types of text compilation in the history of English have not been studied to a large extent from an historical pragmatic perspective.

Questions of genre change and genre dynamics in late medieval and early modern England have been studied by Taavitsainen (e.g. 1997b, 2001 and 2009). She points out the role of differing contexts, text traditions and text transmissions, especially in medieval written culture, which may shape and reshape not only individual texts but also whole genres or subgenres. The study of commonplace books may throw new light on the study of genre change and genre dynamics. The present study has shown that commonplace books should not be seen as genres themselves but, rather, as compilation types that facilitate the transmission and, consequently, the change of texts (and possibly genres). Here, the analysis of the different changes of text functions observed in commonplace books, especially the distinction between constative and performative uses of texts, may prove fruitful in the analysis of genre dynamics and genre change. The period of the late Middle Ages, with its evolving literacy, seems extremely rewarding for studies on the different ways in which texts were re-used under various conditions and settings.

A second perspective concerns the field of historical corpus linguistics. Quite clearly, commonplace books contain inventories of texts and genres that are typical of the written language use of the literate part of the population in late medieval England. In historical corpus linguistics nobody has, so far, looked at the role of the compiler as a typical language user and appreciated the potential of commonplace books as contemporary text collections and, maybe, even corpora in themselves. Further corpus-based studies should explore the various possibilities (and limitations) of including commonplace books in diachronic corpora.[4]

Thus, the study of commonplace books can open up new perspectives on how people communicated with texts and manuscripts in past ages and how such manuscripts can contribute to the compilation of diachronic corpora. But, eventually, it can also change our perception and interpretation of such texts and manuscripts.

---

[4] Samples of Reynes's commonplace book are included in the Middle English section of the Helsinki Corpus. Here they are subsumed under the text-type category 'handbook' (Kytö 1996).

3 Textuality in late medieval England

Two case studies

GABRIELLA DEL LUNGO CAMICIOTTI

1. Introduction

The fifteenth century has been one of the foci of attention for book historians since Marshall McLuhan declared the invention of printing of pivotal importance because it had been responsible for the shift from an oral culture, in which communication was primarily through discourse and group readings of manuscript books, to a visual culture, in which people exchanged ideas through the private, silent reading of printed books (Saenger 1982: 367). The thesis that a technical innovation in fifteenth-century book production influenced ways of reading and the relation between author/scribe and audience, though scarcely nuanced, has long enjoyed scholarly favour. However, in more recent years, this thesis has been increasingly criticised. In the context of a renewed interest in publishing technology in connection with the shift from print to digital media, it has been argued that the medium is not the mode (Hesse 1996: 21), and indeed that print culture should not be considered the inevitable historical consequence of the invention of printing during the Renaissance, but, rather, the cumulative result of particular social and political choices made by given societies at given moments. According to Clanchy (1979: 1), printing succeeded because a literate public already existed; that public originated in the twelfth and thirteenth centuries as a consequence of the production and retention of records. The growth in the uses of literacy eventually resulted in a different 'habit of mind': from hearing written texts to scrutinising the page as a way of concentrating on content (Clanchy 1979: 214–17). From the late fourteenth and particularly in the fifteenth century, writing and individual reading of vernacular texts became far more common than in previous centuries, and the availability of books increased considerably; but reading aloud remained a common practice revealing a preference for a public, shared experience of texts (Coleman 1996: 108). By the seventeenth century, the written (and printed) word was developing its own autonomous identity. However, long after the invention of printing, England appears to have remained largely an oral culture; as pointed out by Baron (2000: 30) 'a culture can have literacy but at the same time essentially function orally'. Within this historical development, the fifteenth century is crucial to the investigation of textual culture: how written texts were shaped according to the processes and practices surrounding their production, transmission and reception. Thus, fresh contributions are needed to give a more detailed account of medieval textuality and, specifically, the changing interaction between written texts, their authors and communities of readers in this pivotal period.

This chapter aims to contribute to this debate by presenting two case studies that tackle the topic from a pragmatic perspective. Pragmatics allows us to approach texts as acts of communication. A number of key assumptions make this possible. Single texts and genres[1] participate in the organisation of ways of thinking and interpreting text cultures – how texts are made and understood – in that they are at once a means and a product of social activity. Texts and genres are historical entities that relate to and reflect the historical context of production and appropriation (Chartier 1995). A pragmatic approach seems particularly suited to the investigation of variation in textual forms in that it centres on the choices made by language users and the world constraints they encounter in using verbal messages. Within this framework, a pragma-linguistic analysis can offer insights into how meaning becomes shaped and ordered as texts within different generic and historical contexts, in that close readings of texts focusing on linguistic and discoursal strategies highlight the range of resources available to text producers for performing particular communicative acts in concrete settings. The awareness of both the pragmatic conventions and the repertoire of linguistic strategies characterising a specific genre in a given cultural context is particularly valuable in reading past texts, in that a text is comprehensible to those who can build around that text a scenario in which it makes sense.[2]

Since changes in textual culture are manifested not only in texts but also, and most importantly, in ways of construing the relationship between author/scribe and intended audience, I will focus here on the

---

[1] Traditionally, only literary genres have received much attention. They have not only been defined as to their properties, but changes over time have also been carefully documented. However, literary genres make up only a very small part of the textual conventions that can be found in a language. For this reason, recent genre research has been broadened and new analytical tools have been introduced which help bridge the gap between literary and non-literary texts. For instance, Monika Fludernik (2000) proposes a model that encompasses the entire range of literary and non-literary texts and integrates narrative with other macro-genres or discourse modes such as argumentative, instructive, conversational and reflective. It is clear that an analytical emphasis on rhetorical/discursive structures of generic as opposed to individual texts can provide insights into the sociocultural settings within which texts are produced and interpreted. Recent approaches to genre are particularly helpful in analysing not only popular and formulaic texts in both contemporary literature and media, but also medieval works, in which conventionality and generic tradition were much more valued than originality of expression.

[2] On some key questions about pragmatic readings or discoursal analyses of historical texts, both literary and non-literary, see Jucker (1995) and Fitzmaurice and Taavitsainen (2007).

Textuality in late medieval England 27

pragma-linguistic investigation of paratextuality,[3] namely, on how the relationship between author and audience is built by exploiting rhetorical conventional resources in the zone of transaction between author/scribe and reading/listening public. As examples, I will consider two single mid-fifteenth-century manuscript works, the *Legends of Holy Women* by Osbern Bokenham and *The Book of Margery Kempe*, respectively representing two extremely popular genres, the saint's life and the life story of a pious lay woman, and belonging to pastoral and devotional discourse, which, in the late Middle Ages, underwent formal changes related to modalities of consumption[4] and illustrate slightly different ways of authoring the text and negotiating meaning with the audience. The changes exemplified by these case studies are connected with the construal of textual space.

Manuscripts and books articulate textual spaces, material and imaginary, in which discourse and narrative can materialise and authorial identity can be developed through both graphic practices such as writing, drawing and printing, and the use of language. Although it lacked our predominant dichotomy of public versus private (Huebert 1997), the medieval organisation of space was no less territorial. The thirteenth century was the period when the control and codification of space was reflected in manuscript culture: the centre of the page layout was the site of reading and monastic *meditatio* on the Word, while the periphery provided extra-textual space for distraction or artistic elaboration, as the idea of text as a written document gradually superseded the idea of text as a cue for speech. With the increase in both devotional and bureaucratic literacy, annotations in the margin might be used not only to illustrate but also to comment upon the adjacent text, and the page became a matrix of visual signs rather than of flowing linear speech (Camille 1992: 21). Slowly, the abundance of marginal images and motifs in Gothic manuscripts, which reached a peak in the first half of the fourteenth century, gave way to verbal notes and comments by scribes as the activities of text writers and book artists were increasingly practised by different individuals and groups (Camille 1992: 22).[5] In the second half of the fourteenth century and in the fifteenth century there was an interiorisation of textual space, which points

---

[3] According to Genette (1987), who coined this term, paratext – typically encompassing cover, dedication, title, preface, blurb, etc. – provides a framework for the written text that shapes its interpretation. It is a privileged site of negotiation with the intended public and is linked to the notion of authority in that it is a way to control the reading of a text. In the Middle Ages, paratextual materials comprised manuscript layout, prologues and authorial interventions, but these elements underwent change in emphasis related to the development of textuality.

[4] In the fifteenth century, novel forms of communicating meaning and changed generic norms regulating textual practices, and the popularity of doctrinal and meditative discourse for a renewed audience, are interrelated in the context of late medieval affective piety. In this period, a growing number of lay people were apprehensive as to their salvation and thus inclined to appropriate monastic practices such as individual meditation on edifying texts, which is one of the factors that may have fostered the practice of individual silent reading.

[5] The shift in late medieval manuscripts from an iconic textuality, where the function of writing is linked to an oral-based culture, to a literate verbal culture is seen not only by the increasing use of devices drawing attention to structural divisions to help readers select

to a textual system where the verbal message and its author acquire relevance: from a marginal space on the manuscript page, the only area available for *glossae* and comments on the part of scribes and readers, textual space came to involve the increasing appropriation of discursive space within the text on the part of the author. Previously, as indicated by Riddy (2000: 2), the hierarchy of scripts and the *mise-en-page* of text and gloss combined to establish relations of authority between different elements and to control the way in which a text was read. An *auctor* was endowed with *auctoritas* through the way the text was presented in the manuscript. This established mode of authoring text gave way to new strategies of controlling the interface between text and reader, including self-authorisation, as illustrated, for instance, by Hoccleve's manuscripts (Thompson 2000). Despite the fact that between these two poles there is a range of intermediate cases where the distinction between the glossator's and the author's voice is not clear-cut, interpolations by the author in the text, with the aim of closely directing its reading, became very common in fifteenth-century vernacular narrative works. Thus, the relationship between writer and scribe was rendered more complex by the dialogue between writer and audience which developed in this period, reflecting the appropriation of literary authority by vernacular writers (Machan 1994: 174).

In what follows, I will present the analysis of two case studies that will help to illustrate how the shift in the construal of textual space in connection with new ways of authoring text had come to completion in the pre-print age. Pragma-linguistic analysis will indicate that in both *The Book* and the *Legends* a novel relationship with the audience, linked with ways of authoring and using written text, is established, thus confirming the thesis that the late medieval textual system represents a particular vision of cultural life and reflects specific modes of construing authorial space, which is not a cultural monolith – indeed, it is forged, in practice, out of the interaction of texts, authors and readers/listeners.

2. Analysis of two mid-fifteenth-century texts[6]

2.1 The Book of Margery Kempe

The Book was written by Margery Kempe together with her confessor in King's Lynn during the 1430s, when she was in her sixties. It is an account of the conversion to the religious life of a wife and mother from a wealthy

---

specific passages, instead of reading the text as continuous narrative (Parkes 1976), but also by the numerous blank spaces left in fifteenth-century manuscripts, which seem to indicate that, even without pictures, text was perfectly intelligible for its intended use (Hardman 1997).

[6] Since the analysis concerns exclusively the use of language, it has been conducted on the edited texts: *The Book of Margery Kempe* by Windeatt (2000) and *Legendys of Hooly Wummen* by Osbern Bokenham by Serjeantson (1971 [1938]).

merchant-class background in her late thirties. Parts of the work recount her conversations with Christ and religious education; parts narrate her pilgrimages and journeys in England and across Europe to Rome and Jerusalem. The work is also concerned with the many difficulties encountered by Margery in gaining acceptance as an unenclosed holy woman and visionary.[7] It aimed to provide repentant sinners with a model life and pious readers with an occasion for meditation.

The Book survives in a single mid-fifteenth-century paper manuscript containing only this text, at one time owned by the Carthusian house of Mount Grace in Yorkshire, where it was extensively annotated, mostly by Carthusian readers. These marginal comments are concerned with Margery's religious experiences and seem to indicate that some readers of *The Book* were familiar with such feelings (Lochrie 1991). Despite the fact that nothing is said about a specific readership of Margery's memoirs in the prologues, the annotations give evidence of the initially positive reception of *The Book*, at least by a circle of readers interested in spiritual texts. However, it never gained a wider audience and later circulated only in reduced form (some excerpts from the work were printed by Wynkyn de Worde in 1501), until the manuscript was rediscovered and edited in the last century.

The surviving manuscript was copied by 'Salthows' soon after it was dictated by Margery to her confessor, from whose copy he may have worked. The respective roles of Margery and her confessor/scribe, as co-authors of the text, have received much scholarly attention. Some have attributed a limited role as author to Margery (Hirsch 1975), while others have opposed this position (Staley 1994; Del Lungo Camiciotti 2008). In medieval women's writings, the scribe is a constant presence and authorship a collaborative effort. In women mystics' writings, a current debate centres on the irresolvable question of exactly what input they had into the texts as we have them today: did the scribes write down verbatim what the devout women said or did they substantially reshape their words? I propose to recognise authority to Margery as the teller of her life story and to the confessor/scribe as intermediary between text and audience. Kempe tells the confessor/scribe the story he writes down, while he incorporates the tale of her life into the system of textual tradition represented by canonical visionary works such as the lives of continental pious women. As a matter of fact, though the actual writer of *The Book* was a priest (a fact that vouched for the orthodoxy of the text), in the longer prologue discursive space is also explicitly attributed

---

[7] In the late Middle Ages, a particular form of female devotion developed, favoured both by women living in religious houses or enclosed in anchorholds and lay women living in the world. Some of them experienced direct contact with the divine through visions and were endowed with the gift of prophesy; many of them managed to get texts recounting their experience made (Zum Brunn and Epiney-Burgard 1989; Dinshaw and Wallace 2003). In England, only two women, Julian of Norwich (McAvoy 2008) and Margery Kempe (Arnold and Lewis 2004), became involved with textual culture as authors.

to Margery as the source of the narrative material and as guarantor of the trustworthiness of her memoirs:

> Thys boke is not wretyn in ordyr, every thyng aftyr other as it wer don, but lych as the mater cam to the creatur in mend whan it schuld be wretyn, for it was so long er it was wretyn that sche had forgetyn the tyme and the ordyr whan thyngys befellyn. And therfor sche dede no thing wryten but that sche knew rygth wel for very trewth. (Windeatt 2000: lines 134–9)

In a textual culture where the perception of language was predominantly auditory, composition was conceived in terms of dictation rather than of manipulating a pen, so Margery's agency could be acknowledged in that she was the oral source of the events reported in *The Book*. Moreover, her voice is directly heard through the many dialogic passages reporting her holy conversations with supernatural beings and exchanges with other characters. It is, however, the confessor who, in addition to writing down her memoirs, develops an explicit rapport with readers/listeners in the paratext. He is apparently the author of *The Book*'s two prologues, where the pact with the audience is established. The longer of these, placed first but written last, gives a detailed account of *The Book*'s genesis (there existed a first scribe's almost illegible manuscript which he partly copied after delaying the task for four years). This prologue can be read as the priest's tribute to the importance of the book he is copying and his attempt to provide it with what he, and perhaps Margery, think a fitting opening, sprinkled with biblical allusions and written in an appropriately formal style (Wogan-Browne *et al.* 1999: 84). The second prologue, written earlier, is a much less elaborate statement of textual origins and authorisations, and the coexistence of both prologues provides good evidence for the contemporary understanding of the function and nature of the prologue as a literary form (on vernacular prologues as sources of literary theory see Wogan-Browne *et al.* 1999). The development of prologue conventions in the more recent prologue may have been perceived by both amanuensis and visionary as serving to enhance authorisation, given the increasing conservatism of English spirituality in the decades between *The Book*'s genesis and its completion (Wogan-Browne *et al.* 1999: 85).

By authoring the prologues and recounting Margery's miraculous and spiritual experiences in the third person, the confessor/scribe contributed to the construction of the public identity of Margery as holy woman and visionary. In addition, he interpolated narration with audience-oriented discursive devices intended to influence the reception of the story. Of particular relevance among these is the paratextual framework of *The Book*, which, in addition to prologues, includes metadiscourse; this represents the role of an author as commentator on the text and guide for the reader, since the ultimate aim of all discourse is to persuade (Crismore 1989). The confessor uses paratextual material to establish a relationship with the audience by furnishing information as to the purpose of the text, the circumstances of its production, explicit commentary and textual orientation. By so doing, he occupies authorial space.

Throughout *The Book*, the confessor gives information as to the structural organisation of the work and refers to extra-textual knowledge, thus providing textual and temporal orientation (examples (1) and (2)):

(1) And so it befel as the ankyr had prophecyed in euery poynt, and, as I trust, schal be wretyn more pleynly aftyrward. (Windeatt 2000: lines 1411–12)

(2) Ferthermore her folwyth a rygth notabyl matere of the creaturys felyng, and it is wretyn her for convenyens, in-as-mech as it is in felyng leche to the materys that ben wretyn beforn, notwythstondyng it befel long aftyr the materys whech folwyn. (Windeatt 2000: lines 1878–81)

The confessor also highlights participation in a shared and active devotion by interspersing the text with pious interjections and emphatic hortatory parenthetical expressions (example (3)):

(3) Nevyrthelesse he lete hir gon to chirche whan sche wolde, . . . thankyd be almyghty God therof! (Windeatt 2000: lines 3718–20)

This is a device which heightens the emotional involvement of readers/listeners, and at the same time confers reliability on Margery's recollections. Other comments help the audience to interpret the text correctly, by offering evaluations of reported miraculous events, as in the following example, where Saint Jerome's appearing to Margery and explaining to her her gift of tears is glossed by the scribe so as better to elucidate the episode (example (4)):

(4) Wyth swech maner of dalyawns he hily confortyd hir spiritys. And also he made gret preysyng and thankyng to God for the grace that he wrowt in hir sowle, for les than sche had an had sweche gostly comfortys, it had ben unpossybyl hir to a boryn the schamys and wonderyngys the whech sche suffyrd pacyently and mekely for the grace that God schewyd in hyr. (Windeatt 2000: lines 3270–5)

The intrusion of the confessor/scribe's voice into the life story dictated by Margery plays a pivotal role in controlling *The Book*'s reception. This indicates that, though the role of the vernacular author of a work was still controversial in the late Middle Ages, he/she was as interactive and important as the devotional text itself and enhanced the role of readers/listeners.

In *The Book*, the authorial role is split between Margery, telling her life story, and the priest, narrating it in writing and commenting on behalf of readers/listeners, with each contributing through different modes. Margery's voice dramatises the remembered events and is directly present in the text thanks to the many conversational exchanges with Christ and other characters in the story. The voice of the confessor/scribe, on the other hand, validates and explains the story, whose orthodoxy he vouches for. In short, the priest directs both the organisation and the interpretation of the text, while Margery controls its content. In the case of mystic writing by women, the intrusion of the narrator in the text to comment on events and address the public is not just a text-organising device, as in other late medieval texts, but also a discursive resource employed to perspectivise the experience of the saintly woman on the part of the scribe. The priests who ministered to women could acquire a deeply admiring interest in their lives, and thereby a personal involvement with them that transcended duty entirely. Very often they formed a close relationship with holy women as their confidants and in most cases confessors, and their voices, directly or indirectly expressed, are an essential element in this genre of medieval narrative (Del Lungo Camiciotti 2008: 27).

The pragmatic analysis of *The Book* shows how, in the mid fifteenth century, the process of production and use of devotional *vitae* enhanced the authoring of a specific text; this was increasingly and openly interpersonal thanks to the presence of devices evoking the reader's attention, which rendered devotional reading an active process that enlisted the reader as co-creator of meaning.

2.2 *The* Legends of Holy Women

A different case is that presented by the *Legends of Holy Women*. Osbern Bokenham compiled this collection of female saints' lives (1443–7) mainly from the Latin *Legenda Aurea* by Jacobus of Voragine (1230–98).[8] The work survives in a small mid-fifteenth-century parchment volume containing only Bokenham's text. This copy was made for Thomas Burgh, an Augustinian friar, like Bokenham himself, who gave the copy to a convent of nuns. However, many of the legends were composed at the request of named female patrons among the aristocracy and gentry. The relationship with readers/listeners is more precise and complex than in *The Book of Margery Kempe*. The *Legends* moves between at least three inscribed audiences: a Latinate clerical peer group represented by Burgh, named female lay patrons, and professed women religious. Bokenham follows literary conventions in adapting scholastic and hagiographic prologue norms, but the tone of his general prologue is partly comic, suggesting that vernacular writing was not taken too seriously by his Cambridge contemporaries (Wogan-Browne *et al.* 1999: 65). The work apparently aimed to offer edifying entertainment to a rather sophisticated audience of lay women and nuns, as well as to gain recognition for Bokenham as a poet.

There is a clear distinction in this work between the voice of the poet and those of the characters. These speak in straightforward dialogic exchanges

---

[8] A longer version of the *Legenda Aurea* by Bokenham was discovered in 2004 in the library of Abbotsford House (Horobin 2007b).

that make everything explicit for the audience, while the narrator intervenes in the paratextual frame and through metadiscursive comments on the story (Del Lungo Camiciotti 2005, 2007a). The paratextual frame of the work, a general prologue and minor prologues to individual lives, has been investigated by Johnson (1994) with a view to highlighting the auto-presentation of the poet as a correct and trustworthy translator, and the expected reception and purposes of his work. In Johnson's words, 'paratext serves the function to protect and advertise the material's inherent utility in its transmission from Latin to vernacular culture' (1994: 121). It is, in fact, a key feature of Bokenham's paratextuality to be self-referential and anectodal, and this aspect makes him an interesting case of appropriation of a morally authoritative Latin tradition.

From a pragmatic perspective, Bokenham's rhetorical strategies are very closely informed by his relationship with the intended readership. The interface between text and audience is revealed by numerous narratorial interventions aimed at directing interpretation of the work. These make frequent use of metadiscourse, which serves to introduce the tale, to connect passages, to interpret the events and to supply a final conclusion or moral. Thus, the narrator *persona* is here both a structural and interpersonal device: his comments provide scaffolding to the boxed stories, which are transformed from a loose collection of saints' lives into a meaningful unit. In addition, they serve the function of establishing a relationship between author and audience. Whenever the narrator intrudes, the sense of storytelling is suspended as he shifts to the present tense and steps in to appeal to his audience. This is a strategy to facilitate empathetic identification on the part of the audience and to increase the explanatory power of the story by using linguistic resources to clarify the characters' motives and values.

The prologues are the site where the negotiation with individual dedicatees is expressed. Here, the narrator marks his presence by using the first person and the present tense, as opposed to the narrative past tense, often signalled by the pro-form *dede* (examples (5) and (6)):

(5)   The matere wych I wil of wryte (Serjeantson 1971: line 73)
(6)   Thys blyssyd virgyne I dede visyte,
      And al the processe I dede owt wryte
      Wych I purpose now to declare (Serjeantson 1971: lines 119–21)

He also signals his involved relationship with the public, in prologues and lives, through exclamations and interjections and by using attitudinal adverbials and pronouns: inclusive *we* and *you* to address a specific public, and *who so* to refer to the general public (examples (7) to (11)).

(7)   Lo! thus ye seen mown (Serjeantson 1971: line 25)
(8)   For treuly, vp-on my conscyence (Serjeantson 1971: line 157)
(9)   But to oure purpoos (Serjeantson 1971: line 29)
(10) who so lyst to here (Serjeantson 1971: line 31)

(11) I you beseche, frend, ryht enterly,
      That ye vouchesaf for me to preye (Serjeantson 1971: lines 228–9)

A third involving strategy to enter an ongoing conversation with both dedicatees and a wider audience is the use of metacomments and parenthetical expressions, both evaluative and text-organising (examples (12) to (19)).

(12) For this, I suppose, all men weel knowe (Serjeantson 1971: line 43)
(13) Thys is fully myn opynyounn (Serjeantson 1971: line 156)
(14) I dare seyn this (Serjeantson 1971: line 138)
(15) But as for the foot, this is certeyn,
      Many a myracle hath ther be shewyd (Serjeantson 1971: lines 144–5)
(16) as ye aftyr shul here (Serjeantson 1971: line 132)
(17) as ye shall se (Serjeantson 1971: line 176)
(18) But, for to drawe to a conclusyoun
      Of thys long tale now finally (Serjeantson 1971: lines 226–7)
(19) But in this mater what shuld I lenger tarye? (Serjeantson 1971: line 4996)

The phrases here that seem to refer to the aural mode of reception, such as examples (10) and (16), have been interpreted as proof that Bokenham anticipates a listening public for his stories (Colemann 1996: 199). Yet, the work is also interspersed with phrases that apparently refer to a literate modality, as where the author refers to writing (example (5)) or employs a metaphorical expression referring to sight (example (17)) to guide his audience. Moreover, it has been shown that pious invocations and exclamations encountered in late medieval narrative are oral formulae adapted to literary use, whose employment seems to indicate an oral–literate interplay rather than dichotomy (Dalrymple 2000: 26). In a nutshell, it seems rather difficult to assign a specific function to each expression: from a pragmatic perspective, all of them serve the function of fostering a participatory dynamic between audience, narrator and text, by uniting them under a single frame of reference.

Before concluding, a final point should be made. Both *The Book* and the *Legends* employ rhetorical strategies such as dialogue and the narrator-in-the-text which render text more interpersonal and enhance audience involvement, but which also shed light on uses of text. Dialogue points to a context of use where text could be orally delivered to a broader audience of listeners, since reported speech is carefully framed by opening, and less often by ending, clauses, which may have the function of signalling to a listening public a clear distinction between narrator and characters' voices (Del Lungo Camiciotti 2007a: 288). As to the narrator-in-the-text, this is a late medieval development in the saint's life. For, in this period, hagiographic tales were reshaped to fit a new context of use by employing this and other narrative devices as they evolved from utilitarian religious writing to literary artefacts for pious entertainment (Del Lungo Camiciotti 2007b). The *Legends* are examples not of anonymous text for exclusive use of preachers, but of authored text. The more recent genre of the life of an extremely devout woman participates in a culture of piety which also conceived text for the edification of both lay and religious people in an empathetic way. Therefore, similar strategies are used to construct the author/audience interface. Of course, there are differences: Bokenham directly addresses his intended readership in prologues and makes frequent use of reader/listener-oriented devices. In short, his narrator persona looms large in discursive space. In *The Book of Margery Kempe*, on the other hand, dialogue is much more prominent than interpolations in the text on the part of the narrator. Such differences depend on the circumstances of production and intended purpose of the two works: a collection of female saints' lives for the pious entertainment of gentlewomen and nuns on the one hand, the life story of a visionary intended for meditation and edification on the other. Yet, both rely on similar rhetorical choices to engage their respective audiences and show narrators firmly occupying discursive space as authors.

To conclude, both *The Book* and the *Legends* testify to the complexity of modes of text production and consumption in late medieval England and illustrate the shift from written text meant only for oral performance to a wider range of uses. The manuscripts that contain the works may not have been meant just for reading aloud within a group, a common practice in the fifteenth century, but also for private perusal on the part of individual readers, in line with new ways of expressing individual piety. Readers of *The Book* could meditate on Margery's mystical experiences. Indeed, that they did so is proved by the marginal annotations. On the other hand, the dedicatees of Bokenham's lives could meditate on the virtues displayed by their namesakes. Both genres are rooted in orality: the hagiographic tale evolves from scripts for preachers, as illustrated by previous collections (Del Lungo Camiciotti 2007b), while the life of a saintly woman is dictated text, thus speech-based narrative. Yet, authority is invested in the specific written text reproduced in the manuscript. In short, orality and literacy are not mutually exclusive culture-types, but mentalities which can coexist despite technological changes relating to circumstances of production and use of manuscripts.

3. Concluding observations

The case studies presented here, which exemplify two popular genres of medieval religious discourse, illustrate what a pragmatic analysis can contribute to our knowledge of late medieval textuality. Firstly, they highlight some aspects of the development of generic conventions; secondly, they can help to shed light on the transition from an oral/aural to a literate culture.

As to the first point, we can say that the analysis has highlighted some linguistic features characterising late medieval religious discourse. The authors of *The Book of Margery Kempe* and the *Legends of Holy Women* avail themselves of rhetorical resources to adapt traditional narrative material so as to make it more suitable for novel audiences in changed cultural conditions. These resources include dialogue and the narrator-in-the-text. In the saintly life and the hagiographic tale, the narrators' direct intervention foregrounds the significance of mystical experiences and miraculous events for new audiences when they step out of the narrative world to comment on the story or signal relevant points through devices aimed at involving readers and listeners. But late medieval saintly and saints' lives also make extensive use of interpersonal strategies which place the reader/listener in relation to the text, the text's author and the social context of use. In both works, paratextual material serves a highly interactional function in constructing rapport with the audience, thus authoring the text. Prologues, in particular, are the site where the pact with the audience is established: credentials are presented and authors' credibility is enhanced by acknowledging their contribution to an ongoing tradition. It is through the appropriation of discursive space that vernacular authors rework both generic norms and their sources in different keys by offering new perspectives to their audiences in a changed cultural context.

This leads to the second point: the transition from an oral/aural to a literate textual culture. To trace the evolution of a genre such as the hagiographic tale is also to trace the relationship between oral and written ways of transmitting and using texts. Despite the growth of lay literacy and the spread of silent reading in the late Middle Ages, most people encountered texts through hearing them read aloud (Coleman 1996). So most people participated in textual culture mainly through performed texts. However, even though the merging of oral and literate strategies is a crucial feature of late medieval narratives, audience-oriented devices clearly point to the use of written text for reading, not merely as script. In fact, the interface of author/audience overtly expressed in the paratext through judgements and comments indicates a shift from the highly unstable medieval text being recreated through oral adaptation for different audiences, in that a situated relationship is constructed between the author of a specific text reproduced in a particular manuscript and its intended audience, as in the case of Bokenham's named addressees and dedicatees or the unnamed audience of *The Book of Margery Kempe*.

To conclude, the shift from an oral-based textual culture, where written English served primarily transcription functions, to a literacy-based one, is far more complex than we tend to realise and cannot be due exclusively to the technological change from manuscript to print in the late medieval and early modern period. For a long time, speech and writing were not divided communicative functions. On the contrary, the oral side of writing remained relevant long after the mainly recording function of the written word and, in the fifteenth century, manuscript authored texts could have a dual use as text to be delivered aloud and read silently. A decisive factor in the emergence of a written English culture may have been the shift from oral to silent reading, which led to the reconceptualisation of the book, which, rather than a technique for encoding speech, came to be seen as self-sufficient. It is not so much the medium as the circumstances in which texts are produced and consumed that shape the message, given that the linguistic properties of both speech and writing vary from one sociohistorical context to another.

4 The significance of now-dispersed Bute 13

A mixed-language scientific manuscript

PATRICIA DEERY KURTZ AND
LINDA EHRSAM VOIGTS

A paper manuscript from the fifteenth and sixteenth centuries was, until 1983, MS 13 in the library of the Marquess of Bute.[*] It has now been broken into four parts and widely scattered, apparently on three continents. This *Sammelhandschrift* had been assembled in the sixteenth century by an anonymous compiler to bring together a range of related treatises in Middle English, Early Modern English and Latin. His choice of astronomical and astrological writings reveals an aim to communicate the knowledge required for, as well as the uses of, astrological calculation. The dismembered parts of this manuscript contain important unique vernacular treatises, but Bute 13 was greater than the sum of its individual texts. Only by considering the integrity of the whole can it be fully understood.

1. History

The codex was assembled in a limp parchment wrapper in the first half of the sixteenth century. The manuscript (c. 190 × 140 mm) combined several booklets on related scientific subjects with a sixteenth-century signature of James Alleyn on the third flyleaf.[1] In the late nineteenth century it was described briefly as part of the collection of the Marquess of Bute, in a report of the Royal Commission on Historical Manuscripts.[2] John Crichton-Stuart, sixth Marquess of Bute (1933–93)[3] sold the manuscript at Sotheby's on

---

[*] With many thanks to Robert Babcock, Bruce Bradley, David Bauer, Luke Demaitre, David McKnight, Mitsuo Nitta, Laura Nuvoloni, Lynn Ransom, Pamela Robinson, Nancy Shawcross, Toshiyuki Takamiya, Lawrence J. Schoenberg and Barbara Brizdle.

[1] Sotheby's Catalogue (13 June 1983, lot 32), pp. 113–15, for Marquess of Bute MS 13. We have not been able to identify a sixteenth-century James Allen/Aleyn/Alleyn/Alleyne.

[2] R. B. Knowles, *Third Report of the Royal Commission on Historical Manuscripts* (London: Her Majesty's Stationery Office, 1892), Appendix, p. 208.

[3] Gavin Stamp, 'Stuart, John Crichton-, sixth Marquess of Bute (1933–1993)', *Oxford Dictionary of National Biography* (Oxford: Oxford University Press, 2004). www.oxforddnb.com/view/article/51532, accessed 28 May 2009.

The significance of now-dispersed MS Bute 13   39

13 June 1983 (lot 13), along with other Middle English manuscripts.[4] The purchaser (for £36,000) was the New York bookseller H. P. Kraus, in whose shop Bute 13 was dismembered (c. 1985) and offered for sale as four newly bound codices.[5] Three of these four manuscripts have been located, but the present ownership of the fourth Kraus unit remains unknown.[6] The first section of the codex was purchased sometime after 1988 by Shozo Asahata of Nara, Japan, who published a facsimile.[7] The second and third Kraus units are now MSS ljs 188 and 191 in the possession of Lawrence J. Schoenberg and Barbara Brizdle and are accessible on-line.[8] See plates 1 and 3.

2. Reconstruction of Bute 13

The following reconstruction of now-scattered texts makes clear the significance of this combination of booklets assembled in a single volume in the sixteenth century. Texts or translations that appear to be unique are signalled with an asterisk.

2.1   Kraus I of IV, now Asahata MS[9]

Flyleaves, including third flyleaf containing signature of James Alleyn (sixteenth century).[10]

---

[4] Other Middle English manuscripts in this sale included Bute MS F.16 (lot 9), which contains 'The Privity of the Passion' and Lydgate's 'Life of Our Lady', now Yale University, Beinecke Library, MS 660. See http://webtext.library.yale.edu/beinflat/pre1600.ms660.htm, accessed 28 May 2009; Mary-Jo Arn, 'The Bute manuscript of "The Privity of the Passion" (Yale University, Beinecke MS 660)', *Manuscripta* 34 (1990): 177–89. The Sotheby's sale also included Bute MS 85 (lot 10), John Gower's 'Confessio Amantis'. See A. S. G. Edwards and T. Takamiya, 'A new fragment of Gower's "Confessio Amantis"', *Modern Language Review* 96 (2001): 931–6.

[5] H. P. Kraus, Typescript Catalogue, 1988. Linda Voigts saw the four small manuscripts in the Kraus salesroom in 1988.

[6] The most recent information known to us concerning the last section of Bute 13, on the elections of times, is found in Catalogue 562 of Hellmut Schumann of Zurich (May 1994), '*Rare Books and Manuscripts*', Item 7, 'With an Early English Geomantic Treatise... On elections of times (in 13 chapters)', pp. 3–4.

[7] *Manuscript of Geoffrey Chaucer's 'Astrolabe' and Other Middle English Documents: (c. 1460–1487)* (Nara: Asahata Barman Lace Co., 1995). The present location of the Asahata manuscript is unknown, but we are grateful that Mr Asahata published this facsimile because he thought 'it better to show this manuscript to Chaucerian scholars than to keep it idle on the bookshelf'. (Introduction, p. 3)

[8] Descriptions of both Schoenberg manuscripts, ljs 188 and ljs 191, along with digital images, are accessible at the Schoenberg Database of Manuscripts, on-line at http://dla.library.upenn.edu/dla/schoenberg.

[9] M. C. Seymour describes the first section of the Bute manuscript (Kraus I), as does Sigmund Eisner. See M. C. Seymour, *A Catalogue of Chaucer Manuscripts, vol. I, Works before the Canterbury Tales* (Aldershot: Scolar, 1995), pp. 127–8; Sigmund Eisner (ed.) *A Treatise on the Astrolabe. A Variorum Edition of the Works of Geoffrey Chaucer, vol. VI, The Prose Treatises, part 1* (Norman, OK: University of Oklahoma Press, 2002), pp. 57–8.

[10] Sotheby's Catalogue, p. 113. The first two blank flyleaves are not reproduced in the Asahata facsimile.

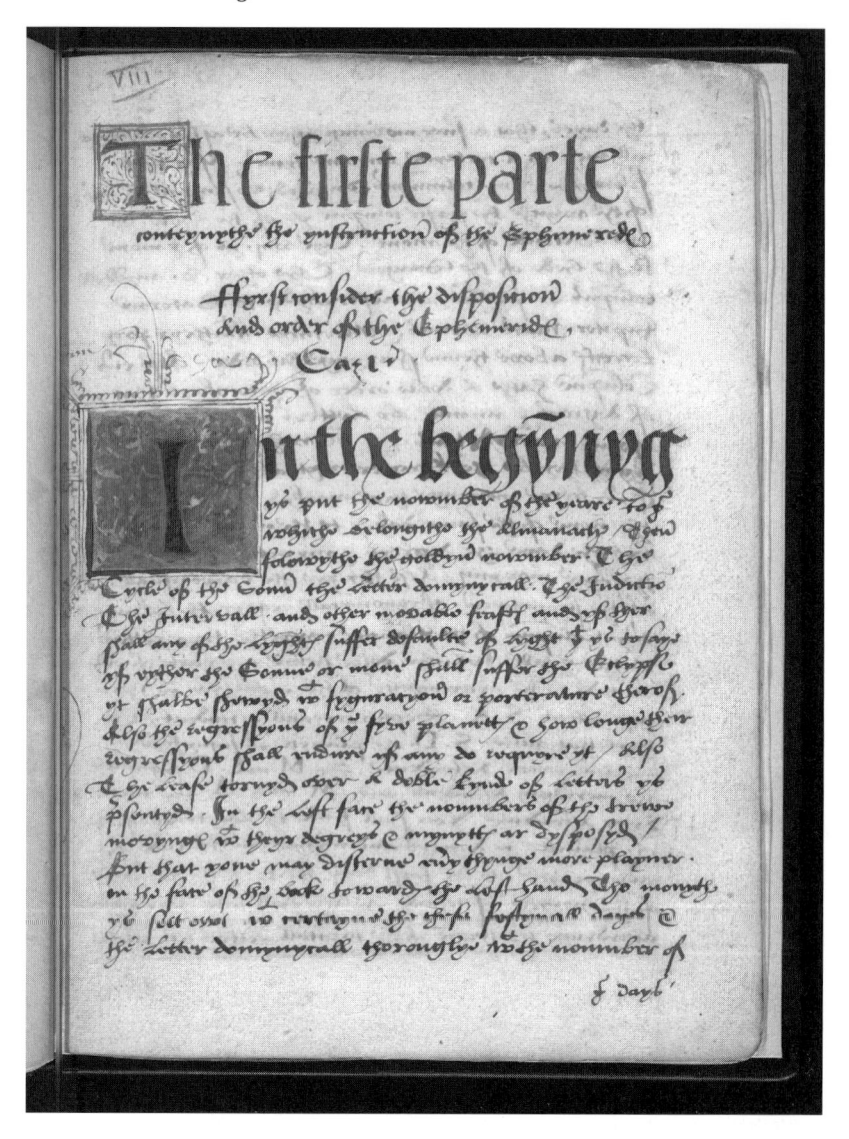

Plate 1 Sixteenth-century English translation of Johannes Schöner, 'Instructio intelligendae Ephemeridos', *Opusculum astrologicum*. Lawrence J. Schoenberg Collection, MS ljs 188, f. 1r. Reproduced with permission of Lawrence J. Schoenberg.

1. *Ff. 1–46v. ME, Prologue, list of contents and text, Al-Qabisi (Alcabitius), 'Introduction to the Art of Astrology',[11] translated from

---

[11] C. Burnett, K. Yamamoto and M. Yano, *Al-Qabīsī (Alcabitius): The Introduction to Astrology* (London: Warburg Institute, 2004), contains editions of Arabic and Latin texts with a

The significance of now-dispersed MS Bute 13   41

French version attributed to Pèlerin de Prusse[12] by Brokhole, 26 April 1460. Colophon, f. 46v: Her endith oure introductory of alcabiteus wt þe louyng of gode translated out of frenche into englysch be Brokhole be þe sayd seignevr the yer of our lord 1460 the 26 day of Apriele and hours [text breaks off]. Other Middle English translations of the Alcabitius treatise can be found in Trinity College Cambridge MSS O.5.26, ff. 1–28 (eVK2 6887.00; 6647.00) and O.7.2C, B (C, ff. 1–8v; B, ff. 1–27; eVK2 7109.00).[13]

a. Prologue and table of contents (ff. 1–4). Incipit: Be the lef of god y hope to do his pleasance and to gefe mynd and understandyng to other of my nacion; Colophon, f. 4: Her endis the Chapturs of Alkabicious of Iugmenttis of the steris and begynyth and begynyth [sic] the first defferens of devisionis (eVK2 1353.00).

b. Text (ff. 4–46v). Incipit: The devysyon of þe firmament in 12 partys egale as the devysyon of the signis and þe 12 partis (eVK2 6666.00); f. 7v, 'The tabule of the termys' showing relationships between signs of the zodiac and planet; other tables on ff. 9v, 12v, 13r-v, 14r-v.

Comments on the codex. Ff. 1–46v, predominantly script A, late fifteenth century; ff. 8v–9v, 20v–22, 23r-v, 27–28? script B, late fifteenth century. Script B at times is introduced mid-line.[14] Medieval foliation apparently began with the flyleaf. Many leaves have been cropped, but fifteenth-century folio numbers are found on ff. 4 (5), 5 (6), 8 (9), 11 (12), 12 (13), 15 (16), 16 (17), 17 (18), 33 (34), 34 (35). Initials on the first twelve leaves of text are red with some use of rubrication thereafter in Text 1. Following Text 1 there is no use of red.

---

modern English translation. See pp. 504–10 for an index to all versions. Bute 13 is omitted in the list of ME translations on p. 508, but the manuscript is described on p. 173. On this widely distributed and influential treatise see also David Pingree, 'Al-Qabīṣī, Abū Al-Ṣaqr 'Abd Al-'Azīz Ibn 'Uthmān Ibn 'Alī', in Charles Gillispie (ed.), *Complete Dictionary of Scientific Biography*, 27 vols. (New York: Cengage Learning, 2008), vol. XI, p. 226. *Gale Virtual Reference Library.* http://find.galegroup.com, accessed 9 June 2009.

[12] Pèlerin de Prusse (Pelerinus de Prussia) may have been the translator of the Alcabitius treatise into French. It is found with two works by him, one on elections and his *De usu astrolabii* (1361–2) eTK 411L, in a manuscript prepared for Charles V of France. See Edgar Laird, 'Astrology in the court of Charles V of France, as reflected in Oxford, St John's College, MS 164', *Manuscripta* 34 (1990): 167–76. See also Edgar Laird and Robert Fischer (eds.), *Pèlerin de Prusse on the Astrolabe* (Binghamton, NY: CMERS, State University of New York, 1995); Lynn Thorndike, *A History of Magic and Experimental Science: Fourteenth and Fifteenth Centuries*, vol. III (New York: Columbia University Press, 1934), pp. 586–7. We have not been able to identify Brokhole.

[13] eVK2 (electronic Voigts-Kurtz, 2nd edn) is a revision of *Scientific and Medical Manuscripts in Old and Middle English*. CD. (Ann Arbor: University of Michigan Press, 2000), now available on-line through a link from the website of the Medieval Academy of America: www.medievalacademy.org.

[14] Our identification and dating of scripts differs from that found in Sotheby's Catalogue, p. 113.

2. *Ff. 47v–71. ME, treatise on astrological prognostication to be used in a variety of circumstances: apprehending thieves and finding stolen objects, hiring servants, building and sailing ships, determining the outcome of battles. It contains an inserted Latin section (f. 58v) and a ME supplement (ff. 68v–71); (eVK2 6780.00).
   a. Text (ff. 47v–67) with authority citations to Messahala, Alkindi and 'Emartibeiaadis'. Headline title: Of the 7 hous; Rubric: Of the significations of the 7 hous; Incipit: The firste lord of his triplicite signat þe first wif þt the sone schale haue The 2 betokenith the 2 wif and þe place þt schale falle to hym.
   b. Inserted Latin passage (f. 58v) on astrological reckoning regarding medical care, in script C as used for Latin texts on ff. 84v–91. Incipit: Et si vellez facere curam corporis manuum et.s. \&/ pedum sit ascendis Capricornus Aquarius vel pisses vel luna in eis.
   c. Supplementary text on interrogations (ff. 68v–71). Rubric: [T]how schalt know þt in þis capter is many priuites þt no man knowes but rightwise men & men þt hath beyn in priuite of that is for to say where þorow þe planet brekis þe planet terme þe fac.

Ff. 67v, 68r, 71v blank
Comments on the codex. Ff. 47v–71, predominantly script A, late fifteenth century; f. 58v, script C, late fifteenth century. Fifteenth-century folio numbers are found on ff. 55 (56), 58 (59), 63 (64), 64 (65), 65 (66), 70 (71).

3. Ff. 72–81v. ME, Geoffrey Chaucer, 'Treatise on the Astrolabe' (text without prologue, in anomalous order). Incipit: Thyne astroloby hath a ring to put onn thi thombe on the left hand in takyng þe heght of þyngis (eVK2 7333.00).[15]

Comments on the codex. Ff. 72–81v, script A, late fifteenth century. Fifteenth-century folio number is found on f. 73 (74).

4. F. 82. ME, verse (incomplete, breaking off in line 12 of 32 lines). One other witness to this text (with slight variants) is British Library, MS Sloane 636, f. 103, which contains sixteen couplets (eVK2 2340.00).[16]

---

[15] See Seymour, *Catalogue*, vol. I, pp. 127–8; Eisner, *A Treatise*, pp. 57–8. For editions of the text with illustrations see Larry Benson (ed.), *The Riverside Chaucer*, 3rd edn (Boston: Houghton Mifflin, 1987), pp. 661–83, 1092–1102, 1193–7; W. W. Skeat (ed.), *The Complete Works of Geoffrey Chaucer* (Oxford: Clarendon, 1926), vol. III, pp. lvii–lxxx, 175–241, 352–67, figs. 1–18. See also Catherine Eagleton and Matthew Spencer, 'Copying and conflation in Geoffrey Chaucer's *Treatise on the Astrolabe*: A stemmatic analysis using phylogenetic software', *Studies in History and Philosophy of Science*, Part A, 37 (2006): 237–68. Apart from Skeat, all these sources were aware of this text in Bute 13.

[16] BL, Sloane 636, a mid-fifteenth century compilation of booklets containing numerous ME and Latin astrological and geomantic texts, is also a witness to the complete treatise on astrological houses, No. 16 (Kraus IV) of Bute and to the Latin text, No. 6 (Kraus I) of Bute.

Incipit: Her y wole youe wise make/ When ye schale a jornay tak (eVK2 2339.00).[17] The poem as it appears in the Bute manuscript is reproduced in Sotheby's Catalogue (13 June 1983), p. 114.

Ff. 82v, 83r–v blank
Comments on the codex. F. 82, script A, late fifteenth century.

5. F. 84. ME, horoscope diagram lacking a date, usually for a nativity, in centre square. Compartments for astrological positions include notes on their significance.

Comments on the codex. F. 84r, perhaps script A, late fifteenth century.

6. Ff. 84v–86v. Latin, text on astrological reckoning relating to thieves (incomplete). Incipit: Et si s[c]ire velis qualiter furis. A closely related Latin text is found in British Library, MS Sloane 636, ff. 117v–118v. Compare eTK 800R, 1464D, and possibly 354J.[18]

F. 87r blank
Comments on the codex. Ff. 84–86, script C, late fifteenth century. Fifteenth-century folio numbers are found on ff. 85 (88?), 86 (89?).

7. Ff. 87v–88. Latin, excerpt from Enoch, 'De 15 stellis de 15 herbis de 15 lapidibus'. The text is organised by stars, each section giving the stone and plant related to the star. In this excerpt we have the first three of fifteen sections. Incipit: Enoke tanquam unus ex philosophis super res (eTK 499G).[19]

Ff. 88v–89 blank
Comments on the codex. Ff. 87v–88, script C, late fifteenth century.

8. Ff. 89v–90v. Latin, Bernard of Gordon?, Tractatus magistri Bernardi de Gordonio ad faciendum sigilla et ymagines contra infirmitates diversas.[20] Headline title: Liber de ymaginibus 12 signorum; Incipit: Aries est signum masculinum igneum incisum membris (eTK 131L). See also 131H-K and 723I.

---

[17] J. Boffey and A. S. G. Edwards, *A New Index of Middle English Verse* (London: British Library, 2005), record this verse as 1201.5, p. 82.

[18] eTK (electronic Thorndike-Kibre), an expanded and updated digital version of Lynn Thorndike and Pearl Kibre, *A Catalogue of Incipits of Mediaeval Scientific Writings in Latin* (TK), rev. edn 1963 with two supplements, now available on-line through a link from the website of the Medieval Academy of America: www.medievalacademy.org.

[19] On the tradition of magic texts attributed to Enoch and others, see Louis DeLatte (ed.), *Textes latins et vieux français relatifs aux Cyranides: La traduction latine du XIIe siècle. Le Compendium aureum. Le De XV stellis d'Herme. Le livre des secrez de la nature* (Liège : Faculté de Philosophie et Lettres, 1942), fasc. 93, pp. 27–88. A copy of this treatise containing all fifteen sections is found in BL, Harley MS 1612, ff. 15–17v.

[20] Luke Demaitre, *Doctor Bernard de Gordon: Professor and Practitioner* (Toronto: Pontifical Institute of Mediaeval Studies, 1980). Although the attribution to Bernard is uncertain, Demaitre points out that this text contains elements associated with his authentic writings (pp. 97–101, 181).

Comments on the codex. Ff. 89v–90v, script C, late fifteenth century.

9. F. 91. Latin, recipe for improving vision, with astrological elements. Below the text is a simple diagram of lines and circles, perhaps indicating celestial positions. Rubric: Ad atuendum [*sic*] oculorum visum in senibus. Incipit: Accipe ova formicarum mixtum et lineas palpebras oculorum. Compare eTK 1331M.

Comments on the codex. F. 91, script C, late fifteenth century.

10. *Ff. 91v–92v. ME, astrological discussion of rain, ice, snow, hail, thunder and earthquake. Headline title: The rewle of Rayne. Incipit: When þe moon is wtin þe radiis of {Saturn} or elis in a {conjunction} or in any oþer aspect[21] (eVK2 8043.00). Compare also eVK2 1439.00; 1874.00; and 4458.00.

F. 93r blank
Comments on the codex. Ff. 91v–92v, script A, late fifteenth century.

11. *Ff. 93v–94. ME, astrological text on chess and other games. Headline title: For to play at Tabullys at ches or any other play. Incipit: If þu wolt haue þe game son broken put the ascender in a mouabul syng & in þe mone also (eVK2 2742.00). For other Middle English writings on chess and table games, see eVK2 7094.00 and 7238.00.

Comments on the codex. Ff. 93v–94, script A, late fifteenth century.

12. F. 94v. ME, horoscope diagram with date in centre square '13 day of may hora 12 pro domino B', equivalent to 1487 based on planetary positions in Tuckerman.[22] Preceded by five lines of ME text beginning 'For to tak a choruþ take hed to the mone'.

Comments on the codex. F. 94v, informal script A?, late fifteenth century, with free-hand diagram.

13. F. 95. Circular diagram containing letters and numbers for onomantic prognostication (*c.* 17?). Sphere of life and death.[23]

Ff. 95v–98 blank (96v, small figure in square, effaced with dark ink)
Comments on the codex. END OF KRAUS MS I. Late addition on formerly blank leaf.

---

[21] Astrological characters in the manuscript are expanded as words within braces.
[22] Kraus, Typescript Catalogue, ascertains the date based on Bryant Tuckerman, *Planetary, Lunar, and Solar Positions A.D. 2 to A.D. 1649 at Five-day and Ten-day Intervals* (Philadelphia: American Philosophical Society, 1964), p. 761.
[23] See Linda Ehrsam Voigts, 'The Latin verse and Middle English prose texts on the Sphere of Life and Death in Harley 3719', *Chaucer Review* 21 (1986): 291–305; Linda Ehrsam Voigts, 'The golden table of Pythagoras' in Lister Matheson (ed.), *Popular and Practical Science of Medieval England* (East Lansing, MI: Colleagues Press, 1994), pp. 123–39.

2.2 *Kraus II of IV, now Schoenberg ljs 188 (ff. 1–20v); see plate 1*

14. *Ff. 100–120/1–20. Sixteenth-century English translation of the first of a series of six Latin texts by Johannes Schöner (1477–1547)[24] together titled *Opusculum astrologicum, ex diuersorum libris, summa cura pro studiosorum utilitate collectum*. The book was printed in Nuremberg by Johann Petreius in 1539.[25] See plate 2. This initial treatise, titled 'Instructio intelligendae Ephemeridos', is a guide to astrological applications of the *Ephemerides* of Johann Müller (Regiomontanus, 1436–76),[26] a large volume of tables providing astronomical positions of celestial bodies for a given period of time. Rubric: The firste parte conteynythe the ynstruction of the Ephimeredes. Incipit: In the begynnyng ys put the nowmber of the yeare to þe whiche belongithe the Almanach. In this manuscript the text contains on f. 117r/17r the date 1540 following a table of lunar movements reading as follows: On the other side folowythe the table of the fyxt sterrys wt þe rysynge & goynge downe and the mediation of þe hevyn rectyfyed to the yere of our Lorde 1540 complet. Before the final table the text concludes, . . . lett hym serche the 57 probleme of the tablys of þe fyrst movynge or 13 of the tablys of dyrections of John de monte Regio (f. 19r). The works and the reputation of Regiomontanus were much more popular in the sixteenth century than during his lifetime.[27] In England, for example, a widely known prediction of a momentous event to occur as the result of the great conjunction of Saturn and Jupiter in 1583 was wrongly attributed to Regiomontanus.[28]

[24] Schöner (b. Karlstadt 1477, d. Nuremberg 1547) was an astronomer, astrologer and geographer known for his early acceptance of the cosmology of Copernicus. See Edward Rosen, 'Schöner, Johannes', in Charles Gillispie (ed.), *Complete Dictionary of Scientific Biography* (New York: Cengage Learning, 2008), vol. 12, pp. 199–200. *Gale Virtual Reference Library*. http://find.galegroup.com, accessed 29 July 2009. See also Thorndike, *A History of Magic and Experimental Science*, vol. III (1934), p. 124, vol. V (1941), p. 361.

[25] We are grateful for the opportunity to use this 1539 Latin treatise in Special Collections at the Linda Hall Library, Kansas City, Missouri.

[26] On Regiomontanus (b. Königsberg 1436, d. Rome 1476), mathematician and astronomer, see Michael Shank, 'Regiomontanus, Johannes', in Charles Gillispie (ed.), *Complete Dictionary of Scientific Biography* (New York: Cengage Learning, 2008), vol. 24, pp. 216–19. *Gale Virtual Reference Library*. http://find.galegroup.com, accessed 9 June 2009. See also Thorndike, *A History of Magic and Experimental Science*, vol. III (1934), pp. 603–4, vol. IV (1934), pp. 419–20, 430–1, 440–3, 530, vol. V (1941), pp. 1–15, 332–77.

Regiomontanus first printed his *Ephemerides* in Nuremberg in 1474, providing tables for 1475–1506 and a brief 'Instruction' (ISTC ir00104500, eTK 1611K). The work had been reprinted eleven more times by 1500. Tables for subsequent years were provided in sixteenth-century printings. See Ernst Zinner, *Regiomontanus: His Life and Work*, trans. Ezra Brown (Amsterdam: North-Holland, 1990), pp. 119, 128.

[27] See 'Aftermath of Regiomontanus', in Thorndike, *A History of Magic and Experimental Science*, vol. V (1941), pp. 332–77; 'the aftermath or afterglow of Regiomontanus belongs properly to the sixteenth century', p. 338.

[28] W. B. Stone, 'The prediction of Regiomontanus: A study in the eschatology of Elizabethan England', unpublished PhD dissertation, Harvard University (1953), pp. 3–6, 232, passim.

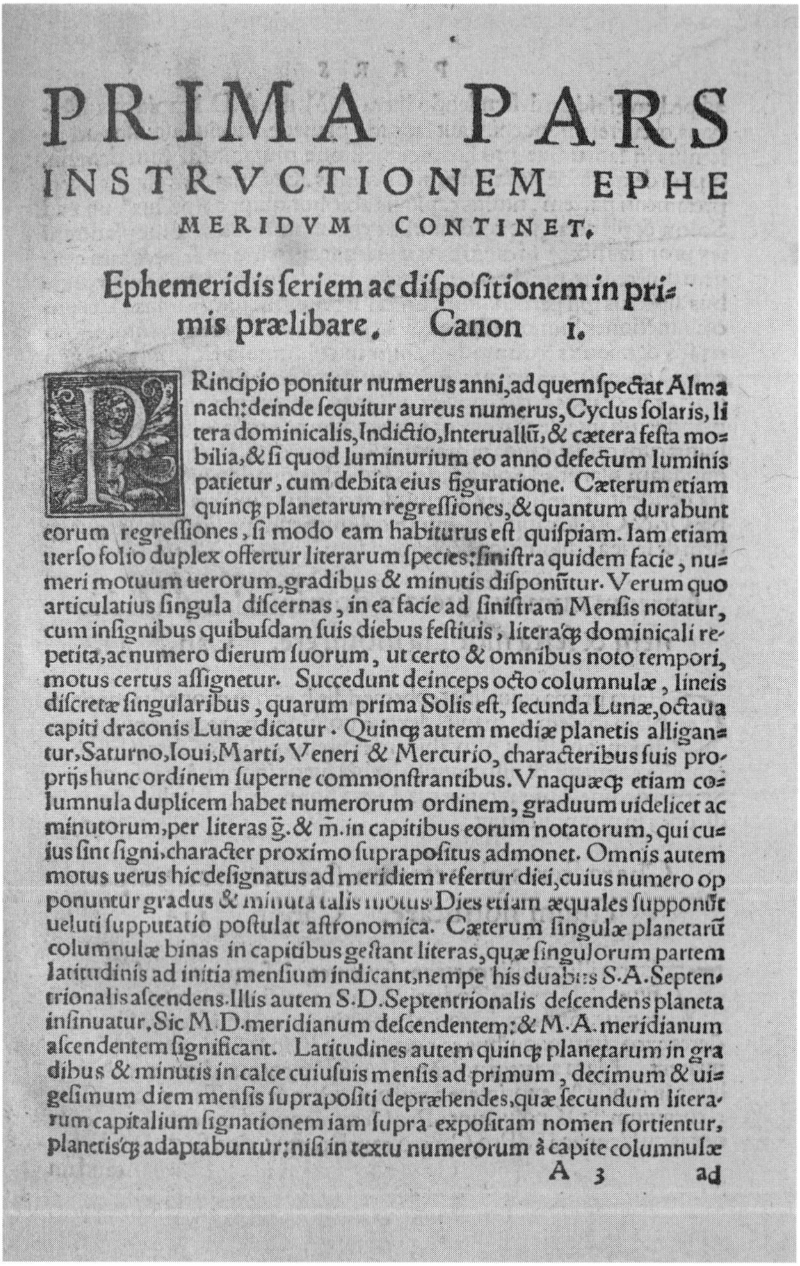

PRIMA PARS
INSTRVCTIONEM EPHE
MERIDVM CONTINET.

Ephemeridis feriem ac difpofitionem in primis prælibare. Canon I.

Rincipio ponitur numerus anni,ad quem fpectat Almanach:deinde fequitur aureus numerus,Cyclus folaris, litera dominicalis,Indictio,Interuallū,& cætera festa mobilia,& fi quod luminurium eo anno defectum luminispatietur, cum debita eius figuratione. Cæterum etiamquincg planetarum regreffiones,& quantum durabunteorum regreffiones, fi modo eam habiturus eft quifpiam. Iam etiamuerfo folio duplex offertur literarum fpecies:finiftra quidem facie, numeri motuum uerorum,gradibus & minutis difponitur. Verum quoarticulatius fingula difcernas, in ea facie ad finiftram Menfis notatur,cum infignibus quibufdam fuis diebus feftiuis, literacg dominicali repetita,ac numero dierum fuorum, ut certo & omnibus noto tempori,motus certus affignetur. Succedunt deinceps octo columnulæ, lineisdifcretæ fingularibus, quarum prima Solis eft, fecunda Lunæ,octauacapiti draconis Lunæ dicatur. Quincg autem mediæ planetis alligantur,Saturno,Ioui,Marti,Veneri & Mercurio, characteribus fuis proprijs hunc ordinem fuperne commonftrantibus. Vnaquæcg etiam columnula duplicem habet numerorum ordinem, graduum uidelicet acminutorum,per literas g̃.& m̃.in capitibus eorum notatorum, qui cuius fint figni,character proximo fuprapofitus admonet. Omnis autemmotus uerus hic defignatus ad meridiem refertur diei,cuius numero opponuntur gradus & minuta talis motus. Dies etiam æquales fupponuelutifupputatio poftulat aftronomica. Cæterum fingulæ planetarũcolumnulæ binas in capitibus geftant literas,quæ fingulorum partemlatitudinis ad initia menfium indicant,nempe his duabus S.A.Septentrionalis afcendens.Illis autem S.D.Septentrionalis defcendens planetainfinuatur, Sic M.D.meridianum defcendentem:& M.A.meridianumafcendentem fignificant. Latitudines autem quincg planetarum in gradibus & minutis in calce cuiufuis menfis ad primum, decimum & uigefimum diem menfis fuprapofiti depræhendes,quæ fecundum literarum capitalium fignationem iam fupra expofitam nomen fortientur,planetiscg adaptabuntur:nifi in textu numerorum à capite columnulæ

A 3 ad

Plate 2 Johannes Schöner, 'Instructio intelligendae Ephemeridos', *Opusculum astrologicum*, Nuremberg, 1539. A3r. Reproduced with permission of the Linda Hall Library of Science, Engineering & Technology, Kansas City, Missouri.

This sixteenth-century translation of the Schöner *Opusculum* appears to have been incorporated in Bute 13 to accompany the fifteenth-century copy of the Mariensüss commentary on the Regiomontanus treatise that followed it (Kraus III of IV, now Schoenberg ljs 191, ff. 1–20v; eVK2 2860.00). Two other ME manuscript witnesses to the Mariensüss commentary also are preceded by texts on the use of the *Ephemerides* tables, but these shorter preceding texts are translations of the brief 'Instruction' from the original 1474 printing of the *Ephemerides*, some portions of which are incorporated in the first chapter of Schöner. These two other manuscripts containing both the ME Regiomontanus 'Instruction' and the ME Mariensüss commentary are Trinity College Cambridge R.15.18 (eVK2 1751.00; 4357.00)[29] and London, Royal College of Physicians 384[30] (eVK2 1751.00; 4359.00; 3788.00).[31]

F. 120v blank
Comments on the codex. END OF KRAUS MS II. Ff. 1–20. Ff. 100–120v/1–20v, script D, after 1540. Tables on ff. 106/6, 108/8, 111v/11v, 117/17, 117v/17v, 119v/19v. Decorated initials: 6-line framed and painted initial with penwork flourishing, f. 100/1; sections demarcated by 3–4 line initials, some painted, some flourished (others wanting). Red strokes and underlining in text. According to the on-line catalogue for ljs 188, a watermark can be discerned, apparently a crown.[32] Many leaves have a catchword at the bottom of the text for the following page: 1r, 1v, 2r, 2v, 3r, 3v, 4r, 4v, 6v, 7r, 8r, 9r, 10r, 10v, 11v, 12r, 13r, 13v, 14r, 15r, 15v, 16r, 16v, 18r, 18v. Catchwords rarely occur when a table or decorative initial follows on the next page.

2.3 *Kraus III of IV, now Schoenberg ljs 191 (ff. 1–20v); see plate 3*

15. Ff. 124–41v/1–18v. ME, late-fifteenth century, translation of Bartholomaeus Mariensüss/Mariensüsz Slesita de Pascua, commentary on the *Ephemerides* of Regiomontanus, lacking prologue and list of contents (eVK2 3789.00), but including the final section, three canons: (1) astrological reckoning for bloodletting; (2) administration of medicines; and (3) planting of trees and vines and sowing of seeds (eVK2 1724.50). This text is a vernacular translation of the Latin treatise that

---

[29] See M. R. James, *The Western Manuscripts of Trinity College Cambridge: A Descriptive Catalogue*, 4 vols. (Cambridge: Cambridge University Press, 1901), vol. II, no. 941, pp. 356–7. This description is accessible on-line at http://rabbit.trin.cam.ac.uk/James/R.15.18.html. See also L. R. Mooney, *The Index of Middle English Prose, Handlist XI: Manuscripts in the Library of Trinity College, Cambridge* (Cambridge: D. S. Brewer, 1995), p. 65.
[30] N. R. Ker, *Medieval Manuscripts in British Libraries*, vol. I, London (Oxford: Clarendon, 1969), pp. 212–15.
[31] Although Bute does not contain a ME version of the complete 1474 'Instruction' of Regiomontanus, as do the T.C.C. and Roy. Col. Physician manuscripts, and as follows the 1481 Mariensüss commentary, it does contain in the first canon of the ME translation of Schöner's 'Instructio intelligendae Ephemerides' significant portions of the 1474 'Instruction'.
[32] http://dla.library.upenn.edu/dla/schoenberg/

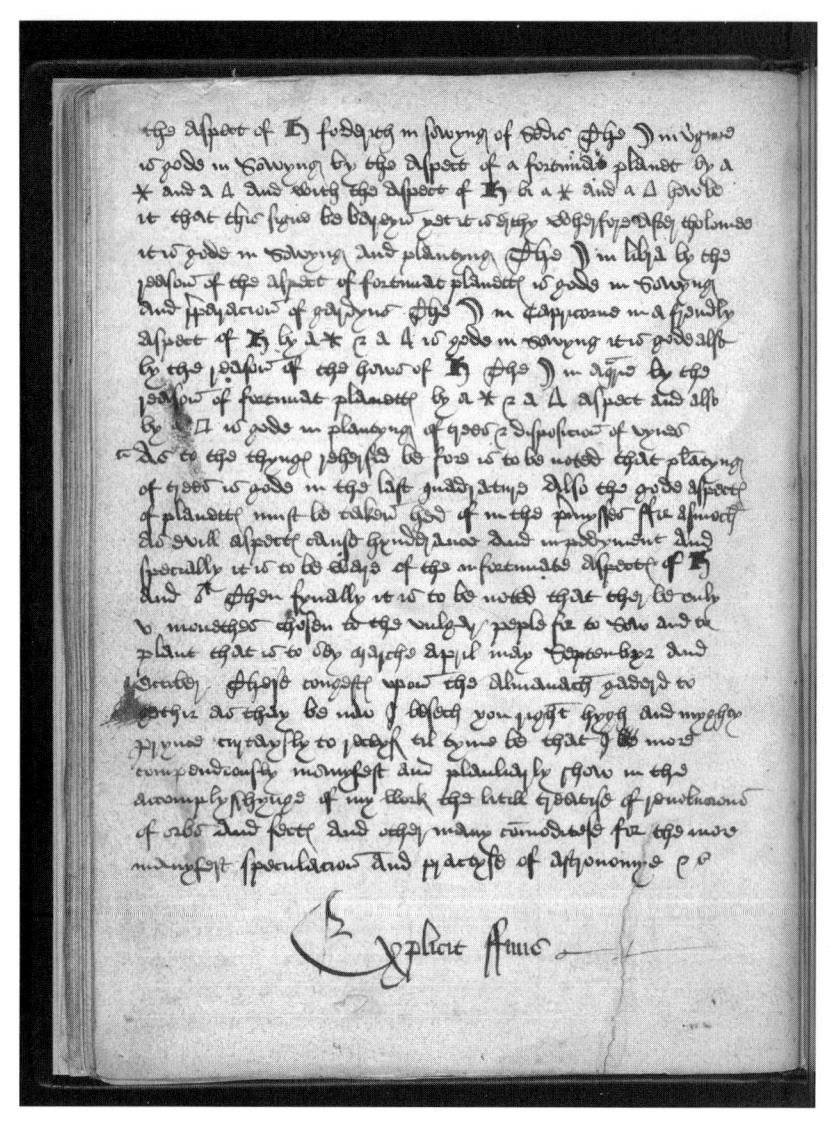

Plate 3 Fifteenth-century English translation of Bartholomaeus Mariensüss, commentary on the *Ephemerides* of Regiomontanus. Lawrence J. Schoenberg Collection, MS ljs 191, f. 18v. Reproduced with permission of Lawrence J. Schoenberg.

accompanied the printing of the Regiomontanus *Ephemerides* by Erhard Ratdolt (Venice, 1481; Latin prol. eTK 1364K, text 948L).[33] Rubric:

[33] Regiomontanus, *Ephemerides*, 1482–1506, with Bartholomaeus Mariensüss, 'Expositiones in Ephemerides et tabula mansionem' (ISTC ir00105000; eTK 948L, 1364K). The volume

The fyrst chapiter of the name of effimerides almanac otherwise called Tacuinum. Incipit: Now to be noted it is principally that these names have \iudiciall/[34] significacioun in maner of cinanyms for ech of them signyfieth a temporal as almanac or effemirides. Colophon (f. 141v/f. 18v): These congestes vpoun the almanach gaderd togethir as thay be now I besech you right hygh and myghty prynce curtaysly to receyf til tyme be that I more compendiously manyfest and planliarly show in the accomplyschynge of my work the litill treatise of reuolusions of orbs and sectis and other many commodiose for the more manyfest speculacioun and practyse of astronomye & c. Explicit ffinis. See plate 3. This prince is apparently also referred to on f. 135v/12v, 'Now I p[r]omyse your magnificence and I shal write an other treatyse of the reuolucions of the worldis and sectis and of folk how the state of the same may be knowen by the signe enteryng in to Aries'. Date found on f. 131/8v in chapter 6 on eleven stars that have influential qualities: 'veryfied the yere of our lorde m^{l}iiii^{c}lxxxx and vi'. The substitution of the English 'right hygh and myghty prynce' in Bute for 'dominus Ladislaw' may be of significance, given the 1496 date in the manuscript. The word 'prince' in medieval England could mean 'a (male) sovereign ruler; a monarch, a king' or possibly 'a male member of a royal family other than a reigning king'.[35] The likeliest candidate for the 'prince'

contains two dedications, the first by Mariensüss for his 'Expositiones' [f. 1], the second by Ratdolt (for the *Ephemerides* tables) to Federico da Montefeltro, Duke of Urbino [f. 11v], followed by the original 'Instruction' from the 1474 printing, [ff. 12r–v]. The Mariensüss dedication is 'Magnifico & generoso domino ladislao de Tschirnahoi d' boskountz & c. Bartholome Mariensüss Slesita de pascua: artium & medicine doctor: salutem plurimam dicit'.

The ME Mariensüss treatise in Bute omits his dedication to Ladislaw, but the dedication is translated in the versions in Trinity College Cambridge R.15.18, p. 7: 'To the ryght high and curtesse estate my lord ladyslawe and zschmahy of boscontz', and in Royal College of Physicians 384, f. 87o: 'To the right highe and curtesse astate my lord ladyslaw and zschmahy of boskontz'.

The Mariensüss dedication in the 1481 printing to 'domino ladislao' was apparently to Wladislas (Ulászló or Vladislaus Jagiello) II (b. 1456), king of Bohemia 1471–1516 (as Vladislau IV) and of Hungary (1490–1516). Interests in prognostication by members of the fifteenth-century Jagiellon dynasty are revealed in a prayer book dealing with divination by means of a crystal (crystallomancy) in the Bodleian Library, MS Rawlinson liturg. d. 6. Although the date of the hand in the prayerbook may link 'Wladislas' with an earlier Jagiellon, the illustrations are from the end of the fifteenth century, during the lifetime of Wladislas II. See Otto Pächt and J. J. G. Alexander, *Illuminated Manuscripts in the Bodleian Library Oxford*, 2 vols. (Oxford: Clarendon Press, 1966–70), I, no. 175 and Plate XIII; Claire Fanger and Benedek Láng, 'John of Morigny's *Liber visionum* and a Royal Prayer Book from Poland', *Societas Magica Newsletter* 9 (2002): 1–4; and Benedek Láng, 'Angels Around the Crystal: The Prayer Book of King Wladislas and the Treasure Hunts of Henry the Bohemian', *Średniowiecze*. http://staropolska.pl/sredniowiecze/opracowania/Lang.html and http://staropolska.pl/sredniowiecze/opracowania/Lang_01.html, accessed 29 December 2009.

[34] The scribe has changed his original 'ydempticall', which was presumably more faithful to the Latin, to 'judiciall'.
[35] See 'prince, n. 1, 7.' *Oxford English Dictionary Online*. Accessed 29 July 2009.

would be Henry VII (1457–1509),[36] but his son Arthur, Prince of Wales (1486–1502),[37] is also a possibility.

The astrological interests of Henry VII are well documented, both in terms of the presence of astrologers at his court,[38] and in terms of astrological manuscripts associated with him. Lewis of Caerleon, M.D. (fl. 1465–95) was a skilled astronomer who served as physician to Lady Margaret Beaufort, Countess of Richmond and mother of Henry VII; to her son Henry (both when he was Earl of Richmond and as Henry VII); and to Elizabeth, Henry's wife. Lewis wrote many astronomical treatises and tables and collected, transcribed and annotated astronomical manuscripts. He was almost certainly valued for his astronomical and astrological skills, and he received considerable remuneration and generous favours from the monarch.[39] John Argentine, M.D. (c. 1443–1508), who studied theology at Cambridge and apparently studied medicine at Padua or Ferrara, also assembled an extensive collection of astrological and astronomical treatises. Perhaps as a royal astrologer, Argentine cast nativities for Edward IV and the ill-fated child, Edward V, and he was employed by the Tudor successor to the House of York. Henry VII also appointed him physician and chaplain to his son Arthur on the birth of the prince in 1486. The last years of Argentine's life were spent as Provost of King's College Cambridge, 1501–8.[40] Two Italian physician-astrologers also attended Henry VII, William Parron (Gulielmus Parronus Placentinus), M.D. was a professional astrologer who served Henry VII from 1490 to 1503.[41] John Baptist Boerio (Boarius), M.D. (fl. 1494–1514)

---

[36] S. J. Gunn, 'Henry VII (1457–1509)', *Oxford Dictionary of National Biography* (Oxford University Press, online edition January 2008). www.oxforddnb.com/view/article/12954, accessed 27 July 2009. See also Mark R. Horowitz (ed.) 'Who was Henry VII? The 500th anniversary of the death of the first Tudor king (1509–2009)', special edition of *Historical Research* 82 (2009): 375–592.

[37] Rosemary Horrox, 'Arthur, Prince of Wales (1486–1502)', *Oxford Dictionary of National Biography* (Oxford University Press, online edition January 2008) www.oxforddnb.com/view/article/705, accessed 27 July 2009.

[38] Hilary M. Carey, *Courting Disaster: Astrology at the English Court and University in the Later Middle Ages* (New York: St. Martin's Press, 1992), pp. 123, 157, 161–4. Carey observes, p. 164, 'Whereas no medieval English king ever pursued the policy advocated by the *Secreta secretorum* to make an astrologer his constant companion... by the reign of Henry VII it had become impossible either to ignore or to dismiss astrology'.

[39] C. H. Talbot and E. A. Hammond, *The Medical Practitioners in Medieval England: A Biographical Register* (London: Wellcome Library, 1965), pp. 203–4; Faye Getz, 'Medical practitioners in medieval England', *Social History of Medicine* 13 (1990): 269; Carey, pp. 156–7. See also Linda Ehrsam Voigts, 'Scientific and medical books', in Jeremy Griffiths and Derek Pearsall (eds.), *Book Production and Publishing in Britain 1375–1475* (Cambridge: Cambridge University Press, 1989), pp. 345–402, especially ills. 44 and 45, showing astronomical tables and commentary thereon by Lewis.

[40] Talbot and Hammond, pp. 112–15; Getz, p. 263; Carey, pp. 157–60; Peter Murray Jones, 'Argentine, John (c. 1443–1508)', *Oxford Dictionary of National Biography* (Oxford: Oxford University Press, 2004) www.oxforddnb.com/view/article/642, accessed 29 September 2009.

[41] Carey, pp. 161–2; C. A. J. Armstrong, 'An Italian astrologer at the court of Henry VII', in E. F. Jacob (ed.), *Italian Renaissance Studies: A Tribute to the Late C. M. Ady* (New York: Barnes and Noble, 1960), pp. 432–54.

The significance of now-dispersed MS Bute 13 51

attended both Henry VII (after 1498) and Henry VIII. Erasmus praised his astrological skill as 'superior to all others'.[42]

Evidence of astrological books linked to Henry VII is also particularly rich. Among the entries referring to books in Privy Purse expenses, 1491–1505, is one of 1499 'To Master William Paromis, an astronymyre, £1', apparently a reference to William Parron, mentioned above.[43] On some occasion Parron apparently gave three decorated astrological manuscripts to Henry.[44] The most important astrological book written for Henry VII is a spectacular illuminated manuscript, British Library, Arundel 66, a very large and copiously illustrated astronomical-astrological manuscript of some 293 folios, probably completed in London in 1490.[45] Arundel 66 contains many astronomical tables, including the canons and tables for Oxford of John Killingworth, perhaps the most important of fifteenth-century English astronomers.[46] It also includes (ff. 48–249) the *Liber introductorius ad judicia stellarum* of the late thirteenth-century Guido Bonatus [Bonotti] de Foralivio, a work that in this manuscript was signed 30 June 1490 'per me Johannes Wellys compositus et renovatus' (f. 249).[47]

Ff. 142v/19v, 143r-v/20r-v blank.
Comments on the codex. END OF KRAUS MS III. Ff. 124–41v/1–18v, script E, *c.* 1500 (after 1496). F. 124 is soiled and badly rubbed, indicating that it circulated as the first text in an unbound booklet or manuscript. Leaves are foliated in an early sixteenth-century(?) hand. Scribal calligraphic capital letters at beginning of sections. Table, f. 126/3. F. 142/19. First of

[42] Talbot and Hammond, pp. 117–19; Getz, p. 264; Carey, p. 161.
[43] H. R. Plomer, 'Bibliographical notes from the privy purse expenses of King Henry the Seventh' *The Library*, Third Series 4 (1913): 291–304, p. 302. On Henry's Library see also T. A. Birrell, *English Monarchs and their Books: From Henry VII to Charles II* (London: British Library, 1987), pp. 5–7.
[44] Armstrong, 'An Italian astrologer', pp. 432–54; Kathleen L. Scott, *Later Gothic Manuscripts 1390–1490*, Survey of manuscripts illuminated in the British Isles, vol. VI, parts 1 and 2 (London: Harvey Miller, 1996), part 2, pp. 364–7. The manuscripts in question are BL, Royal 12.B.vi; Bodleian Selden supra 77, and Paris, B.N. lat. 6276. Scott also points out that the *Prognosticum* of Johannis Michael Nagonius, addressed to Henry VII, survives in York Minster Library XVI N. 2, a manuscript containing a frontispiece depicting the monarch in a chariot, and his coat of arms on f. 5v.
[45] Scott, *Later Gothic Manuscripts*, part 1, figs. 504–5, Colour Plate 17; part 2, pp. 364–7.
[46] J. D. North, 'The Alfonsine tables in England' in Y. Maeyama and W. Saltzer (eds.), *Prismata: Naturwissenschaftsgeschichtliche Studien* (Wiesbaden: Steiner, 1977), pp. 269–301. Rpt. in North, *Stars, Minds and Fate* (London: Hambledon, 1989), pp. 325–59. In his discussion of Killingworth, also spelled Chillingworth, (b. *c.* 1410, d. 1446), pp. 343–8, North addresses the 'new system' of Alfonsine tables created by this short-lived Merton College astronomer. He points out 'the sheer utility of the tables. The medieval scholar was an intensely practical man.... The compiler of ephemerides was a man in whose debt many considered themselves to stand', p. 348.
[47] John Welles, a common name, may refer to a scholar. See A. B. Emden, *A Biographical Register of the University of Oxford to A.D. 1500* (Oxford: Clarendon, 1957–9), s.v. Wells, Welles, Wellis, Wellys. However, John, Viscount Welles, d. 1498/9, was a half-brother of Lady Margaret Beaufort. See M. K. Jones and M. G. Underwood, *The King's Mother* (Cambridge: Cambridge University Press, 1992), pp. xxiii, 125–34. On John Willis, M.D., Cambridge, fl. 1456–80, see Talbot and Hammond, pp. 194–5.

two originally blank flyleaves containing on the recto seventeenth-century(?) Latin notes on astrology and diseases.

2.4 Kraus IV of IV, present whereabouts unknown,[48] ff. 145–61/1–17

16. Ff. 145–148v/1–4v. ME, incomplete text on thirteen astrological houses as confirmed by geomancy.[49] Incipit: The first howse ys clepid ascendant and the hirne off the est & it is the howse of liffe & hit signifieth bodies & life (eVK2 6756.00). Similar texts are found in London, BL, Sloane 636 (eVK2 6758.00) and London, Wellcome Library 510 (eVK2 6757.00).[50]

Comments on the codex. Ff. 145–60/1–17, indeterminate hands, dated to *c.* 1500 in catalogue descriptions.[51]

17. Ff. 149–160/5–16. ME, on astrological elections of times, prologue and text (eVK2 1948.00; 3195.00). Other ME versions are eVK2 1945.00–1947.00 and 3196.00–3199.00; 4578.00; 7729.00; 7730.00. Of particular significance is the text in Royal College of Physicians, MS 384 (eVK2 7729.00).[52]
   a. Prologue (f. 149/5). Incipit: For as moche as every science or craft oon art for his utilite (eVK2 1948.00).
   b. Text (ff. 149–60). Incipit: It is to knowe that ther ben 7 planetis þe whiche (eVK2 3195.00).

F. 161/17 blank
Comments on the codex. END OF KRAUS MS IV. Ff. 145–60/1–17, indeterminate hands, dated to *c.* 1500 in catalogue descriptions.

3. The relationship of Bute 13 to other surviving manuscripts

Bute 13 shares intriguing patterns of common texts with other manuscripts. Such combinations are important because they illustrate why Bute 13 should be understood as a whole and why its dismemberment is so unfortunate.

---

[48] Catalogue 562, Hellmut Schumann of Zurich (May 1994), Item 7, pp. 3–4.
[49] For records of forty ME treatises on geomancy, see eVK2.
[50] This astrological-geomantic treatise is found in a fuller version (fifteen houses) in the mixed English-Latin mid-fifteenth century codex, BL, Sloane 636, 32–37v (eVK2 6758.00). Sloane 636 is also the only other codex known to us containing the poem that is No. 4 (Kraus I) and the Latin text that is No. 6 (Kraus I) in Bute 13. It contains numerous astrological and geomantic texts. Another incomplete version of this treatise (twelve houses) is found in Wellcome Library, MS 510, ff. 32–34v (eVK2 6757.00).
[51] Sotheby's Catalogue, p. 113; Schumann, Item 7, p. 3.
[52] Lister Matheson and Ann Shannon (eds.), 'A treatise on the elections of times', in Lister Matheson (ed.), *Popular and Practical Science of Medieval England* (East Lansing, MI: Colleagues Press, 1994), pp. 23–59 (based on Oxford, Bodleian, MS Ashmole 337, ff. 1v–19), contains a discussion of six manuscripts, including Bute 13, pp. 27–8.

British Library, Sloane 636, like Bute, a compendium made up of booklets, contains some thirty Middle English texts, most on astrological prognostication, along with numerous Latin writings on the subject. This codex shares three texts with Bute 13: No. 4 (Kraus I), No. 6 (Kraus I) and No. 16 (Kraus IV). No. 4, the ME verse prognostication for journeys, is found only in these two codices and is complete only in Sloane 636. No. 6, the Latin astrological text concerning thieves, is found in both manuscripts. No. 16, the ME treatise on astrological houses confirmed by geomancy, is complete in Sloane 636 and occurs in incomplete versions in Bute 13 and Wellcome Library 510.

Two other Middle English manuscripts are particularly significant in clarifying how the sixteenth-century Bute 13 compiler made his choices in assembling his texts: Trinity College Cambridge MS R.15.18 and London, Royal College of Physicians MS 384.[53] Like Bute, the Trinity manuscript contains a late fifteenth-century copy of Chaucer's *Treatise on the Astrolabe* (No. 3, Kraus I), the commentary by Bartholomaeus Mariensüss on the *Ephemerides* of Regiomontanus (No. 15, Kraus I) and the 'Instruction' of Regiomontanus, parts of which are incorporated in the Schöner compilation in Bute (No. 14, Kraus II). These three texts are the only Middle English works among the Latin treatises in the Trinity manuscript.

Royal College of Physicians MS 384 is a large paper codex from the end of the fifteenth century or beginning of the sixteenth, written by a single scribe. In it are found more than thirty-five Middle English and Latin tables and treatises ranging from more learned Arabic astronomy to popular astrological prognostication. Royal College of Physicians MS 384, like No. 17 (Kraus IV) in Bute 13, incorporates a Middle English text on election of times. More important, it includes, like Trinity, the commentary on the *Ephemerides* of Regiomontanus by Bartholomaeus Mariensüss in the same translation as found in Bute, No. 15 (Kraus III). Royal College of Physicians, also like Trinity, contains the 'Instruction' of Regiomontanus, parts of which are incorporated in the Schöner compilation in Bute, No. 14 (Kraus II).

4. Bute compilation: significant individual texts

The importance of Bute 13 lies in part in its individual works. It appears to contain a number of unique texts: No. 1 (Kraus I), Brokhole's 1460 translation of Alcabitius; No. 2 (Kraus I), a long ME work on astrological prognostication; No. 10 (Kraus I), ME astrological predictions of weather; No. 11 (Kraus I), ME astrological work on chess and other games; and No. 14 (Kraus II), an Early Modern English translation of Schöner's Opusculum, part 1 (which includes parts of the Regiomontanus 'Instruction').

[53] Linda Ehrsam Voigts, 'What's the word? Bilingualism in late-medieval England', *Speculum* 71 (1996): 813–26, describes the three manuscripts containing the Regiomontanus text and accompanying commentary in Middle English as evidence that the vernacular had achieved credibility for the transmission of sophisticated scientific writings (p. 817).

Also of considerable interest is the modification of the commentary by Bartholomaeus Mariensüss on the *Ephemerides*. Unlike the Trinity or Royal College of Physicians versions to which it is closely related, text No. 15 (Kraus III) in Bute 13 deletes the preliminary address in the Mariensüss commentary to 'my lord ladyslawe and zschimahy of boscontz'. However, in the body of the work the English translator inserts references to a 'right high and mighty prince' rather than to the 'dominus' in Mariensüss 1481 Latin (and 'lord' in Trinity and Royal College of Physicians versions). This prince is also addressed at the end of the text as 'your magnificence' in the section where the author promises to write another treatise. It is quite possible that this commentary was adapted to address an English 'prince', and the date 1496 in the English version of Bute should not be overlooked, given the well-attested interest in astrology of Henry VII (r. 1485–1509).

5. Bute compilation: the whole greater than the sum of its individual texts

Bute 13, even though now scattered, remains a manuscript of considerable value for our understanding of late medieval English scientific writing, both because of the unique texts it contains and because a sophisticated sixteenth-century compiler brought together in this manuscript a unified and purposeful compendium for astronomical and astrological calculation and prognostication. This unity is evidenced in complementary texts, such as the English and Latin writings dealing with astrological calculations regarding theft (Nos. 2 and 6, Kraus I). It is also evidenced in the range of information of value to astrologers, from advice on use of the astrolabe in Chaucer's treatise (No. 3, Kraus I), to instructions on using the tables in the *Ephemerides* of Regiomontanus (No. 14, Kraus II) and the Mariensüss commentary on those *Ephemerides* (No. 15, Kraus III). Skilled astrologers were of necessity skilled astronomers, and to this end they required astrolabes, astronomical tables and treatises on the use of tables and on astrological calculation.[54] Bute 13 in its entirety must have been created to fulfil the promise of the colophon of the Mariensüss treatise: 'for the more manyfest speculacions and practyse of astronomye'.[55]

---

[54] Physicians in the Faculty of Medicine at the University of Paris – designated for some time as 'Facultas in medicina et astrologia' – were urged to possess an almanac with astrological tables and an astrolabe for accurate astrological calculation. See Thorndike, *A History of Magic and Experimental Science*, vol. 4, pp. 141–2.
[55] Text 15 (Kraus III), f. 141.

5 Communicating attitudes and values through language choices

Diatopic and diastratic variation in *Mary Magdalene* in MS Digby 133

MAURIZIO GOTTI AND STEFANIA MACI

1. Introduction

In previous analyses of the Middle English play *Mary Magdalene* in Bodleian Library, MS Digby 133, no satisfactory interpretation of diatopic and diastratic variations has been offered: deviation from the norm has usually been classified as scribal inconsistency. Indeed, the framework within which the play has been persistently explored seems to have been outlined by literary and philological studies rather than by linguistic investigation. Such types of research range from an account of the textual history of MS Digby 133 in which scribal hands are compared, to suggestions regarding both diachronic and diatopic aspects of the play (Bowers 1965; Baker and Murphy 1967; Bennett 1978; Baker 1989; Bush 1989), as well as to the geographical location for the staging of the play, which seems to have been Lincoln because of the liturgical tradition of this town and its St Mary Magdalene Cathedral (Ritchie 1963). Further investigation has been directed towards the performance of the play during the late Middle Ages, apparently staged in Chelmsford in the early 1560s, as evidenced by a detailed analysis of the Chelmsford play book and the Chelmsford list of properties (Coldewey 1975). In this area of research, studies have flourished concerning both the way the play has been staged (Wickham 1972; Jeffrey 1973; Jones 1978) and the possibility of a present-day production of *Mary Magdalene* (McKinnel 1984). Special attention has been given to the themes that characterise the play: the importance of the allegory of the castle, regarded as the fortress where the conflict between Good and Evil is fought (Cornelius 1930); the imagery of banqueting and clothing, by means of which the differences between good and evil characters are emphasised (Coletti 1979); as well as the imagery of sleep and waking, darkness and light characterising the play and symbolising the passage from sin and death to eternal life (Maltman 1979) and linked to the motif of temporal and spiritual sovereignty (Velz 1968). The religious role found in *Mary Magdalene* has been compared with that emerging from other liturgical, secular, Latin and vernacular English and Continental medieval plays dealing with the Magdalene figure (Elton 1948; Garth 1950; Chauvin 1951; Davidson 1972) and connected to the role offered by canonical and apocryphal gospels (Malvern 1969). Such a role is omnipresent in the play and apparently derives from both historical and biblical sources supported (or romanced) by the *South English Legendary* (Grantley 1983) and by an eleventh-century manuscript (Misrahi 1943).

Linguistic analysis has been marginally carried out by the editors of the play (Furnivall 1882; Schmidt 1885; Pollard 1890; Adams 1924; Devlin 1966; Bevington 1975; Baker and Murphy 1976; Donovan 1977; Baker et al. 1982; Grantley 1983). Apart from Pollard's edition, which only covers the first part of the play, all the other editions seem to be emendations of Furnivall's. Although all editors describe every aspect of the play, they never seem to offer original contributions, as they hardly differ from Furnivall's first description of the play. Indeed, every edition is a replica of the first, with the classical division into sections dealing with the manuscript description, language, versification, sources and editorial method. As to the linguistic section, all editors describe the type of language used in *Mary Magdalene* but none offers a plausible interpretation for the variants found in the play, which are all dismissed as the result of scribal mistakes and bad copying. What is missing is an in-depth analysis of the language of *Mary Magdalene* by means of which deviations from the norm can be justified.

These linguistic 'discrepancies' should be carefully scrutinised according to a change of perspective. Our chapter will indeed show that what has traditionally been regarded as scribal carelessness actually derives from a modern misunderstanding of medieval scribal practices (Laing and Lass 2003). The purpose of the following investigation is, therefore, to make a contribution to the understanding of the language of the Digby play of *Mary Magdalene*, its use and meanings connected to dialupic variations, which have revealed certain pragmatic and sociolinguistic variables connected to codes, registers and situational contexts, by means of which social status, pious intentions and religious credo are revealed through language. Indeed, the significant combination of Southern, Midlands and Northern elements featuring in the language of *Mary Magdalene* does not imply scribal sloppiness, but is, instead, the result of the scribe's desire to faithfully reproduce the author's design, i.e. to communicate a religious message thanks to the negotiation of certain linguistic traits.

2. MS Digby 133

This study is based on the text of *Mary Magdalene* preserved in MS Digby 133 (Bodleian Library), a quarto volume containing other unrelated texts brought together by chance: Galileo's *Discorso del Flusso e Reflusso del Mare*, dated 1616; a tract of Roger Bacon's *Radix Mundi*, dated 1550; *The Conversion of St Paul*; tracts of *De Theorica Trium Superiorum* (*Planctarum*), *De Epiciclo Lunæ* and *De Capite et Cauda Draconis*, all of them written in a seventeenth-century hand; the incomplete *Trattato dell'Arte Geomantica*, probably dating from the early seventeenth century; *Mary Magdalene*; *Candelmes Day and the Kyllyng of the Children of Israelle*; and the incomplete fragment of *Wisdom*. The contents of this manuscript were put together in the seventeenth century and rebound in the nineteenth century in a seventeenth-century style (Devlin 1966: ii; Baker and Murphy 1976: vii; Baker *et al.* 1982: ix). The various texts are physically distinct and the paper used is of varying sizes. The only evidence of a continuing hand in the manuscript seems to be provided by the fact that (a) the initials of Myles Blomefylde are on *The Conversion of St Paul*, *Mary Magdalene* and *Wisdom*; (b) probably the main scribe of *The Kyllyng* was also the scribe of *Wisdom*; (c) lines 217–24 of *Mary Magdalene* seem to have been borrowed from *The Kyllyng* (lines 97–104).

Little is known about the history of the manuscript. It bears the initials K.D., which scholars (Devlin 1966; Baker and Murphy 1976; Baker *et al.* 1982) have attributed to Kenelm Digby. Much of Sir Kenelm Digby's library was donated to him by his own tutor at Oxford, Thomas Allen, who was an enthusiastic collector of scientific and alchemical works; Digby 133 is a typical Allen-Digby book, since it is a collection of alchemical, magical, astrological and religious-literary works. None of the Digby 133 texts was, however, listed in the catalogue of the Allen Library. Only the Galileo, Bacon and geomancy treatises were listed as the contents of the book when the formal Bodleian Catalogue was compiled in 1634. A first catalogue description of *The Conversion*, *Mary Magdalene* and *The Kyllyng* can be dated back to the 1640s; the *Wisdom* fragment appeared as a text in the 1697 catalogue. Therefore, as Baker and Murphy (1967: 165) state, 'there is the possibility that the plays were very late acquisitions by Digby's librarian and were simply lumped together with the treatises after the catalogue had already been made for the formal presentation to the Bodleian'. Nevertheless, from the numbering of the various texts throughout, the original work seems to have comprised the Galileo tract, *Radix Mundi*, the treatise on geomancy and *Mary Magdalene*. At some time, this book was broken up and enlarged with the other plays, which bore the initials or the name of Myles Blomefylde and therefore showed some sort of relationship with *Mary Magdalene*.

2.1 Description

Mary Magdalene occupies ff. 95r–145r of MS Digby 133; it is in octavo and the paper used has a watermark throughout, representing an elaborately drawn pot of flowers quite similar to a French design described by Briquet (1968: 612), which dates this manuscript to around 1510–25.[1] Scribal conventions apparently follow the tradition of the early sixteenth century. The copy appears to be in a single hand throughout and the scribe seems to

---

[1] The date identified, thanks to the watermark, seems to indicate the date of the copying, as the original text may have been written earlier.

have written in Gothic *littera cursiva* Secretary *currens* with a few Anglicana features.

The first page bears the initials M.B., identified as those of Myles Blomefylde; the words *explicit oreginale de Sancta Maria Magdalena* at the end of the text have been taken by editors to mean that the manuscript was the text used in dramatic representations (Baker *et al.* 1982: xxvii). Since the text of *Mary Magdalene* in MS Digby 133 is not the original one but a very bad and hurriedly made copy, it seems likely that the scribe copied the inscription found at the end of the original text. Baker *et al.* (1982: xxxii) claim that the text was copied under stress conditions: apart from spelling mistakes, more than thirty lines are missing, most of which are tail-rhyming lines; stage directions were copied in the wrong place (as, for example, those after lines 1796 and 2107); lines were placed in the wrong order (such as lines 1438–9); pages were skipped (ff. 141v–142v); sometimes, the same lines were repeated (such as lines 427 and 437). In short, there seems to be such a lack of care in copying that *Mary Magdalene* might be the earliest 'pirate' copy of an English play (Baker 1989).

2.2 Authorship, date and provenance

The initials of Myles Blomefylde at the beginning of the play might lead to the conclusion that he was the author of the play. Yet, the watermark described above confutes the supposition of Myles's authorship, since Myles was born in 1525. The fact that the text of *Mary Magdalene* is a copy, as said before, makes identification of the author of the play impossible.

Mary Magdalene is written in a single hand throughout and the scribal practice follows the tradition of the 1520s. This, combined with the date of the watermark, led some scholars (Baker and Murphy 1967, 1976) to the conclusion that the play had been written in the second decade of the sixteenth century, and therefore later than the supposed date of composition given by Furnivall (1882: 301) as 1485. Yet, even though the scribal tradition and the watermark would suggest an early sixteenth-century date, this might refer to the date of the copying whereas the original play might be dated several years earlier than the surviving manuscript (Donovan 1977).

A linguistic study of the text reveals an East-Midland provenance as the dialect used resembles that of Norfolk. Schmidt (1885: 385) suggests that *Mary Magdalene* was a Midland play written in a Kentish dialect. Bennett (1978: 6) observes that the language used in *Mary Magdalene* is strikingly similar to that of *Promptorium Parvolorum* (1440) from an orthographic, morpho-syntactic, semantic and metaphorical point of view, and that such a language seems to be the dialect of Lynn. A provenance of Bury St Edmunds seems possible, but, as Ritchie (1963) rightly assumes, the great number of scenes and characters in *Mary Magdalene* certainly make a performance of the play too expensive for the Abbey of Bury. Ritchie then suggests that probably the location of the play's performance was Lincoln, the largest diocese in England, where religious plays had been acted since the second decade of the fourteenth century; this suggestion is strongly supported by the fact that in the fifteenth century this religious dramatic tradition was controlled by the powerful St Anne's Guild and that St Mary Magdalene Chapel is in Lincoln Cathedral. Basically, however, the geographical area of provenance might be the area of East Anglia, probably extended to Cambridgeshire, Suffolk and part of Essex (Baker 1989: 21).

Although scholars (Furnivall 1882: xiv, 53; Schmidt 1885: 385; Pollard 1890: 193; Devlin 1966: iv; Bevington 1975: 689; Donovan 1977: xv; Baker *et al.* 1982: xxxvi; Grantley 1983: 442) have identified the language of *Mary Magdalene* as belonging to the East-Midland dialect, with features pointing either to Norfolk, Lynn, or Lincolnshire, there is, however, an interesting mix of Southern and Northern features, such as the Southern infinitive ending *-en* typical of monosyllabic verbs (as in *gon*, deriving from OE *gā*, line 1011), which in the manuscript is also found for disyllabic verbs (as, for example, in *leuen*, line 65), and the use of infinitives with no final morphemes (as in *bring*, line 288); the occurrence of the Southern ending of the third-person singular *-þ*, *-th* (*holdyth*, line 126), together with the Northern form *-es*, *-ys* (*dwellys*, line 125), though sporadically used; plus the occurrence of the Northern spelling 'qw-' (*qwat*, line 523) for 'wh-', used along with 'wh-' (*what*, line 512) and 'w-' (*wos*, line 6). There is a noticeable presence of Old French loanwords, which apparently points more to a South-Eastern provenance than an East-Midland one. These variations in diatopic features, which cannot be immediately justified, have been considered by scholars (Furnivall 1882; Pollard 1890; Adams 1924; Devlin 1966; Baker and Murphy 1976; Donovan 1977; Baker *et al.* 1982) as scribal inconsistencies.

2.3 Scribal practice

Scribal practice is more complex than it appears. Middle English (henceforth ME) scribes were inventing a new spelling system. Indeed, the Norman Conquest certainly influenced the use of written English in Britain. Before the Conquest, English was the language of both government and literature, and was used, in particular, in recording legal and administrative documents (in this, it differed from the rest of Europe, where Latin was used). The Conquest influenced the use of written English so much that Latin and French replaced English in the written language of government, law and literature. Yet, the drawing up of documents in English did not cease completely: copying such records was important in order not to tear original registers when handling documents (which were not replaced by their copy but kept as proof in case of litigation). When, in early ME, the recording of documents in English flourished once more, it could well occur that scribes found the original Old English (henceforth OE) spelling incomprehensible and felt obliged to invent their own (Laing 1991: 33–9). ME scribes, therefore, were spelling reformers by necessity (Laing 2008: 11).

While copying, scribes had to decode the original texts or manuscripts and re-encode them in such a way as to offer different encoding solutions. Sometimes spelling systems could include variant solutions adopted by a single scribe (Laing 1999: 251). The scribe could then invent a spelling system and use it (a) to compose rather than copy (as Orm); (b) to copy someone else's work (and thus decode the language of the author and then re-encode it in his own language); (c) to copy someone else's work which he also had to translate (and thus decode the language of the author, re-encode it in his own language and to a greater or lesser extent translate the original text or manuscript into his own dialect (Laing 1999: 251–70; see also McIntosh et al. 1986: 12–23). Undoubtedly, in many cases scribes knew the different dialects and had no difficulty in copying the text. This was a necessity because texts and scribes were not physically linked, they were able to move around freely: texts passed from one region to another, and dialectal translation was necessary so as to allow the text to be understood by its audience or readership; scribes from other regions, and therefore speaking different dialects, had to understand (i.e. to translate) the text in order to copy it (Beadle 1991: 93; see also McIntosh et al. 1986: 12–23 and Laing 2008: 11–14). For instance, a scribe from Norfolk could work in Kent, and while copying his Kentish exemplars could use a Norfolk spelling system to produce a Kentish translation; the same scribe, when working in Norfolk, could come across a Northumbrian text and, while copying it, have to translate the Northumbrian dialect and its spelling systems into the Norfolk systems in order to make the text accessible to other Norfolk people. Sometimes they probably did not care whether they understood the words and simply tried to copy the text in exactly the same way as it was written. If this was the case, even in late ME, they reproduced the OE spelling features perfectly since they did not grasp the exact sense of words and were worried about losing the meaning of the text unless they reproduced it word for word. In other cases, scribes copied the text less carefully and even invented nonsensical spellings because they did not understand the language in its strange, archaic forms (Laing 1991: 39).

We are not able to say whether the scribe of *Mary Magdalene* can be regarded as either the 'translator' of his exemplars or as the inventor of some spelling system which was used to copy someone else's work. It seems, however, that *Mary Magdalene* has strong Norfolk features (Beadle 1991: 90). Modern editors of the play (Devlin 1966: iv; Bevington 1975: 689; Donovan 1977: xv; Baker et al. 1982: xxxvi; Grantley 1983: 442) claim that native words appear to have a modified orthography because, apparently, the scribe(s), while copying the manuscripts, tended to change the spelling of words into that of his/their own dialect. In the opinion of these scholars, to preserve the rhythmical pattern of the stanza, such changes were not made when lexemes were in a rhyming position. Overall, the general opinion about the manuscript of *Mary Magdalene* is that it was copied by a single scribe who used such an inconsistent style – probably because his exemplar was inconsistent, too – that *Mary Magdalene* may be regarded as a very hurried, poor copy of the original manuscript (Baker *et al.* 1982: xxxi–xxxii). In other words, a consistent feature of *Mary Magdalene* seems to be its inconsistent spelling, which is so varied as to confirm the impression of scribal carelessness. Indeed, the same word may occur in different forms and spellings. Examples are 'daughter(s)' spelt as *doctors* (line 68), *dowtter* (line 99), *dowctor* (line 416), *docctor* (line 877), or 'variance' spelt as *weryoūs* (line 36), *varyawñs* (line 767), *waryawns* (line 1903), *waryovñs* (line 2004), *weryawñs* (line 2097). The causes of these graphical discrepancies are accounted for by Blake (1979: 40), who links them to the absence of a universally accepted standard, where no norms of spelling, inflectional use or syntax existed to which writers and copyists felt they had to adhere. The scholarly opinion according to which graphic variations in *Mary Magdalene* are indeed expressions of chaotic and misleading irregularities (from which no geographical and dialectal identification of the play can be inferred) has not adequately recognised that the principles upon which the spelling of the play is based may reveal the strong relationship existing between orthography, on the one hand, and phonology and morphology, on the other. A typical example of the use of *d* for *th* is *ded*, 'death' (line 1319), which both the *Oxford English Dictionary* and the *Middle English Dictionary* record as a thirteenth- to sixteenth-century variant in ME Northern dialects (but not confined to just these, as indicated by Dobson 1968: 954–5; and Brunner 1970: 38); the spelling found in the play suggests a plosive form since the word rhymes with *godhed* (line 1321). However, a less dialectally marked use of 'th' is possible when the word is not in a rhyming context, as revealed by *deth*, 'death', found in the stage direction after line 775.

Although any scribal variance could be accounted for by historical reasons as it was mainly caused by a rupture of the English writing tradition that took place after the Norman Conquest (Blake 1979; Laing and Lass 2007), scribes were native English-speakers who wrote professionally for a native English speaking audience with whom they shared linguistic knowledge; the apparent carelessness and confusion which have always been attributed to medieval scribes are 'an artefact of our own present lack of understanding' (Laing and Lass 2003: 258). The fact that ME scribes did not feel any obligation either to preserve the original spelling or to 'observe complete consistency in adapting the spelling of their original to make it conform to their own practice' (Brook 1963: 56) is not synonymous with inferior quality of the represented language. Therefore, *Mary Magdalene* should not be regarded as 'corrupted' and its scribes should not be considered incompetent in their work. Variation is thus not an indication of the scribe's carelessness but rather of its being part of the author's precise linguistic design whose communicative function was that of highlighting differences in social status and moral standing.[2] In copying his original, the *Mary Magdalene* scribe was not actually incompetent and careless but, rather, followed a precise, authorial, refined, poetical style without which the play could not have been so successful.

3. Communicating attitudes and values through morpho-syntactic features

As far as ME is concerned, complications result from the fact that not only did changes vary diatopically but they also varied to a considerable degree within the different linguistic areas themselves, given the presence of manifold scribal practices and parish-related amanuensis systems that did not necessarily coincide with the scribe's own idiolect (Smith 1996: 29). This is clearly attested to in *Mary Magdalene*, where different morphological variants – both innovative and conservative – are used. An in-depth investigation of the morphological and syntactic features of the play has instead revealed that such variations seem to derive from the communicative interaction existing between the author of the play and his targeted audience. Indeed, no other factor can explain the variety of morphological and syntactic alternatives. The shift from one form to another can be explained on the one hand by the social effect, and on the other by the poetic effect the author of the play wants to achieve. Since *Mary Magdalene* is a religious play, in which the heroine is proposed as the best example that Christianity had to express notions of sin, repentance and salvation, language has to be a powerful and effective tool in order to convey and describe such concepts. Therefore, evil characters can also be identified by means of certain (socio)linguistic features conveyed by particular grammatical structures. Usually, the most conservative linguistic forms in the play are those used by pious characters, the most innovative ones by pagans. As we will see in the following sections of this chapter, the speeches of pagans are characterised by Northern features. In other words, morphological innovation and syntactic variation are influenced by the pragmatic function that language performs in revealing the real religious *gnosis* and can therefore be seen as the result of a struggle between Good and Evil, expressed in words.

3.1 Southern infinitive endings

The play contains some infinitive verbs with the Southern ending *-en*,[3] which have always been regarded as scribal misspellings (Baker *et al.* 1982).

---

[2] Regarding these issues, see also a more detailed analysis of the text in Maci (2008).
[3] In the South, the ending *-en/-n* (<OE *-an*) used for the infinitive remained until the end of the fourteenth century and somewhat longer in monosyllabic forms, whereas in the Midlands *-en/-n* disappeared earlier (Mossé 1958: 76; Brunner 1970: 71). Jefferson (2005) suggests that the presence of an *-en* desinence for the infinitive form, which in the North had disappeared by the fourteenth century, was maintained by the Northern scribal schools as a marker for alliteration. LALME (McIntosh *et al.* 1986) does not describe any linguistic profiles related to the presence of an *-en/-n* desinence in the form of the infinitive.

Variation in *Mary Magdalene* in MS Digby 133   63

Table 5.1 *Breakdown of Southern ending* -en *in* Mary Magdalene

	Monosyllabic		Disyllabic	
	Occurrences		Occurrences	
Rhyming				
	beyn (l. 55), *seyn* (ll. 166, 883, 1327), *ten* (l. 535), *sen* (l. 536), *gon* (ll. 1011, 1234)	8	*houkkyn* (l. 1160)	1
Non-rhyming				
Before vowel	*werkyn* (l. 152), *seyn* (ll. 166, 1132), *leuyn* (l. 198), *leuen* (ll. 65, 1524), *leven* (l. 1997), *dwellyn* (l. 327), *restyn* (l. 568), *sen* (l. 700), *lyyn* (l. 597), *ben* (l. 714), *synkyn* (l. 746), *sawen* (l. 852), *gon* (l. 1142), *syyn* (l. 1972), *wepyn* (l. 1972), *shewyn* (l. 898), *rewlyn* (l. 1689)	19	*abydyn* (l. 16)	1
Before consonant	*werkyn* (l. 380), *gettyn* (l. 370), *shewyn* (l. 1550), *sekyn* (l. 613)	4	*abydyn* (ll. 301, 1989), *obeyyn* (l. 2017)	3

However, the possibility of a scribal mistake in the play may be indirectly confuted by the fact that the Southern ending is a feature characterising monosyllabic verbs, as in the case of *shewyn* (lines 898 and 1550) and *rewlyn* (line 1689). An investigation using WordSmith Tools (Scott 2007) has revealed that the final Southern ending *-yn/-en* has been added to monosyllabic verbs, which accounts for thirty-one 'regular' occurrences of the Southern ending *-en*. However, five occurrences of disyllabic verbs have the Southern infinitive ending. Overall, nine infinitives are in rhyming positions; the other twenty-seven are in non-rhyming position. Of these, twenty infinitives have the Southern ending when the following word begins with a vowel, and seven before a word starting with a consonant. The data seem to suggest that the distribution of the Southern morpheme *-en* may be determined by the vocalic context. A summary is offered in table 5.1.

As indicated in table 5.1, there are, however, three out of five occurrences of disyllabic infinitives with an *-en* desinence in a consonantal environment. As to why the final infinitive Southern ending can be added to disyllables in a linguistic environment that usually does not allow it, an explanation can be offered in sociolinguistics terms, since it can be observed that the ending occurs only whenever such important characters as Herod, the Emperor, Jesus, Mary Magdalene and the converted King of Marseilles speak. Secondary characters never use the final *-en*. It seems therefore that the *-en* acts as a social marker indicating aureate diction. Furthermore, such a form seems to be related to the metrical scansion of the play: the presence of the unnecessary Southern desinence may be regarded as a way of creating an additional syllable for the author's metrical purposes. This appears to be the case in *the agreement of grace her shewyn I will* (line 898): the line is spoken by Jesus when asking Mary and Martha to accompany him to Lazarus's burial place. Since it is the scene of Lazarus's resurrection, solemnity is created by means of Christ's words, pronounced with special intensity and clarity, and emphasised by the alliteration of the phonetic cluster [gr] in *agreement* and *grace*. Here, the line has a regular metrical pattern where the sequence of anapaestic feet could have been lost if the final *-yn* of *shewyn* had not appeared. The occurrence of a final unnecessary Southern syllable is even more striking in the case of a disyllabic infinitive verb in *In þis deserte abydyn wyll wee* (line 1989). Here, Mary Magdalene is revealing her desire to spend the rest of her life as a hermit in the desert. Thanks to the presence of the final *-yn* of *abydyn* the line is resolved in an anapaestic trimeter (in which final *wee* is accented for rhythmical reasons). The presence of a final anapaest is confirmed by the fact that all the lines (lines 1989–2002) forming the stanza in which Mary Magdalene speaks end with an anapaest: it seems, therefore, that anapaests are an expression of perfection in language, as they are used in Christ's discourses. Just like Jesus, Mary Magdalene can use anapaests because by now she has been raised to the stature of a saint thanks to her purification obtained through thirty years of ascetic life.

3.2 Plural forms of the present indicative

By the end of the fourteenth century, the plural paradigm of present indicative verbs of all dialects tended either to be reduced to a final *-e* or to disappear (zero-forms).[4] There was, however, the occurrence of *-eþ* forms in various late ME texts whose scribes belonged to the *-en* area. In the Midland dialects, for example, traces of the morphemes *-eth/-ith* were still present, as the *Paston Letters* indicate (Davis 1971). According to McIntosh (1983), these forms did not derive from the traditional OE *-iaþ* paradigm, but were, rather, innovations modelled on the inflection that occurred north of the Chester-Wash line, where the operating rule required the present indicative plural form *-es*, *-en*,[5] unless the subject of the verb was a personal pronoun immediately preceding or following it. If so, the ending was reduced either to *-e* or to zero. Northern Midland dialect was so strongly influenced by this paradigm that its own present indicative plural forms were modelled on it: the present indicative plural forms ending either in a final *-en* or final *-es* were substituted by *-eth*, unless the subject of the verb was a personal pronoun in contact with the verb itself. If so, the ending was *-en*, or reduced either to *-e* or to zero (see also McIntosh *et al.* 1986: 309).

---

[4] Brunner (1970: 71) states that levelling to zero was adopted throughout England when the subject was a pronoun positioned after the verb.
[5] According to Wright and Wright (1928: 176), in modern Northern Scottish and most Northern Midland dialects, all the singular and plural persons take final *-s/-z* when not immediately preceded by pronouns (i.e. when the subject is a noun, a relative or interrogative pronoun, or when the verb and the subject are separated by a clause). See also De Haas (2008) and Filppula (2008).

Table 5.2 *Breakdown of plural present indicative forms in* Mary Magdalene

		Subject = person pronoun		Subject = non-person pronoun	
Rule	Desinence	subject–verb adjacency	subject–verb non-adjacency	subject–verb adjacency	subject–verb non-adjacency
Midland (standard)	-*es* ending	0	0	0	0
	-*en* ending	2	7	3	1
	0 ending	40	0	5	3
Innovative	-*th* ending	0	0	7	0
Southern (conservative)	-*th* ending	1	0	0	0

In *Mary Magdalene*, there are only sixty-eight occurrences of the plural form of the present indicative. Only seven cases present the innovative Northern ending -*eth* or its spelling variant -*yt*/-*yd* (see examples (1) to (7); our italics):

(1) Here *answerryt all þe people* at onys 3a my lord 3a (stage direction to line 45).
(2) Swych *desepcyouns potyt* peynys to exsport (line 458).
(3) Here *aperytt to dyvllys* before þe mastyr (stage direction to line 726).
(4) Here *goth Mary and Martha* and mett wyth Jhesus (stage direction to line 794).
(5) Here *goth Mary and Martha homvard* (stage direction to line 819).
(6) Yower *dilectabyll dedys devydytt* me from dyversyte (line 955).
(7) Here *devoyd all þe thre Maryys* (stage direction to line 1133).

There is one Southern form ending in -*th* immediately preceded by a personal pronoun subject (line 1527). Yet, in the play there are also thirteen occurrences of a more standard Midland paradigm in which the plural of the present indicative is marked by morphemes ending with -*en*. All the other forty-eight plural forms of the present indicative have no morpheme at all. A summary of all occurrences is offered in table 5.2.

Despite the operating rule described by McIntosh (1983) and McIntosh et al. (1986), in the play itself the adjacency of the verb to its subject does not seem to be relevant from a morphological viewpoint. The low rate of -*th* endings may be indicative of the fact that levelling of all endings towards the zero-form was the standard procedure by the time *Mary Magdalene* was written. As we have seen, in *Mary Magdalene* the innovative paradigm occurs mainly in stage directions, where the language has more free rein as it does not follow the metrical pattern of the play. The only two occurrences of the new -*th* desinence in the play can be justified if we admit that the author of the play needed an extra syllable for the sake of metre. The same opportunistic search for extra syllables in order to accomplish the metrical structure of the play is the main reason explaining the presence of thirteen present indicative plural forms ending with a final -*en*, the Midland dialectal paradigm used during ME.

Yet a further possible reason for this choice may be that the innovative Northern paradigm was here employed to stress a character's negative message by means of irregular morphology. This trend is confirmed in other Digby plays, namely *The Conversion of St Paul* and the *Wisdom* fragment. In *The Conversion of St Paul*, a final -*th* is found in speeches made by characters that are not to be taken as models by a religious, Christian audience: line 391 is spoken by Anna, a pagan priestess, and lines 444, 446 and 488 by the Devil himself. In *Wisdom*, apart from the stage direction (after line 164), the other two present indicative plural morphemes in -*th* are when Man is temped by the Devil: the first is spoken by Lucifer himself (line 401); the second one is by Understanding, one of Man's five senses that had already abandoned God's teachings to follow the Devil's (line 587). By employing -*th* forms, probably representing a low-class or vulgar kind of language that does not suit an honest, religious person, the author of the play connotes the Devil's discourse or the sinful speeches pertaining to the five senses. The use of this morphological device performs not only a religious function but also a social one, i.e. that of identifying pagan characters and of stigmatising them by attributing to them the language spoken by members of other linguistic communities.

3.3 *Interrogative constructions*

As far as interrogatives are concerned, they are generally formed by inverting the subject–verb position: *wy wepest þou?* (line 1057). The form *do* had not yet begun to be used as a grammatical marker with a semantic function (i.e. that of signalling either a question or a negative structure, which were respectively realised with an inverted verb–subject adjacency and the apposition of *nat* to the main verb in order to negate the sentence).[6] Indeed, the use of *do* as an auxiliary is found only twice in questions, i.e. *Who agens me don dare?* (line 61) and *Why so hastely do ʒe for me send?* (line 410). The fact that in these two cases *do* is used by, respectively, the pagan Emperor and Flesh seems to suggest that the auxiliary may have a social marker function in underlying the heretic speeches of these two negative characters, whose boasting is also emphasised

---

[6] According to Roberts (1985) and Kroch (1989), English completely lost subject–verb inversion in the middle of the sixteenth century. Ever since then, only *be*, auxiliary *have* and the modal verbs (*can*, *may*, *must*, etc.) could be inverted. Based on the behaviour of indicative sentences, Roberts argues that the rise of *do*-forms is a reflex of the loss of the verbal movement. As to the sociolinguistic implications of the rise of the periphrastic *do* in affirmative and negative declarative sentences, see Nurmi (1999).

by alliteration.[7] Such a 'modern' use of *do* must have clearly been seen as a subversive pattern destroying the traditional frameworks of both language and religion. This strengthens the hypothesis formulated above: characters are also identified by means of certain (socio)linguistic features conveyed by particular grammatical structures. Usually, the most conservative linguistic forms in the play are those used by pious characters, the most innovative ones by pagans.

4. Conclusion

Our analysis of the ME play *Mary Magdalene* has thus shown that the diatopic and diastratic variations found in the text are not to be attributed to mere scribal inconsistency. On the contrary, what has traditionally been regarded as scribal carelessness actually derives from a modern misunderstanding of the scribe's practices. Indeed, the significant combination of Southern, Midlands and Northern elements featuring in the language of *Mary Magdalene* does not imply scribal sloppiness, but is instead the result of the scribe's desire faithfully to reproduce the author's linguistic design. This was anything but chaotic, as it was meant to fulfil the playwright's aim to depict the endless battle between Good and Evil through the figure of Mary Magdalene; in order to achieve this goal the author also employed language variants to underline negative attitudes and to highlight noble values, thus conveying precise messages to the audience.

Indeed, in the text, evil characters are linguistically identified by means of certain structures reflecting morpho-syntactic innovations or features belonging to different diatopic varieties, whereas pious characters use more conservative linguistic forms in line with local usage. The most innovative structures are sometimes overused by evil characters, who are generally recognisable because they use a linguistic variety belonging to a different English dialect. As has been seen, alliteration is also generally associated with pagans, who represent a threat to Christianity, to its beliefs and its power. Other variants have a clearly marked social function: they are used when the nobility speaks, when Jesus is on stage, when important characters play a crucial role in the play itself.

At times, extensive use of these linguistic 'variations' seems to represent a mocking of linguistic variants belonging to other regional communities; this is done in order to strengthen the recipients' sense of belonging to the Christian community. This results in a parody of other dialectal variants

---

[7] Typically and traditionally in ME religious drama, alliteration is employed to show non-Christian characters as being arrogant and impertinent (Berger 1999). To the medieval audience, therefore, a strong use of alliterative verse is immediately recognisable as a linguistic marker for the identification of blasphemous and heretical speech, which is contrary to the aureate diction of the Bible. In *Mary Magdalene*, all evil characters speak alliteratively. As to the function of *do* as a metrical prop-word, see Nurmi (1999) and Maci (2008: 110–12).

and encourages the author to present irreverence through worthless, pagan discourse and, at the same time, to better focus on the sacred. The shared laughter provoked by the mocking lines has not only a religious function – that of identifying pagan characters – but also a social one – that of stigmatising the pagans by means of the language commonly used by members of other linguistic communities.

As our investigation has shown, linguistic patterns and variations thus represent important sociolinguistic tools that are employed very effectively by the author to connote the characters of *Mary Magdalene*. Thus the diatopic and diastratic variants found in the text are far from being inconsistent imperfections of the manuscript, but, rather, prove to be an effective means adopted by the scribe to communicate specific messages to its audience and to better represent the different religious and social identities of the characters of the play. In light of these considerations, we can thus reconsider the role the *Mary Magdalene* author had as a metrical and prosodic artist, who apparently exploited language in a very creative way and whose ability has, so far, never been adequately recognised.

6 Constructing the audiences of the Old Bailey Trials 1674–1834

ELIZABETH CLOSS TRAUGOTT

1. Introduction

One of the objectives of recent work in historical discourse analysis has been to investigate ways in which the writer's perspective shapes and constrains the ways in which his or her words can be interpreted (Taavitsainen and Fitzmaurice 2007: 22).* In this chapter, I discuss how the trial reporters whose reports constitute the *Old Bailey Corpus 1674–1834*[1] sought to construct and engage with their audiences. Shoemaker (2008) hypothesises that these audiences were property-owning middle- and upper-class readers seeking to improve themselves. Over the years, what began as a commercial enterprise became increasingly subject to regulation by the Mayor of London, and therefore more official in tone and intent. By the nineteenth century, the proceedings were read primarily by lawyers and public officials.[2] A gradual shift in appeals to readers can therefore be expected.

In thinking about how readers are selected by writers, and indeed constructed by them, it is useful to think in terms of a concept of textual voice that is grounded in the work of Bakhtin and Vološinov. This textual voice acts 'to acknowledge, to engage with or to align itself with respect to

---

* Many thanks to Magnus Huber and Robert Shoemaker for comments on the work of the reporters, and to Susan Fitzmaurice for insights into the meaning of 'conversation' and 'politeness' in the late seventeenth and early eighteenth centuries. Thanks also to two anonymous reviewers for helpful comments.

[1] This corpus is a subset of the *Proceedings of the Old Bailey, 1674–1913*, compiled by Magnus Huber for linguistic analysis. However, I used the on-line version of the *Proceedings* for the same years for searches (www.oldbaileyonline.org/ edited by Clive Emsley, Tim Hitchcock and Robert Shoemaker). This has the disadvantage of limiting searchable material because words of three or fewer letters cannot be searched. Most problematic is the inability to search for personal pronouns; however, combinations such as *I shall* are searchable, as are *thou*, *thee* and *your*. Review of the front matter of the *Proceedings* and of many of the trials suggests I was able to retrieve the most relevant strings for the investigation of how audiences were constructed. Use of the on-line corpus has the advantage of allowing comparison of the scanned transcriptions with the associated original printed text. Where there are discrepancies I followed the original (in example (4) *they self* of the transcription was changed to *thy self* of the original, and in example (8) *susfice* was changed to *suffice*). The on-line *Proceedings* were accessed for purposes of writing this chapter from February to April 2009.

[2] www.oldbaileyonline.org/static/Publishinghistory.jsp.

69

positions which are in some way alternatives to that being advanced by the text' (White 2003: 260), and also uses a 'set of engagement resources which act to reject, counter, confront, head off or rule out actual or potential dialogic alternatives' (White 2003: 268). In the case of the Old Bailey Trials, up to 1760 most proceedings were selected from the whole set of trials, and although some early texts are about robbery, most are about rape, sodomy and murder – topics that were expected to shock or, alternatively, appeal to the prurient sensibilities of readers, but in any event to contradict the expected norms of civil and polite audiences. In the first years of the trial proceedings, reporters clearly sought to position themselves in very specific ways with their readers. The main question I address is what linguistic strategies they used to do so, and how these changed over time. I will consider to what extent regulation by the Mayor in the seventeenth century and by the City in the eighteenth may have had a direct impact on this engagement.

In particular, I explore address to the reader, both direct and indirect. To the extent that the focus is on appeals to the reader, hence the intersubjectivity of the texts, this study complements Doty's, where the focus is on how the scribes of the Salem Witchcraft Trials 'interposed subjective or evaluative elements in the examination records' (Doty 2007: 26), hence the subjectivity of those texts. It also complements Koch (1999), which models, but does not expand on, scribe–reader verbal communication in early Romance court trials records.

Section 2 provides some historical and textual background about the *Old Bailey Proceedings*. Direct address to the reader is explored in section 3, indirect address in section 4, and attempts to allay readers' scepticism in section 5. Section 6 serves as a conclusion.

2. Some background about the *Old Bailey Proceedings*

A detailed account of the history of the *Proceedings* is provided at the online website for *The Proceedings of the Old Bailey, 1674–1913*.[3] A few key points relevant to the issue of creating a readership have been drawn from this resource and from Huber (2007), as background to the discussion that follows.

The Old Bailey was London's central criminal court from 1673, when the courthouse was built, to 1843, when it was renamed the Central Criminal Court. It was completely rebuilt in 1907, and continues in use. The *Proceedings* published from 1674 to 1834 contain 'over 100,000 trials, totalling *c*. 52 million words' (Huber 2007: 1). They were a commercial enterprise, and somewhat sensational. Already in 1679, the Court of Aldermen ordered that accounts be approved by the Lord Mayor and other justices. A century

---

[3] www.oldbaileyonline.org/.

later, in 1778, the City 'stipulated that they should represent "true, fair, and perfect narrative" of what happened in court' (Huber 2007: 2).

I am not concerned in the present chapter with the authenticity of the material as a source of data about the Early Modern English period. However, there would be little purpose in investigating how the reporters constructed their audiences if the trials were not of value for insights into the language of the period. The importance of trials as sources of linguistic data has been discussed at some length (see e.g. Culpeper and Kytö 2000; Kryk-Kastovsky 2000, 2006b and 2007) and the substantial value of some of the trials is by now well established. Langbein's rather dismissive comments from a lawyer's perspective on the *Proceedings* were that they are 'sensation-mongering pamphlets written by lawyers, usually anonymously, for sale to the general public' (Langbein 1978: 267, cited in Archer 2007), and that they are problematic because they do not give full details of individual trials. However, he granted that they probably provide some of the best materials on English trials before the end of the eighteenth century (Archer 2007: 188–9). Reliability as a legal document does not equate with reliability as a linguistic one, however (Huber 2007: 14). Using the example of negative contraction, Huber (2007) gives a detailed account of the usefulness of the *Old Bailey Corpus 1674–1834* for linguistic analysis. He finds that from 1720 on, when trials were reported in first rather than third person, about 85 per cent of text is first-person (Huber 2007: 5). Negative contraction was extensively used in the early period, suggesting close attention to the speech of trial participants, and that the 'verbatim passages are arguably as near as we can get to the spoken word of the period' (Huber 2007: 1). Huber notes a dramatic decline of *don't*, from 74 per cent in the 1730s to 12 per cent in the 1830s. Negative contraction was virtually zero in 1780, rose moderately in 1790, but after that continued to decline, except that there was a slight rise in the case of *shan't*. Huber suggests the decline at the end of the eighteenth century may be related to the fact that the *Proceedings* became an official document at that time (Huber 2007: 25).[4]

The texts represent not only negative contraction, but also features of varieties of English (1a), and even a lisp (1b):

---

[4] Fitzmaurice (2010a) notes that negative contraction was regarded in the early part of the eighteenth century as a feature of 'polite talk', so much so that its use, especially after auxiliaries (*can't, han't, shan't, didn't, coodn't, woodn't, isn't, en't*) was parodied by Swift in his *Treatise on Polite Conversation* (1738); this might suggest an alternative reason for the use of negative contraction in the early texts of the *Proceedings*, if a correlation could be found between negative contraction and the speech of more educated and 'genteel' participants. However, at least some instances are clearly attributed to (relatively) uneducated people, so 'politeness' does not appear to be a reason for the use of contraction in the *Proceedings*. For example, Baker says 'I can't write nor read' in the Trial of Alexander Watson and William Howard (28 June 1733, t17330628–30).

72   Traugott

(1a) His Leg vas vary mush more queek dan mine, so dat I no coud cash him; but I call out to de Peoples to stop a de Teef, and da stop him prasaant. (Trial of John Palmer, 11 October 1732, t17321011–42)

(1b) I am a Thilver-Thmith by Trade, and the Dith wath left me to make a Cover to it. (Trial of Alexander Watson and William Howard, 28 June 1733, t17330628–30)

Even if not entirely accurate, such representations suggest the reporters were, at least until the nineteenth century, aware of the linguistic practices of participants in the trials, and thought them worthy of representation.

I refer to the writers as 'reporters' rather than 'scribes', since they claim to provide summary or verbatim reports of trials. While most wrote up their own shorthand notes, sometimes this may not have been the case, as implied by the following correction:

(2) THE Short-Hand Writer having omitted to take the several Questions put to the Witnesses, with their Answers in the Words they were deliver'd, that Defect cannot now be supply'd.

But we having perus'd the following Tryals do certify, that the Substance of the Evidence given by the several Witnesses is faithfully taken. (16 January 1748, f17480116–1)

Solid information about which reporters were also transcribers at the trials is not always available before 1773; only then did names of reporters and their responsibilities begin to be specified in the front matter (Huber 2007; Shoemaker 2008). Furthermore, we do not have information about whether the front matter was composed by the reporter or the printer. In so far as the present chapter investigates front matter (appeals to readers and titles), the texts are assumed not to be part of the original court transcript (a shorthand manuscript) but, rather, of the discourse frame written for publication with the printed transcription. For the purposes of this chapter, I assume the front matter was written by the transcriber/reporter.

The *Proceedings* were not the only documents of the time directly associated with the trials. There were also 'advertisements', especially from 1729 to the 1750s, which reporters used not only to advertise the contents of upcoming reports, but also, to some extent, to negotiate their relationship with their readers.[5] Advertisements will be included in the discussion below when they relate to the *Proceedings* and therefore to the reporters' texts.[6] There is also a third type of text associated with the trials. During the years 1679–1772, the 'Ordinary' (the chaplain of Newgate Prison) had 'the right to publish an account of the prisoners' last dying speeches and behaviour on the scaffold, together with stories of their lives and crimes'

---

[5] www.oldbaileyonline.org/static/Advertising.jsp.
[6] Advertisements covered a large variety of offerings, including publications by the Ordinary (see below), medical cures and corn prices, as well as the *Proceedings*.

(www.oldbaileyonline.org/static/Ordinarys-accounts.jsp). These accounts had explicitly moral purposes. Sometimes they suggest how a reader should or might react to the content of the accounts (3a), or to the reporting of them (3b) and the reader is even occasionally invited to think like a member of the jury (3c):

(3a)   Such a Scene of complicated Wickedness, will I presume, surprize the Reader; it may neither be unpleasant nor unuseful to him, if I set down here what past betwixt us relating to this. (R. Wykes, Ordinary's account, 20 July 1700, OA17000720)
(3b)   If there seem to be any Contradiction in the above Confessions, 'tis hop'd the candid[7] Reader will not impute the same to the Writer hereof; but to the disingenuous and base Way of acting and speaking such vile and naughty People use. (James Guthrie, Ordinary's account, 28 May 1733, OA17330528)
(3c)   In this Light he looked upon the Matter to the last, nor would he be persuaded to see it in any other; and I leave the Reader to determine, whether or not, according to his own Account of the Matter, there is the Appearance of a felonious Intent. (John Taylor, Ordinary's account, 17 June 1751, OA17510617)

Since these accounts were not written by reporters, they will not be included in discussion. They are, however, relevant, as they were among the discourses about trials and their outcomes to which readers had access, and are a significant part of 'the historical conditions in which a text is constructed, transmitted and received' (Taavitsainen and Fitzmaurice 2007: 30).

3. Direct address to the reader

As will be discussed in more detail in section 5, the first set of reports were thought of as *News*. The term *News* was dropped later in 1674, and *Narrative* or *Account of Proceedings* came to be preferred. After the highly successful publication in December 1678 of a detailed account with a more objective tone, and the subsequent decision to publish reports only after approval of the Lord Mayor and other justices, the term *Proceedings* appears almost without fail in the title.[8] The titles themselves suggest a shift within a few years from reports that aligned themselves with earlier chap-books to more objective accounts. Is there evidence that there was a shift to a different audience as well?

The first surviving publication, of 29 April 1674, has a double frame. First is the title, which claims the truth and correctness of the report (*exact and*

---

[7] 'Open-minded'.
[8] www.oldbaileyonline.org/static/Publishinghistory.jsp#origins. Titles are discussed in more detail in section 5.

true accompt) while subjectively evaluating the contents (*remarkable trials of several notorious malefactors*). This is followed by direct address to the reader (see example (4)). The speech-act moves in this address are a subset of those identified for the letter: greet, query, narrate/report/inform (Taavitsainen and Jucker 2007: 115). Example (4) is a loaded question (note the *more*), and, since the interlocutor is not present, serves as an invitation to engage in a particular way with the text:

(4) READER, Wherein canst thou more experience thy self for the ordering of a good Conversation, than by seeing the follies of those, who either by their own idle or extravagant living are forced to seek out those ways and means, which either are destructive in themselves, or purchase shame and destruction in their end? (29 April 1674, f16740429–1)

Key here are experience and conversation, not explicit moral improvement.

To understand what 'conversation' means in this context, we need to investigate how it is used elsewhere in the trials, and in the period. In the front matter of the *Proceedings* the word *conversation* is used only one other time (the next year), and then with reference to the conversation of *malafactors*:

(5) AT the Sessions... were Tryed a great number of Malafactors, for Crimes of various and sundry natures, as Murthers,... Libellers, and other Enormities; whereby we see that Vice hath not only an infectuous quality of spreading its Venome; but that it's Poison, like that of a Viper, or Adder, doth taint the conversation of sinful Societies, with varigated and multiform tinctures of Impieties, so that it is strange to see what a speked mass of loathsome crimes present themselves at these times amongst the wicked Heard that are brought before this great Tribunal, to receive the due reward of their wickedness. (7 July 1675, f16750707–1)

In the years immediately following, *conversation* appears within the reports in two collocations. One is with negatively evaluating adjectives such as *idle*, *loose* and *suspicious*, always with reference to talk by those indicted. The lone occurrence of *good* ('attesting his former good Conversation, Credit, and Estate', 11 July 1677, t16770711–3) appears to be an early variant of the second type of collocation. From 1681 to 1695, there are thirty-six instances of the phrase *life and conversation*. These are preceded by adjectives like *good*, *honest*, *unblamable* or *wicked*. Those who could give testimony that their lives and conversation were of the positive type, or who gave a detailed (and presumably credible) account of their lives and conversations, were usually acquitted. After 1695, *conversation* occurs only infrequently with *life*. It usually refers to talk (X had a conversation with Y, the conversation was in Welsh, etc.).

The usage in the early part of the trials suggests that 'conversation' was construed by the reporters and participants in the trial setting in terms that match Brewer's concept of eighteenth-century politeness as achieved by 'a manner of conversing and speaking with people which by teaching one to regulate one's passions and cultivate good taste, would allow one to realize what was in the public interests and for the general good' (Brewer 1997: 102, cited in Fitzmaurice 2010a).

One of the purposes of Fitzmaurice's article is to show that Brewer's view of politeness is not nuanced enough to provide an account of the varieties of politeness practised, and contested, in the eighteenth century, or the changing attitudes toward it as the century wore on. In the *Proceedings*, the concept of 'conversation' as a generalisation over moral conduct and verbal interaction with others occurs not in the eighteenth but in the late seventeenth century. What counts is whether people interact civilly or are given to quarrel and lies, and who the interlocutors are (respectable people or thieves). The reporter assumes that language use is directly correlated with morality. So the reader constructed in example (4) is one who engages in good (therefore moral) and presumably polite interactions, and the reports will serve to fill his or her arsenal of civil, unblamable and moral talk with more moral messages. The reports appear not to be intended to change lives, but, rather, to reinforce them. Even though not directly invoked in example (5), the reader is invited to share the reporter's assumptions (*we see that* . . .). What is *strange* 'unexpected, remarkable', is the mass of crime (eleven persons were on trial that day, one of whom was condemned to be burned for the murder of her husband).

Direct address to the audience in their role as reader occurs in the front matter of only the first Proceeding (cited in example (4) above) and in the form *To the Reader* in the front matter of the proceedings of 6 April 1692 (f16920406–1). More personal direct pronominal address also appears only in the earliest years. The first report is addressed not only to *Reader*, but to one addressed as *thou*, in other words, a specific imagined interlocutor with whom the reporter is on sufficiently good terms as to be able to use the informal singular form. Example (4) goes on: 'The first thing I shall shew thee is about a Robbery on the High-way' (29 April 1674, t16740429–1). From then on, however, only *you* is used, whether out of politeness or out of a desire to reach out to a larger set of interlocutors, as in: 'I Shall, with as much brevity and truth as may be, give you a candid account of the trials of the several Prisoner XX' (14 January 1676, t16760114–1). I have found no second-person examples after 1678.[9] Imperatives appear to be used only in the advertisements of the Ordinary's reports.[10]

---

[9] This is no doubt in part a function of the search restrictions. However, whereas *you* occurs in the early years in the context of first-person *I shall*, it does not in later years when *I shall* appears (1710 and 1749).

[10] e.g. Advertisement, 21 February 1733 (a17330221–1).

In sum, direct address to the reader by reporters of the *Proceedings* is limited to the first two years of publication, 1674 and 1675. The reader is constructed as one who seeks the truth at the same time as being interested in remark-worthy stories, and, in the first report, one who seeks to display morality through good conversation in the sense of moral and civil conduct.

4. Indirect appeal to the reader

If readers are rarely addressed directly, they are frequently invoked in the third person as *the reader* or *the public*. In general, the reader is in the early years expected to be impatient with, or uninterested in, reports that are *tedious* and *impertinent*, and to wish to read only of that which is *remarkable*, for example:

(6) Not to trouble the Reader with a tedious Relation of things trivial or impertinent, the most considerable or remarkable Transactions of this Sessions were as follows. (17 January 1677, f16770117–1)[11]

However, one early report suggests that the intended reader might not be quite as upright a person as was invoked in the first report (see (4)). This particular reader is envisioned as aligning himself with a hard-line position against anyone accused of criminality, and yet being intrigued by stories of crime, and secretly relishing tales of horror. This highly dialogic strategy is used in the front matter to the 1675 trial of three men suspected of robbing a gentleman but acquitted because they could prove they were *honest Labourers*:

(7) These two instances, though they may not give the Reader that satisfaction he expects, because there is no condemnation or Execution in the case, yet my design in the reciting them is rather to warn all people that they take care how they wander late in the Evening about the out-skirts of the City, than to satisfie the curiosity of such as take delight to see and hear of the tragical ends of those miserable wretches, that are the Authors of such mischief. (9 September 1675, t16750909–2)

Rather than being invited to approve of justice (an honest labourer can be acquitted), the reader is expected to be disappointed that there was no condemnation (presumably the reporter is implying that he did not agree with the verdict in the case). The lame justification for reporting the trial so that it should serve as a warning to people who travel at night is embedded in the evocation of a reader whose morality is upheld by delighting in punishment (justified or not, it appears).

In subsequent years, there are virtually no more overt appeals to readers' prurient tastes, but a sodomy trial in 1727 prompted the reporter to write the following:

---

[11] See also 15 January 1675 (f16750115–1).

(8) Here they went to Bed, (where the Writer of this paper would draw a Curtain, not being able to express the rest with Decency, but to satisfy the Curiosity of the Reader let this suffice, he did all that a beastly Appetite could prompt him to, without making an actual penetration.) (Trial of Charles Hitchin, 12 April 1727, t17270412-41)

A search for the word *reader* (in the relevant sense)[12] shows that from 1727 until 1777 the reader is called on mostly to correct errors in prior reports, or to refer to other reports. There is the occasional invitation to evaluate the narrative. Commenting on a statement by a witness named Timms, the reporter adds a parenthesis that engages the reader (though this engagement may be primarily an excuse to add a detail of which the reporter became aware post-trial):

(9) (Timms.) Then he gave it me, saying, there it is; and resigned quietly. (It must seem strange to the reader, that the two armed prisoners should resign so quietly. Note, Timms had in his hand a pistol when he demanded Jackson's hanger, which he did not mention till the trial was over.) (Trial of John Conquest and William Jackson, 2 July 1755, t17550702-6)

After 1777, there is no entry for *reader* in the relevant sense. This is a year before the City required that reports be fair and true, and may be taken as a further shift in reporting practices away from direct interaction.

One of the most interesting reports for our purposes is that of Muggleton's trial. Muggleton was a religious imposter, who apparently formed and led a heretical sect. He had, according to the reporter, 'a strange enthusiastick head'. When the indictment was read out, many passages of his writings were recited. They were

(10) so horrid and blasphemous, that we think fit to spare the Christian modesty of each pious ear, by not repeating the same here, where there is no necessity for it. (Trial of Lodowick Muggleton, 17 January 1677, t16770117-1)

The reporter further injects himself into the report in various ways; for example, by generalisations about persons of Muggleton's type, and by evaluating the counsel's statement:

(11) And as all Hereticks covet to be Authors and Ring-leaders to a Sect, so by divers printed Books and Corner conferences, he easily seduced divers weak and instable people (especially of the Female-Sex) to become his Proselytes... The Prisoner pleaded not guilty, but frustrated the general expectation, by saying nothing further either

---

[12] Other senses include reference to (proof-)readers and to individuals with the surname Reader.

to excuse or justifie himself, but had a Counsel appear'd for him, who ingenuously declar'd himself asham'd to speak a word in favour of such a Cause. (Trial of Lodowick Muggleton, 17 January 1677, t16770117–1)

This kind of reporter evaluation ceased after 1677. A century later, the formula 'too indecent/indelicate for publication' came to be used from time to time to flag the kind of content that was omitted. During the late eighteenth and nineteenth centuries, the more neutral term 'unfit' came to be preferred.

5. Attempts to allay readers' scepticism

The greatest anxiety in the early years appears to have been to ensure that readers would accept the reports as true. Front matter seeks to validate the text by claiming that what follows is *An exact and true accompt* (29 April 1674), *a/the true account* (nine instances between 1675 and 1683), *a/the (full and) true relation* (five instances between 1674 and 1681) or *a/the true narrative of the Proceedings* (forty instances between 1675 and 1683). There are sixty instances of *true* in this sense in the front matter from 1674 to 1683, after which this kind of self-validation is used only once, referring to true copies of letters (6 December 1706, f17061206–1).[13]

There was clearly awareness of scepticism on the part of the public, and the reporters sought to counter it overtly in the early years. By the end of the seventeenth century, however, the strategy used to allay such scepticism was to omit any obvious reporter's voice addressing the reader. *Vile* is used in front matter and in reports as a comment on offenders only until the 1720s. After that it is found in quotations of insults ('you are a vile Toad', 'a vile old Baud', Trial of Mary Burness, 28 June 1733, t17330628–7). As for *loathsome*, which appears in the front matter cited in example (5), it does not appear again except in quotations. Only such subjective judgemental terms as were also used by judges; for example, *malefactor(s)*, continued to be used in front matter until 1800 (the few instances of *malefactor* in the nineteenth-century materials are in quotations of trial participants).

Titles of *Proceedings* are especially indicative of the changes. As mentioned at the beginning of section 3, the first Proceedings were entitled *News*, for example:

(12) News from the SESSIONS-HOUSE IN THE OLD BAILY, OR A full and true Accounpt of the Tryals and proceedings this last Sessions, holden at the Old-Bayly. (14 April 1675, f16750414–1)

Even after the term *News* was abandoned later in 1674, titles continued until 1684 to include such terms as *Narrative*, *Account* and sometimes *Relation*; all,

---

[13] Two later advertisements from 1733 deny additions of 'feigned and romantick adventures', but these are for the Ordinary's reports, not the *Proceedings*.

Constructing the audiences of the Old Bailey Trials   79

but most especially *Narrative*, implying an act of storytelling and hence the possibility of subjective interpretation. Not surprisingly, evaluative adjectives like *true*, *truest*, *exact* and *full* were used as well to counter possible scepticism about the veracity of the telling, for example:

(13a) AN Exact and True ACCOUNT OF THE PROCEEDINGS OF THE SESSIONS, Begun at the OLD-BAYLY, On Wednesday January the 17th. 1682. (17 January 1783, f16830117–1)
(13b) THE TRUE NARRATIVE OF THE PROCEEDINGS AT The Sessions-House IN THE OLD-BAYLY. (10 October 1683, f16831010–1)

In 1679, we find one title in which only *Proceedings* appears, without any evaluation of the text, and without a term referring to a narrative act:

(14) THE PROCEEDINGS AT THE SESSIONS At the Old-Baily, August the 27th and 28th, 1679. CONTAINING The Several Tryals of a great number of notorious Malefactors ... and all other remarkable Occurrences there. (27 August 1679, f16790827–1)

Between 1679 and 1684, only two other titles like this appeared (24 November 1681 and 29 August 1683). However, from September 1684 on, the title is consistently *The Proceedings of*, or occasionally *The Trials of*. Such changes suggest a shift toward presenting the materials as objectively as possible. In 1773, a further major shift to accountability occurred with the naming of the shorthand transcribers.

Two other related shifts should also be noted. One is that, from 1760, all *Proceedings* came to be *whole* (rather than the excerpts of earlier years that focused on those trials that the reporter deemed *remarkable*, and deliberately excluded those alleged to be *tedious*). Another is that, by the 1730s, part of the concern of front matter became financial – readers are assured that the contents will fit into a three-penny book (a four-penny book from the late 1740s on, with higher prices as the century progressed). This suggests appeal to a reader who is more concerned about economics than about truth.

We must conclude that active and overt intersubjective construction of the reader was concentrated in the very early years, and declined significantly after the Lord Mayor's approval was required in 1679. By hypothesis, the Ordinary, whose reports appear from 1679 on, may have taken over many of the intersubjective strategies of earlier reporters.

Further study will no doubt reveal more subtle ways in which the readership was shaped, but this will require detailed investigation of the shorthand transcripts themselves, the reporters' additions, and comparison, where possible, between different accounts of the same trials (see Huber 2007: 19–20).[14]

---

[14] See also Hiltunen and Peikola (2007) on differences between transcriptions of the same trials, and between transcriptions and published text in the case of the Salem Witchcraft Trials.

6. Conclusion

We may conclude that reporters' attempts to engage the reader were remarkably short-lived. The audiences cultivated and constructed in the early years, especially the first five years, were expected to improve themselves not only morally (by education), but also socially (by having recourse to noteworthy conversation points in polite society, especially in the coffee houses of the period). For this they needed to be sure that the reports were 'true'. By the mid 1730s, however, audiences appear to have been expected to be more concerned about economics.

Regulation by the Mayor in 1679 had a significant effect on the ways in which reporters engaged with audiences. Shifts to a relatively more objective tone in the following decades meant that no significant change can be correlated with further controls in 1778, at least in the frame of the front matter. The requirement that year that reports should provide a 'true, fair, and perfect narrative' might be expected to have triggered a large number of new claims to veracity, but this was, in fact, not the case.

Part II

Communicating through handwritten correspondence

7 A defiant gentleman or 'the strengest thiefe of Wales'

Reinterpreting the politics in a medieval correspondence

MERJA STENROOS AND MARTTI MÄKINEN

1. Introduction

Gruffuth ap Dauid ap Gruffuth[1] is a minor figure in the history of the Welsh Uprising (1400–14). However, unlike most of those who took part in the uprising, he has not vanished without a trace. He survives in a small correspondence, consisting of three letters: one written by himself, another written to him as a reply and a third one referring to him. The second correspondent is a much better-documented historical person: Reginald Grey, third Lord of Ruthin and one of the most powerful English lords in North Wales by the time of the uprising. The two correspondents represent opposite sides and have strongly conflicting interests: put very simply, Gruffuth wishes to make a living, while Grey is seeking royal authority to take a hard line against the rebels. The letters concern appointments to local offices, as well as the theft of some of Grey's horses.

The letters belong to the aftermath of the uprising. They have been edited several times and were characterised by early editors as 'barbarous' and 'savage' (e.g. Ellis 1827: 5; Hingeston 1860: xxii), in line with the general conception of the Welsh Uprising. Gruffuth is mentioned in numerous historical works, as well as in fiction, as a 'thief' or 'Welsh bandit'; references to him often bear a tone of contempt or amusement.

It is suggested here that the stereotypical characterisation of Gruffuth in modern historiography is a remarkable example of the communication of politically charged texts to readers across several centuries. It derives from readings that take Grey's letters largely at face value, without considering critically the political agenda behind them. The image of Gruffuth as a bandit has, in its turn, coloured the interpretation of the historical happenings referred to in the texts.

The aim of this chapter is to reconsider the evidence for the status and characterisation of Gruffuth ap Dauid ap Gruffuth, based on a new reading

---

[1] The spelling adopted here is that used by Gruffuth himself. The present-day Welsh spelling is Gruffudd ap Dafydd ap Gruffudd.

of the correspondence. It will seek to evaluate the evidence for the prevailing image of Gruffuth in the literature as 'rude' and 'barbaric', a 'Welsh bandit' whose language is 'rude and rugged'. It will be suggested that this characterisation reflects the attitudes of the modern editors and historians rather than anything found in the text itself.

As the terms of characterisation are highly subjective, they can only be evaluated through a careful critical consideration of the material, placing it in its context with regard to genre, language, history and society. The conventions of late medieval English letter writing are fairly well known. As the letters form a correspondence, we can deal with the actual communication between the writers: it is possible to retrieve at least some of the perlocutionary effects of speech acts, usually lost forever. On the other hand, even though the historical context is relatively well documented, there are gaps in our knowledge that make interpretation difficult: most notably, all our information about Gruffuth, including his social status, has to be extracted from the correspondence itself. It will thus be important to take into account all the available evidence gleaned from the dialectal forms and the physical text, as well as the intratextual evidence.

Section 2 of this chapter will outline the contents and the general historical context of the correspondence, while section 3 will describe the characterisation of the letters, and of Gruffuth as a person, by modern editors and historians. The letters will then be reconsidered, using three different approaches, which are dealt with in sections 4, 5 and 6 respectively: the dialectal analysis of scribal texts, the analysis of pragmatic units and historical source criticism. The pragmatic analysis will apply the framework for the study of insults developed by Jucker and Taavitsainen (2000), as well as the traditional concepts of politeness theory, such as face and face-threatening acts. The findings of the three analyses will then be considered together in order to evaluate the traditional image of Gruffuth.

2. The letters and their historical context

The Welsh Uprising began in September 1400, when the Welsh aristocrat Owain Glyndŵr had himself proclaimed Prince of Wales. During the peak years of 1403–5, the uprising involved all of Wales, and it had strong supporters including, for a short time, the French. Glyndŵr's army had some spectacular victories and managed to shake off most of the English rule in Wales. From 1406, the tide started to turn against the Welsh, as outside support failed, and English rule began to be re-asserted. By 1410, the Welsh Uprising as a national movement was waning; however, the unrest continued at the local level for another decade.

Reginald Grey, third Lord of Ruthin, was one of the most powerful English lords in Northern Wales. The Grey family had been engaged in continual border disputes with their Welsh neighbours during much of the late fourteenth century, and near-contemporary sources suggest that Grey's actions towards Glyndŵr, one of his neighbours, functioned as a catalyst for the start of the revolt. The town of Ruthin was the first target attacked by the rebels in September 1400.

In 1402, Grey was captured by Glyndŵr and later released for a sizable ransom (10,000 marks); he was then made to swear never to take up arms against Glyndŵr again. However, in 1409, he was granted a royal commission and ordered to go to his Welsh lordship to deal with the rebels and to enforce submission. As Smith (1967: 251–3) has shown, it is within this historical context that the present letters belong.

The letters are found in British Library MS Cotton Cleopatra F.iii, a compilation of originally detached documents relating to public affairs in the reigns of Richard II, Henry IV and Henry V. The compilation includes numerous items connected to the Welsh Uprising. The letters are bound in the reverse order of their implied order of composition, and may be listed as follows:

1. A letter from Gruffuth ap Dauid ap Gruffuth to Reginald Grey (f. 104r)[2]
2. A letter from Reginald Grey to Gruffuth, in reply to 1 (f. 102v)
3. A letter from Reginald Grey to the Prince of Wales, referring to letters 1 and 2 (f. 102r)

The contents of the letters may be briefly summarised as follows. In the first letter, Gruffuth admits to being in possession of two horses belonging to Grey, and reports a hearsay that Grey plans to mete out punishment on Welsh people because of the theft. He promises to retaliate: *as mony men þ^t ӡe slen and as mony howsin þ^t ӡe bran for my sake, as mony wol J bran and sle for ӡour sake* 'as many men as you will kill and as many houses as you will burn for my sake, as many will I burn and kill for your sake'. All this is preceded by a long narrative that seems to act as an explanation for Gruffuth's need of horses. He complains about having been deceived by John Wele, an administrative officer in the lordships of Chirkesland and Oswestry. Wele had offered him a 'king's charter', that is, a pardon, and a position as Master Forester and *keyshat*[3] in the lordship of Chirkesland (adjoining Ruthin), if he joined a military expedition overseas. Gruffuth had procured himself the required horses and men, but the offer had turned out to be a trap to catch him in an area where he had no safe conduct.

---

[2] The manuscript has two running sets of foliation; the one chosen here is also referred to in the *Linguistic Atlas of Late Mediaeval English* (McIntosh et al. 1986). According to the other foliation, the letters are found on ff. 70r, 70v and 72r respectively.

[3] The term *keyshat* seems to represent a Welsh official's title, corresponding approximately to Middle English *serjeant*. The forms *caisead, kysead, kysett* and *kysseid* appear in later documents as the name for a particular community rent or fee, 'rendered in lieu of the maintenance of the *Cais* or serjeant, who carried out police duties ... and who in medieval days had had the right to impose himself on the community during his tenure of the office' (Rees 1953).

Lord Grey's reply to Gruffuth consists for the most part of a point for point repetition of the contents of the former letter, using the phrase *as þu seiste* 'as you say' to mark reported speech. He then points out that whatever harm others have done to Gruffuth, it does not justify his violation of Grey's property. He denies having any plans of punitive action directed on the population, and indicates that the false accusations will be made known to the king. Finally, he points out that Gruffuth's letter is a confession of horse-theft, and expresses his hope to see him hang, in verse form:

> we hoepe we shall do the a pryve thyng: a roope, a ladder and a ryng, heigh on gallowes for to henge and thus shall be your endyng. And he that made the be ther to helpyng, and we on our behalfe shall be welle willyng.
>
> 'we hope to do you a secret thing: a rope, a ladder and a ring, high on the gallows to hang, and that will be your ending. And may He who made you be there to help [you], and we, on our part, will be keen and willing.' (letter 2)

The supreme command over the war in Wales had, in 1403, been given to the young Prince of Wales, the future Henry V. Grey's other letter, written to the prince, discloses that Grey had received the king's privy seal, with letters from the prince, commanding him to enforce peace within his lordship. He assures the prince that he is doing his best, but claims that peace will depend on bringing all officials in North Wales and the Marches under English control. To achieve this, he begs the prince to grant him a fuller authority, stretching over all the lordships and counties of North Wales. He then refers to his correspondence with Gruffuth, calling him *the strengest thiefe of Wales* 'the most blatant thief in Wales'; he explains that he is attaching Gruffuth's letter, together with a copy of his own reply, so that the prince will *knowen his goode wyll and gouernance* 'know his [Gruffuth's] good intent and behaviour'.

Grey's motive for attaching Gruffuth's letter must be seen in conjunction with the main point of his letter to the prince: the importance of bringing the local officials under control. The policy of appointing former rebels as local officials had been pursued in many parts of Wales and generally seems to have worked well, as Davies points out:

> Indeed the most striking feature of the social landscape and pattern of governance in Wales by 1421 was the degree to which it was dominated by men who had once been prominent supporters of Glyn Dŵr... it must have been painfully obvious that local governance could only be restored... by vesting it once more in the hands of those who had exercised it before the revolt. (Davies 1995: 312)

This policy was opposed by the parliament, who already in 1402 had wished to exclude all Welshmen from the major local offices (Davies 1995: 205). It was also, it seems, opposed by Grey, who had suffered great personal losses during the uprising, and whose relationship to the local Welsh population was, by all accounts, a highly strained one. It would seem likely that Gruffuth's letter was here used to illustrate the unsuitability of former rebels for holding local offices.

All three letters were sent to the Prince of Wales at the same time, the first two as appendices to the third. Letters 1 and 3 are dated to 11 and 23 June respectively; however, there is no reference to the year. Ellis (1827: 2) dated the letters to *c.* 1400, a date still cited by numerous reference works, including the *New Index of Middle English Verse* (Boffey and Edwards 2005) and the *Middle English Compendium*. However, it is now recognised that the historical references in the letters do not suit the early period of the revolt, nor the months preceding it. Smith (1967: 253) dates the letters convincingly to the period 1410–12, based on the historical persons mentioned.[4] Davies (1995: 297) states that they 'almost certainly' belong to 1411, while Smith suggests that either 1411 or, preferably, 1412 would fit with an expedition to France led by Arundel in the autumn of 1411.

At this point, the English were keen to end the war, and willing to negotiate about pardons to individual rebels. The villain of Gruffuth's story, John Wele, seems to have carried out unauthorised negotiations on his own account. In 1414, he was charged for such negotiations, involving, among others, a rebel named as Gruffudd ap Dafydd ap Llywelyn of Iâl (Yale), esq.; negotiations with him were said to have taken place in April 1409. It is worth noting that this other Gruffudd, while presumably not identical with the present one, was a Welsh aristocrat involved in a very similar situation to that described in the present correspondence.

3. The portrayal of Gruffuth in earlier scholarship

The Glyndŵr revolt is not an easy period of English history from the point of view of objective historiography. The panic it caused among the contemporary English was considerable. Popular rumour held that the Welsh intended to bring about 'the destruction of the kingdom and the English tongue' (Davies 1995: 157); Owain Glyndŵr claimed that it was unsafe for him to approach the English border because of such rumours (Davies 1995: 157). A tendency to see the Welsh as a dangerous 'other' has persisted through centuries, and even some relatively recent textbooks tend to portray the happenings of 1400–14 as a story of the English kings defending civilisation against the barbarians. Such views are much in evidence in most of the earlier scholarly references to the correspondence, and it may be argued that they still colour historians' reading of the letters.

---

[4] Most importantly, Gruffuth mentions Piers Cambre as the receiver of Chirkesland; Peter Cambrey entered this office after Michaelmas 1409. As Grey's letter is addressed to the prince, it must have been written before the death of Henry IV in March 1413.

The first modern editor of the letters was Ellis (1827), who introduced both the erroneous dating to 1400 and another, more remarkable, mistake that continued to haunt historical writings for quite some time. Ellis attributed both letters 1 and 2 to Gruffuth, not realising that the second was Lord Grey's reply:

> If the letter which is pasted at the back of Lord Grey's [to Prince Henry] be that which he alludes to as written by 'the strongest thief in Wales,' that personage must have been Griffith ap David ap Griffith, one of Glyndowr's most strenuous partisans. His epistle, indeed, is of a barbarous character, and breathes more of savage warfare than of chivalry, **but such was the general feature of Glyndowr's campaigns.** (Ellis 1827: 5, emphasis added)

It is astonishing that anyone who had actually read the letter could make this mistake. The name 'Gruffuth ap Dauid ap Gruffuth' appears at the beginning and clearly refers to the addressee rather than the sender. The letter refers throughout to the earlier letter by Gruffuth to Grey (which seems to have escaped Ellis's notice), answering it point by point; further, it promises to inform the king and refers to 'our lordship' and to horses stolen 'out of our park', expressing the wish to see the recipient hang for horse-theft. Finally, both Gruffuth's letter and Grey's reply to it are referred to in Grey's letter to the prince.

Ellis clearly expected the followers of Glyndŵr (and not English lords) to write 'barbarous' things: accordingly, the letter threatening a hanging had to be written by Gruffuth, even though the contents could not possibly make sense to a careful reader. The mistake was repeated by other writers, including the anonymous reviewer in *The Edinburgh Review* (1827: 196), who pours scorn upon the presumed Welsh writer, as well as on contemporary romanticists.

> such courtesies as that of the brutal savage, Glyndower's lieutenant... in his letter to Reginald Lord Grey de Ruthyn, may excite a smile... His name is Griffith ap David ap Griffith; and he is of the true cast, which our sentimental lovers of 'the olden time,' who regret all improvement, would have us regard as the genuine race of men, high-minded men. 'We hope,' says Griffith, or, as he signs his name, Gruffuth, 'we hope we shall do the a privy thing; a rope, a ladder, and a ryng...' In which fine poesy of the true time of chivalry, be it observed, in passing, there is some little trace of the versification of its modern eulogists and imitators. (Anon. 1827: 196)

The *Transactions of the Cymmrodorion* (Honourable Society of Cymmrodorion 1828) likewise reported on Ellis's edition, and characterise the letter as a 'Swing letter' or 'Captain Rock's notice', referring to a nineteenth-century practice of harassing farmers and landowners by sending them threatening letters. The same mistake is repeated in several mid-nineteenth-century historical works, including Tyler (1838) and Wright (1852). Both repeat the characterisation of Gruffuth as the greatest thief in Wales and cite the 'rude rhymes' with disapproval; Tyler (1838: 97–8, fn. g) notes that they 'indicate the character of [the] author and the spirit of the times'.

In 1860, Hingeston pointed out that the person behind the 'rude rhymes' was Lord Grey himself, and that the letter was 'addressed to, not written by, Griffith ap David ap Griffith' (Hingeston 1860: 38, fn. 1). While this settled the authorship question for good, the characterisation of Gruffuth as a rude and savage Welshman lived on, and few mentions of him omit the epithet of thief or bandit; a notable exception is Smith (1967). The characterisation is also translated into fiction in the novel *Owen Glendower*, first published in 1940, by John Cowper Powys, in which Gruffuth appears as a minor character, referred to as 'the slipperiest thief on the border' (Powys [1940] 2002: 346).

As late as 1994, a revised history of Henry IV still dates the letters to 1400, and the characterisation of Gruffuth echoes the earlier comments:

> Early in 1400... Grey of Ruthyn was engaged in a dispute with a man named Griffith ap David ap Griffith, who, incensed at not receiving the office of bailiff of Chirkland, had trespassed onto Lord Grey's lands and stolen two of his horses... **Griffith might be a rude, even barbaric man**, but Lord Grey lacked all pretence of diplomacy and courtesy in his dealings with Griffith (Bevan 1994: 80, emphasis added)

Davies (1995: 297) finally dispenses with the adjectives 'rude' and 'barbaric': however, even he characterises Gruffuth as 'a Welsh bandit'.

The negative characterisation of Gruffuth through 180 years of history writing is remarkable considering the actual evidence. Only Bradley (1902: 115–16), who shows little sympathy for Grey, seems to take the thief-epithet in its context: 'a defiant gentleman of North Wales... the "strengest thief in Wales", Grey calls him, which is to say that he accuses him of carrying off some horses from his park at Ruthin'. Most historians seem not to have allowed for the possibility that Gruffuth could have had any social standing, a presupposition that has had important implications for the interpretation of the letters.

4. The dialect of the letters

Before proceeding to discuss the contents of the letters, their linguistic and physical aspects should be considered, as any information thus gleaned might significantly affect the evaluation of the content. Most importantly, the letters clearly represent two distinct linguistic usages, as well as scribal hands: the letter from Gruffuth differs from the two others, suggesting a different origin. There is thus no *a priori* reason to doubt the authenticity of Gruffuth's letter. The most salient dialectal differences are shown in table 7.1. Letters 1 and 3 seem to be originals; both were originally folded

Table 7.1 *A comparison of distinctive dialectal forms in the three letters*

	1 (GDG to RG)	2 (RG to GDG)	3 (RG to Henry)
ASKED	askyt 2	asked 2	–
BURN	bran 3	brenne 4	–
HAD	hade 6 hedde 1	hadde 5	hadde 1
IF	ȝyf 1	giffe 2 gife 1 if 1	if 1
KNOW *pres.pl.*	knoyn 2	knowen 1	–
LIVING *n.*	leuyng 3	lyvyng 1	–
MANY	mony 3	many 3	many 1
MUCH	muche 1	moche 1	–
OWN	own 1	oun 2	oun 1
SAID	saed 3 seide 1	seide 3	–
SHOULD	schuld 5	sholde 2, shold- 4	sholde 1
SH-	sch- 16	sh-	sh-
THEM	ham 2 hem 1	hem 3	hem 2
TRUE	truw 1	trewe 2	trewe- 2
WHETHER	qweþur 2	whether 2	–
WHICH	qwich 1 qwych 1	which 3, whiche 2	which 1, wich 1
YE	ȝe 5	ye 1	ye 8
YOUR	ȝour 8	your 1	your 6, youres 3
-GHT	-ȝt 6	-ght 4	-ght 3

with the recipient's name written on the back. Letter 2 is said to be a copy; the implication is that the original was sent to Gruffuth.

In the *Linguistic Atlas of Late Mediaeval English* (LALME; McIntosh, *et al.* 1986), the letter from Gruffuth is mapped as Linguistic Profile 1363 in the Ruthin area; it is presumably an 'anchor text', placed on the map on the basis of external evidence.[5] A comparison with other material in LALME shows that the assemblage of dialectal forms agrees with northernmost Wales and the Northwest Midlands: key forms include *mony* 'many', *ben* 'are', *qwich/qwych* 'which' and *qweþur* 'whether'. Some spellings seem to reflect Welsh orthographic conventions: thus <ae> for the diphthong commonly spelt <ay/ai> in *saed* 'said', *maester* 'master', *forsaede* 'aforesaid', *fael* 'fail' and *araement* 'arrayment' (see Black 1998: 63).

The letter is said to have been *j-wrettin in grete haste at þe parke of Brinkiffo* 'written in great haste at the Park of Brinkiffe'. According to Grey's reply, it had been sent to him by a tenant of his, Deykus Vaghan. The letter may have been written by Gruffuth himself. The text contains numerous changes and corrections that suggest that it was composed while being written. Some suggest a Welsh speaker correcting himself when producing un-English constructions:

---

[5] The Welsh material is too scanty in most areas to make detailed localisation using the 'fit-technique' feasible. Neither is there reason to suppose that written English in Wales would display an unbroken dialect continuum: English settlement and rule was relatively recent, patchy and manifested through absentee landlords and isolated boroughs.

J was redy and wylly for [to] a-gon w^t him hedde he be truw
'I was ready and willing [to] go with him, had he only been true'

And [a] gode frend come and told me þis
'And [a] good friend came and told me this'

The infinitive marker and indefinite article were added afterwards by the writer; Medieval Welsh had neither.

The letters from Grey are written in one hand and seem to represent a single scribal usage. In LALME, this was defined as 'colourless North Midland language'. While not obviously 'colourless', containing several regionally marked features, the usage is certainly difficult to localise. The forms *oun* 'own', *heigh* 'high' and *other* 'or' occur scattered in the North Midlands, but their main area of distribution is more southern; with *ben* 'are' and *dud* 'did' they suggest a Southwest Midland localisation. Other forms, including *agayn* 'against' and *giffe* 'give' suggest a more northern area. The assemblage does not seem to fit the English dialect continuum, but could indicate an individual usage (McIntosh *et al.* 1986: 22) or, indeed, a variety of immigrant English in Wales. As such, it could represent the usage either of Lord Grey himself (who had partly grown up in Ruthin) or an amanuensis.

It may be concluded that the linguistic usages agree well with what we know about the background of the correspondents: a Welshman and an Englishman from the Ruthin area. Hingeston (1860: xxii) characterised Gruffuth's language as 'rude and rugged'. At the structural level, it is difficult to see what he might have referred to. Certainly, Grey's orthography looks more 'modern' in its avoidance of the letter yogh; however, its use in this period was the default, and Hingeston must have been familiar with it. A comparison of the syntax of the two letters does not produce any support for Hingeston's characterisation: rather, the numerous neatly made corrections in Gruffuth's text suggest that he showed particular care for the language. Grey's text contains some infelicities of reference (suggesting for its part a composition in haste), as well as features that might well have struck a nineteenth-century scholar as 'rude', such as the generalisation of *was* in the past indicative *(thu was, we was)*. It is possible, however, that Hingeston was characterising the pragmatic level of the letters; this should be turned to next.

5. Rude and rugged? Analysis of insults and politeness strategies in the correspondence

5.1 Introductory remarks

This section looks at the correspondence strategies adopted by Gruffuth and Grey, in order to evaluate the early editors' claims that Gruffuth's language is 'rude and rugged' and that the correspondence in general is 'barbarous' and 'savage'. As the characterisations do not seem to reflect structural incompetence, it might be expected that they would then refer to a general lack of politeness, as well as, perhaps, some form of active insult.

The following analysis considers insults, the recorded reactions to them and politeness strategies in general. The main focus will be on Gruffuth's letter and Lord Grey's reply, as they form two adjacent 'turns' in the correspondence. The letters are a rare case of late Middle English correspondence, in that we have first-hand information both of the pragmatic units and the addressee responses to them. The analysis is based on Jucker and Taavitsainen's article on the speech acts of insults, in which they outline the pragmatic space to analyse verbal aggression (2000: 72–6; see also Taavitsainen and Jucker 2007). It also refers to Brown and Levinson's (1987) theory on face and politeness.

Jucker and Taavitsainen's approach holds that any realisations of speech acts are relational, that is, they are bound to their context, culture and time (2000: 92). Speech acts must be studied in the context of adjacent speech acts, as well as in their social and textual context (2000: 70). This entails that, in order to interpret the illocutionary force of a speech act, one must consider the culture and the person that produced it, pay attention to any evidence of the perlocutionary effect, if available, and look for genre conventions that may play a role in the linguistic realisation of the speech act. Similarly, texts must be studied in the context of adjacent texts, that is, within the intertextual continuum of which they form part. In this particular chapter, the implication is that the meaning potential of the letters unfolds best when seen as part of the correspondence.

Jucker and Taavitsainen (2000: 73) define insults as having two obligatory elements (i and ii), and one optional (iii). The speaker needs to utter a proposition that characterises the addressee or hearer (i); the hearer must perceive the proposition uttered as inappropriate (ii); and the hearer must believe that the proposition was uttered with an intention of hurt (iii). In the pragmatic space devised for the study of insults, Jucker and Taavitsainen (2000: 74) distinguish eight dimensions that operate on five levels. The levels are defined by the form of insults, their semantics, their context dependence, the speaker's attitude and the addressee's reaction.

The formal level of the pragmatic space enfolds the dimensions from ritual or rule-governed to creative insults, and from typified to ad hoc insults. The semantic level holds the dimension from truth-conditional to performative insults; the former would be insulting propositions that can be shown to be true or false (such as slander), whereas the latter would be insults that are directed at a person and are meant to be offending, but have no relevance to the reality (name-calling would fall under this category). The level of context dependence is realised by one dimension, from conventionalised, speech community-bound insults to particular, situation- and reaction-bound insults. The fourth level focuses on speaker attitude, and enfolds the dimensions ludic–aggressive, intentional–unintentional, and irony–sincerity. The fifth and final level pays attention to the addressee reaction, which may range from a reply in the same form to denial, silence or violence.

The concepts in politeness theory relevant for this chapter are face and face-threatening acts (FTAs). Negative face is the individual's wish to remain unimpeded. Positive face enfolds the individual's self-image and the desire to be appreciated by others (Brown and Levinson 1987: 61–2). Positive politeness includes strategies in which speakers focus on the maintenance or establishment of the other person's face. Strategies of negative politeness usually aim at redressing a FTA so that the impact on the face of the addressee is minimised. The linguistic manifestations of negative politeness tend to become formalised, such as the choice of pronoun and form of address (Brown and Levinson 1987: 129–30, 198–9). However, even politeness conventions are culturally and temporally bound, thus the well-known preference for negative politeness strategies in Present-day English cannot be generalised to late Middle English, let alone to other languages (Jucker 2008b; for discussion of Brown and Levinson's theory, see e.g. Kopytko 1995 and Locher 2004). Applying the politeness theory to the English of a native Welsh speaker does not, however, need to be problematised here: Gruffuth had adopted the use of a code that he knew would be understandable to the recipient and this would encompass communicative strategies, as well as linguistic structure.[6]

FTAs may threaten either the positive or negative face of recipients. Acts that compromise their freedom of territory or actions, such as requests or commands, are FTAs against their negative face. FTAs against their positive face vary from criticism and disagreement to contempt and non-cooperation in communication. A FTA may also be aimed at a speaker's own face; this generally involves manifestations of negative politeness from the speaker's side. The decision to commit a FTA is always the speaker's to make: he or she must decide whether the benefits are greater than the anticipated disadvantages.

5.2 The interchange between *Gruffuth* and *Grey*

Gruffuth's letter to Grey begins with a conventional form of address: *Worschipfull lord J recomande me to ȝou and to ȝour lordschip* 'Worshipful Lord, I recommend myself to you and your lordship'. The form of address is the appropriate one addressing a nobleman in the late Middle English period (Raumolin-Brunberg 1996: 168–71). It is an act of deference striving to maintain Grey's negative face (Kopytko 1995: 526–7); Gruffuth also uses the formal pronoun of address throughout.[7] The conventional sequence of

---

[6] As regards Gruffuth's training in English, see section 6.
[7] Even though the use of *ye/you* as the pronoun of formal address was established during the late Middle English period, there was much fluctuation in the usage and address terms

salutatio and *captatio benevolentiae* (see Davis 1965: 236) is cut short: Gruffuth does not express a desire to hear of Grey's welfare nor is he saying anything of his. The brevity is, however, excused by a conventional formula at the end claiming that the letter was written in haste.

Grey, on the other hand, begins his reply by stating Gruffuth's full name, with no honorifics or titles. This is acceptable in a letter to a social inferior, as is the informal pronoun of address, *thou*. They would form a potential insult unless the unequal relationship was accepted by both parts. Gruffuth has already submitted himself by his formal address, thus Lord Grey's form of address may have been appropriate.

Even though Lord Grey's address formula was not a FTA, the following *salutatio* certainly was: *We send þe greting welle, but no þyng wiþ goode hert* 'we send you a greeting, but not at all with a good heart'. Grey here employs the convention of *salutatio* but breaks with its form, signalling his hostility, and thus threatens the positive face of Gruffuth. In terms of Jucker and Taavitsainen (2000), this insult is creative on the formal level and conventional in the sense that all the members of the speech community would have understood it as an insult. It is performative (there is nothing in it that would be truth-conditional) and the speaker's intention or attitude is certainly aggressive. Lord Grey's assumed social superiority indicates that he has nothing to lose even if he commits a FTA, thus redressive action is unnecessary.

In Gruffuth's letter, the *salutatio* is followed by the request *J wold pray ȝou hertli þ^t ȝe wold her how þ^e fals John Wele serued me* 'I would pray you heartily that you would hear how the fals John Wele treated me'. The request restricts the freedom of Grey, thus it is a FTA against his negative face. However, it is redressed by the use of conditional forms that take the focus away from the direct request: Brown and Levinson would call this conventional indirectness (1987: 131). Further, the requesting verb, *pray*, and the modifying adverb, *heartily*, are both intended to ensure the addressee of the speaker's sincerity (Jucker 2008b: 20). Here, the expressions of sincerity are a FTA against the speaker's negative face: he admits that he needs the addressee's attention in this matter. The expressions can also be analysed in terms of extended social distance, i.e. affect, intimacy, importance and cunning (Kopytko 1995: 536). In this case, the importance of the matter to Gruffuth overrides any reasons for choosing a more redressive action.[8] In contrast, Grey's letter contains no *captatio benevolentiae* nor transition from *salutatio* to *narratio*; rather, it continues in *in medias res* style, a further indication of the inequality of the correspondents. As noted earlier, if both the correspondents accept

---

could vary even within a single dialogue (see e.g. Burnley 2003: 32, 33). In the current correspondence, Gruffuth's use of *ye/you* is consistent, as is Grey's use of *thou/thee* when addressing Gruffuth but *ye/you* when addressing the prince; here the address terms clearly mark social status.

[8] This is an example of the dynamic and situation-bound nature of social distance (see Locher 2004: 39–40, 47).

the roles suggested by their respective letters, the mode of communication is appropriate and acceptable.

Gruffuth continues with a lengthy passage relating the story of his dealings with John Wele. This is not a FTA in itself, although where Grey disagrees with Gruffuth he may feel his positive face threatened. The account of Gruffuth's coming into possession of the two horses concerns an issue where disagreement is unavoidable; his admission is in itself a FTA against Grey's positive and negative faces. Gruffuth here tries to assure Grey of his goodwill in order to diminish the effect: *for no hatered þ^t J hade to ȝou or ȝour lordschip þei wern taken* 'they were not taken because of any hatred that I had to you or your lordship'. This is a combination of positive and negative politeness strategies: Gruffuth is both giving reasons for the taking of the horses while rendering the FTA impersonal, moving it away from the person of the addressee (Brown and Levinson 1987: 128, 190). Grey makes no comment on the truth value of Gruffuth's account. He simply repeats it, marking the reported text with the insertion of *(as) þu seiste* '(as) you say'.[9] Lord Grey does not express overt disagreement until the point where Gruffuth turns to the matters concerning his lordship.

Gruffuth then relates a rumour about Grey's intended actions: *hit was told me þ^t ȝe ben in purpos for to make ȝour men bran and sle in qwadesoeuer Cuntre þ^t J be and am reseued in* 'I was told that you intend to make your men burn and kill in whatever country where I am or where I am received'. The FTA against Grey's positive face is here related to the truth value of the statement and thus this would constitute a truth-conditioned insult or slander. For this reason, Gruffuth is very careful in his formulation of the proposition: he does not claim that the proposition is true, nor even his, only that he had received such a piece of information. The follow-up passage is the only directly threatening part of the letter: here Gruffuth promises to burn and kill in retaliation for Grey's acts: *as mony men þ^t ȝe slen and as mony howsin þ^t ȝe bran for my sake, as mony wol J bran and sle for ȝour sake* 'as many men as you will kill and as many houses as you will burn for my sake, as many will I burn and kill for your sake'. This is a commissive speech act, a threat: Gruffuth commits himself to a certain future action if the conditions mentioned earlier are fulfilled. The passage adds aggressive speaker intention to the assumed insult in the earlier passage.

For Grey, the claim that he plans to burn houses and kill men is the most important point that needs refuting: it is the one part of Gruffuth's letter that could be harmful to himself. He categorically denies the proposition's truth value: *we was neuere so mys avised to worch agayn the kyng no his lawes* 'we were never so unwise as to act against the King or his laws'. It cannot

---

[9] This remark should be taken literally, as a marker of reported speech, and not to mean 'these are your words, but I disagree': the marker is used throughout the letter, and even though Lord Grey may disagree with Gruffuth's report, it would be assuming too much to assign that function to the marker.

be true because it would constitute treason. He then states that Gruffuth has been misinformed, and thus treats the claim as slander (Jucker 2000: 374–6). His promise to inform the king and his councillors seems to betray a worry that the accusations might reach the king through other channels. The refutation is meant to establish Grey's positive face and to threaten Gruffuth's. Whether Gruffuth deemed this an insult would depend on his evaluation of the situation.

Gruffuth continues with a directive that is as close as one comes to an actual insult in his letter: *doutes not J wolle haue boþ^e bredde and ale of þ^e best þ^t is in ȝour~ lordschip* 'have no doubt that I will have both bread and ale of the best that is in your lordship'. The use of a directive *doubt not* in itself constitutes a FTA against Grey's negative face in the form of a command: there is no reason to resort to redressive action, as the following commissive is a threat to Grey's lordship.

After repeating Gruffuth's statement that he will have bread and ale in Grey's lordship (whether by stealing or simply by being 'received' among the Welsh people), Grey states simply that it is *agayn our wyll* 'against our will'. Grey's comment suggests that the FTA does take place, but not necessarily the insult. However, this is a question of definitions: if the threat to the lordship is equal to a proposition that characterises Lord Grey, and he believes it was intended to hurt him (which it obviously did), then this exchange establishes an insult.

Finally, Grey turns to the matter of horse-theft. As a Marcher Lord, Grey held legal power within his jurisdiction, and had the right to both arrest and condemn Gruffuth on the basis of a confession. He makes clear that he considers Gruffuth guilty, and does not accept his explanation: *þegh John Welle haþ doon as þu abouen has certefied vs thynkeþ þat þat sholde noght be wroken towarde vs* 'even though John Welle has done as you say, it seems to us that should not be avenged on us'. The letter is finished with the much-quoted verse in which Grey expresses his wish to see Gruffuth hang, followed by the simple statement: *for þy lettre is knowlechyng* 'for your letter is a confession'.

As a speech act, the verse is an expressive that functions as an insult: it is creative in its formulation[10] and displays an aggressive speaker attitude. The light tone also underlines the powerful position of Grey. This is a FTA against both the positive and negative faces of Gruffuth: capital punishment is the ultimate threat to one's freedom. As Grey has established himself as socially superior since the beginning of the letter, he has no need for redressive actions: his loss is minimal, even though Gruffuth would be insulted. The main insult in this passage is the form of punishment, fit for a thief. The addressee reaction is lost to us, but at least we can say that this is a

---

[10] The formulation of the insult is creative, even though it may be quoting a popular rhyme of the era.

truth-conditional and conventional insult. The complete absence of any closing formula or even a signature would constitute a final insult; however, they may simply be lacking in the copy.

The closing of Gruffuth's letter employs a short form of a conventional formula: *J can no mor but gode kepe ȝour worschipffull astate in prosperite* 'I can [write] no more, but God keep your worshipful estate in prosperity'. In itself this would contribute towards the negative politeness expected from a social inferior. However, in the context of the preceding speech act, it may also be interpreted as an expressive, adding a further jab to the preceding insult or threat: 'may your estate prosper, so that I can benefit from it'. Bradley (1902: 116–17) took it as a humorous jab; however, this may simply reflect the modern reader's tendency to read meaning into formulae that have lost their conventionality.

The last line of Gruffuth's letter uses a conventional place-and-date formula: *j-wrettin in grete haste at þe parke of Brinkiffe* 'written in great haste at the Park of Brinkiffe'. The phrase '*in grete haste*' is common in short contemporary letters, and at least partly functions as a politeness formula, providing a reason for brevity that might otherwise be perceived as insulting. Whether intentional or not, the indication of place might have added a touch of defiance: Brinkiffe was a forest belonging to Grey's area of jurisdiction.

5.3 Grey's letter to the prince

Letter 3, Grey's letter to the prince, stands formally in contrast to his letter to Gruffuth, being addressed to a superior. The *salutatio* and *captatio benevolentiae* form a textbook example of letter-writing formulae, including all the elements listed by Davis (1965: 236). In the form of address (*Right heigh and myghty prynce, my goode and gracious lorde*), honorifics are multiplied and modified by adjectives denoting deference and respect.

At the same time, Grey is not afraid to employ very direct address: *J shall trewely do my power to do our liege lorde þe kynges commaundement and youres but worshipfull and gracious lorde ye most commaunden the kynges officeres in euery cuntree to do þe same* 'I shall truly do my best to carry out the commandments from the king and yourself, but, worshipful and gracious lord, you must command the king's officers in every jurisdictional area to do the same'. The demand here is a FTA against the prince's negative face, and it stands apart from the rest in its directness; however, like all FTAs in this letter, they are balanced with negative politeness strategies: the phrase *gracious lord* is repeated in every sentence that contains an FTA of any kind. Lord Grey ends the letter with a recommendation of the carrier, a brief recapitulation of the main points and a closing formula very similar to that used by Gruffuth.

In his letter to the prince, Lord Grey shows that he is not oblivious to politeness strategies, nor to letter-writing conventions, and that he knows how to modify his writing according to the recipient. This implies that, in both letters, he has chosen the mode of writing that he has deemed appropriate. Both letters show him as an audacious writer, not afraid of employing blatant FTAs, even though this may be more obviously visible in the letter to Gruffuth, which employs no politeness strategies to modify the effect.

5.4 Gruffuth and Grey as correspondents

A comparison of the two correspondents shows Grey as by far the bolder writer. Gruffuth's letter does not mark defiance through its form. His choice of form of address would have been the default when writing to a superior. In the loci where a FTA is hazarded but not wished for, Gruffuth tries to tone down the effect by redressing the most delicate information contents in phrases that contribute towards negative politeness.

The edge to his letter comes clear close to the end, where he delivers his conditional threat to Grey; however, as Gruffuth is throughout careful in his claims about Grey, he makes it, at least in principle, possible for the recipient to ignore his threat. Gruffuth employs negative politeness strategies in a creative way, striving to give Grey an opportunity to accept his letter without losing face.

Grey is less preoccupied with negative politeness. He is familiar with politeness formulae but also exploits the effect of ignoring them: in both letters he at times deems the benefits gained by a frank style to be greater than the polite strategies that would lead one to avoid FTAs; this is particularly true of his letter to Gruffuth. The absence of politeness formulae is in itself unremarkable in this letter, as it merely marks his social status; however, it makes his insults, in particular the verses at the end, stand out with a stronger effect than the more guarded expressions of aggression in Gruffuth's letter.

Again, there are no grounds for accepting Hingeston's (1860: xxii) characterisation of Gruffuth's language as 'rude and rugged'; rather the contrary. It may be concluded that the characterisation relates not so much to the actual language of the texts as to expectations about the characteristics of a Welsh rebel, including his linguistic usage.

6. The letters as evidence of Gruffuth's status: a critical reading

It remains to address the question of Gruffuth's social status. Most historians seem to have pictured him as a kind of common thief with no social standing. Such a view seems to be implied in the conclusions drawn by Davies about the situation in North Wales at this time, involving 'demeaning bargains' from the point of view of the English:

Gruffudd was willing to submit but clearly not on any terms: he wanted a royal charter of pardon, an important local office, and arrangements to go on military service overseas. Such demands may sound outrageous, but it is clear that lords and their officials were driven into demeaning bargains in order to secure the final extinction of the revolt. (Davies 1995: 297)

As Davies notes elsewhere (1995: 312) that the appointment of former rebels of local standing to official positions was common in the aftermath of the rebellion, and in fact often the only workable solution, the 'outrageousness' here must then reflect his assumptions about Gruffuth's social status and suitability for such a position.

The correspondence contains much indirect evidence about Gruffuth's status, as well as indirect evaluations about his suitability for office. However, as all this derives from interested parties, it has to be treated critically. Most earlier scholars, it was noted, accepted Grey's characterisation of Gruffuth as *þe strengest thiefe of Wales*. This characterisation can hardly be expected to be objective, especially considering what we know of Grey's situation and thus his likely agenda. Financially ruined by the ransom, he could only benefit from a hard-line approach towards the Welsh, also advocated by the King's Council. At the same time, any reports to the king or the Prince of Wales about his overstepping his authority could be damaging. He would need to present Gruffuth (and thus the Welsh) in as unfavourable a light as possible, justifying both his own actions and his request for more authority.

On the other hand, there is no reason to doubt the general veracity of Gruffuth's account of his circumstances. The facts are not contested by Grey, and the letter would have had little purpose unless they were verifiable.

The most striking statement with implications about Gruffuth's social status is his claim that he was offered not only the king's pardon but the offices of Master Forester and *keyshat* in Chirkesland. Davies (1995) seems to suggest that all the demands came from Gruffuth himself. However, Gruffuth's letter states unequivocally that the offer came from John Wele, who had approached him 'by trety of' his cousins, Master Edward and Edward ap David:

> he wold gete me þᵉ kyng-is Char*ter* and J schuld be Maes*ter* Fors*ter* and keyshat in Chirke-is lond ... Aft*ur*ward he askyt me qweþ*ur* J wold go ouer see wᵗ hym And he wold gete me my Char*ter* of þᵉ kyng~ and bring me to hym sounde and saff and J schuld haue. wages as muche as any gentilman schuld haue þᵗ went wᵗ hym

> 'He would get me the king's charter and I should be Master Forester and *keyshat* in Chirkesland ... later he asked me to go overseas with him, and he would get me my charter from the king and bring me to him

sound and safe, and I should have as much in wages as any gentleman that went with him' (letter 1).

Gruffuth makes clear that the overseas service was part of the deal with Wele: *J nold a-gon for no wages w^t hym ouer see but for to haue my Charter of þ^e kyng and sum leuyng þ^t J my3t duel in pees and in Rest* 'I did not wish to go overseas with him for the sake of wages, but in order to get my charter from the king and some means of living, so that I would be able to live in peace and quiet'. The implication is that Gruffuth is keen to submit and make peace in exchange for a position of office: however, he consistently portrays John Wele as the active player in the negotiations. This may, of course, be simply a way of justifying his own case; however, what we know of John Wele's dealings otherwise fits well with the narrative as it stands.

The offer may have been a trap; however, in order to work, it must have had some credibility. Offices such as these were extremely attractive: they provided a good income and the officers generally wielded the real power locally. Gruffuth must have had reason to believe that the offer was made seriously; this belief must also have been shared by his cousins, as well as the Bishop of St Asaph, who were involved in the negotiations.

Suitability for office would have required some social standing in Wales. That Gruffuth is likely to have had such standing is suggested by his account of the dealings in Oswestry, where he claims to have 'sent' Piers Cambre, the receiver of Chirkesland (and thus a fairly important person), three times to speak to Wele. That Gruffuth was regarded as a member of the gentry is also indicated by his preparations for military service overseas, procuring men and horses, as well as by Wele's promise about wages: *as muche as any gentilman schuld haue þ^t went w^t hym* 'the same amount in wages as any gentleman that went with him'.

Finally, Gruffuth's letter (whether penned by himself or dictated) suggests considerable literacy skills, familiarity with English letter-writing conventions and a fluent command of English. For a member of the Welsh gentry, this would not have been exceptional; many had gone to England for their education, and Owain Glyndŵr himself had studied law at the Inns of Court. The title 'Master' used of his cousin Edward also suggests either university learning or, more generally, high social status; the English name probably indicates intermarriage between Welsh and English families.

All these points taken together suggest a person of some social standing and education. There would thus be no need to consider the negotiations 'outrageous' or 'demeaning'; they only appear so if we accept the premise that he was a common thief. There is, of course, no inherent contradiction in a gentleman stealing horses,[11] or turning to a life of marauding in the aftermath of a rebellion. Gruffuth himself complains that he has no means

---

[11] The 'confession' by Gruffuth depends in fact on an 'I' [*J*] inserted above the line at a crucial point: *And as J. herd þer ben taken ij horses of 3our men þ^t wern pyte in 3our parke þoo horsys*

of living but must find it *as [gode] wolle ordeyn for* 'as God will provide it'; a complaint that in itself presupposes that this had not always been his situation.

7. Conclusion

The strands of enquiry may, finally, be brought together. The dialectal analysis has shown that there is no reason to assume that the letters are anything but authentic. Comparing letters 1 and 2, the slips and corrections show Gruffuth as the more careful writer, more intent on giving a good impression. The pragmatic analysis confirms this difference. Apart from the conditional threats towards the end of Gruffuth's letter, he is consistently careful in employing politeness strategies and avoiding blatant FTAs. Grey's letter to Gruffuth shows neither careful polishing nor the employment of politeness strategies. This is to be expected in a letter to a social inferior (which Gruffuth would be no matter how high his status in Wales); however, in addition, his letter contains insults that make the tone overtly aggressive. Even in his letter to the prince, Grey comes across as the bolder writer of the two, something easily explicable considering his more stable position. On the whole, there is nothing in Gruffuth's letter that would seem to justify the adjectives 'rude', 'rugged' and 'barbaric': even the threat of burning and killing is conditional on what would have been outrageous action by Grey.

The intention here is not to elevate Gruffuth ap Dauid ap Gruffuth to a hero, although he might deserve that after centuries of vilification. Rather, the point is that the letters present a very intricate weave of politics and agenda, which should be taken into account when interpreting them as historical evidence. Presenting Gruffuth as *þe strengest thiefe of Wales* suited Lord Grey's purposes. We do not know how the prince received the letters, but there is no doubt that they communicated well their original purpose to their early English editors. The present chapter has attempted to produce a reading of the letters without accepting Grey's phrase as a starting point; it might be concluded that the combined force of historical, dialectal and pragmatic evidence suggests that Bradley's (1902) phrase of 'a defiant gentleman' might fit the context much better than the stereotype of the bandit.

J wod qwer þei ben / but for no hatered þ^t J hade to ȝou or ȝour lordschip þei wern taken but my men toke ham and [J] boȝt ham of hem 'And as I heard there have been two horses taken from your men, which were placed in your park: I know where those horses are, but they were not taken because of any hatred that I had towards you or your lordship, but my men took them and [I] bought them from them'. It is impossible to tell whether the 'I' was inserted by Gruffuth himself as a correction or by Grey as a means of 'improving' his evidence. Similarly, it is difficult to know whether Gruffuth's promise to get bread and ale in Grey's lordship refers to guesting or theft. The correspondence is thus open for different interpretations, depending on the reader's expectations.

8 Sociopragmatic aspects of person reference in Nathaniel Bacon's letters

MINNA PALANDER-COLLIN AND
MINNA NEVALA

1. Introduction

People are one of the most central topics of discussion in everyday discourse. Consequently, texts abound with person reference, but the frequency and type of reference varies. Cultural practices, politeness norms, genre/textual conventions and situation-specific communicative needs influence the ways we refer to people. Whether we call our interlocutor *you* or *your Highness* carries a lot of social meaning, as does referring to a colleague as *Mary* or *Professor Smith*. The meanings are both situation-specific and may reflect the speaker's personal orientations but they also stem from a societal system of established hierarchies and social distinctions. Similarly, whether we can talk about ourselves in particular contexts and what we can say is a matter of interpersonal negotiation on several levels. Mühlhäusler and Harré (1990: 5) suggest that 'grammatical rules for the use of person-indexing expressions in most languages include reference to specific social relations'. Their model of person reference, like, for example, Layder's ([1997] 2003) social theory, incorporates the macro- and micro-levels of analysis within the same framework in recognising that there are macro-societal conventions and categories affecting our behaviour on the one hand, and that writers make meaning and strategic choices in local contexts on the other hand.

In our discussion of person reference in Nathaniel Bacon's sixteenth-century letters, we aim to show how person reference works towards placing individuals in the broad societal framework of appropriate social roles and relations, creating a certain type of text genre and expressing the writer's persona and local communicative needs. As a theoretical model we have been particularly inspired by Layder's sociological domain theory suggesting that there are four domains in everyday social life that relate to each other and are always present in interaction ([1997] 2003: 2–5). These are (i) psychobiography, (ii) situated activity, (iii) social settings and (iv) contextual resources. The four domains situate individuals in a complex web encompassing personal feelings, attitudes and predispositions, the current face-to-face transaction, the particular setting of a specific location or social organisation, and the society-wide distribution and ownership of resources along gender, race and class lines. We set out to explore whether and how these domains are reflected in the way person reference is used.

Our understanding of the sociopragmatics of person reference comprises going beyond the immediate situational context into the social dimension. Historical sociopragmatics is used here to cover not only diachronic variation and change at the social and societal level of language use, but also in the individual and contextual dimensions. In other words, we aim to study the macro-level of social, sociocultural and sociological factors, as well as the micro-level of personal, situational and stylistic factors.

On the personal, psychobiographic level, we focus on Nathaniel Bacon, whose general life history can be reconstructed on the basis of Hassell Smith and Baker (1987–1988) and Hassell Smith ([2004] 2005). As a situated activity, we deal with the letter genre and its conventions. Personal letters are a highly interactive genre both in the type of linguistic features they exhibit (such as first- and second-person pronouns) and as a social practice, allowing us to explore characteristics of past communicative patterns between identifiable individuals. Bacon's letters can be accessed as manuscripts in archives, but we have relied on a selection of letters sampled on sociolinguistic principles from *The Papers of Nathaniel Bacon of Stiffkey* (Hassell Smith and Baker 1987–1988) and included in electronic format in the *Corpus of Early English Correspondence*. Arguing for the sociopragmatic nature of person reference, we do not particularly illustrate or discuss the use of corpus tools in this chapter, although we refer to our previous research where corpus tools and methods were extensively employed.

Bacon's letters encompass the sixteenth-century family context, the business of estate management and county administration as specific social settings. Finally, the broad societal context can be approximated on the basis of sociohistorical research that helps us create an understanding of the more permanent factors defining the moral order of the period and its people. At a minimum, a person's social rank and gender are important identity and relational factors, as England was a highly stratified society where people of different rank and gender participated in partly different activities and had different legal rights. Wrightson ([1982] 2003: 25), for example, writes that in early modern England 'the most fundamental structural characteristic of English society was its high degree of stratification, its distinctive and all-pervasive system of social inequality'. The separation of civil and domestic life was also evident (Bryson 1998: 167). Different types of language registers for addressing people of various ranks were advised in letter-writing manuals and conduct books of the period (Bryson 1998: 166–8). According to manuals, superiors should, for instance, be allowed the initiative in discourse, while inferiors should avoid blunt questions and direct contradiction. In response to a superior, the inferior should use the appropriate title, avoid direct address with the pronoun *you*, insist on the superior's freedom from any obligation to the inferior, and show submission. The normative ideas express the expectations placed on a gentleman's verbal behaviour and clearly show that a varying portrayal of the self and other was the prescriptive norm, depending on the situation. Our analysis shows that the choice of person reference relates to micro-interactional contextual needs, genre and macro-societal structures alike.

2. Nathaniel Bacon and his letters

Nathaniel Bacon (1546?–1622), a Norfolk 'county magnate' and local politician educated at Trinity College, Cambridge, and Gray's Inn, is the central informant in this study (Hassell Smith [2004] 2005). Living in a country estate in Norfolk, Bacon was concerned with the business of farming and estate management, matters that his letters to servants and local yeomen largely deal with. Altogether, the sample contains seventy-nine letters, of which twenty-nine were addressed to Bacon's father, Sir Nicholas Bacon, who was Lord Keeper of the Great Seal to Elizabeth I. The letters to Sir Nicholas mostly deal with the management of the Stiffkey estate, matters such as farming, the sale of corn and the measuring of the ground. Bacon's judicial and administrative duties as a Justice of the Peace placed him within a wider community locally, but not nationwide (Hassell Smith and Baker 1987–1988, III: xvi). Many letters to noblemen and other gentlemen deal with administrative matters. In addition to those to his father, the family letters are addressed to Bacon's younger brother Edward, sister Elizabeth and in-laws. These letters also typically contain some family 'business', such as money or negotiations concerning the placement of Bacon's young wife.

Bacon represents the social rank of lower gentry writing to his social superiors, equals, inferiors and family members. The letters date from the years 1571–1594 when Bacon was first a young husband in his twenties and later a father in his late forties arranging his daughters' marriages. He can be found as Sir Nathaniel Bacon in the *Oxford Dictionary of National Biography*, but since he was knighted only in 1604, we shall refer to him as Nathaniel Bacon or Bacon (Hassell Smith [2004] 2005).

3. Person reference

We shall deal with first-, second- and nominal third-person reference, excluding third-person pronominal forms. First- and second-person reference is usually regarded as fundamentally different from third-person reference as, for example, first and second persons are primarily referred to only with person markers, whereas reference to third persons can be achieved with various lexical and pronominal means (Siewierska 2004: 5). In terms of the psychological principles operating in person reference, recognition and economy apply to third-person reference – as also illustrated in our discussion – but do not apply in the same way in first- and second-person reference (for the principles, see Levinson 2007; Sacks and Schegloff 2007). The principles of recognition and economy suggest that the primary purpose of (third-person) reference is to achieve recognition with minimal expressive means, i.e. to use a single referring expression whenever possible, to use a name rather than a description if possible, and to use only one name of a binomial construction if possible. First and second persons are generally known from the context and they are referred to economically by pronouns. In practice, person reference does not fully follow the principles of recognition and economy, and Levinson (2007: 31) additionally identifies circumspection as the third principle leading us to 'observe further local constraints', such as to 'say "Mr Williams" rather than "Jim" if the school rules forbid pupils to use the teachers' first names' (see also Allerton 1996 and Dickey 1997). It is precisely in this area of social and pragmatic constraints that we find a joint discussion of first-, second- and third-person reference useful.

3.1 First- and second-person reference

Acts where the interactants refer to one another are typical of even brief interactions. As the person speaking or writing is the 'default origo' of such an act and the addressee its 'focus', these acts always index '*some* social relation between speaker and addressee' (Agha 2007: 280). In personal letters, the writer–addressee relationship can be regarded as primary, and consequently letters abound with first- and second-person pronouns, such as in example (1) below where *I* acts on, or in relation to, *you*. The idea of the first person as a linguistic feature relating to identity and relational functions of language can be based on Mühlhäusler and Harré's (1990: 87–105) thesis of double indexicality for *I*, by which 'I and other first-person expressions are used not to denote anything, but as indices of location' (Mühlhäusler and Harré 1990: 92). These locations are of two kinds as *I* indexes the speaker's utterance in place and time, and with the person to be held morally responsible for it. Mühlhäusler and Harré (1990: 94–5) suggest that speakers are always located in both ways, physically and morally, and that physical location tends to be universal, stable and independent of cultural conventions, whereas moral geography is local, variable and embedded in different registers. The location of speakers in the moral order of speaking is defined by various permanent as well as temporary factors. More or less permanent factors include the rights, duties and obligations of the speakers and hearers, and relate to their social roles in the context, while temporary factors refer to the moment-by-moment presentation of self as confident, shy, competent, arrogant and so on.[1] For instance, in (1) below, 'I am content he shall bargaine with yow' locates the

---

[1] As Jucker and Taavitsainen (2003: 10) point out, the use of address pronouns and nominal terms alike is 'susceptible to synchronic and diachronic variation', meaning that changes in the context of the utterance vary situationally as well as socially, and any generalisations can only be approximations.

act of being content at the writer Nathaniel Bacon and specifies the time as simultaneous with the writing. The responsibility indexing specifies the impact of the utterance in relation to the writer's position in the situation – a master writing to a local yeoman – and the responsibility for the outcome is taken by the writer (i.e. what kind of consequences the writer's state of satisfaction may have, or what would happen if he were not content).

(1) Aldred, yf the rentes of West Somerton be ready & gathered, **I** wold have them delivered to Momforth, the bearer hearof. Touching **your** rent corne **I** am content he shall bargaine with **yow** either for the whole or for **your** part... Thus far **yow** hartely well... **Your** very friend Nathaniel Bacon. (Nathaniel Bacon to Goodman Aldred, 1570s, I: 93, emphasis added in all examples)

Many languages grammaticalise social relationships in the second person (T/V systems), or, alternatively, third-person systems signal respect for the addressee (Mühlhäusler and Harré 1990: 135–48). In earlier periods and in some dialects in this period, the opposition of *thou* and *you* served to indicate distance, intimacy and power as a T/V system.[2] This is not the case in Bacon's letters, where a third-person system of deferential titles is used. *Your Lordship*, *Your Ladyship*, *Your Honour* and *Your Worship* include reference to the addressee's gender and social status: *Your Lordship* was reserved for the nobility and *Your Ladyship* to titled ladies. *Your Honour* could be used to address 'any person of rank or quality' and *Your Worship* to address 'a person of note' (*Oxford English Dictionary*; see also Postles 2005; Busse 2006: 61–5). The use of titles was recognised in contemporary conduct books, and, for instance, their repetition to superiors at intervals was recommended (Bryson 1998: 165).

3.2 Third-person reference

According to Hanks (1992: 55), dynamism and contextuality are the basic features of interaction: as the interactants shift, the indexical framework of reference changes. The use of third-person reference belongs to one of the deictic means that can be used to move between different viewpoints. Basically, there are two kinds of reference forms that convey deictic information: recognitional forms, which have unique reference throughout the communicative situation, such as personal names and recognitional descriptions (e.g. *the guy who is standing beside you*), as well as non-recognitional reference

---

[2] The findings of many studies on YOU/THOU variation (e.g. Busse 2002; Walker 2007) indicate that in broad terms the choice between these pronouns corresponds to relative power relations between the interactants, as inferiors tend to be addressed as THOU and superiors as YOU, although there is considerable room for manoeuvring to show shifts in feelings, attitudes, level of intimacy, etc., to the point that not every individual shift between YOU and THOU can be accounted for (Nevala 2004a: 177–8).

forms, which shift according to the situational context, such as pronouns (Schegloff 1996: 459; also Smith and Jucker 1998; Clark and Bangerter 2004: 37–8).

Levinson (2007: 33) suggests there is a scale of decreasing ambiguity of reference, which is at the speaker's disposal in each interaction. The recognition continuum ranges from those reference forms that refer to an open group of possible referents (such as pronouns), via minimal description terms (*that man, the neighbour*) and kinship terms to personal names, which in turn refer to a highly restricted group of possible referents. Referential terms may be used, for example, to alter distance in respect to the addressee and/or the referent. The speaker may also use reference for shifting power relations by, for example, mitigating the self by focusing on other interactants more than on oneself. In general, there are a number of factors that may influence the use of person-referring expressions, such as 'those which govern the way in which the conversation is organised, the topic of conversation, and any social factors, which may include power and distance differences between the participants' (Wilson and Zeitlyn 1995: 80).

Some of the non-recognitional forms, in particular, can be used ambiguously, and often require some serious interpretive skills on the part of the addressee. According to Lerner (1996: 292), the pronoun *you*, for example, can be used for both reference and address at the same time, leaving the listeners to solve who is being referred to and who directly addressed. In Schegloff's (2007: 131) view, nominal terms, such as personal names, are most typically used when directly addressing the hearer. However, when used in contexts in which the speaker asks the hearer to introduce him/herself, e.g. at the beginning of a phone call ('Hello, is this *Mrs Thomas*?'), the term is used as a reference to the addressee, not as a form of address.

So, the dynamic nature of reference means not only that recognitionals and non-recognitionals are used to shift between different deictic positions but also that they can be used to express, for example, the speaker's attitude towards the referent. Stivers (2007: 85) found this to be true of the so-called alternative recognitionals, in particular.[3] Whereas the name is considered the unmarked reference form for recognitionals, alternative terms not only refer to a person but are also markedly used to perform a certain pragmatic action, such as complaining. Demonstrative prefaced descriptions like *that next door neighbour*, for example, do not actually associate the referent to either the speaker or the addressee; the demonstrative *that* is used to show that 'the referent is outside of the speaker's interactional focal area or "here-space"' (Stivers 2007: 86). Stivers finds that, in her material, the expression '*that* next door neighbour' is used instead of '*our* next door neighbour' to mark the beginning of a complaint sequence. It not only asserts that the neighbour is not in the 'here-space', but also foregrounds the complaint before any actual

---

[3] These are what Schegloff calls 'recognitional descriptions' (1996: 459).

complaint has been made.[4] The phrase in itself does not suggest that there is a problem, but adding the demonstrative determiner does so, since it distances the referent from the speaker. As Stivers notes, alternative recognitionals differ from other types of recognitionals in that they are 'designed to assist in conveying the action and accounting for the action in which they are embedded' (2007: 89). This sort of critical disassociation can also be found in the use of third-person reference in our material, and we shall discuss some of these contextual factors more closely in section 4.3.

4. Person reference in Nathaniel Bacon's letters

4.1 First- and second-person reference

In Nathaniel Bacon's letters, first- and second-person pronouns, as well as addressee reference in the form of third-person titles, can be interpreted on several contextual levels referred to in the introduction, including Bacon's local communicative needs in the current transaction, rhetorical conventions of the letter genre and the social settings Bacon takes part in, and more general social relationships and hierarchies important in early modern society. In the following discussion we shall illustrate the interplay of these contextual aspects in the use of first- and second-person reference starting from the level of broad societal hierarchies and proceeding through genre and institutional conventions to characteristics of individual interactions, although in practice the levels are intertwined and interrelated.

Palander-Collin (2006, 2009) explored the use of first- and second-person reference in Nathaniel Bacon's letters in relation to sixteenth-century social hierarchies in particular, showing that the first and second persons were important loci for the coding of social hierarchies, as the frequencies of self-mention (*I*) and direct addressee inclusion (*you(r)*) were higher in letters to social inferiors than superiors, while indirect addressee inclusion (*Your Lordship*) was used in letters to superiors, including Bacon's father, Sir Nicholas. This tendency towards self-evasion perhaps reflects a hierarchical distance between father and son, which is also expressed in the repetition of the title *Your Lordship* and the use of other elements of the humiliative style (see example (3) below). The use of deferential titles was a salient feature of civil speech and writing in the sixteenth century (see Bryson 1998: 166–8), whereas relatively high frequencies of first-person reference may stem from increasing involvement and a less restrained style used in informal, familiar and friendly relationships, where there is no hierarchical distinction between the writer and the recipient, or the writer is socially superior to the

---

[4] Gernsbacher and Shroyer (1989: 537, 539) found that the indefinite *this* is also used as what they call 'a cataphoric device', in that it often influences the way in which the referent is mentally represented and thus makes it easier for the listener to access that mental image in the subsequent narrative (also Jucker and Smith 2003: 408–9).

recipient. In register studies, the frequent use of first- and second-person pronouns – together with other involvement features like private verbs, present tense verbs, *be* as the main verb, contractions, general emphatics, hedges and amplifiers – has been shown to be characteristic of spoken and speech-related registers, including personal letters, whereas written registers and formal speech are clearly less involved (e.g. Biber 1988, 2006: 50). These tendencies seem to hold across time periods, but increased stance marking, involvement and subjectification in various genres in the history of English from around the seventeenth century onwards have also been observed (Biber and Finegan 1989; Taavitsainen 2002; Biber 2004).

Since the writer and the addressee are the central interactants in a letter, it is no wonder that the first- and second-person forms are used in letter formulae that conventionally establish their mutual relationship. This genre-specific phraseology is characteristic of the contemporary discourses of servitude and friendship and it relates to wider societal structures reflecting the writer's and the recipient's superior or inferior status. (Semi-)formulaic phrases involving the writer and/or the recipient typically occur as opening (example (2)) and closing formulae (examples (3)–(5)) emphasising duty and humbleness towards a superior (examples (2) and (3)) or friendship and goodwill towards a familiar (example (4)) or inferior recipient (example (5)).

(2) **My** dutie [in humble wise] remembred {unto **your honour**}. It pleased **your honour** and Mr Attorney by {your} letters of the xiii of this presente in Her Majestes name to commande **me** to graunte by coppie of courte rolle to Thomas Lichefeilde, esquire, one of the gromes of Her [Highenes] privey chamber, and his heires all the copyhold landes and tenements late in the tenure of John and Gregory Smyth. (Nathaniel Bacon to Sir Ralph Sadler, Chancellor of the Duchy of Lancaster, 1582, II: 219)

(3) Thus wishinge **your Lordship** continuall health, **I** leave with humble askinge of **your** blessinge. (Nathaniel Bacon to his father, Sir Nicholas Bacon, *c*. 1571, I: 18)

(4) Thus requiring to be hartely commended to Sir Henrie, **I** wish **you** both long well to do. (Nathaniel Bacon to his sister, Lady Elizabeth Neville, 1592, III: 217)

(5) Thus desyeringe **you** that the deputaconship maie be dispached, **I** bid **you** hartelie fare well. (Nathaniel Bacon to William Smythe, Customer of Yarmouth, 1570s, I: 84)

A comparison of letters written to the same recipient further highlights the importance of the topic and the writer's personal involvement with it in triggering frequent self-reference. Nathaniel Bacon's three letters to his father-in-law, Sir Thomas Gresham, are a case in point. The one with the highest and the one with the lowest frequency of the first-person subject *I*

(24 vs. 5.2 instances per 400 words)[5] both deal with estate management, but the letter with the highest frequency of *I* expresses Bacon's disappointment at the decision of the recipient and the father, Sir Nicholas Bacon (*my Lorde*), which does not grant him the right to govern certain estates in the way he had anticipated (example (6)).

(6) Sir, **I** received **your** letter the seconde of this moneth, wherin was enclosed the surrender mad aswell by **yow** as by my Lorde. Upon the readinge of **your** letter . . . **I** finde that which **I** litle loked for. **I** see that [**your**] meaninge is that notwithstandinge **your** surrender **I** shall not have to do with the maners either of Langham or of Combes, but that **I** shall stande to an annuell pencion or the just some of which valewe **yow** covenaunted **your** landes [to] be. (Nathaniel Bacon to Sir Thomas Gresham, 1572, I: 34)

On the other hand, in the letter with the lowest frequency of *I*, Bacon's role has been to obtain information about a surveyor of the Duchy, who had surveyed Sir Thomas Gresham's manor of Wighton, and he reports the findings. These dealings also involve problems as they may, at worst, lead to a trial between Sir Thomas and the Queen, but the situation is not Nathaniel Bacon's fault or particular concern. The surveyor as well as Wighton men, tenants, farmers, the Queen and Sir Thomas (*Sir, you*) are then the focus of Bacon's account, while Bacon himself has a consolatory role in the process, illustrated in example (7).

(7) These speatches of **the Surveior** have caused **me** to suspect that **he** hath surveied that pece of ground of **yours** for **the Quene**, which, yf **he** have done, than **yow** shalbe driven to try **your** right with **the Quene**, which will bread some busines, how good soever **your** title be. The speatches used by **the tenauntes** . . . **Sir**, yf the matter cold not otherwise be holpen but a tryall shold be therof betwene **yow** & **the Quene**, **I** am easily abl[{e{] to compasse **yow** the sight of the best evidens belonginge to [{the{] manor of Wighton. (Nathaniel Bacon to Sir Thomas Gresham, 1576?, I: 189)

Bacon's orientation in the situation can also be analysed in terms of the rhetorical functions performed in the first person. Two salient orientations can be pointed out: orientation to real-world events, when Bacon narrates personal experiences and actions, and stance, when he expresses opinions and attitudes. Stance in the first person is typically expressed with mental verbs like *think*, *know*, *desire*, *wish* and *doubt*, and these cover 30 per cent of first-person subject + verb expressions. Stance expressions often align Bacon with the recipient and/or modify the force of the utterance. Thus, they seem to have an important interpersonal role. In Bacon's letters to Sir Nicholas in

---

[5] The average letter length is 400 words.

particular, his role in managing the family estate of Stiffkey on Sir Nicholas's behalf – often in the way the father has wanted him to do – becomes clear in the actions he describes. Example (8), for instance, illustrates how he has *sent* (action) the copies enclosed in the letter because the father has *willed* him to do so. He also explains why he has postponed going to Stiffkey, resorting to information received from Mounford, their family servant.

(8) **I** have sent herin enclosed the copie of a letter hertofore written, which **your Lordship** willed **me** to send. **I** have appointed my goinge over to Styfkey for keapinge the court & {measuringe} treadinge out the feild boke until Witson weake. **I** thought to have gone soner, but Momford hath written **me** worde that before that time the tenauntes will not be at leysure for sowinge ther sommer corne. (Nathaniel Bacon to Sir Nicholas Bacon, 1573, April 23–8, I: 67)

4.2 Third-person reference: nuclear family and relatives

The correspondence of Nathaniel Bacon contains a vast array of different reference forms to people both close and distant. Interestingly, the nuclear family members, relatives and servants are also the most common 'possession' in Bacon's letters as over 60 per cent of *my* precedes such person references. Example (9) is an extract from Bacon's letter to Anthony Stringer, which shows a typical variety of terms normally used at the time to refer to relatives and thus also easily identifiable to the intended addressee, who happened to be a servant to Bacon's father-in-law, Sir Thomas Gresham. The modern reader may, however, have difficulty working out the identities of some of the referents. For example, the term *my father* does not refer to Bacon's own father, Sir Nicholas, but to his father-in-law. Bacon did refer to Sir Nicholas with the same term, but also used his title, *my Lord* (see example (6) above).[6] Similarly, *my Lady* is used here to identify Bacon's stepmother, Lady Anne Bacon, instead of what would have also been an acceptable term to use in this context, i.e. *my mother*. The other members of his kin referred to in the example, his wife (Anne Bacon) and aunt (Lady Anne Gresham), are more easily interpretable.

(9) I litle mistrusted [afore] first [I tried that] **my father** wolde have ben unwillinge in the matter; [first] my Lorde likinge of it, [againe] **my Lady** well content with all, & havinge promised to {take paines with}[have a care of] **my wife** when she came, & [lastly] **myne Aunt** not against it. (Nathaniel Bacon to Anthony Stringer, 1570s, I: 10–11)

Example (10) shows the way in which Bacon refers to his close family members, i.e. his brothers, when he writes to William Cecil, who became

---

[6] See e.g. Nevala (2004b: 2140).

Bacon's uncle by his father's second marriage, to Anne Cooke. He uses kinship term + first name of his half-brother Anthony, possibly to separate and to distance him either from his full brothers or from another half-brother, Francis. With the form *my eldest brother*, Bacon refers to Nicholas Bacon.

(10) Your Lordship knoweth howe for the {matters}demaundes in question betwene **my brother Anthony** and **my eldest brother**, together with my self, I yelded to sondrey pointes by your Lordships earnest perswacion. (Nathaniel Bacon to William Cecil, 1579, II: 102)

(11) I did, as I sent your Lordship worde I wolde, writ to **my sister Woodhouse,** & I have alredie received aunswere againe. She sendeth me worde that she thinketh it best for me to seake to be with **my brother Windam,** not knowing what I had alredy done therin. (Nathaniel Bacon to Sir Nicholas Bacon, 1571?, I: 18)

Since the group of other relatives is larger than that of close family, the identification of more distant kin is often aided by the use of a kinship term + last name combination. It is also very common that the last name is used to refer to one's sisters. In example (11) above, Bacon refers to his sister Anne (Woodhouse) and his brother-in-law Francis Wyndham, the latter with whom Bacon and his wife, Anne, were lodging at the time of the letter. Whether the use of the last name in reference to Bacon's sister, Anne, denotes greater interpersonal distance is not certain, since it can also appear here simply because of the need to identify the referent. One of Bacon's sisters-in-law was also called Anne, and using, for example, the term *my sister Anne* would not have greatly helped the addressee in recognising the referent's identity.

4.3 Third-person reference: other referents

Whereas the forms used to refer to family and other relatives are more clearly concerned with identifying the referent, those used to point at distant referents appear to be influenced more by either social or contextual factors. In examples (12) and (13), we can see the use of such referential terms, which not only identify the person but also put him in a certain social position relative to both the writer and the addressee. In the first example, Sir William Paston is acknowledged as a knight and the sheriff of Norfolk, whereas other referents in the passage are only referred to by their (full) names. What is particularly interesting is that the person who is being examined in the case in question is referred to with the term *one James Borne*, which already gives the reader the impression that he is not socially equal to the writers, the addressees or to the other referents.

(12) It pleased your honours to directe your letters to **Sir William Paston, knight, shreif of Norfolk,** and [to] us, or any two of us, for the

examynynge of **one James Borne** touchinge an arrest by processe at his suite oute of the corte of the Viceadmyraltie within Norfolk of a ship laden with Newe Castell coale, whereof the ownors be **Richard Walsingham & Mathewe de Heere,** as doth appere by theire peticion. (Nathaniel Bacon and Thomas Farmer to William Cecil and Sir Walter Mildmay, 1583, II: 255)

The following passage shows an even clearer example of social inequality in respect to the referent. At the time of Bacon's letters, it was very common to use only the last name with reference to people of lower ranks, and so here Sir Nicholas's servant is called *Hill* instead of giving his full name. Moreover, Bacon makes sure that the addressee understands who the 'Hill' in question is and what his position is by introducing him as *Hill, your Lordship's servaunt*.

(13) For in Easter terme I sued out a common latitat against him, which by **Hill, your Lordship's servaunt**, was served upon him somwhat before Midsomer terme, & **Hill** for the more speade sent not the bond taken for his apparaunce to me, but sent it directly to London to my brother Edward, who delivered it unto Clerk. (Nathaniel Bacon to Sir Nicholas Bacon, 1575, I: 179)

Examples (14)–(16) in turn show how third-person reference can be used for more contextual than purely social purposes. In the first extract, Bacon writes to his father, telling him about the 'adversary' of his acquaintance William Heydon and the strife between the two. Once he has stated who Grick is and how he is related to the matter, Bacon changes the reference term into plain last name. The negative attitude towards the whole issue, and his reluctance in taking part in it, is further intensified by Bacon's use of the form *this Grick*, which distances the referent further from his 'herespace'. This also makes it clear to the reader that he is somehow taking the side of Heydon, who, on the other hand, is referred to as *Mr William Haydon*.

(14) I have joyned with **Mr William Haydon** in a letter to your Lordship in the behalf of this bearer, whom I humbly desier your Lordship to be good unto. Both he & **his adversarie Gricke** dwell in Langham just by me, & I have sought by sutch meanes as I cold devise to end the cause betwene them, & the wilfullnes of **Grick** is so great as he wilbe brought to no agrement. Therfore yf it shall be your Lordship's pleasure to call **this Grick** before yow, onlesse your Lordship apoint him to be bound to [abide] the order mad, no end wilbe in the cause. (Nathaniel Bacon to Sir Nicholas Bacon, 1576, I: 184–5)

(15) I have enquired what **this Twynyhoo** is, & I heare no accompt [be] mad of him in any respect. [I am told he will drink sack as a man drinketh [ale]. Sir Henry Lee use[th] him for his instrument to find

out bond men within the Duchie. (Nathaniel Bacon to Sir Thomas Gresham, 1576?, I: 189)

In example (15), the use of the *this* + last name construction is even more visibly negative. Bacon refers to Edmund Twynho with the form *this Twynyhoo*, which serves as an opening to a characterisation sequence. The term used foregrounds what is to come: it is no surprise to the reader that Twynho is described as a person not deserving of much respect, because of his drinking habits and otherwise. The addressee is thus predisposed to a negative opinion of the referent by a single term alone.

(16) I certefied your Honour in my last letter of **one Mr Henry Caru & one Thomas Hobbert**, who live & spoile along this cost & warraunt ther doinges by the Spanish Kinge's licens, notwithstanding the last winter's proclamation. **This Caru** hath latly laid up his ship, but **Hubbert**, being furnished with men & artillery out of **Caru** his ship & going as his agent (for the licens is only unto **Caru**), continueth his trad & bringeth in the spoile, or prises as thei terme them, into the portes of Blackney & Cley, & ther be attending **Caru** & his freindes to receive them. (Nathaniel Bacon to Sir Nicholas Bacon, 1576, I: 205)

A mixed type of reference can be found in example (16). Henry Carew and William Cotton received letters of marque by the Duke of Alva, Spanish commander in the Netherlands, to capture rebels against the King of Spain and to sell any goods confiscated from them. As Bacon notes, Thomas Hobbert did not actually have a licence for this, so he acted as Carew's 'agent'. The tone of the passage is again negative, and although Bacon starts by using the form *one* + name to simply introduce his father to both men and the issue in general, he quickly changes into the form *this Caru*, and finally refers to them with only *Caru* and *Hubbert*. Once the identification itself is over and done with, Bacon emphasises the negative impression he wants to give of the two men to the addressee by using such terms that decrease the referents' power within the context.

(17) Uppon this my absens Mr Sidneys councell refused to have the courte kepte, notwithstandinge that **Mr Spratt the knowen officer, and aucthorised by my Lord North**, was reddy there to execute the place. I have taken the advise of some which understand the lawe and have opened unto them the hole state of the cause, and ther opyneon is that the exercise of the place by **the said Sprat** is to be warraunted by lawe. (Nathaniel Bacon to John Brograve, 1583, II: 232)

The last example here is (17), from Bacon's letter to his attorney, John Brograve. The style of writing is more official than in Bacon's more personal letters, and he uses the types of referential terms that often appear in legal contexts, i.e. *Mr Spratt the knowen officer, and aucthorised by my Lord North* and *the said Sprat*. He does this to distance himself not only from the referent and the addressee but also from the matter itself.

5. Discussion

Person reference – including first, second and third persons – in Nathaniel Bacon's sixteenth-century letters creates both personal and contextual meanings pertaining to the current interaction as well as broader social meanings relating to a certain social setting, such as a family, administrative or legal context, and societal structures such as status hierarchies (see Layder's [1997] 2003 domains discussed in the introduction). As the writer and the addressee are the primary interactants in most personal letters, first- and second-person pronouns are frequently used. However, they tend to be even more frequent in intimate and symmetrical relationships, while status differences are overtly coded with deferential third-person titles, in particular. In the sixteenth century, status differences are evident not only in professional and administrative settings but also in the family sphere, at least in gentry families. This is highlighted in Nathaniel Bacon's letters to his father, Sir Nicholas Bacon, which employ self-reference less frequently than his letters to his siblings, for instance, and use the deferential title *your Lordship* rather than the pronoun *you* (Palander-Collin 2006, 2009). Moreover, first- and second-person expressions are used in genre-specific formulae that conventionally establish the writer–addressee relationship, resorting either to a humiliative or a friendly style.

As to topic, first-person reference seems to increase when the matter at hand is personally important to the writer, thus reflecting the level of psychobiography. Rhetorically, first person may perform different functions in letters. Letter formulae can be regarded as having a highly conventionalised rhetorical function, but other salient functions include the writer narrating experiences and actions in the first person and the writer taking a stance.

If we look at the occurrence of third-person reference in general, most of the instances appear in Bacon's letters to his father and to William Cecil, both his power superiors. In this sense, third-person reference seems to be more typical in contexts where first-person reference is avoided to some extent. The references to third persons increase each time Bacon asks the addressee for a favour to himself or deals with some matter on behalf of somebody else. Not surprisingly, there are also many references in those passages in which he reports on what other people have said or done, as in the telling of general news.

In the material, there are some clear factors influencing the choice of referential term. Firstly, often when referring to the members of his family and kin, Bacon's main impetus seems to be identifying the referent and helping the addressee to do so as well. Identification, naturally, helps the recipient of the letter to position him/herself in respect to the referent interpersonally, and possessive pronouns, like *my* and *your*, can also be frequently used as a part of the referential term to increase the sense of being either included in or excluded from the writer's/referent's in-group. Secondly, the more distant the referent is from the writer and/or the addressee, the more there appear to be both social and contextual factors at work. Bacon tends to use only the last name when the referent is either his social inferior (e.g. servant) or his distant power superior. He also often feels the need to clarify the referent's social status by adding further information, as in example (12) above.

Thirdly, the contextual mood of the referential sequence affects most clearly the choice of the term: for example, Bacon's negative attitude, whether it be contempt, hostility or hatred, shows in the range of possible terms. This becomes most visible in his use of the *that* + last name construction, which he uses only in critical contexts. In a way, we can see in this similarities to what Nevala (2010) found in her study on self- and addressee-oriented reference. In addition to the social and contextual aspects of 'appearance', 'attitude' and 'authority', which Nevala found affecting the choice of referential terms, she proposes a fourth factor, 'perspective'. Appearance is a mainly social aspect and concerns the writer's or the addressee's status or role as an inferior or superior participant in the interaction; attitude relates to the contextual mood of the writer, which may or may not be influenced by the addressee's initiative or previous response; authority relates to claiming one's position, often in the context of impersonalising or distancing oneself from the other. A good example of the aspect of perspective, however, is a situation in which the writer anticipatingly speaks, one might say, on behalf of the recipient and predicts the words s/he assumes the addressee will make. Often in these cases, the writer's attitude is inherently critical. Similarly in the use of *that* + last name for third person, the addressee can easily become predisposed against the referent under the influence of the writer, because s/he already foresees a negative remark about to appear in the immediate context. As noted above, Stivers (2007: 87) suggests that the demonstrative determiner *that* works as a kind of a pre-complaint booster, which influences the addressee's attitude towards the referent. In Bacon's letters, this kind of creating of predispositions is sometimes evident also in those contexts where he refers to a third person with *one* + name.

6. Conclusion

In our study of person reference in Nathaniel Bacon's sixteenth-century letters, we found that person reference works not only as an agent in placing individuals within the societal and hierarchical framework, but it also creates and maintains a certain type of text genre and, most importantly, helps the writer to express his/her own interactional persona and local communicative needs.

The four domains in Layder's sociological theory – psychobiography, situated activity, social settings and contextual resources – appear to be working in our material as well, since, for Bacon, person reference seems to function at least as a tool for identification (either purely deictic or inherently interpersonal), for personal feelings, attitudes and predispositions towards the addressee and/or the referent, as well as for the particular setting of a specific location or social organisation. Thus, our analysis indicates that the choice of, and variation in, person-referential terms relates to both macro-societal structures and micro-contextual needs, and only further study will show how deeply these two levels are intertwined in the letters from other writers within the same genre.

9 Poetic collaboration and competition in the late seventeenth century

George Stepney's letters to Jacob Tonson and Matthew Prior

SUSAN FITZMAURICE

1. Introduction

> I had gott as far as Wesel when I receivd yr letter, & had indeed layd aside all thoughts of writing upon this melancholy Subject; but at yr desire & Sr W. Trumbull's command (to wch I always pay great deference), I have tryd wt I cou'd do & here send it you, such as I cou'd hammer out between Wesel & Lipstadt; you will find by the \coursness &/ flatness of it, that it is ye product of Westphalia Dyet & no sleep; But they that will have a Poem, must have a Poem, as Busby used to say of a May-pole. (Stepney to Tonson, 24 February 1695)

> I have carefully perus'd thy Ode & must honestly confess it is in my Mind the worst piece I ever saw of yr's: Do not think I speack this out of Envy for your Poetry, or in Revenge for ye severe reflexions you made on mine, but upon Mature & impartial Considerations (Stepney to Prior, 2 April 1695)

These extracts are taken from the autograph manuscript copies of two letters written by George Stepney in 1695. The first is to Jacob Tonson, his publisher, fellow Whig and Kit Cat Club member, on his arrival in Lipstadt, having spent the journey by post-chaise writing a poem 'upon this melancholy Subject', namely, the death by smallpox of Queen Mary.[1] The second is to his old friend Matthew Prior, after reading the latter's poem commemorating King William's return to the European battle theatre after Mary's death.[2] He declares he has no great regard for or opinion of the poems

---

[1] The manuscript letter is held in the Folger Library, MS X.d.7. I transcribed the letter on 3 November 2000. For brevity's sake, all quotations from this document will be identified as S1.
[2] The manuscript is in the Public Record Office, in the *Stepney Papers*. All references to this letter are taken from Swedenburg's transcription (1946: 25–6), and are identified as excerpts by S2.

that occupy his attention in these letters. However, while his depreciation of his own poem can harm nobody, his apparent depreciation of another poet's work has the potential to damage that poet's self-worth. So, although Stepney's apparent modesty about his own poem might seem disarming and even endear him to his addressee, his direct criticism of another might seem caustic and have the opposite effect.

Stepney begins his letter to Tonson by suggesting that although he had decided not to write a commemorative poem, 'yr desire' and his friend William Trumbull's 'command' have conspired to change his mind. He warns his publisher that his poem is 'ye product of Westphalia Dyet & no sleep'; having been hammered out during a journey spurred on by obligation rather than inspiration, it is not one of his best. He concludes this somewhat apologetic introduction with an aphorism that underlines the fact that his apology is more gestural than substantial. The saying consists of a pair of clauses that are identical in every respect except that the first has *will* and the second has *must*. He then attributes the aphorism's form (rather than its subject) to Dr Richard Busby, the redoubtable headmaster of Westminster School, who educated John Dryden, Charles Montagu, the Earl of Halifax, and Stepney himself (Spens 1997: 14).[3] Addressing his friend Prior, Stepney insists that his negative view of his friend's poem is born solely of 'Mature & impartial Considerations'. However, his keenness to assert that he is not reciprocating his friend's 'severe reflexions' suggests that he has anticipated that Prior will indeed interpret the criticism as reciprocal treatment, and so he tries to cancel the thought. The problem is that by mentioning Prior's criticism at all, he inevitably draws his addressee's attention to it. Stepney dissects both poems in these letters, pointing out what he identifies as their 'faults' and suggesting possible improvements to them. His letters exhibit features that are characteristic both of his epistolary habits and of his handwriting, including abbreviations, variable spellings, emendations and crossings out.

However, these manuscript letters are different from the types of letters that Stepney writes as a career diplomat to William Blathwayt, from the European cities where he designed and brokered treaties for his Whitehall masters (Fitzmaurice 2006). They are also different from the letters he pens in the tricky rhetorical task of seeking patronage from the great men of English politics, such as the Duke of Shrewsbury (Fitzmaurice 2006). They are also different from his sociable correspondence with fellow poets, many of them members of the Kit Cat Club, the fellowship of senior Whig politicians and the ambitious young men they patronised, overseen by its secretary, Jacob Tonson.[4] Stepney would correspond with colleagues such as Joseph

---

[3] See Knighton (2004) for a biography of the headmaster of Westminster.
[4] For a detailed description of the Kit Cat Club, see Carter (2005), and for a description of the Kit Cat Club as a social network, see Fitzmaurice (2000, 2010b).

Addison and close friends such as Charles Montagu when he was far away and unable to enjoy their fellowship at the Kit Cat's hub, Christopher Cat's pie shop.[5]

The two letters examined here reveal the use of the personal letter for a different communicative act. They shed light on the nature of literary labour in the period and they illuminate Stepney's own critical practice. Stepney's letter to the publisher Tonson allows the possibility that literary production involves collaboration and sociability. Stepney's letter to Matthew Prior, fellow diplomat and poet, seems to support this impression but invites the additional inference that this kind of consultation can be destructive as well as constructive. Certainly, Stepney practises the same critical method in evaluating his friend's poem as in reviewing his own. I will consider how these letters reflect writers' competitiveness as well as their collaborative inclinations, specifically when praise for literary products could mean tangible rewards as well as enhanced reputations. Stepney's letter to Tonson poses the question of how far his own reading of his poem confirms his receptivity to the critical reaction of friends and colleagues. How far do his remarks reveal a sincere (as opposed to mock) interest in seeking editorial help? How does his epistolary autocriticism compare with the kind of criticism he offers to his fellow poet? And how far does his approach chime with the attitudes and practices of fellow poets like Matthew Prior?

In this essay, I compare Stepney's critical method in his letters to his publisher and friend to ascertain how consistent this method is. I also compare his criticism with the printed versions of the poems to ascertain how effective his comments were. I argue that, read carefully in their specific historical circumstances and literary milieu, these letters illuminate the practice of what I shall call 'critical friendship' in an enduring friendship that involved competition for patronage as well as social and political camaraderie. The linguistic and rhetorical evidence for this claim lies in the directness of his address, his explicit request for advice from his addressees and his friends, and his frank and routine reference to a shared bank of knowledge. Stepney's letters illustrate cogently how self-criticism and criticism of others contribute to the role of critical friend, a role he performed honestly, directly and openly, in letters only recently discovered and made public.

2. Poems on 'this melancholy Subject'

The death of Queen Mary on 28 December 1694 occasioned 'a predictable flood of elegies', including poems by well-known poets like William

---

[5] The *Network of Eighteenth-century English Texts* corpus includes a sub-corpus of out-letters from Stepney to these social contacts as well as in-letters from them to him. See Fitzmaurice (2007) for the most detailed description of the corpus.

Congreve, John Dennis, William Walsh and George Stepney, as well as lesser lights like Edmund Arwaker, Robert Gould and Samuel Cobb (Sutherland 1969: 156; Winn 1987: 477). As a diplomat abroad, Stepney wrote to William Blathwayt on 21 February 1695, to inform him of how he proposed to treat the subject of the queen's death when he got to Dresden to consult the Elector of Saxony about preparations for war. Examined in this light, the death of the queen threatened to be a diplomatic obstacle to getting the job done. He decides to allow Blathwayt's 'circular' to suffice and

> when I come to speak with ye Electr, I shall only en passant touch a word or two on this melancholy subject, & not ask a particular audience, wch (to keep up to ye Ceremony) I shou'd have, in a long mourning Cloak, & this wou'd constrain ye Electr & his Court to yt same uneasy formality; wch (I know) they are not pleasd with (Stepney to Blathwayt, 11/21 February 1695/4, Wesch; British Library, MS 9719. [gsleto21])

Stepney had more weighty diplomatic matters to attend to than satisfying the public's demand for eulogies. So the composition of what Spens (1997: 297) characterises as his 'longest and most successful composition' (*A Poem Dedicated to the Blessed Memory of Her Late Gracious Majesty Queen Mary*) barely occupied his mind at the beginning of 1695.[6] Nevertheless, he dashed off a draft and asked James Vernon to deliver the poem with a cover letter to Tonson. In his letter, he requests Tonson to send twelve copies of the poem to his sisters 'because I'm sure they will be fond enough to like it, thô nobody else shou'd' (S1). He marks his self-consciously deprecating approach to his work by implying that fondness for their brother, not critical acumen, obliges his sisters to love his work. His strategy might strike the reader as one calculated to protect his positive face; on the one hand, this stance protects him against disappointment and humiliation if his addressees view the work negatively, as he would be able to point out that he had a low regard for the poem from the outset. On the other hand, if his addressees praise his poem he can duck their condescension by claiming that he is not a very good critic. In either case, his letter is designed to appeal to multiple addressees with potentially different perspectives.

Let us examine this matter further. He asks Tonson to show the poem to his friend Charles Montagu, who he thinks 'may have leisure to peruse it, & with a cast of his Eye will tell you where it most fails', and to William Congreve, because he had 'read his Pastorall with so great satisfaction' (S1). However, among the 'best judges' of the poem's quality, he names John Dryden. Stepney approaches the question of Dryden's looking at the poem somewhat tentatively; he hazards that the subject of the poem might not be 'agreeable' to Dryden, 'yt I am persuaded he is so much my friend as to deal impartially with me, & I hope will alter several places in the many

---

[6] Hereafter, I refer to the version printed by Tonson in 1695 with the abbreviation *Poem*.

that want to be corrected' (S1). Stepney's judgement was spot on. Dryden was one of the few poets not to commemorate the death of Queen Mary in verse.[7] Winn (1987: 477) quotes the anonymous *The Mourning Poets* (1695) thus:

> Ev'n *Dryden* mourns; tho yet he does refuse
> To mourn in public, and exert his Muse;
> Nor can we well his Want of Love suspect,
> Who kindly could an absent Muse correct.

Winn's guess that Stepney was the 'absent Muse' fits the circumstances. Stepney's elaborate set of requests and instructions situates him as Tonson's client, and their manner and substance suggest that Stepney trusted Tonson. He was sufficiently confident to impose upon his publisher and fellow Kit Cat member and leave him to exercise his own judgement. Tonson, in turn, was at liberty to carry out his friend's requests or not.

In a postscript, Stepney asks Tonson to send a copy of his poem to Prior too: 'I scribble over a Copy to send to Mr Prior, who perhaps may send you some amendments' (S1). Prior was also a client of Tonson's, and, like Stepney, had been asked to produce a poem to mark Queen Mary's death. However, like Dryden, Prior did not immediately do so, excusing himself by saying, 'I am as yet so afflicted for the death of our dear Mistress, that I cannot express it in bad verse, as all the world here does' (Prior to Lord and Lady Lexington, the Hague, 1 March 1695).[8] Prior might as well have included Stepney's poem among the 'bad verse' for when he received it, he did not spare his friend's feelings or his face in his criticism. When Prior got around to composing a poem three months later, it was written 'on his Majesty's Arrival in Holland, After the Queen's Death'. Stepney's first impression of Prior's poem was that 'the style is not heroic but very good of its sort'.[9] However, after further careful reflection, Stepney assumes the stance of a critical friend, unpicking Prior's poem in much the same way that he had dissected his own. Let us examine the role of critical friend as Stepney performs it in these literary critical letters to his publisher and friend, respectively.

---

[7] Winn (1987: 477) suggests that Dryden's silence was 'primarily motivated by his unwillingness to praise a queen he regarded as an undutiful daughter'. Specifically, Mary was the daughter of James II, the Catholic king who was displaced in the 1688 'Glorious' Revolution, and the wife of William of Orange, the uncompromising Protestant with whom Mary assumed joint sovereignty of England (Holmes 1993: 195). Despite Dryden's apparent antipathy towards the post-revolution monarchy, he was generous with his consideration for the poetry of its admirers.

[8] Quoted by Eves (1939: 94).

[9] Stepney to his sisters, Frances and Dorothy Stepney, Dresden, 19/29 March 1694/5. Cited by Swedenburg (1946: 28).

3. 'I shall now tell you wt faults I my self find with it'

Stepney's letter to Tonson consists of detailed critical comments giving the impression that he doesn't regard his poem as being quite finished. It seems to be at best provisional, possibly the basis for a poem to be completed in collaboration with his friends. His letter to Prior is constructed in the same way, consisting of a general critical assessment of the whole poem, followed by a brief though pointed appraisal of each stanza. His flippant summary of the poem's meaning is brutal in its directness:

> I have anatomizd [your Stanzas], & find their meaning to be 'That ye King shou'd no longer bewail ye Queen, but think of Heading his Army: Even Albion, who wou'd formerly have kept him from making ye Campayne, now advises him to go for Flanders, being of the Physitians opinion that Action may divest his Grief. Then Holland comes in (God knows how) & wou'd say some tender thing, but is afraid of making ye King Cry, afresh for the Lady newly deceased, & therefore chuses to put him in mind of his Ancestors who have been dead much longer; & presses him to excel them in Virtue, How? by taking a noble resolution of going to ye Feild in Spight of his dead Wife, who (as you say) is only gone before to prepare a place for him, –If this be Sense I honestly own I have lost mine. (S2)

By reducing the poem to its bare bones in this manner, Stepney ridicules the idea that it should take up as many as forty-one four-line stanzas. He offers a *precis* delivered in the historic present and he adopts parenthetical comment clauses to convey his mock disbelief at the poem's premise. His dismissal of the poem as nonsense would insult the most tolerant addressee, but he seems confident that he can talk straight to a close friend without offending him. After all, he treats aspects of his own poem in a similar fashion; while he does not summarise his own poem he deprecates and mocks his poetic skills. He complains immediately that the first four lines are 'too stiff & the next four too flat' (S1). He insists that 'all Beginnings come hard to me' but concedes breezily that once 'into ye right road, I can make shift to Canturbury it on, as Sir Godfrey calls it' (S1). Stepney constantly refers to his social circle, enhancing the familiarity established directly with his addressee and indirectly with those friends to whom he expects Tonson to show his letter. So in the same manner that he drops Busby into his conversation, here he alludes casually to the Kit Cat portraitist, Sir Godfrey Kneller.[10] Stepney's discussion of the first eight offending lines of his poem illuminates how hard it is to start a poem. His comments are couched in hypotheticals and counterfactuals, asserting that instead of the existing second line, 'May it prove lasting, as *Maria*'s Praise;' he would have written, 'On the firme

---

[10] Kneller painted likenesses of Stepney together with forty-seven other Kit Cats to be hung in Tonson's Barn Elms house to commemorate the Club. See Carter (2005).

Basis of Maria's praise' (S1). The first five syllables of the line clearly present difficulties – both disyllabic words 'lasting' and 'basis' change the distribution of the stresses, with a decidedly clunky effect. Here are the first eight lines as published:

> Once more, my Muse,–we must an Altar raise;–
> May it prove lasting, as *Maria*'s Praise;
> And, the Song ended, be the *Swan*'s thy Doom;
> Rest ever silent, as *Maria*'s Tomb.
> But whence shall we begin? Or whither steer?
> Her Virtues like a perfect Round appear,
> Where Judgment lies in Admiration lost,
> Not knowing which it should distinguish most.
>   (*Poem*, lines 1–8)

Stepney pretends despair – 'take yr choice, I am sensible all ye 4 are wrong: So are the 5th & 6th' – but he is optimistic that Dryden 'at one minute can sett them right' (S1). He reflects on line 6, offering alternative ways of expressing the conventional association of perfection and the perfect shape – a circle – to express his subject's virtue. What seems to present the greatest challenge is getting the stress right; his choice of 'circle', while lexically apt, is rhythmically awkward, prompting several alternatives, none of which quite works because each fails to achieve the constructional and rhythmical parallelism needed for the heroic line:

> Her virtues being like a continued Circle or
> Her virtues a continued Circle show or
> Her numerous Virtues like a Circle show.
>   (S1)

The substitution of 'perfect Round' for 'continued Circle' makes the five iambic foot heroic couplet balanced, both semantically, Virtues = circle (a perfect round), and rhythmically on either side of the caesura:

```
x    / x     / x    //   / x     /      x /
her  virtues like a //  perfect round  appear
```

It is little wonder that Stepney appears to admit defeat, repeating, 'None of 'em are right, & yet a little matter may mend them, thô I cannot do it; & I'le assure [you] they've given me more trouble than all ye rest' (S1). He is quite amusing on the matter of the necessity of some sort of a beginning, observing wryly that had there been no 'Exordium', 'ye 9th line woud have come too quick upon you' (S1).

Having dispensed with the problem of how to manage the opening of his poem, Stepney selects individual lines for attention. He volunteers his dissatisfaction with his diction, asks his publisher for his opinion and gives him the liberty to make changes as he sees fit. Scrutiny of the printed poem in light of Stepney's comments suggests that his friends did intervene to make felicitous changes. So coming to line 13 in his manuscript, he suggests that one past tense verb form ('carry'd') be replaced with another ('bore'), and then offers yet another alternative: 'challenged'. The line that Tonson published allows us to infer that Tonson sought Dryden's help to solve the poet's dilemma by composing a new line: 'A Mien compos'd of Mildness and of State' (*Poem*, line 13). However, Tonson does not act on the suggestion that line 22 be 'altred thus: To Mortalls, did in shapes like theirs appear' or that 'meant' be replaced by 'came' in line 24:

> To visit Men, like Mortals did appear:
> Least their too Awful Presence should affright
> Those whom they meant to bless, and to delight.
> (*Poem*, lines 22–4)

Stepney compares lines 30 and 31 with 'shoeing-horns, to pull on ye 2 following lines' and so recommends their deletion (S1). Tonson disagreed. This couplet and the following two (lines 32–3) exhibit imperfect rhymes. Stepney makes the long back close vowel of 'sought' rhyme with the short back half open vowel in the second syllable of 'forgot', and then rhymes 'Retreat' with 'Great' to give the impression of a mid-close rather than a fully close front vowel in 'Retreat'.

> Reliev'd not only those who Bounty sought,
> But gave unask'd, and as She gave, forgot;
> Found modest Want in its obscure Retreat,
> And courted tim'rous Vertue to be Great.
> (*Poem*, lines 30–3)

Stepney was also dissatisfied with line 55, commenting, '<u>Did in this Couple</u>, or <u>Did in their Union</u> for Couple is a mean word' (S1).[11] The printed poem shows the substitution of the more obviously poetic 'Nuptials' for the 'mean' word, thus acknowledging Stepney's sentiment: 'Did in Their happy Nuptials well agree' (*Poem*, line 55).

Stepney also gives specific instructions for formatting the poem for publication. He discusses the possibility of key words being 'printed in a Roman Character' to highlight their relevance to the subject. He specifies lines 41 and 42 as 'they summe up the 3 foregoing Paragraphs, wherein her Personal Maty. is describd from 9 to 24. Her Charity from 25 to 33 & her Piety from 34 to 40' (S1). The printed version italicises the key words rather than the entire couplet:

[11] I follow Stepney's own practice of underlining words as a way of either quoting material or highlighting it. I also use (below) Stepney's practice of striking out words to indicate how he crosses out items in his letter. However, to indicate the insertion of a word above the line, I insert the word on the line between two slashes, as, for example, \might/.

> Since She was *Form'd*, and *Lov'd*, and *Pray'd* like you,
> She shou'd, alas! have been *Immortal* too:
>
> *(Poem*, lines 41–2)

Stepney's attention indicates that the visual impact of the printed poem would be as important as its language. He implies that highlighting selected words attracts and focuses the reader's attention not only to their presence but to their significance. So he directs that in lines 51 and 52, 'Balance & Sword must be distinguishd by particular Characters, least otherwise it ~~woud~~ \might/ not be perceivd that I hint at ye 2 Ensigns of Justice' (S1). Here, Stepney refers to the conventional symbols of justice – a pair of scales and the sword – aligning them with feminine and masculine qualities respectively. The extended gender contrast culminates in line 54 with the conjunction of William, the 'God of Battel', and Mary, the 'Queen of Love', in marriage.

> Of Justice *She* at home the *Ballance* held,
> Abroad, Oppression by *His Sword* was quell'd;
> True Emblems of the *Lyon*, and the *Dove*;
> The God of Battel, and the Queen of Love
> Did in Their happy Nuptials well agree;
>
> *(Poem*, lines 51–5)

Stepney was known and admired for his classical learning and his facility with languages, a result of Busby's training. Much of his poetry, like that of his peers, was translated from or fashioned in imitation of the classics. The key models included 'Horace's epistles, satires or odes, or of the *Ars Poetica*; of Virgil in pastoral or Georgic; of Ovid in fable, or especially metamorphosis, or the Heroical Epistle, and in the *Ars Amatoria*; of Lucretius in the philosophic poem; of the comic epic' (Dobrée 1959: 127). He shared this background with Prior, whose early success in translating Horace into English metre had reputedly attracted first the interest and then the patronage of Lord Dorset (Eves 1939: 14). Stepney's privileging of classical formal models shapes his critique of Prior's ode: 'For 1st you have chose Measures wch are neither proper for Heroick nor Elegy; & are often reduced to ye necessity of forcing unnaturall Rhimes, wch indeed cannot be avoided in Alternate' (S2). He seems to be anxious to judge Prior's poem in terms of its fidelity to appropriate classical genres. This is congruent with the formal preoccupations of public poetry in the period. Sutherland (1969: 156) observes that 'the poets were at work, writing for the most part funeral-pindaric odes, but also pastoral elegies and straightforward panegyrics'. Stepney thus feels quite justified in chastising him for the absence of classical form in his poem: 'You have thrown away all ye Classick Learning, & have not imitated any Roman Poet' (S2). The only classical element in Prior's poem was the Latin motto, quoted from Horace's ode 'on Virgil's grief for the unexpected death of Quintilius' (Eves 1939: 96), which Stepney notices. 'Yr Motto seems to me to be ye best of ye Piece: If I was in yr Place, I'de print it alone, & leave out ye Poem' (S2). By arguing that the only estimable aspect of Prior's work is his choice of the Horatian motto, he implies that the poet's own composition has no value. His directness suggests that he is confident that his friend will not take his comments badly. Alternatively, he might judge that having received Prior's critique of his poem in good faith, he has earned the right to mete out equivalent treatment, and in this game of tit for tat, Prior's response is of no consequence.

Stepney draws on his classical education for his own inspiration and offers some explanation at the same time as asking Tonson to check the accuracy of the names. So he admits that 'I know not rightly if Æmus shou'd be writ with an H', offering the clue, 'see, 'tis a mountain in Thessali, where Mars & Venus used to lye together' (S1). Taking a different tack to help his readers understand his potentially obscure classical allusions, Stepney provides details of this allusion, which is designed to foreground King William's virtues in peacetime:

> 64. The Latin Hind [*sic*] is a known story in Livy & Thonis. 11th Chapt. & 1 book. Lucius Quinctius was made dictator from a Plowman & was sent in an ensigncy out of State agst ye Æquos & Voleios, whom he defeated, & then returnd [scribbled out] as it were in hast to his former occupation. (S1)

Tonson pays lip service to Stepney's request by signalling the story's reference in a sidenote, simply noting the name Lucius Quinctius.[12] Stepney asks Tonson to check the accuracy of other details too. So, getting to line 80, he conjectures that 'You have read the Bible later than I; & must know best, if the Prophet's name who was snatchd away, was Elija or Elisha' (S1). Tonson evidently did as he was bidden, finalising the name as *Elijah*.

Stepney continues to mine his classical stock in the poem as he draws attention to the impact of Mary's death on William, the 'great Soul'. He compares the bereaved William with Homer's 'Illustrious' but 'mortal' hero, Achilles, in a complex simile in which he argues that whereas a lost Mistress incapacitates the hero, the death of a friend catapults him into murderous action. Stepney uses the visual presentation of the poem to draw attention to his classical references. He asks Tonson to use 'Roman letters' to highlight the word 'Soul' in line 98:[13] 'Left likewise in his *Soul* one mortal Part', 'to mark that by \his/ Soul likewise I do not mean in His Soul as well as

---

[12] Fifth-century BC Roman patriot. He was consul in 460BC and dictator twice (458BC and 439BC). According to tradition, in his first dictatorship he came from his farm to defeat the Aequi and Volscians, who were threatening the city from the east and southeast. He returned from battle, resigned his dictatorship and went home to his farm. In 439BC he came out of retirement to put down the plebeians. www.cc.columbia.edu/cu/cup/; accessed 15 June 2009.

[13] It appears in line 100 in the published version of the poem.

the King's but In His Soul as well as in his Body' (S1). He also wants to foreground 'Soul' to focus on Achilles' mortality without resorting to the anatomical term for that mortal part of his body – heel. And he concludes: 'That Simile I think is very just & proper to ye Subject' (S1).

In contrast, Stepney is not convinced of the justness of Prior's poetic language in his commemorative ode. As he 'take[s] each Stanza to pieces', he passes swift judgement:

> The 1st may pass: The 2d is pretty, but does not follow; The 3d is stark nought, for it signifyes nothing: The 4th is well but in my mind it shou'd be backd to ye first: The 5th wants connexion. The 6th is a Hackney thougt tag'd with unnaturall Rhymes. The 7. 8. & 9th are well enough & to ye purpose; But your 10th & 11th are a greater sheet of Sunshine than mine was (S2).

He is direct and unambiguous in his opinion. His praise, when he offers it, is lukewarm at best. His praise is attenuated when he considers the poem's logic and structure, observing the lack of 'connexion' between stanzas. He also deploys a tellingly negative adjective, 'Hackney', to condemn the thought as commonplace, trite and worn out.[14] However, Stepney is prepared to acknowledge the good parts in Prior's poem – emphasising their superiority by comparing them favourably with his own efforts. His comparison of his own sun simile with Prior's extended metaphor of the monarchy as the sun ('Great Sun') conveys the implication that his criticism is even-handed and impartial. He implies that he takes criticism well because as well as taking Prior's harsh judgement, he is enough of a critic to see when it is justified. He demonstrates to his friend that he applies the same critical standards regardless of the author's identity. So he continues, handing out approbation ('25th is very well') and opprobrium ('You must have scribbled wt follows in ye 22. 23. & 24th for they are sad Stuff') in turn (S2). He also comments on the political context and likely reception of the poem, warning that 'in Politicks you are not much to be commended for beginning to make yr Court so early to Princesse in yt manner' (S2). Stepney here assumes the diplomat's stance, alive to the complex political relationships that may be highlighted and jeopardised by a poet's public comment, however obliquely it may be expressed.[15]

Stepney's own writing is profoundly influenced by his immersion in his literary milieu, as evidenced by his attention to Prior's poem. As well as asking Tonson to check minor historical and literary facts and to consult

[14] See *Oxford English Dictionary Online*. '*Hackney* 7.B. As *adj*. Worn out, like a hired horse, by indiscriminate or vulgar use; threadbare, trite, commonplace; hackneyed. *Obs.*'; accessed 28 June 2009.
[15] This reference is quite oblique. 'The stanza reads: That Freedom which all Sorrows claim,/ She does for Thy Content resign:/ Her Piety itself would blame;/ If Her Regrets should waken Thine'. It is possible that Stepney is referring to his suspicion that Prior is trying to insinuate himself into a position to gain patronage from Queen Mary's younger sister, Anne, who succeeded to the throne on William's death in 1702.

with his friends to improve the composition, he asks his publisher to assess the matter of potential plagiarism. Stepney is quite candid in questioning the originality of his work. So he volunteers that 'either Mr Dryden or Mr Otway have a line on K. Charles like my 44th ... theirs runs <u>confirme our hopes</u>' (S1). But he continues: 'However I will not alter it'. In fact, the line he remembers occurs in Edmund Waller's *A poem on St. James's Park*, published in 1661, as 'Confirm our hopes we shall obey him long'.[16] Tonson changes the line to avoid a complete match. Stepney admits to being suspicious of the ease with which he composed lines 92–3:

> Blush not, great Soul, thus to reveal Thy Woe;
> Sighs will have vent, Eyes too full o're-flow;
> (*Poem*, lines 92–3)

So he comments, 'upon my Soul I know not if I made or stole them' (S1). He then tries to trace the memory of the lines, concluding with a request to Tonson to delete them if he discovers that Stepney has plagiarised another poet:

> You lent me Waller a little before I left England, & I likewise read in London a Poem of Mr Arwaker's upon ye Queen's death; but having neither of those Author's by me, I cannot call to mind if either of them have lines like these two. You have a better Memory, & if You find I have purloin'd, 'tis but just to strike 'em out; there will be no gapp in ye connexion. (S1)

A search of *Early English Books Online* reveals no matches despite the lines' highly conventional flavour; however, a search for selected phrases generates a large number of hits in verse published between 1650 and 1700. For example, Stepney's phrase 'great Soul' occurs 177 times in 144 records. Closer scrutiny indicates that it is a stock phrase for addressing or referring to the subject of an elegy or a panegyric. Similarly, the imperative 'blush not' occurs very frequently in verse of the same period (46 hits in 43 records). In fact, the pair of lines is uniquely Stepney's, although their components evidently belong to the poetic genre of the public elegy so popular in the period.

Stepney's final comment on the poem's detail has to do with another potential plagiarism, this time from Prior's *Ode in Imitation of Horace*, the first of Prior's poems published by Tonson, in 1692. The detail concerns the last four lines of the poem, which effectively call upon William to return to the European theatre. Stepney writes: 'If I am not mistaken, Mr Prior has something like this Line in the Ode he made in Imitation of Horace: If he had, you may leave out the 4 last; for the Period will be as compleat

---

[16] 'Here a well-polisht Mall gives us the joy/ To see our Prince his matchless force imploy;/ His manly posture and his graceful mine/ Vigor and youth in all his motion seen,/ His shape so comely and his limbs so strong/ Confirm our hopes we shall obey him long'.

without 'em' (S1). He may be referring to a specific line but the poem's final four lines seem to echo much of Prior's poem, a composition celebrating the rare Anglo-Dutch defeat of a French invasion expedition at Barfleur and La Hogue in May 1692, thereby ending the danger of invasion (Holmes 1993: 196). We can do no more than speculate that Prior dealt directly with this matter in his critique of the poem, very likely confirming that Stepney's line was original although similar to the poetry of the moment. Additional evidence that the line was probably Stepney's own is Tonson's decision to keep the poem's ending as drafted, regardless of his client's concerns.

4. 'If ye world judges better of it, I shall submit, & be very agreably surprizd'

Stepney is quick to express his negative opinion of the poems in his letters to Tonson and Prior. Before embarking on his detailed critique of his own poem, Stepney suggests that it be printed without his name because 'I am persuaded neither my Name nor Poem can help one another' (S1). Despite his apparent desire for anonymity, there is another reason. The poem's conclusion recommends that the king return to the war in Flanders. Stepney asks Tonson to delete his recommendation 'if the Parliament shou'd prevail with him to ye contrary' (S1) because to be seen to advise the king to do the opposite would seem absurd (and politically damaging). Tonson left the ending intact. At the end of his detailed commentary on his own poem, Stepney reiterates his suggestion that the poem be printed anonymously. This suggestion might seem to sit oddly with his request that Tonson give published copies 'in my name' to his friends Charles Montagu and Sir William Trumball, his boss, William Blathwayt, and fellow civil servant, James Vernon, expecting the latter to pass on a copy to the Duke of Shrewsbury. How do we judge this apparent incongruity? It is possible that he judged that friends and competitors alike might regard a signed elegy from him as an ostentatious bid for preferment, and result in his being ridiculed or, worse, shunned by his peers. However, the publication of a 'bad-tempered poem, *Urania's Temple: Or, A Satyr upon the Silent Poets*, castigating those who had failed to contribute to the national mourning' amidst the published commemorative poems suggests that it was an appropriate occasion for public acts (Sutherland 1969: 156). His repeated suggestion that his name not be attached to the published poem seems to be a strategy to avoid condemnation by his friends and peers while passing on responsibility for the decision to his publisher. He exhibits a diplomat's savvy in requesting the poem's distribution to key people, as the act reaped rewards. James Vernon wrote to him in March:

> You will see by the Gazett you are got into Print & I'le assure you tis to the Encreas of your Reputation. I must confess I was concernd before to see so great a Subject so poorely treated but now I am satisfied for the rest of the poets omnes dehire ex animo debeo, Congreve was

> thought to have done well onely for Hanging the Roomes & painting a dismall Scene, but tis Mr Stepney onely shews the Queen (P.R.O. *Stepney Papers*, 105/82, 12 March 1694/5. Quoted by Swedenburg 1946: fn. 91).[17]

Stepney must have been aware of the positive public reception of his poem by the time he wrote to Prior in April 1695. However, this was evidently insufficient balm to soothe the sting of Prior's criticism. He cannot help referring to his friend's comments as he compares Prior's efforts: 'No, Mat, if I spoyld my Poem by writing too fast; you have spoild yrs by dreaming too long. In short, I have no opinion of it, & if ye world judges better of it, I shall submit, & be very agreeably surprizd' (S2). Stepney readily acknowledges, from personal experience, that others may regard the poem differently. But he presses on, urging his friend, 'I leave you to yr 2d thoughts whether you will print, or not: you have not my consent, liberavi animam meam' (S2). In fact, although Prior presented the forty-one verses to King William, who was expected at The Hague in April, they were not printed until later. Prior 'sought to comfort the King by reminding him of his duties to the nation' (Eves 1939: 96), and he arguably achieved this goal. Because his verses reached their real addressee (the king), he had nothing tangible to gain from the poem's publication, in contrast to Tonson, who would profit from every poem sold.

5. Conclusion

Scrutiny of Stepney's letters illuminates the highly interactive, and indeed sociable, nature of literary labour in the late seventeenth century among the members of a social network. Stepney and Prior remained close friends till Stepney's death in 1707, to judge from the evidence preserved in their correspondence and in the historical record. Their relationship was marked by the political and social camaraderie of being, with Charles Montagu, first Dorset's protégés and then promising poets seeking favours from the Whig grandees in the Kit Cat Club (Fitzmaurice 2000, 2008). At the same time, because they were seeking patronage in the same quarters, they found themselves in direct competition, particularly in the race to offer literary pearls on public occasions, such as the death of a monarch. Stepney's letters reveal the extent to which self-criticism, on the one hand, and criticism of others, on the other, were part of the practice of critical friendship. The 'critical friend' was a role that Stepney and Prior reciprocated – honestly, openly and directly – in letters that remained private for their lifetimes, as evidenced by the manuscripts' relatively recent discovery. Unlike

---

[17] Swedenburg (1946: fn. 91) reports that Stepney made direct reference to more tangible rewards than praise for his public poetry. It is clear that the ultimate award of a gold medal in 1698 was recognition for continued service rather than for the impact of any single work.

Addison's carefully wrought letters to his protégé Ambrose Philips (Fitzmaurice 2002), or Pope's obsequious letters to the grand dictator Addison (Fitzmaurice in press), these manuscripts may be more revealing of how close friends approach openness to criticism and the desire for editorial advice in private than the letters published as ostensible models of communication.

10 Handwritten communication in nineteenth-century business correspondence

MARINA DOSSENA

I hope this pen will write; it is the third I have tried.
Robert Louis Stevenson to Sidney Colvin
(Edinburgh, [Autumn] 1875)

1. Introduction

This contribution aims to supplement the studies of early handwritten communication provided in other chapters of this collection. In particular, I intend to provide an overview of the traits observable in late modern business correspondence, just before the modes of formal communication were affected by new technological developments, such as the invention of the modern typewriter in 1855.

While manuscripts continued to be in normal use for familiar correspondence until the rise of electronic mail in the late twentieth century, in business exchanges the use of handwriting decreased as new tools allowed for greater speed in the preparation of documents. Surviving manuscripts, however, allow us to study the correlation between the purpose of the exchange, the respective social roles of the participants (Dossena 2010), the hands in which the documents were drawn up (Dury 2008) and the greater or lesser use of the conventions of specialised communication (such as the use of abbreviations and/or crystallised salutation formulae at the beginning and at the end of texts). In addition to letters between participants of varying status (such as managers and agents, sellers and clients, or business partners), reference is also made to management records (meant for company use only) and printed circulars in which specific details could be added by hand so as to personalise the text.

All the examples discussed in this study are drawn from the authentic documents currently being transcribed for inclusion in the *Corpus of Nineteenth-century Scottish Correspondence* (19CSC; see Dossena 2004; Dury 2006, 2008).[1] At the time of writing (April 2009), the corpus comprises

---
[1] I gratefully acknowledge permission to quote from MSS held in the National Library of Scotland, the Archives of Glasgow University, and the Bank of Scotland Archives; such

c. 400 letters (comprising drafts, fair copies[2] and copies, equally distributed between familiar and business letters), with a total of *c.* 100,000 orthographic units.[3] Given the relatively small size of the corpus and the nature of my investigation, focused on barely quantifiable traits, my analysis will be primarily qualitative; it is nonetheless hoped that it will contribute to the scientific debate concerning the methodology of corpus studies.

2. Nineteenth-century business correspondence: between personalisation and standardisation

The nineteenth century appears to have provided a gateway to modernity from many different points of view. As far as vocabulary is concerned, for instance, the Industrial Revolution had a significant impact on the legal, social and economic spheres; legal innovations were introduced by the copyright[4] and trademark laws, by Acts concerning postage,[5] and by Acts on workers' rights and compensation (see Tompson 2000: 170–6). Business correspondence also began to change. While in earlier times business transactions were conducted either by means of spoken language or by means of letters in which the personal dimension was already quite prominent (as shown, for instance, by the inclusion of personal comments, personalised greetings, or formulae that epitomised the relationship existing between participants), the ideology of self-improvement that had started in the eighteenth century, and that was to become so widespread in Victorian times, affected the ethics of business exchanges. Within this framework, greater attention was given to the kind of 'gentlemanly behaviour' discussed by Del Lungo Camiciotti (2006), and politeness strategies were employed according to the social roles taken on and attributed to each other by the participants. Such roles could fluctuate, and greater or lesser modesty or authority could be displayed, in relation to

---

permission does not extend to third parties, so the quotations presented in this paper should not be used elsewhere. I am also indebted to Richard Dury for his help in the design and compilation of 19CSC, and for valuable comments throughout the investigation process.

[2] By 'fair copies' I mean letters that were actually sent. In some cases, fair copies were, in fact, the first and only draft, as time or financial constraints did not afford encoders preliminary drafts.

[3] In eighteenth- and nineteenth-century manuscripts, words were often linked up, therefore the label 'orthographic unit' is deemed to be preferable to 'word'. Still on terminology, note the use of the term 'encoder', as opposed to 'writer'. The latter can only be applicable to holograph letters: when the contribution of an amanuensis cannot be excluded, or is, in fact, expected, as in the case of managers dictating to secretaries, the person who actually 'writes' the letter is not necessarily the person whose meanings are conveyed. Concerning 'recipients', this is deemed to be a better term than 'addressees', as the person to whom the letter was actually addressed was not necessarily the only person who read it – in fact, as is well-known, in late modern times letters were often circulated among friends and family.

[4] The first copyright act was issued by Queen Anne in 1709, and was later repealed by the Copyright Act 1842.

[5] The Uniform Penny Post started in January 1840.

the purpose of the exchange (see Dossena 2006 and 2010), which implies variation in the relevant linguistic choices.

The encoders of business letters thus found themselves needing to reconcile possibly conflicting aims: on the one hand, communication should be as efficient as possible, and time-saving opportunities offered by the 'new technologies' of the time had to be grasped; on the other, the recipient had to be shown appropriate consideration, lest his positive face be threatened – indeed, his positive face should be enhanced, if at all possible, and any impression of haste should be avoided, so as not to imply inadequate consideration. The degree of personalisation afforded by handwritten documents thus proved very valuable, and appears to have been preserved even when documents such as circulars could actually be printed. As a result, correspondence is a rather varied text type also from the point of view of its physical appearance: at the same point in time and place we find handwritten documents, printed documents, and printed texts in which handwritten details are provided. It is a somewhat complex picture, worth discussing in greater detail in the next sections, on account of the potential influence of varying traits on the pragmatic quality of the texts.

2.1 Handwritten letters: personalisation and intra mœnia communication

Handwritten messages have been the object of several investigations concerning personal letters (whether relating to familiar or financial matters; e.g. see Fairman 2003, 2007). Such studies have been extremely important for the study of vernacular usage on the part of minimally schooled encoders,[6] and have contributed to our understanding of everyday language in various parts of southern England.[7] Specialised communication, however, does not appear to have raised the same kind of interest until very recently, probably on the assumption that its linguistic features, so close to the morpho-syntactic models provided by contemporary grammars, would not yield significant results as far as language variation is concerned. However, it is not just grammar and lexis that may vary, and we need to go beyond widespread beliefs in the attempt to find out more about as many facets of the text as possible.

First of all, when we study handwritten letters in business exchanges, it is very important to make distinctions between their sources: in particular, we

---

[6] While these encoders wished to avoid dialect forms, which were thought to be unsuitable for written communication, they nonetheless expressed themselves according to their level of education. This meant they were often unaware of spelling mistakes, and though they attempted to employ the polite formulae recommended by letter-writing manuals, their syntax was somewhat idiosyncratic. The resulting text was therefore a reflection of their semi-spontaneous usage, as the attention given to formulae was quickly superseded by the urgency of the matters at hand (see Dossena in press).

[7] Concerning Scotland, see Dossena (2008).

136   Dossena

should distinguish between letters preserved in personal archives (whether of agents, clients or business partners) and letters transcribed in companies' letter books for archival purposes. Such distinctions account, for instance, for the presence or absence of abbreviations, the greater or lesser attention that appears to have been given to the use of an elegant hand, or the occurrence of any self-corrections in the text. While drafts may have been preserved in personal archives, in company archives these are practically non-existent: any self-corrections recorded in letter books are therefore witnesses of authentic 'slips of the pen', which would have hardly been acceptable in the actual letters sent to the clients or agents.

2.1.1   Handwritten letters in personal archives
Personal archives include a very wide range of texts, and sifting through them for the identification of business letters may not be easy. However, it may be a good starting point to focus first on the archive of somebody whose professional interest was known to be in the business sector, such as a printer, a publisher[8] or a wine dealer, and then outline the network of his correspondents. It is, of course, very likely that such archives will include large numbers of personal letters as well, but it is exactly the mixture of business and personal issues that may prove to be of great interest in such cases. Indeed, it is not infrequent for personal remarks to occur in a letter in which the main point is a business-related one, and for business observations to be found in otherwise largely personal notes; in example (1), for instance, we have a humorous remark on a rather talkative mutual acquaintance, while in example (2) the writer uses the familiar name of the subject under discussion (Johnny).

(1)   Edinburgh
      Aug. 26th 1852
      My Dear Sir A . . .[9]
      Along with this I enclose our offer for the first edition of your new His-tory, which will I hope prove agreeable to you [. . .]
      We had as I told you Miss S[. . .] – staying with us who is a most amusing person
      I never heard any woman talk so much & so well. It is true that <u>the much</u> rather gets the better of <u>the well</u>

(2)   45 George St. Edinburgh
      21st Octr 1852
      My dear W[. . .]

---

[8] In recent years, noteworthy resources have been made available to scholars; among these, it is certainly important to mention the Murray and Bartholomew Archives in the National Library of Scotland (see www.nls.uk).

[9] In examples, most names are abbreviated or omitted for reasons of privacy; in order to save space, line and page breaks in the body of the letter are not indicated either.

I got Mr Spieris letter this morning telling me you would not be able to write this month [...]. Johnny is over at St Andrews so you can't have his opinion but I ~~will~~ think he will agree with me as to the advisability of your not attempt-ing to hurry off a short paper.

In such exchanges the relationship between participants is not influenced by the object of their communication, but by other factors rooted in their mutual background. Their manuscripts thus maintain the same quality as far as hand and overall structure and presentation are concerned. Indeed, it is not infrequent to come across metacommunicative comments on this point when encoders feel sufficiently confident with each other; for instance, such a comment as that given in the epigraph above, on the quality of pens, is also found in the letter written by a young lady to a publisher, enquiring about possibilities of working as a copyist or a secretary – see example (3).

(3) [...] I hope you will excuse my troubling you, but I thought perhaps you wouldn't mind my writing to you. I thought you might be in the way of knowing of some secretary work, or copying that one could do__
I want just now to make a sum of money outside my own allowance, & as I can write pretty quickly & as a rule legibly I think, I thought that would be the best way, and thought of you at once as possibly being able to put me in the way of it__ [...] I fear this note is not particularly legible but I have a horrid pen and very little ink. (Edinburgh, 8 October 1893)

The recipient is a close acquaintance of the encoder's parents, which makes her application less inappropriate from the social point of view, and which enables her to address him directly, though very modestly and paying great attention to his negative face. Despite the object of her letter and her claims to write legibly, the encoder then contravenes the recommendations of letter-writing manuals and adds a comment on the supposedly bad quality of her current letter, saying that she has 'a horrid pen and very little ink'. The comment personalises the message and grants it an immediacy that allows the reader to witness the moment in which the message is encoded; despite, and in fact because of, its blemishes, it is a very powerful personalisation strategy, enhancing the positive face of the participants, who can afford to share even the perception of a less than perfect text.

Another important personalisation strategy in nineteenth-century manuscripts is the use of specially black-profiled letter-writing paper when the family was in mourning. Although the recipients are not necessarily informed of the details, they can infer that the encoder has suffered a loss, and act accordingly; the letter, just like clothes and arm-bands, could convey meaning on the private status of the encoder and become a metonymy of such status.

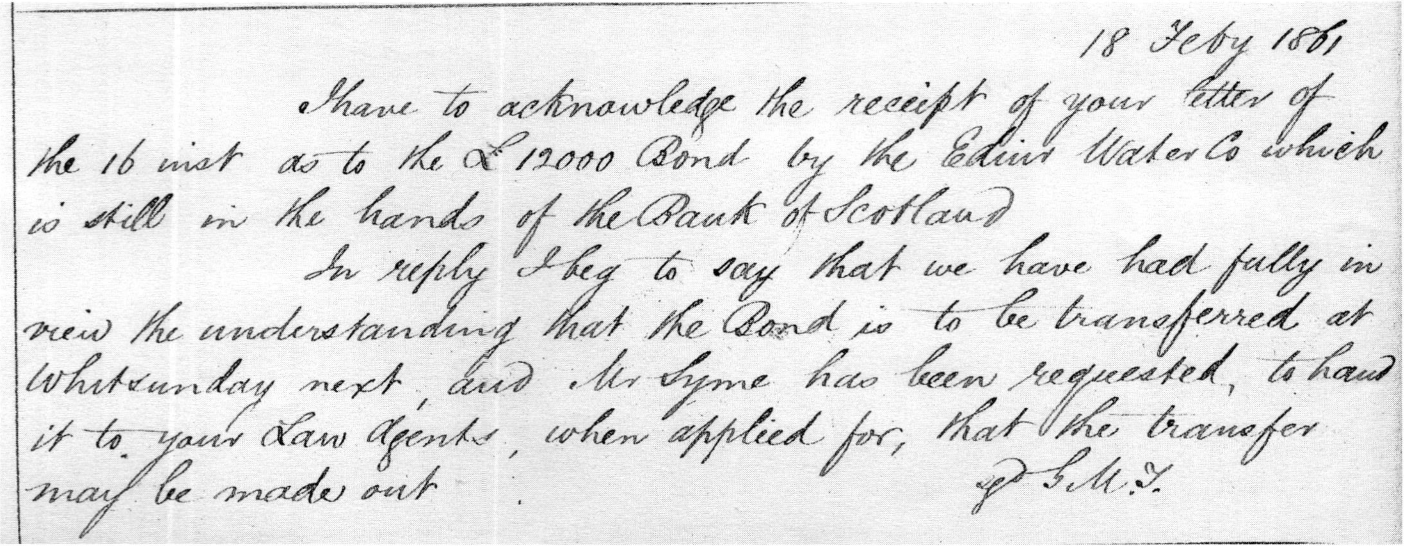

18 Feby 1805

I have to acknowledge the receipt of your letter of the 16 inst as to the £12000 Bond by the Edin.l Water Co which is still in the hands of the Bank of Scotland

In reply I beg to say that we have had fully in view the understanding that the Bond is to be transferred at Whitsunday next, but no time has been requested to hand it to your Law Agents, when applied for, that the transfer may be made out.

J.M.L.

Plate 4 Text in Bank of Scotland letter book no. NRAS945/1/146/44 (courtesy of Lloyds Banking Group plc Archives)

As for the hands that are employed in business letters of this kind, these may be somewhat idiosyncratic, and – while ensuring legibility – make few, if any, concessions to the stylistic prescriptions of 'corporate' correspondence. Far from being standardised Secretary hands, they are typically cursive hands, and constitute another very important personalisation strategy – so important that graphological investigations are often the basis for the assessment of a document's authenticity. Indeed, these are normally holograph letters, and when scribes are employed owing to the encoder's bad health, it is the encoder's scruple to indicate this in the text, as in example (4).

(4) A pity for you that my amanuensis is not on stock to-day, and my own hand perceptibly worse than usual. (R.L.S. to J. M. Barrie, Vailima, 5 December 1892, http://en.wikisource.org/wiki/The_Letters_of_Robert_Louis_Stevenson_Volume_2/Chapter_XI)

Finally, it may be taken as a sign of deference to the recipient when businessmen who could afford to dictate to secretaries actually wrote in person. In such cases it is not a matter of confidentiality, as secretaries could certainly be assumed to be trustworthy; it is more a case of professional relationships in which the mutual status of the participants is constructed also by means of the channels employed for communication, and whether these require greater distance (as implied by the contribution of a mediator, such as the secretary to whom the text is dictated) and standardisation (the same letter may be dictated for a variety of recipients) or greater proximity and personalisation, as each holograph letter is, in fact, unique.

2.1.2 *Handwritten letters in company letter books*

In relatively large companies, such as those in the insurance, banking and trading sectors, the plurality of interactants (typically clients, agents, suppliers and third parties addressing the company on legal issues) made it vital for encoders to be able to keep track of what messages had been issued. While in-coming letters were filed according to different criteria (for instance, there could be one file per branch of the company), out-going ones were copied into letter books in chronological order. We do not know who actually copied these letters – the names of these copyists, like those of medieval scribes, have not come down to us. However, their 'toils obscure', as Robert Burns labelled the work of ordinary people, have preserved huge quantities of potentially very valuable data.

These scribes' hands are usually very neat and highly legible secretarial ones – see plate 4.[10] Individual idiosyncrasy in the formation of graphemes can, of course, be detected, but the level of standardisation is considerable. The reason is that such records were expected to be accessible to other members of staff, whether at present or in the future, and too much personalisation

---

[10] Instances from other texts are provided by Dury (2008: 134–5).

in handwriting could have a negative impact on the legibility of the words, thus possibly violating the Gricean maxim of Manner and posing a threat to the reader's positive face.

As for content structure, the name and qualification of the addressee is usually placed in the outer margin of the page, together with the date on which the letter was sent. The vocative form is usually a standardised 'Sir', while closing formulae are typically abbreviated and often replaced with 'I am etc etc etc'. This seems to point to the fact that formulae were so crystallised in company usage that there was no need for the copyist to waste time, paper and ink writing them out in full – any reader within the company would have known what was supposed to follow that elliptical 'I am'. Similarly, signatures (both names and qualifications) were abbreviated and preceded by the participial form 'signed' (between round brackets): e.g. '(signed) Geo. Sandy Sec^y'.

What was actually preserved and transcribed accurately was the body of the letter, in which specific information, comments, evaluations and proposals were conveyed in the words of the encoders themselves, occasionally referring to them explicitly, as in example (5).

(5) The Directors do not allow any dispensation [...] But whether to do or forbear immediate diligence, the Directors leave meanwhile to you. (Edinburgh, 20 December 1826)

Letter books themselves were then filed in order, and could be very valuable sources of information when branches were acquired or suppressed, or when companies merged. In present-day archives, such as the ones consulted for the creation of 19CSC, these materials have provided data to business and social historians, but remain largely unexplored by linguists, despite their great potential interest.

2.2 Printed letters: circulars, appeals and early advertisements – addressing the general public

If we ask who wrote business letters, the obvious answer is that they were written by businessmen; however, ordinary people might actually have written their own business letters, though perhaps without following the conventions of business communication very closely. This is the case, for instance, for paupers seeking financial help (see Fairman 2003), for prospective contractors, or for correspondents providing references for job applicants (see Dossena 2006). Nor was it the case that ordinary people never received business letters unless it was for matters of economic or legal import (such as those sent by banks to their clients). Business letters could be addressed to the general public as circulars, appeals for subscriptions and as advertisements; in this way, even ordinary readers could gain access to the conventions and formulae of business English, albeit at the receptive level, and the message reached as wide a readership as possible while maintaining its generic features in lexis, syntax and textual organisation. Clearly, this meant that personalisation had to be sacrificed, but the opportunity to circulate content both widely and effectively was more important in the trade-off.

Concerning this type of letter, archives preserve circulars and appeals for subscriptions, while early advertisements are available in newspaper archives and (ideally) in the digital editions of their early issues.[11] Dealing with printed materials always poses far fewer problems to transcribers, who do not have to interpret uncertain graphemes, indicate linked-up words, or solve interpretation problems when unclear abbreviations are offered. However, with printed materials we cannot exclude editorial interventions that were not necessarily submitted to the encoder – i.e. the person who wrote the draft or prompted the letter – for approval; in fact, printers have often been known to amend the text according to what was assumed to be the standard form, so these letters cannot be assumed to be direct evidence of their encoders' actual linguistic choices.

On the other hand, anything addressed to the general public is of indisputable pragmatic interest. In the case of circulars, for instance, the politeness moves selected by the encoder had to cater for the needs of an addressee who was both an individual and a member of a possibly large group with an identity of its own. As a result, such moves had to show deference to both identities of the recipient: showing consideration for the group, while acknowledging the individuality of the reader.

In example (6a) below the recipient is not named, but is addressed directly with the second-person pronoun featuring as the subject of the passive clause expressing the invitation to attend the meeting ('you are desired to attend'). Nor is the encoder named explicitly, as the letter is signed by the 'officer', 'by Order of the Keeper': we do have an individual addressing the recipient, but the identity of the 'Keeper' is only known to the recipient as a contributor to the fund, i.e. as a member of the group of recipients.

(6a) Signet-Hall,
Edinburgh, 12th June 1844.
SIR,
You are desired to attend a Stated General Meeting of the Contributors to the Widows' Fund, and of the Society, on Wednesday next, the 19th current, at Two o'Clock, afternoon, in the Signet-Hall.
A view of the Business for consideration is annexed.
By Order of the Keeper,
[...], Officer.

[11] On nineteenth-century promotional discourse, see Bailey (1996: 26–8) and Görlach (1999: 147).

The case illustrated in example (6b) is similar, as far as the naming of encoders and recipients is concerned (though this time the collector appears to write on his own behalf); however, the second part of the letter expands the announcement of the meeting, and stresses the importance of attending, lest another adjournment should be required.

(6b) Edinburgh, 29th June 1844.
SIR,
I beg to intimate, that in terms of the resolution adopted at the Meeting of Contributors to the W.S. Widows' Fund, held on 19th instant, a Meeting of said Contributors will be held within the Signet-Hall, on Wednesday 3d July next, at Twelve o'clock noon, for the purpose of considering the Petition of Mrs M[...] to be admitted to the benefit of the Fund.

I have to mention, that a very strong hope was expressed at last Meeting, that every resident Contributor would endeavour to be present, so as to prevent any farther adjournment in consider-ation of the claim from want of attendance of the requisite number of Contributors.
I am,
SIR,
Your most obedient servant, [...], Collector.

While in (6a) the most prominent personalisation strategy was reader-oriented (the text began with 'you', and there were no occurrences of 'I'), in (6b) the situation is reversed: there are no instances of 'you', whereas 'I' occurs twice, both times at the beginning of a paragraph. In addition, both sentences are modalised; in particular, they convey deontic modality: in one the encoder asks for permission to inform ('I beg to intimate'), in the other he expresses obligation to say ('I have to mention'). In both cases, the encoder appears to be employing negative politeness moves conveying greater deference to the recipient, probably on account of the fact that attendance is required at another meeting just days after an earlier one, and to stress the importance of such attendance. The message, in its apparent redundancy and urgency, might therefore pose a greater face threat than the previous one, and requires the encoder to accept responsibility for it, without addressing the recipient directly.

On the other hand, politeness moves are also a function of the purpose of the text. In the intimation transcribed below (example (7)), dated 1834, the encoder (a 'sub-collector') is very direct in his address to the recipient: not only does he refer to terms set down by an Act of Parliament, which grant inescapable legal validity to the proceedings, but he also tells the recipient that any further expenses will be the sole responsibility of the recipient himself. The encoder thus presents himself as having greater authority than the recipient and, despite the passive clauses in the first section of the letter, he does not hesitate to threaten the recipient's negative face – first by making it clear that the letter is about 'his' road-money, and then by predicting the results of any reluctance to pay ('you will have yourself to blame'). Although the prediction is non-factual, as the recipient might pay in time after all, the encoder avoids any hypothetical structure, to prevent the request from being weakened.

(7) **FINAL NOTICE**
INTIMATION is hereby given, that, unless your ROAD-MONEY for the year 1834 to 1835 is paid to me at my house within Fourteen Days from this date, in terms of the Act of Parliament, the Sheriff's Warrant will be applied for, and you will have yourself to blame for the Expenses which will be incurred. (Comely Green, 15 December 1834)

It would, of course, be very difficult to ascertain when circulars were sent to recipients whom encoders knew personally; in any case, even when they were, the relationship existing between participants is not made visible in the text. For the encoder of a printed circular, all recipients are equal, and politeness moves do not relate to the social roles of the participants as individuals, but to their status and social roles as members of specific groups with specific functions within the groups themselves.

2.3 Print and handwriting: self-(re)presentation and self-promotion

A type of letter in which handwritten communication mixes with printed text is found when encoders use headed paper for their messages. In the case of more affluent encoders, even private letters could be written on personalised paper; see example (8), for instance, in which the printed part imitates an especially elegant hand.

(8) *Pembroke Lodge,*
 Richmond,
 Surrey.
 March 24
 1884
 My dear Catherine
 I have received the sad announcement of yr husband's death –

In personal archives, letters of this kind are quite frequent, and when encoders moved, but new stationery was not yet available, the printed address at the top of the page could be crossed out, and replaced with the new one in handwriting. Similarly, it is possible to come across letters written on the headed paper of a hotel, showing that the letter was sent while away from home – in fact, the letter may then include a promise to visit the recipients upon return, thus showing polite consideration on the part of the encoders, who might otherwise be seen to boast of their location.

Concerning business exchanges, headed paper has always been a very valuable tool of self-presentation and self-promotion. Companies may even include a small image of their premises, so that the impression of an *in situ* exchange is created, and the distance between participants may be reduced, albeit virtually. The fonts employed in headed paper may also reflect the company's attitude to business; we may go from earlier instances, employing traditional, ornate fonts, to later ones, in which sans-serif, more rational-looking lettering, is preferred; instances of these various cases are given below (examples (9a), (9b) and (9c)).

(9a) Pharmaceutical Society of Great Britain.
BOARD OF EXAMINERS FOR SCOTLAND
36 YORK PLACE, EDINBURGH
March 19th 1895.
Dear Sir,
The Board will meet in the Society's House, 36 York Place, Edinburgh, at 10 a.m. precisely on the 6th + probably 8–9- + 10th April. [. . .]

(9b) D. & F. Marshall.
Chartered Accountants
30 S^t. Andrew Square.
Edinburgh 21st Jany 1895
Dear Sir
Referring to my recent interview with you [. . .] when you mentioned that you were willing to sell [. . .]

(9c) Highland & Agricultural Society of Scotland
Edinburgh 6 Albyn Place 27 March 1851
Gentlemen
I should sooner have communicated to you the decision of the Publication Committee in reference to [. . .]

In (9a) the text is printed, except for the details underlined in the transcription, which are handwritten by the sender of the message in order to adapt a standard form to the requirements of a specific case and recipient. Similarly, in (9b) the firm's heading is supplemented by printed details concerning the address and the date, in which only the day, month and year are handwritten. Finally, in (9c) the name and address of the sender are printed, but the whole date is handwritten.

The range of possibilities represented by these examples makes it difficult to argue that some strategies were more widespread or more suitable for business correspondence. In fact, they seem to indicate that the quantity of printed text featured in a letter was a function of several factors, basically of an economic type. First of all, it depended on how much, and in what fonts, the company could afford to have it printed: if, in the date, the millennium, century and decade were printed, the headed paper had to be reprinted every ten years, but if it was just the millennium and century that were printed, then reprints could be much less frequent. It also depended on how often the company could expect to send the same message to a variety of recipients: yearly meetings of a society, held at the same premises and at the same time every year, albeit on different days, could be advertised employing mostly printed messages; in other cases, when the message was occasional, only a totally handwritten letter had to be issued, no matter how frequent the exchanges between the same participants.

3. Concluding remarks

This brief overview of handwritten documents at the time and in the genre in which typed and printed messages began to spread in the late nineteenth century has allowed us to glimpse the importance still attributed to manuscripts in that context. While speed and efficiency were, of course, crucial for the preparation of business correspondence, cost-effectiveness was not the only consideration, as legibility and clarity were also greatly valued. Skilful penmanship, calligraphy, ornamental lettering, the use of special fonts in headings, and even the inclusion of images, contributed to the self-representation that encoders conveyed by means of their messages. Neat, elegant and error-free manuscripts showed deference to the recipient by means of their own 'good-looking' presentation; at the same time, they allowed the encoder to personalise the message, so that it would suit the requirements of a specific interlocutor.

The Gricean maxim of Manner thus seems to apply to this kind of genre. Moves in the epistolary exchange made themselves acceptable to the recipient, and were designed to ensure that their clarity would facilitate the recipient's decoding tasks. This meant that scribes had to avoid unclear graphemes, smudgy self-corrections, unnecessary redundancies and cramped lines. Indeed, letter-writing manuals could provide exhaustive guidance on the use of blank lines before the salutation, the body of the letter, and the signature: the bigger the gap between these elements, the greater the deference shown to the recipient and, indirectly, the more affluent the encoder, or so he was made to seem, who could afford to waste so much writing paper. Even printed circulars adopted this philosophy, and often left large blank spaces on the page.

Another very important consideration was related to the personalisation of the message. Such personalisation was often both encoder- and recipient-oriented. It was encoder-oriented when encoders personalised the letter by employing headed paper, thus drawing attention to their own individual or corporate identity (their name, qualifications, address, and, on occasion, a tiny image of their premises); it was recipient-oriented whenever the recipient was addressed directly, possibly indicating his surname and address.

As a result, politeness and face-enhancing moves appear to go beyond linguistic choices: even such seemingly marginal paralinguistic traits play a part in the way in which a message is made to be interpreted. It would be as impolite to send a badly handwritten business letter as it would be to shout in a conversation or to use only capital letters in a present-day blog entry or e-mail message, and even minimally educated encoders did their best to compose 'standard' letters. The 'dress-code' of the genre in Victorian times appears to have dictated interesting requirements for manuscript, typed and printed documents. Although encoders could be creative in their choice of fonts and graphemes, what remained foregrounded was the role of the recipient as a reader who could rely only on what he saw for the assessment of both the value of the message and the business credibility of the encoder.

Part III

From manuscript to print

11 The relationship between MS Hunter 409 and the 1532 edition of Chaucer's works edited by William Thynne

GRAHAM D. CAIE

1. Introduction

This chapter will look at how early printers communicated with their audience; in particular, how they made manuscript texts accessible as printed books to the new reading public, and how they treated the manuscripts that were their exemplars. In this way, we can assess the communicating power of the handwritten texts from the late medieval period and the challenges these manuscripts posed for early printers. In order to do this, it is helpful to compare the early printed text with the exact manuscript the editor and printer used. This task is greatly helped by the increasing number of manuscripts available in digitised facsimiles. It is now possible to display the facsimile of the manuscript, the early printed text based on the manuscript and a diplomatic or critical edition side-by-side for easy comparison.

2. Glasgow University Library, MS Hunter 409 and Thynne's edition

The University of Glasgow possesses the sole remaining witness of the Middle English *Romaunt of the Rose*, a work frequently attributed to Geoffrey Chaucer.[1] As we do not have the opening folio of this unique manuscript, we do not know if Chaucer's name appeared on it. We do know, however, that all early editors, such as William Thynne in the early sixteenth century, claimed that it was by Chaucer. But, as its authorship was later called into question and the issue has never been successfully resolved, it is generally referred to as 'The Middle English *Romaunt of the Rose*'.

This text is in Glasgow University Library, MS Hunter 409 (V.3.7) (hereafter MS G), written in the first quarter of the fifteenth century, as can be seen by the handwriting and illumination.[2] A number of leaves have intricate and delicate marginal illustrations, largely of foliage, and there are many

---

[1] The question of Chaucer's authorship of parts or all of the *Romaunt of the Rose* is still hotly disputed. The arguments are summed up by Charles Dahlberg in his edition of the *Romaunt* (1999: 32–46). I am indebted to Charles Dahlberg for a number of observations in this article.
[2] A summary of editors' suggested dates is given by Dahlberg (1999: 46).

illuminated capitals. The manuscript is written by one scribe throughout and he has made a number of corrections himself. There are emendations by other scribes, for example the later completion of lines left blank by the main scribe, and there are later marginal additions. It is written in an early fifteenth-century hand that might be described as hybrid anglicana formata as it has elements of cursive formata with some textura features, for example in the minim letters and capitals. The hand is consistent and clear throughout and is written in black ink.[3]

Of specific interest to the editors and indeed to any study of the *Romaunt of the Rose* are the early printed editions, especially because MS G has some folios missing. Glasgow University Library has a number of early printed editions of Chaucer's works, including the 1492 edition of the *Canterbury Tales* printed by Richard Pynson (Hunterian Bv 2.12) and based on Caxton's second edition. The first printed edition of the collected works of Chaucer, including the *Romaunt*, is by William Thynne in 1532, which is entitled 'Chaucer *The workes of Geffray Chaucer newly printed, with dyuers workes whiche were never in print before*', and it was printed in London by Thomas Godfrey. It is almost certain that Thynne used MS G as his main source. There was a second edition by Thynne in 1542.[4] Thynne largely re-used Caxton's blocks from his second edition of *c.* 1483 for illustrations in his edition of *The Book of the Duchess*, but some woodcuts, e.g. those depicting the Knight and the Squire, were newly made.[5] William Thynne claims in his introduction to have collected 'trewe copies or examplaries' of Chaucer's manuscripts, and his son, Francis, reveals that his father searched all libraries in England for Chaucer's works.

3. The missing folios

As MS G has missing folios, and the earliest printed text by Thynne in 1532 is complete, it seems sensible that modern editors fill in the manuscript lacunae with the relevant sections from Thynne. It is highly likely that the missing folios were present when Thynne made his edition, but the question of whether Thynne used other manuscripts when MS G failed him or simply

---

[3] A digitised facsimile of the manuscript is easily accessible at: www.memss.arts.gla.ac.uk. Glasgow University Library also houses a manuscript copy of the *Canterbury Tales* (Glasgow University Library, MS Hunter 197 (U.1.1)) and the colophon of this text states that it was made by father and son, Geoffrey and Thomas Spirleng, and completed in January 1476. In addition, Chaucer's poem, *An ABC*, is also in this collection in a fifteenth-century manuscript (MS Glasgow, Hunter 239 (U.3.12)) along with a copy of *The Pilgrimage of the Lyfe of the Manhode*.

[4] A digitised facsimile of this edition from the Glasgow copy (Sp Coll Hunterian Bs. 2.17) can be found at www.memss.arts.gla.ac.uk. See Caie (2006). The text in the missing folios of MS G is replaced by the text in this edition.

[5] These woodcuts can be seen at: http://special.lib.gla.ac.uk/exhibns/chaucer/works.html. Digitised images of other early editions of Chaucer's works by Pynson, Speght and Islip can also be seen at this site.

filled in missing lines with his own translations from the original French *Le Roman de la Rose* is still disputed (Dahlberg 1999: 56). It is interesting that Francis Thynne also cites the French original when criticising some readings in the later edition by Speght in 1598 (Pearsall 1984: 83–90).

Alfred David in the Textual Notes to the edition of the *Romaunt* in *The Riverside Chaucer* (David 1988: 1199) states that he prefers to leave blank the additions to the MS G text made by Thynne, whereas in my on-line transcription, which accompanies the digitised *Romaunt*, I have added Thynne's version, as did F. N. Robinson in his 1957 edition. I am inclined to believe that the missing folios – the first folio, which might have had Chaucer's name, and the eleven other folios, which were torn out – were still in the manuscript when Thynne printed the text and, as I am sure that Thynne used MS G as his major source, I can see no reason why Thynne's text should not accurately reflect the manuscript reading.

It is likely that the missing leaves in MS G were as attractively illuminated as f. 57 and hence removed. These comprise f. 1, which contained lines 1–44; the folio following the present f. 5, lines 333–80; two folios following f. 27, lines 1387–482; one following f. 47, lines 2395–442; one after f. 71, lines 3595–690; three folios following f. 148, lines 7383–574.

4. The relationship between MS G and Thynne's 1532 edition

Skeat (1899) and Robinson (1957) claimed that Thynne did not use MS G as his source text, but that both came from a common ancestor, now lost. Robinson in his edition states that 'the two authorities are independent but closely similar. The present text is based upon G [MS G], completed and corrected by T [Thynne]' (1957: 924). Ronald Sutherland in the Introduction to his parallel translation of the *Roman* and the *Romaunt* states that the Glasgow manuscript 'was not the codex used by Thynne, for his edition contains readings for lines either missing or originally omitted and later filled in by a sixteenth-century hand' (Sutherland 1968: ix). Sutherland claims that MS G was corrected later from a manuscript 'superior to his original source'. This assumes that Thynne did not make the corrections himself. More recently, the view presented by James Blodgett (1979: 97–113) that Thynne had indeed based his edition largely on MS G has been generally accepted for reasons that are outlined in the remainder of this section.

Anyone working with MS G or the digitised edition can see the printer's marks on it. Naturally they need not have been made when the 1531 printing was taking place, but it is clear that it has gone through printers' hands. One of the key clues to the fact that we are dealing with the actual manuscript Thynne's printer used is the fact that he, probably Thomas Godfrey, marked with a marginal stroke the line in the manuscript that corresponded to a new column in his edition. The manuscript is in one column and the printed book in two. At the point in the manuscript where the second column begins in the printed edition, the printer has written 'coll' for 'column' in the margin (see plate 5).

These marks are relatively consistent throughout the manuscript (there are, however, some omissions of 'coll') and such a habit is common practice for sixteenth-century printers. In every occasion, the occurrence of 'coll' in the manuscript relates to a new column in the printed edition. There are other traces of printers' marks and ink smudges that could have been done by any printer using this manuscript as his source, but there is no way that any other printed edition would have columns ending on precisely the same line in the text as those marked in this manuscript.

There are other printer's marks that show Thynne was aware of certain textual problems; one example is on f. 17v, line 892, which has a marginal note 'lat [or 'lak'] a lyn' between two lines which have 'flourettes' and 'scochouns' in rhyme position.[6] (See plate 6.) The passage describes the flowers embroidered on the coat of Amant, and Thynne must have realised that these lines did not rhyme, so he added the line: 'Ypainted al with amorettes', thereby restoring the rhyme. The Riverside edition omits this line and adds a line of dots to show that something is missing, but Dahlberg includes it. Did Thynne invent the rhyme himself, or is Sutherland correct in saying that he was working from another manuscript? In addition to the theory that Thynne had two manuscripts and between them derived a sensible reading when he encountered problems in the text of one, there is the strong possibility that Thynne himself translated the line, after referring to the original *Roman de la Rose* text. In this case, the French text has '*fete par fines amoreites*', which seems to be a fitting source for 'Ypainted al with amorettes'. As Thynne frequently added the archaic 'y-' prefix to the past participle, I am inclined to think that he invented this line and that he must have had his inspiration at least for the rhyme word from a copy of the *Roman*.

Another major clue to the link between MS G and Thynne's edition is the fact that Thynne is obviously confused by the text of MS G at the point where lines 7109–58 appear before lines 7013–108 and lines 7159–206 come after lines 7207–302 in the manuscript. One can but assume that the leaves containing these lines were misplaced in the exemplar from which the MS G scribe copied before he began his work and that he was totally unaware of any problem. The leaves are not misplaced in MS G as the errors occur in mid-folio. The scribe turned a leaf in his copy text and was apparently not troubled by the lack of rhyme or the break in sense, so slavishly continued his copying. However, at line 7110 he leaves a blank line, as he realises there is no rhyme and assumes a line is missing.

---

[6] Blodgett (1979: 100) and Dahlberg (1999: 55) claim that the notation is 'lat a lyn'; I believe it is a 'k', and 'lack a line' makes better sense. However, 'lat' could have the sense of 'leave'. See Dahlberg (1999: 103).

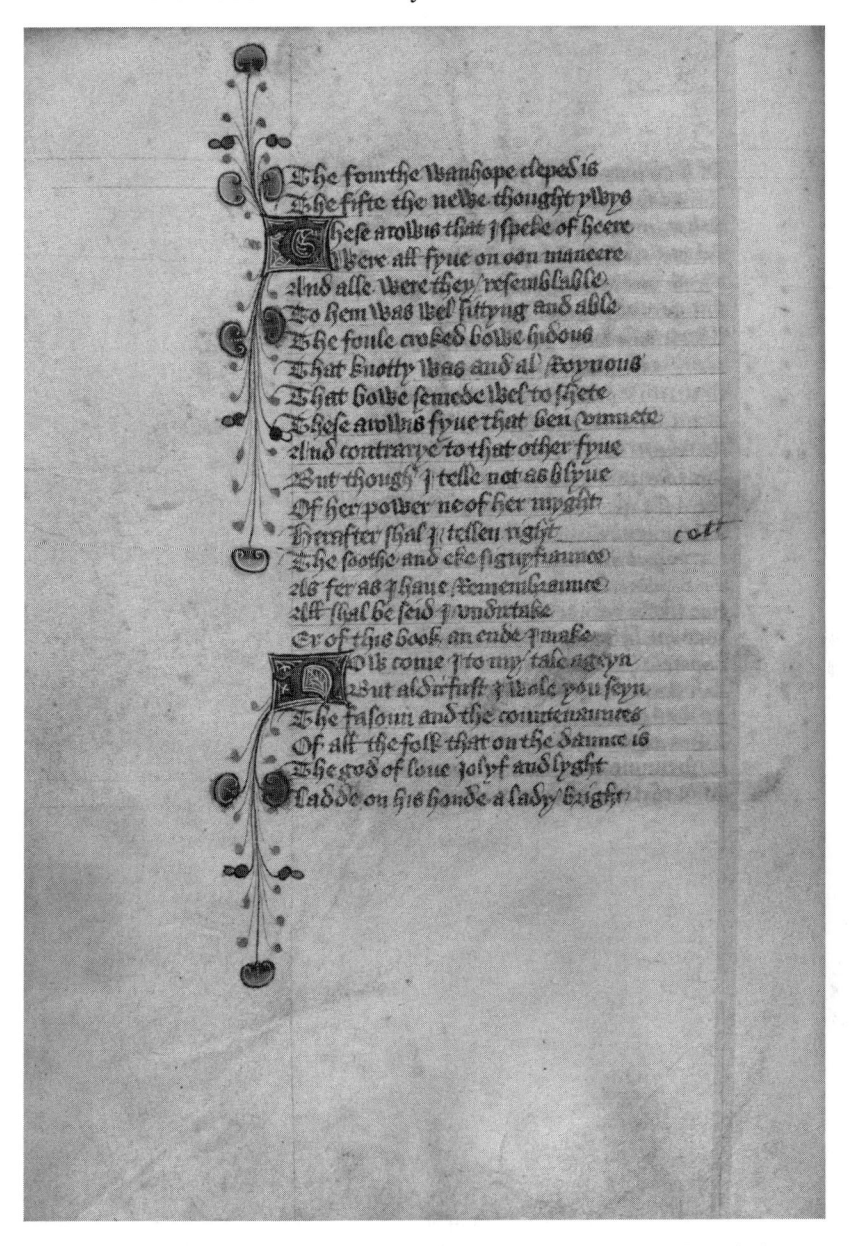

MS Hunter 409 and Thynne's 1532 edition of Chaucer 153

The fourthe wanhope clepeð is
The fifte the newe thoughte pleys
These a trollis that j speke of heere
were all fyue on oon maneere
And alle were they resemblable
To hem was wel fyttyng and able
The foule crokeð bowe hidous
That knotty was and al toynous
That bowe semede wel to shete
These arowis fyue that ben unmete
And contrarye to that other fyue
But though j telle not as blyue
Of her power ne of her myght
Hereafter shal j tellen ryght
The soothe and eke signyfiaunce
As fer as j haue remembraunce
All shal be seið j vndirtake
Er of this book an ende j make
Now come j to my tale ageyn
But aldirfirst j wole you seyn
The fasoun and the countenaunces
Of all the folk that on the daunce is
The god of loue jolyf and lyght
Ladde on his honde a lady bright

cott

Plate 5 Glasgow University Library, MS Hunter 409 (V.3.7), f. 115r.
By permission of Glasgow University Library.

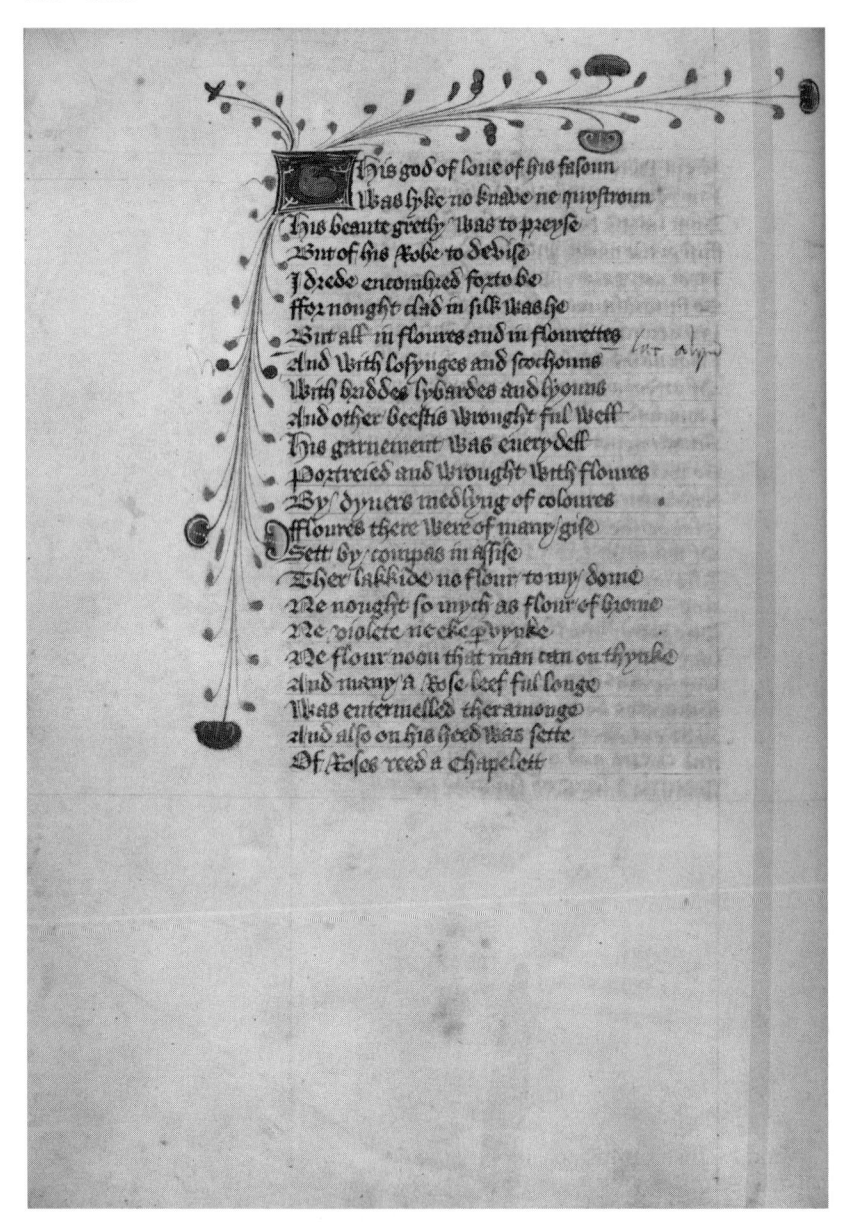

This god of loue of his fasoun
Was lyke no knaue ne muystroun
His beautee gretly was to preyse
But of his robe to devise
I drede encombred for to be
ffor nought clad in silk was he
But all in floures and in flourettes
And with losynges and scochouns
With buddes lybardes and lyouns
And other beestis wrought ful well
His garnement was euery dell
Portreied and wrought with floures
By dyuers medlyng of coloures
ffloures there were of many gyse
Sett by compas in assise
Ther lakkide no flour to my dome
Ne nought so mych as flour of brome
Ne violete ne eke pynke
Ne flour noon that man can on thynke
And many a Rose leef ful longe
Was entermelled ther amonge
And also on his heed was sette
Of Roses reed a chapelett

Plate 6 Glasgow University Library, MS Hunter 409 (V.3.7), f. 17v. By permission of Glasgow University Library.

The fact that Thynne makes the same error is strong proof that he used the Glasgow manuscript as his exemplar. Unlike the scribe of MS G, however, Thynne was obviously aware that something was wrong as he makes clear printer's marginal marks at the point in the passages where the lines in the misplaced folio begin and end (see f. 145r, plate 7.). There is a large printer's E-like mark with four horizontal lines indicating an error, although he apparently does not solve the problem or realise what has gone wrong.

5. The National Library of Scotland fragment

Although I said that there was only one extant manuscript of 'The Middle English *Romaunt of the Rose*', there was a recent discovery of a single leaf of another *Romaunt* manuscript. A few years ago, two Edinburgh research students, when reading the papers of a nineteenth-century Scottish minister in the National Library of Scotland, discovered in an envelope a manuscript leaf folded amongst his papers.[7] The leaf (hereafter NLS fragment) is about the same size as the MS G folios, written on both sides, in single columns, in a Secretary hand. On the envelope appears the wording '?Lydgate *c.* 1460', not a bad guess as to the date. Simon Horobin has analysed the fragment and suggests that it might be dated mid-fifteenth century (2006: 205–15).[8] It is in fact a leaf from a *Romaunt of the Rose* manuscript and of course we initially suspected that it was one of those cut and missing from MS G. This suspicion was increased when we saw that it covered part of the text of the poem that was on one of the missing leaves, lines 2395–442. However, closer examination showed that it was not from the same manuscript, although the writing space and the hand are very similar, but not identical, and the text overlapped that of MS G by a few lines. The NLS fragment covers lines 2403–50, but the few lines of overlapping text are crucial for direct comparison between the two manuscripts, although there are extremely few differences. It did, however, point to the fact that there was more than one manuscript made of this poem and so the hunt is now on for the remainder of this manuscript – or indeed others. How it landed up in the north of Scotland is anyone's guess. Because of the scribal errors in MS G and the textual errors caused by the missing folios, we did know that MS G was not the original witness. Horobin suggests that the dialect 'represents a type of London English of this period' (2006: 208).

As it is most likely that the folios were cut out of MS G after Thynne had printed his edition, we can be sure that the text in Thynne reflects that in the missing folios with the usual minor changes Thynne was accustomed to make. It is therefore helpful to compare the text in the NLS folio with that

---

[7] The discovery was made by Helen Brown and Anna Tindley of Edinburgh University in the National Library of Scotland. Sally Mapstone identified the leaf as containing lines from the *Romaunt*.

[8] I am indebted to Dr Horobin for his analysis of this fragment.

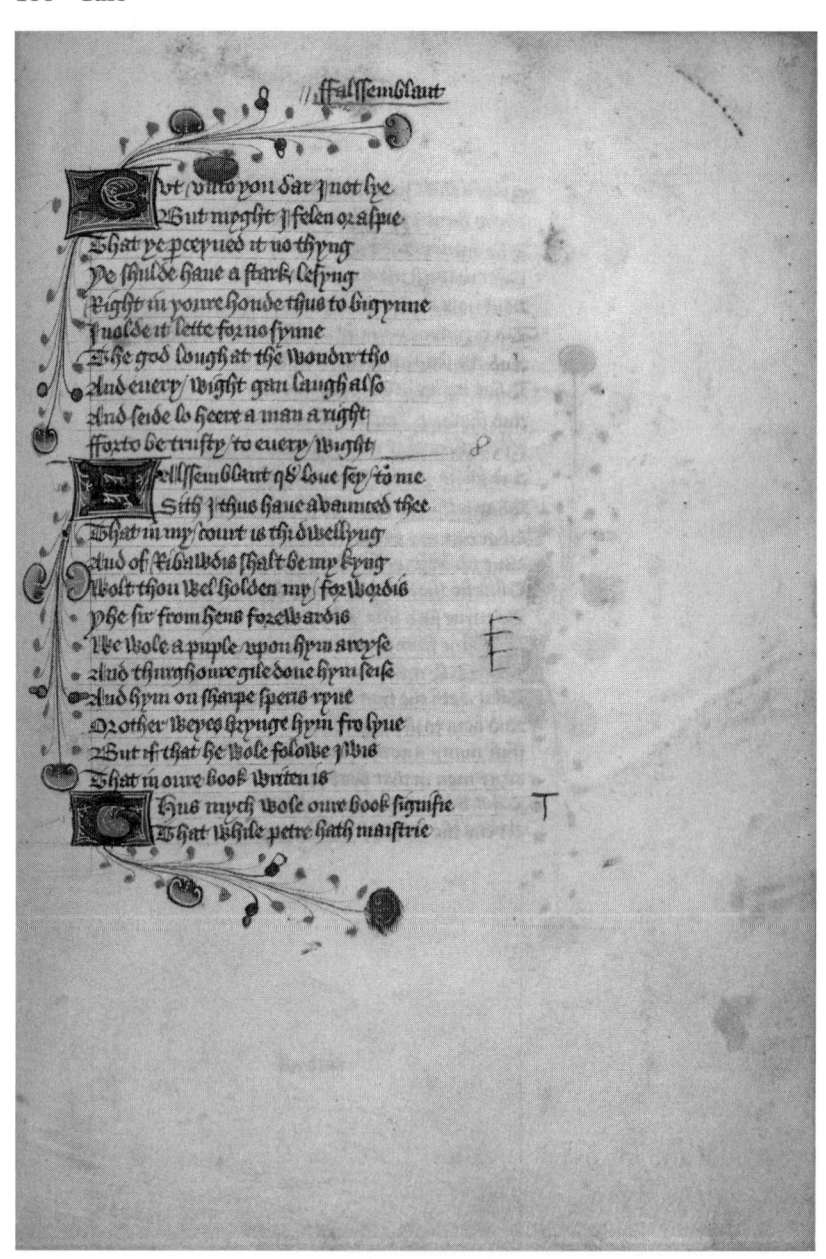

Plate 7 Glasgow University Library, MS Hunter 409 (V.3.7), f. 145r.
By permission of Glasgow University Library.

in Thynne. The differences between Thynne and the fragment are slight, as are Thynne's changes to MS G throughout his editorial work. There are, however, a few interesting discoveries made by a comparison of the Thynne edition and the NLS fragment.

In line 2427 of the *Romaunt* we find:

Thynne: Alas myne eyen sene I ne may

NLS fragment: Allas myn eyghen sende I ne may

The French original has '*envoier*' 'send' and the Riverside edition has made the editorial emendation of 'sene' to 'sende' too, as it makes more sense, although there is a semantic link between 'eyes' and 'see'. This suggests that the MS G scribe also had 'sene', a mistake that Thynne followed, but the NLS fragment scribe did not. This find, then, confirms the change made by the Riverside editors to 'sende' as being correct and the NLS fragment represents a more accurate reading.

In line 2450 of the *Romaunt* we find:

Thynne: That no itching pricketh so.

MS G: That no yecchyng prikketh soo

NLS fragment: That noon yrchon ne pryketh soo

Here we are lucky, as the line comes at the end of the fragment, to have both MS G and NLS fragment readings. The French has '*Qui poignent plus que heriçons*' (2328 of *Roman de la Rose*). *Heriçon* is French for 'hedgehog', and is correctly translated in the NLS reading by the Middle English *yrchon*, 'hedgehog'. MS G and Thynne have 'itching', but it makes better sense that a hedgehog pricks, as itching does not prick, but irritates. There is a chance that the MS G scribe was unaware of the archaic word *yrchon*, which was very rare in the fifteenth century, or it could have been dictated to him and one can appreciate why he changed it to 'itching' (Horobin 2006: 211). The key question is whether Thynne had other manuscripts of the text present or whether he referred back to the original French version. In the 'itching' case he appears to have followed MS G and not looked at other manuscripts (assuming that others did not follow MS G's reading) or at the *Roman de la Rose*.

6. Thynne and his use of the French *Roman de la Rose*

The many changes that Thynne made, for example when he filled in the missing lines in the MS G, may well be attributed to Thynne's own ingenuity and perhaps his reading of the French original rather than consultation of other manuscripts.[9] An example of this occurs at line 6786, which is blank in MS G, and a later hand, which would not have been seen by Thynne, has

---

[9] See the comments on this issue in David (1988: 1198).

added 'Of thyngis that he beste myghte', which does not really make sense in the passage:

> He made a book, and lete it write
> Of thynges that he beste myghte.
> (lines 6785–6)

Thynne, however, fills in the blank line in his edition with:

> Wherin his lyfe he dyd al write.

This uses the same rhyme word, but it appears to be based on the French (Dahlberg 1999: 285):

> *ou sa vie fiste toute escrivre* ('where he had his entire life written').

One cannot be certain that Thynne referred to the *Roman* to complete the line, but his solution is a close translation of the French. Another example where Thynne appears to have referred to the *Roman* occurs at line 193 (MS G f. 6r) where we find the confusing reading 'And she hadde usage', which is metrically deficient and without meaning, but it is corrected by Thynne to 'And she had a foule visage', which echoes the French '*mauvé uisage*', thereby restoring the metre and sense.

7. Misplaced folios

The biggest challenge to Thynne occurred at the passages made illogical by the above-mentioned misplacement of folios. At lines 7009–12 in MS G f. 140r we read:

> Of Antechristes men am I,
> Of whiche that Crist seith openly,
> They have abit of hoolynesse,
> And lyven in such wikkednesse.
> [MISPLACEMENT HERE: Blank line]
> To copy if him talent toke.

This is followed by a blank line in MS G, possibly because the scribe could not make sense of it, but Thynne added a line to give rhyme and some sense and cohesion: 'To the copye if him talent toke/ **Of the Evangelystes booke**.' There is no equivalent in the French text, so it must have been his own inspiration.

Thynne again had problems with the abrupt change in subject at line 7108 (f. 143r), where the misplacement makes the text appear disrespectful to 'oure Lady', so he invents a couplet to make the transition less awkward. MS G has:

MS Hunter 409 and Thynne's 1532 edition of Chaucer

> Biforne oure Lady, at parvys,   (line 7108)
> But I wole stynt of this matere   (line 7207)
> For it is wonder longe to here,   (line 7208)

Thynne adds (shown in bold):

> Biforne our Lady, at parvys,
> **That they ne myght the booke by**
> **The sentence pleased hem wel trewly.**
> But I wyl stynt of this matere.

In this way, Thynne creates slightly better sense and deflects the criticism from the lady to the book. There are other occasions where there are MS G gaps but where Thynne's reading does not reflect the French text, e.g. lines 1890–2 on f. 36v. The section describes ointment that might help heal the wounds of the heart. MS G reads:

> Somdell to yeve aleggement
> Upon the woundes that he hadde
> That he hadde the body hole made.   (line 1892)

And Thynne:

> Somdele to yeve alegement
> Upon the woundes that he hade
> Through my body in my herte made.   (line 1892)

It would appear that line 1892 was blank in MS G when Thynne read it, although the later hand that writes 'That he hadde the body hole made' is an extremely good copy of the original scribe's hand. The French version is quite different at this point. One can guess that Thynne used common sense to suggest that the wounds were made through the body to the heart. Alfred David in the Textual Notes to the Riverside edition states that Thynne's addition 'makes a kind of sense but has no equivalent in the French, which says that the God of Love made the ointment with his own hands to comfort pure lovers: "*Amors l'avoit fair a ses mains/Por les fins amanz conforter*" ' (David 1988: 1107).

Another example of Thynne following MS G where one might suspect that he would have spotted an error in his source is at line 421:

MS G: And semeth a seemly creature.

Thynne: And semeth a seemly creature.

Some *Roman* manuscripts have 'simple criature' and others 'seinte criature'; it would appear that the MS G scribe is influenced by the preceding 'semeth', rather than translating 'simple' (a reading adopted by Dahlberg and in Riverside) or 'seinte'. But on many other occasions, as mentioned above, Thynne seems to prefer the *Roman* reading to that of MS G, e.g. at line 185:

> MS G: And that is that for usure
> Leneth to many a creature.
>
> Thynne: And that is she that for usure
> Leneth to many a creature.

The French has '*c'est cele*', 'it is she' and so Thynne better reflects the French original. Similarly, in line 508, MS G has 'daunws of love' being sung, while Thynne follows the *Roman* and substitutes 'Daunces'. It would appear that the MS G scribe was confused by the minim letters in his source manuscript, but Thynne corrects the reading.

8. Other changes by Thynne

Thynne makes many spelling changes and introduces weak preterites for strong ones, reflecting linguistic change in the hundred-year gap, e.g. 'wepe' appears in MS G for the preterite form, which is changed to 'wept' by Thynne (line 332); 'wexe' for 'waxed' (line 691) and 'wext' in Thynne. He also prefers the 'y-' prefix on past participles. Examples are:

> MS G: The botme paved everydell (line 126)
>
> Thynne: The botome ypaved everydele

and:

> MS G: ffrounced foule was hir visage (line 155)
>
> Thynne: Yfrounced foule was her visage.

The only reason for Thynne to do this is to make the text more archaic or at times he might feel that an extra syllable is needed (David 1988: 1198). David points out that the changes Thynne makes are much more frequent in the first 1300 lines and suggests that his 'interest and editorial initiative began to decline after some 1200 lines' (David 1988: 1198). For example, nearly all the 'y-' prefixes (twenty-one in all, according to Dahlberg 1999) occur in the first 1600 lines. The other minor changes that Thynne makes are largely orthographical.[10]

9. Marginalia

Thynne does not include the marginalia in the manuscript, but there are interesting clues as to ownership from the names in the flyleaves and elsewhere. On f. 1r is the inscription 'Thomas Griggs, possessor huius libri' ('Thomas Griggs, the owner of this book'), but nothing is known about Griggs. We know from the above examples that the manuscript must have

---

[10] These are listed by Dahlberg (1999: 58).

MS Hunter 409 and Thynne's 1532 edition of Chaucer 161

been in the hands of Thomas Thynne in London by the early 1530s. On f. 60r the name 'Ihon thin' appears, and this might refer to Thynne's nephew, John Thynne. Lord Mountjoy's name appears on f. 139r; this is possibly the father or son, Charles or William Blount, Baron Mountjoy (d. 1534 and 1545, respectively). We can only be sure of ownership once the manuscript was purchased by William Hunter in the mid eighteenth century and passed to the Hunterian Museum in 1807.

10. Conclusion

Much more about sixteenth-century editors' methods can be gleaned by a close comparison of MS G with the 1532 edition, but I hope to have established that Thomas Thynne definitely used the Glasgow manuscript as his source, resorting to the French original when in doubt, and may not have consulted any other manuscripts. A detailed comparison between the early fifteenth-century scribe's spelling and that in the 1532 edition would also be worthwhile and this would be greatly facilitated by the digitised images of both books. One would have to remember the later editor's desire to make his text more archaic, as witnessed by the 'y-' prefix to past participles. The above detailed comparisons are but a few of those that tell us more about how early printers treated their manuscript sources – and it would appear that they had no qualms about writing over them or even, I suspect, destroying them after their purpose was fulfilled. [One hopes that our libraries today are not depleted because of the preservation of texts electronically.] It also shows how Thynne tried to make his text more accessible to his reading public by attempting to correct scribal errors. There is a final interesting comparison, and that concerns marginalia. MS G has many marginal comments in addition to those by the printer; one is a poem that has nothing to do with the text, others are practice letters and lines copied to imitate the scribe's hand, while the printed editions generally have no or very few handwritten additions. It would appear that the manuscript had a greater communal function; the text after all moved in every manuscript witness and the reader participated in its development, as the text was not fixed or 'set in print', unlike the later printed edition. Comparison between these two works, then, provides an endless source of information on how we can assess the communicating power of the handwritten texts from the late medieval period and the challenges these manuscripts posed for early printers.

12 The development of play-texts

From manuscript to print

JONATHAN CULPEPER AND JANE DEMMEN

1. Introduction

It is an axiom of historical linguistics, and indeed historical studies generally, that our present-day assumptions are not a reliable basis for the analysis and interpretation of language data from earlier periods. Assumptions, not just about language but about any kind of human experience, help people make sense of the world in a cognitively efficient way. But those very assumptions interact with the phenomena to which they pertain, and together they change over time. Present-day assumptions form the endpoint of diachronic change. The first task for the historian is to describe earlier states of the language and its contexts, including the likely assumptions of contemporaries, and begin to understand why it is as it is. The second task is to explain the processes of change that have led to the situation today. This chapter aims to show how present-day assumptions about early modern play-texts are inappropriate or misleading. It explores how the dialogue of earlier plays was shaped by particular manuscript practices, and compares this with the dialogue of present-day plays that are shaped by the context of printing.

The present-day reader is likely to take some of the conventions of play-texts for granted, including that the play exists from the outset as an entire visible entity, available to all readers. Indeed, plays are now generally written as a whole, rapidly reproduced for people to read as a whole and published as a whole. For example, Henrik Ibsen's play *Ghosts* was published in 1881 before it had been performed, and this was the case for the remaining plays he produced (Holland 2006: 1). Ibsen looked forward to the profits from publication, as he was writing in a period in which the reading public had rapidly expanded and was to expand further (something which, in the UK, was assisted by the Education Act of 1870, making school compulsory). With regard to historical plays, although there is sometimes an acknowledgement of different manuscript variants and imprints, in present-day works they are also generally discussed as a whole and edited as a whole. However, historically, from the earliest plays through to fairly late in the early modern period, the play-text had a very different existence. It was written in manuscript form for performance, and only printed later, if at all. Moreover, and crucially

Development of play-texts: from manuscript to print

for the actors who performed it, it did not exist as one complete text. It is more accurate to think of an early play as a bundle of fragments rather than a unitary whole. Only in performance did those fragments unite as a whole. In this chapter, we argue that such differences in textual history had a number of implications for how the play was written – implications that linguists, historians and critics have generally ignored. In particular, we explore implications for turn construction, especially turn length, and the cohesiveness of the dialogue (including implications for the diversity of vocabulary and the role of terms of address).

This chapter focuses on five plays written and performed in the time of Shakespeare. For obvious reasons, character-part manuscripts have not generally survived from this period, though 'foul papers' are thought to be reconstructions from them and the memories of actors. However, there is no evidence to suggest that manuscript plays written for performance, like the five plays we analyse, were then radically revised before they were subsequently printed, to remove traces of the fact that they were originally written in manuscript form, physically fragmented and then united in performance. In section 2, we will review the early play manuscript practices, the outcome of this review being a set of hypotheses about how these practices are likely to have shaped the language of the play. In the sections 3 to 5, deploying both quantitative and qualitative analyses, we will test some of these hypotheses with respect to specific linguistic features.

2. Plays: manuscripts and performance

As Stern (2004) argues, the early modern play is a patchwork in a number of ways. For one, it was quite normal for a writer to gather disparate bits of material from various sources, especially the commonplace book, and weave them together. For another, it is never a unitary whole in the same way as, for example, a poem. Plays were not only formed as patchworks but were written to be so. The audience would in part be listening to plays for turns of phrase or passages that could be recycled in other contexts – in commonplace books, other literary texts or even just in everyday discourse. Stern writes that plays

> were to a certain extent written to be resolved into commonplace books. For a play that was not published, indeed, quotation was the way it would be promulgated amongst the audience – and thus the mark of its success. (Stern 2004: 156)

Moreover, Stern points out that the

> printed layout of surviving text raises the suggestion that some plays were transcribed, kept, learned, revised, and even written, not as wholes,

> but as a collection of separate units to be patched together in performance. (Stern 2004: 156)

Stern (2004) observes that songs, and some letters, were often printed in a different typeface, and were kept separately from the rest of the play. The same goes for prologues and epilogues. Did the play ever exist as a whole? The answer to this is yes, most likely as

> a loosely tied bundle of papers, consisting of the book of dialogue (or several if the play were submitted piecemeal...), some separate sheets containing songs and letters, other separate papers containing prologues and epilogues (unless kept elsewhere as no longer relevant), and finally, perhaps, a separate bill/title page providing the lure that attracted the audience. (Stern 2004: 166)

There must have been some kind of 'complete' text submitted to the Master of the Revels (Stern 2004: 166). In 1581, the Master was granted significant powers to censor and licence plays for performance. In fact, the Master's commission only required that 'players' and their 'playmakers' 'present and recite' their plays to the Master (from the commission cited in Gurr 1992: 73). However, even as early as the 1580s, when the job was less textual in nature, Stern (2000: 52) points out that it is unrealistic to suppose that the Master of the Revels had the time to listen to private performances of all plays being produced in London. Instead, manuscripts were brought in for inspection, and this accords with the contemporary accounts of how the Master of the Revels 'perused, & neccessarely corrected and amended' plays (Feuillerat 1908: T III 71, a collection of documents relating the revels, cited in Stern 2000: 52).

If early modern plays were written for performance, what matters, then, is how the text equipped the actors for performance. Once the playwright had completed the manuscript, it was in fact read to the actors, during which casting would take place (Stern 2000: 60–1). Thereafter, actors would receive their individual parts. Having said that, actors could be given parts to learn even before the play was finished, i.e. before it could be read out as a whole (Stern 2000: 62). What actors never received was the whole text, partly because it was expensive to produce multiple manuscript copies and partly because with more full copies in circulation there was an increased risk of the play being stolen by a rival company or printer (Palfrey and Stern 2007: 1). Thomson summarises what happened to the Elizabethan play manuscript:

> In the best-conducted companies, the scribe (or scribes) had made not one but at least two fair copies of the manuscript. The first would become the property of the company, serving as what we would now call a promptbook: the second, to save further transcription, could then be cut up into individual 'parts' and the scraps of speeches pasted onto a scroll, with short cues added... Only when the parts had been

assembled on their individual scrolls could the play conveniently be given its first reading by the company. (Thomson 1997: 322)

The actor's 'part', then, had the more literal meaning of part of the play-script, and not simply the character in the play, as is more often the case today; also, the word 'role' may derive from the 'roll' of paper containing the actor's part. Thomson does not elaborate on what the 'short cues' consisted of, but fortunately Stern, especially in collaboration with Palfrey, has studied this in detail (see Palfrey and Stern 2007).

The cue was a prompt for a speech in an actor's part. It consisted of one to three words preceding each speech (Palfrey and Stern 2007: 95). However, there was no explicit indication of:

- the speaker of the cue,
- the length of gap between one speech and another (i.e. how long one might have to wait before one heard one's cue), or
- having been cued, to whom one should direct one's speech and in what capacity. (Stern 2000: 61; Stern 2004: 166)

Let us look at an example of an early part, the part of Orlando in Robert Greene's play *The Historie of Orlando Furioso*, which dates from the early 1590s. The dashed lines precede the one- to three-word cues that were provided for the speeches that comprise Orlando's part.

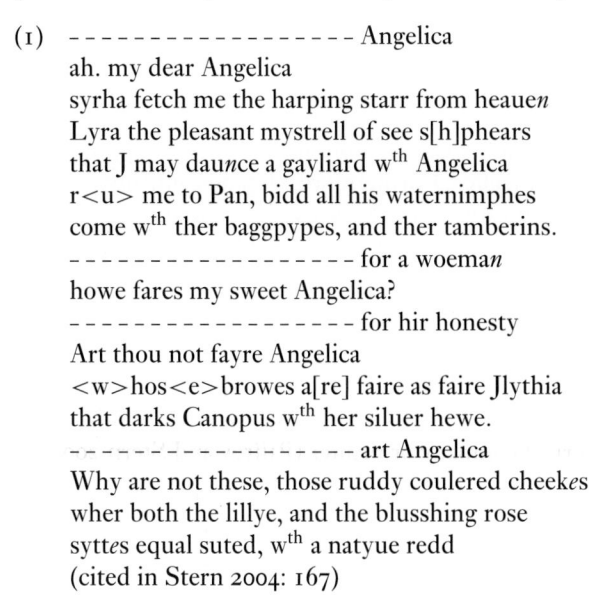

(1) ------------------ Angelica
    ah. my dear Angelica
    syrha fetch me the harping starr from heaue*n*
    Lyra the pleasant mystrell of see s[h]phears
    that J may dau*n*ce a gayliard wth Angelica
    r<u> me to Pan, bidd all his waternimphes
    come wth ther baggpypes, and ther tamberins.
    ------------------ for a woema*n*
    howe fares my sweet Angelica?
    ------------------ for hir honesty
    Art thou not fayre Angelica
    <w>hos<e>browes a[re] faire as faire Jlythia
    that darks Canopus wth her siluer hewe.
    ------------------ art Angelica
    Why are not these, those ruddy coulered cheek*e*s
    wher both the lillye, and the blusshing rose
    sytt*e*s equal suted, wth a natyue redd
    (cited in Stern 2004: 167)

From the first cue in the part version of Orlando's dialogue in example (1), we can gather that Orlando is talking to an unknown interlocutor who mentions or introduces a second interlocutor, Angelica, to whom Orlando subsequently addresses himself. It is not clear from the second and third cues whether these lines are spoken by Angelica or the first interlocutor. The fourth cue suggests it is the other interlocutor speaking, unless Angelica is talking about herself in the third person. Also, in the part version, it is not clear whether Orlando's question 'Art thou not fayre Angelica' seeks to confirm her identity or her opinion of her own beauty. We compared this to the corresponding extract from the earliest printed version of the whole play, dated 1594, on Early English Books Online,[1] shown below in example (2).

(2) Org: Excellent: come see where my Lord is.
My Lord, here is Angelica.
Orl: Mas thou saist true, tis she indeed;
How fares the faire Angelica?
Cl: Well, I thanke you hartely.
Orl: Why art thou not that same Angelica,
Whose hiew as bright as faire Erythea
That darkes Canopus with her siluer hiew?
Cl: Yes forsooth.
Orl: Are not these the beauteous cheeks,
Wherein the Lillies and the natiue Rose
Sits equall suted with a blushing red?

The wording of the lines is not identical to that in the part version and a direct comparison is therefore not possible. Nevertheless, we can immediately glean a lot more information about what is going on: notably, the identities of Orlando's interlocutors. Although the cues in the part version suggest that Orlando is talking to Angelica, we can see from the full version that in fact a clown is pretending to be Angelica. Furthermore, Orgalio contributes to the deception by identifying the Clown as Angelica to Orlando in the first turn. It is hard to see how the actor playing Orlando would have known that he is talking to the Clown in disguise and not to the real Angelica at this point in the play from the part version alone. It may well become apparent later in the part version, the full text of which we have not seen, and it would not of course have stopped the actor from learning his own character's lines. However, limited access to the other characters' speech must clearly have severely limited the actor's ability to prepare fully for the role in advance of the play coming together as a whole.

Given the pressures, not least of all financial, of producing a huge repertoire of plays, group preparation and rehearsals were a 'luxury' (Stern 2000: 64). Actors ended up with little sense of the play as a whole. All this may lead one to suspect that performances, particularly first performances, were a disaster. However, two things helped hold some aspects of the performance

---

[1] See http://eebo.chadwyck.com.

together. One was a 'plot', a sheet of paper on cardboard hung backstage, containing essential dramatic information, the sequence of scenes, the actors' entrances, others in the scene, and so on (see Palfrey and Stern 2007: 72). Perhaps the present-day parallel would be the film storyboard. The other was a prompter, who had responsibility not just for the words but also for the action, e.g. giving notice of actors' entrances and properties, and also of important events, such as music, dances and songs.

We believe that early modern playwrights were likely to have conceived plays in a more fragmentary way. Furthermore, the production of the manuscript for distribution as parts would also have influenced the language of the plays. Stern (2004: 168) comments that the fact that plays were learnt by actors in fragmentary form is likely to have affected the way they were written. Let us consider some specific areas of influence. Firstly, given the fragmentary nature of the text, one would expect less cohesion across the dialogue. In particular, one would expect less of the cohesive repetition that characterises so much conversation, with one interactant recycling words and phrases from the previous one. 'Lexical cohesion' is amongst Halliday and Hasan's (1976: 324) classification of 'types of cohesive relations', a subcategory of which is 'reiteration', e.g. through lexical repetition; see also Hoey (1991: 3–25). This would lead to the hypothesis that early modern plays have greater lexical richness compared with present-day plays. Secondly, the fact that the manuscript was to be cut up had implications for the way turn-taking was represented. The 'new speaker = new line' rule was a practical necessity. Interestingly, early printed plays periodically departed from this for another practical reason, namely to save space and thus reduce printing costs. An example is given in (3):

(3) *Went.* We shall honor thee.
     Bar. But how Butler. *Bu.* I am now
     going to their place of residence, scituate in the choicest place in
     the City, and at the sign of the Wolf iust against Gold-smiths-row
     (George Wilkins, *The Miseries of Inforst Mariage*, 1607, G1V)

Furthermore, rapid turn-taking, involving short turns, would have required much more cutting and pasting. This would lead to the hypothesis that early modern plays have longer turns on average compared with present-day plays. The cut-up manuscript also reduced potential for representing simultaneous talk and interruptions. Playwrights would use designations such as 'omnes' to signal that a group should speak, or would indicate an interruption through an incomplete sentence, a dash or the interrupting character using an item such as 'hush', though these do not always signal interruptions, of course. Thirdly, given that an actor would only get to read his[2] own character's part of the dialogue, hearing the rest of the dialogue at possibly just one

---

[2] In this period, all actors, of course, would have been male.

rehearsal, there was pressure on the playwright to provide the actor with sufficient evidence in the part he received, particularly in the cues, as to how the dialogue would cohere, both for the actors and for the audience. One way in which this could partly be achieved was through reliance upon terms of address. Terms of address also have the advantage of providing relational information − information about relative social status and other social groupings. This would lead to the hypothesis that early modern plays not only contain a greater number of terms of address compared with present-day plays, but, more particularly, that those terms of address were available as implicit cues for actors.

In the following three sections, we will put these three hypotheses to the quantitative test. Of course, there may well be other factors that contribute to lexical richness, average turn length and frequency of terms of address, but we will also provide some supporting qualitative evidence of a causal relationship.

3. Data and methodology

3.1 Corpora of present-day and early modern plays

In order to test our hypotheses, we compare our five early modern plays with a similar sample of present-day plays, using corpus analysis methods. We matched our corpora as closely as possible in size and structure, and selected plays that were generally successful and popular in their time. Both corpora span as few years as possible, in order to minimise the influence of changing trends and styles of writing over time. Our present-day drama corpus was originally constructed for comparison with early modern drama in *A Corpus of English Dialogues, 1560–1760* (hereafter, CED). Both corpora were compiled by Merja Kytö (University of Uppsala) and Jonathan Culpeper (Lancaster University); for further details on CED, see Kytö and Walker (2006).[3] The present-day corpus contains samples from five award-winning comedies spanning a ten-year period, 1974 to 1984, and comprises 38,190 words of direct speech. Samples are drawn from the plays listed in table 12.1.

For our early modern corpus, we used five plays from the Drama Comedy section of CED. Samples are drawn from the plays listed in table 12.2.

Given that our quantity of material is relatively small, we were very careful in our selection of plays. We avoided playwrights whose work was particularly stylistically distinctive or idiosyncratic and, regarding the early modern plays, those who wrote with a view to publication rather than performance, e.g. Ben

---

[3] The plays of the present-day corpus were selected and scanned by Jonathan Culpeper and proofread by Merja Kytö. The corpus was prepared for personal research and, for reasons of copyright, is not publicly available. In contrast, the CED has been deposited at the Oxford Text Archive (see http://ota.ahds.ac.uk/; access is free, though signing a user agreement will be required), and will be available on the forthcoming ICAME CD-ROM.

Development of play-texts: from manuscript to print

Table 12.1 *The present-day plays: five comedies, 1974–1984 (word counts from WordSmith Tools)*

Date published	Title	Author	Word count of sample
1974	Absurd Person Singular: A Comedy	Alan Ayckbourn	6563
1981	Educating Rita: A Comedy	Willy Russell	9197
1982	The Real Thing: A Comedy in Two Acts	Tom Stoppard	8651
1982	Noises off: A Play in Three Acts	Michael Frayn	7120
1984	Run for Your Wife: A New Comedy	Ray Cooney	6659
			38190 (*total*)

Table 12.2 *The early modern plays: five comedies, 1594–1607 (word counts from WordSmith Tools)*

Date of first printing	Title	Author	Word count of sample
1594	A Knacke to Knowe a Knaue	Anonymous	9097
1595	The Old Wiues Tale	George Peele	5870
1599	An Humerous Dayes Myrth	George Chapman	7258
1602	How a Man May Chuse	Thomas Heywood	7778
1607	The Miseries of Inforst Mariage	George Wilkins	8002
			38005 (*total*)

Jonson. We included plays for which the dates of the first performance, first printing and our source texts coincided as closely as possible. The plays in CED are based on the earliest available extant printed versions of the plays. In fact, the source texts for the five early modern plays we use are, as far as we know, the very first imprint. The present-day plays are based on the earliest published versions. As far as scholarship can tell, no play, whether early modern or present-day, was performed more than two years before it was printed, and in most cases it was printed in the same year as it was performed. Indeed, it is quite possible that some plays were printed whilst still being performed, as is suggested by the title page of Wilkins's play: '*The Miseries of Inforst Mariage as it is now Playd by his Maiesties Seruants*'. We trimmed an equal amount from the ends of each of the five early modern play samples from CED, in order that the overall size of both corpora would be approximately the same.

3.2 Regularising early modern spelling variation

Variation in spelling is a known problem for corpus linguists using historical texts and investigating results based on the matching of orthographic word

Table 12.3 *The present-day plays: number of words, turns and average number of words per turn (word counts from* WordSmith Tools; *turn counts from* Microsoft Word [TM] 2007*)*

Title	Number of words	Number of turns	Average number of words per turn
Absurd Person Singular: A Comedy	6563	665	9.9
Educating Rita: A Comedy	9197	595	15.5
The Real Thing: A Comedy in Two Acts	8651	725	11.9
Noises off: A Play in Three Acts	7120	853	8.3
Run for Your Wife: A New Comedy	6659	1004	6.6
	38190 (*total*)	3842 (*total*)	10.4 (*overall mean*)

forms. We applied the spelling variant detecting software *VARD2* (version 2.1.5) to our early modern data. *VARD2* was developed at UCREL[4] (see Archer *et al.* 2003: 26) and continues to be tested and improved (see Rayson *et al.* 2005, 2007; Baron and Rayson 2008). *VARD2* regularises early modern spellings by applying a set of disambiguating rules, including the comparison of spellings with an extended dictionary. The user can choose the level of confidence with which *VARD2* regularises spellings: at higher levels, the programme requires more evidence from the disambiguating rules in order to change the spelling. We used the default threshold of fifty per cent, which requires evidence from the dictionary plus one of two other sources in order to replace a spelling variant.

4. Turn length compared

Table 12.3 and table 12.4 display the average number of words per turn in our present-day and early modern plays.[5] We had hypothesised in section 2 that early modern plays would have longer turns on average compared with present-day plays, on account of the practicalities of deconstructing the written manuscript into parts: rapid turn-taking, involving short turns, would have required much more cutting and pasting. Moreover, even if the manuscript was not literally cut up and pasted together for an actor but instead written out, that still would involve the addition of cues. If the speech length, i.e. the turn length, begins to get close to the cue length, the result could be confusion. This hypothesis is clearly supported by our results. The

---

[4] UCREL: the University Centre for Computer Corpus Research on Language, Lancaster. See www.comp.lancs.ac.uk/ucrel.
[5] Turns were counted by getting the computer to identify the speaker name preceding each speech. For this task we used the fairly powerful 'find' facility in *Microsoft Word*[TM] 2007, which allows wildcards. We checked at least 25 per cent of the results in every file to ensure accuracy. Turn totals were derived by temporarily conducting a 'replace all' operation; the number of replacements was the number of turns.

Development of play-texts: from manuscript to print   171

Table 12.4 *The early modern plays: number of words, turns and average number of words per turn (word counts from* WordSmith Tools; *turn counts from* Microsoft Word^{TM} *2007)*

Title	Number of words	Number of turns	Average number of words per turn
A Knacke to Knowe a Knaue	9097	138	65.9
The Old Wiues Tale	5870	237	24.8
An Humerous Dayes Myrth	7258	436	16.6
How a Man May Chuse	7778	289	26.9
The Miseries of Inforst Mariage	8002	398	20.1
	38005 (*total*)	1498 (*total*)	30.9 (*overall mean*)

average turn length for early modern plays is almost exactly three times that of present-day plays; even excluding *A Knacke to Knowe a Knaue* (with its very high turn length), the result is still twice as high. Of course, this is not to deny that other factors, apart from the practicalities of the manuscript, may contribute to this result. As we pointed out in section 2, playwrights were less likely to have been thinking in terms of cohesive, quick-fire, naturalistic conversation, but more in terms of fragments: set pieces that might become quoted in other sources. This is not to say that early modern drama was completely devoid of rapid turn-taking. However, if such rapid turn-taking appears, it is a temporary deviation from the norm, and often designed for particular rhetorical effects. A good example is the rhetorical technique of stycomythia, in which single lines or half lines are given to two alternating characters, usually in violent dispute. An excellent example can be found in Act I Scene II of Shakespeare's play *Richard III*, where Richard of Gloucester encounters robust resistance from Lady Anne.

5. Lexical richness compared

Having confirmed in section 4 that there were fewer, longer turns in early modern plays compared to present-day plays, we now investigate our second hypothesis arising from the labour-intensive production process of cutting and pasting speech turns for the distribution of parts to early modern actors. To investigate our expectation in section 2 that early modern drama would have been less cohesive and featured relatively less repetition and recycling of words than present-day drama, we began by obtaining type-token ratios for the play samples in both corpora. These show the relative lexical richness of the plays by calculating the number of unique words (types) in every 1,000 running words (tokens) in the texts (see Scott 1996–2009). Higher type-token ratios indicate greater lexical richness, and therefore lower levels of word repetition. We used standardised type-token ratios because the

Table 12.5 *The present-day plays: number of words and standardised type-token ratios* (*word counts and type-token ratios from* WordSmith Tools)

Title	Number of words	Standardised type-token ratio
Absurd Person Singular: A Comedy	6563	36.8
Educating Rita: A Comedy	9197	36.7
The Real Thing: A Comedy in Two Acts	8651	38.8
Noises off: A Play in Three Acts	7120	33.5
Run for Your Wife: A New Comedy	6659	38.4
	38190 (*total*)	36.9 (*overall mean*)

Table 12.6 *The early modern plays: number of words and standardised type-token ratios* (*word counts and type-token ratios from* WordSmith Tools)

Title	Number of words	Standardised type-token ratio
A Knacke to Knowe a Knaue	9097	40.5
The Old Wiues Tale	5870	42.7
An Humerous Dayes Myrth	7258	37.8
How a Man May Chuse	7778	42.9
The Miseries of Inforst Mariage	8002	43.1
	38005 (*total*)	41.4 (*overall mean*)

play-texts in our corpora vary in length, i.e. the figures are calculated per 1,000 words. The results are shown above in tables 12.5 and 12.6.

As tables 12.5 and 12.6 show, type-token ratios were generally higher in the early modern play-texts, although the type-token ratio of *An Humerous Dayes Myrth* was lower than the others and more similar to those of the present-day play-texts. Though the overall mean type-token ratios of early modern and present-day play-texts do not show a huge numerical difference, a t-test showed that the results were statistically significant (significance probability level 0.011, two-tailed, conducted using *SPSS*). This confirms that our early modern play-texts show greater lexical richness than the present-day ones. We therefore pursued our hypothesis of less lexical repetition/recycling and lower levels of cohesion further, through some qualitative analysis.

All the present-day comedy samples showed evidence of sequences of short turns where characters repeat and echo each other's words. One of many examples is given below. In the examples in this section, we have added turn numbers to the original play-text, and have highlighted the repetitions for clarity and convenience.

Development of play-texts: from manuscript to print 173

(4) 1. HENRY. **It's no good.**
 2. ANNIE. You mean it's not **literary**.
 3. HENRY. It's not **literary**, and **it's no good. He can't write.**
 4. ANNIE. You're **a snob**.
 5. HENRY. I'm **a snob**, and **he can't write.**
 6. ANNIE. I know it's raw, but **he's got something to say.**
 7. HENRY. **He's got something to say.** It happens to be something extremely silly and bigoted. But leaving that aside, there is still the problem that **he can't write.** He can burn things down, but **he can't write.**
 (Tom Stoppard, *The Real Thing*, 1982: 56–7)

In example (4), Henry and Annie, a couple, are in disagreement, and effectively constructing opposing arguments. However, their strategies for doing so involve picking up and borrowing one another's words and phrases, rather than introducing new ones. Turns 1 and 3 are linked through 'it's no good'; turns 2 and 3 through 'literary'; turns 3, 5 and 7 through 'he can't write', repeated twice in turn 7; turns 4 and 5 through 'a snob' and turns 6 and 7 through 'he's got something to say' ('something' is also repeated in turn 7). These links are, in Halliday and Hasan's (1976) terms, reiteration, which strengthens the cohesiveness of the text.

In contrast, the early modern drama shows fewer of these links, with characters introducing more new words and phrases rather than echoing each other's words, as in the following example of a male and a female character, Lemot and Florila, again in some dispute:

(5) 1. *Flo.* Why let vs be gon my kind *Lemot*, and not be wondered at in the open streets.
 2. *Le.* Ile go with you through fire, through death, through hell, come give me your own hand, my own dear heart, this hand that I adore and reverence, and loath to have it, touch an old man's bosom, O let me sweetly kiss it; [*he bites*]
 3. *Flo.* Out on thee wretch, he hath **bit** me to the bone, O barbarous Canibal, now I perceive thou wilt make me a mocking stock to all the world.
 4. *Le.* Come, come, leave your passions, they cannot mooue me, my father and my mother died both in a day, and I rung me a peal for them, and they were no sooner brought to the church and laid in their graves, but I fetched me two or three fine capers aloft, and took my leave of them, as men do of their mistresses at the ending of a galliard; *Besilos manus*
 5. *Flo.* O brutish nature, how accursed was I ever to endure the sound of this damned voice?

6. *Le.* Well, and you do not like my humour, I can be but sorry for it, I **bit** you for good will, and if you accept it, so, if no, go.
7. *Flo.* Vilain, thou didst it in contempt of me.
(George Chapman, *An Humerous Dayes Myrth*, 1599, F2r–F2v)

As example (5) shows, within the seven speech turns, the only repeated lexical (content) word linking turns is 'bit', in turns 3 and 6. Otherwise, the two characters make their points using fresh sets of words and phrases, introducing more variety but reducing the cohesiveness of the text. Note that the turns are much longer, too, in the early modern example than in the present-day example, as discussed in section 4.

It may well be that the short turns and lexical repetition we observe in the present-day drama are particularly characteristic of comedy, since it was clear from our data that the serial echoing of words and phrases is often exaggerated so as to be amusing. This is demonstrated in example (6) below.

(6) 1. MRS. CLACKETT. What's he **saying**?
2. FLAVIA. He's **saying** . . . ring the police!
3. ROGER. **Ring the police?**
4. OMNES. **Ring the police!**
   ROGER picks up the receiver, finds the body of the phone missing, and hands the receiver to LLOYD.
5. ROGER. It's for you. LLOYD puts the receiver to his ear and tries to dial.
6. FLAVIA. No **phone**?
7. MRS. CLACKETT. To TIM: **Fetch a phone**!
8. TIM. **Fetch a phone**? Exit TIM through the front door.
9. FLAVIA. Here's the **phone**!
10. ROGER. We've found the **phone**! LLOYD puts the receiver back on top of the phone. At once it rings.
11. FLAVIA. **Pick it up!**
12. LLOYD. faintly **Pick it up?**
13. OMNES. **Pick it up!**
14. FLAVIA. picks it up It's **the police**! I'll tell them **we're just missing a young woman!**
15. ROGER. Yes! **We're just missing a young woman!**
(Michael Frayn, *Noises off*, 1982: 169–70)

Several series of echoes, i.e. repeated words and phrases, are clear in the above sequence of fifteen turns; indeed, all except turn number 5 contain a word or phrase which is repeated. It goes beyond strengthening the cohesiveness of the text to adding a farcical quality to the proceedings on stage. Quick-fire, sequential repetition as a comic strategy is perhaps something that only became fashionable in drama at a time when it no longer added to the effort involved in producing and distributing the script. In any event, we can see

Table 12.7 *The present-day plays: number of terms of address, turns and average number of terms of address per turn (word counts from* WordSmith Tools; *turn counts from* Microsoft Word^{TM} *2007)*

Title	Number of terms of address	Number of turns	Average number of terms of address per turn
Absurd Person Singular: A Comedy	59	665	0.09
Educating Rita: A Comedy	38	595	0.06
The Real Thing: A Comedy in Two Acts	53	725	0.07
Noises off: A Play in Three Acts	130	853	0.15
Run for Your Wife: A New Comedy	138	1004	0.14
	418 (*total*)	3842 (*total*)	0.11 (*overall mean*)

Table 12.8 *The early modern plays: number of terms of address, turns and average number of terms of address per turn (word counts from* WordSmith Tools; *turn counts from* Microsoft Word ^{TM} *2007)*

Title	Number of terms of address	Number of turns	Average number of terms of address per turn
A Knacke to Knowe a Knaue	224	138	1.62
The Old Wiues Tale	145	237	0.61
An Humerous Dayes Myrth	207	436	0.47
How a Man May Chuse	128	289	0.44
The Miseries of Inforst Mariage	132	398	0.33
	836 (*total*)	1498 (*total*)	0.56 (*overall mean*)

from example (6) how quickly and easily repetitions accumulate in parts of present-day comedy, helping to account for the lower levels of lexical variety seen in the present-day type-token ratios in table 12.5.

6. Terms of address compared

We manually inserted a tag of one symbol not otherwise used in the texts, a forward slash (/), immediately before each term of address in the plays in both corpora. Using the *WordSmith Tools* Concord function we could then isolate all the terms of address in our corpora simply by conducting an automated search for anything immediately preceded by /.

Table 12.7 and table 12.8 display the numbers of terms of address, turns, and average number of terms of address per turn in our present-day and early modern plays.

As can be seen from tables 12.7 and 12.8, there are exactly twice the number of terms of address in the early modern plays as in the present-day plays: in total, 836 and 418, respectively. Given that the number of terms of address may be influenced by the number of turns in the data, we calculated the average number of terms of address per turn. For present-day plays, about one in ten turns contains a term of address; for early modern plays, on average every second turn contains a term of address. This clearly supports our hypothesis that early modern plays feature a greater number of terms of address compared with present-day plays. This is not surprising, as the systems of terms of address differ between the two historical periods we are looking at: the early modern period relied on terms of address to express deference much more than is the case today. Nevertheless, for the early modern actor the cohesiveness of both the turn-taking system, e.g. who was talking to whom, and the social system, e.g. in what capacities characters spoke and received talk, hangs upon the system of terms of address that was available at the time. In effect, terms of address acted as implicit cues within the speeches of the actors' parts, giving them information about how to orientate the speeches when the play came together as a whole in performance. Example (7) shows how this works. Moreover, here we have comparatively short turns and more than two participants in the dialogue; consequently, the need to orientate the actors is greater.

(7) *Eum.* Thanks **my fine eloquent hostess**.
Iack. But hear **you master**, one word by
the way, are you content I shall be halfes in all
you get in your iourney?
Eum. I am *Iack*, here is my hand.
Iack. Enough **master**, I ask no more.
Eum. Come **Hostess** receive your money,
and I thank you for my good entertainment.
Host: You are heartily welcome **sir**.
Eum. Come *Iack* whether go we now?
Iack. Mary **master** to the coniurers presently.
Eum. Content **Iack**: **Hostis** farewell.
(George Peele, *The Old Wiues Tale*, 1595, E3v; emphasis added)

7. Conclusion

In this chapter we have argued that the evolution of plays from manuscript to print may have had an impact on the language of the plays. In particular, early modern plays were not the unified wholes that plays are now, in the sense that (a) playwrights were likely to have been more focused on 'set pieces' and individual character/actor parts, and (b) plays were literally fragmented into parts for distribution to the actors, only coming together in performance. We hypothesised three ways in which the impact of this would be manifested in the language of early modern plays compared with those from the present day:

Development of play-texts: from manuscript to print

(i) Early modern plays have longer turns on average compared with present-day plays, because longer turns would have minimised the amount of cutting and pasting of speech turns when preparing an actor's part, and also maintained a visual distinction between the speech itself and the short preceding cue.

(ii) Early modern plays have higher levels of lexical richness, since they were more like a stack of speeches working relatively independently towards a particular end than an interlocking, overlapping discourse.

(iii) Early modern plays contain a greater number of terms of address compared with present-day plays, and these would have usefully provided implicit cues to actors learning their parts in isolation about the discourse and social relations between characters, which would be needed to unify the play in performance.

In sections 4, 5 and 6, we tested these three hypotheses quantitatively and qualitatively. Quantitatively, we found supporting evidence for all three. However, other factors may well have played a role in shaping the language of plays and, consequently, our findings. Nevertheless, our qualitative examples and analyses support the idea that there is a causal link, at least in part, between the different media (manuscript and print) and the different linguistic characteristics we observed.

Our study has merely scratched the surface of what might be an issue of considerable importance. It is surprising that the constraints and practices of early modern play script production are so woefully neglected not only in historical studies but also in texts on the stylistics of drama (e.g. Herman 1995; Culpeper *et al.* 1998). As a result, a full understanding of the linguistic characteristics of the plays cannot be achieved.

Needless to say, there are other ways in which the medium of the plays would probably have affected their language, including, as we mentioned, that the cut-up manuscript also reduced the potential for representing simultaneous talk and interruptions; compare the elaborate transcription notation system of the present-day playwright Caryl Churchill. Such effects would be worth investigating. Furthermore, we have considered only comedy plays here; our results could usefully be compared with those from a wider range of genres.

13 Communicating Galen's *Methodus medendi* in Middle and Early Modern English

PÄIVI PAHTA, TURO HILTUNEN,
VILLE MARTTILA, MAURA RATIA,
CARLA SUHR AND JUKKA TYRKKÖ

1. Introduction

This chapter examines three early English versions of an ancient medical text by Galen of Pergamon (*c.* 129–216), the ultimate authority on Western medicine well into the modern era.[1] The three texts, dating from three different centuries, give a unique insight into how Galen's canonical knowledge was communicated in English during the medieval and Renaissance periods. The text in focus is *Methodus medendi*, the *Method of Healing*, a long and substantial work on therapeutics, consisting of fourteen books (edited by Kühn 1825). As Galen's chief therapeutic manual, offering 'the most sustained account of [his] attitude towards medical theory and practice' (Nutton 1991: 1), *Methodus medendi* is remarkable in the history of medicine, discussing a wide range of diseases and providing philosophical arguments and presuppositions that in the author's view should govern the doctor's therapeutic activities. The original target audience was medical professionals of the most advanced level; the work demanded a comprehensive knowledge of medical terminology and ideas as an essential preliminary and, possibly, clinical experience (Nutton 1991: 5). The text remained important among learned physicians across centuries. It was used in teaching therapeutics in medieval and early modern universities (Bylebyl 1991; McVaugh 2006); the last books, in particular, were used in surgical education long after the sixteenth century (Nutton, personal communication).

The three English versions of *Methodus medendi* date from a transition period characterised by large-scale sociocultural changes affecting the domain of medicine. The scientific paradigm was experiencing a major epistemological shift, with medieval scholastic, logocentric science heavily dependent on ancient texts giving way to a new scientific thought-style relying

---

[1] Many thanks to Vivian Nutton for sharing his knowledge of Galen's life and works with us and for helpful comments on the article. The research reported here was supported in part by the Research Unit for Variation, Contacts and Change in English, funded by the Academy of Finland and the University of Helsinki.

more on empirical methods and explanatory principles based on observation and cognition (see Crombie 1994; Taavitsainen and Pahta 1995). The domain of science and medicine was also undergoing a process of vernacularisation whereby English emerged in medical writing from the shadow of Latin, first in texts used in non-institutional contexts, and gradually replacing it as the language of institutional medical science (see e.g. Voigts 1989; Pahta and Taavitsainen 2004). At the same time, communication technology was revolutionised by the advent of printing, with the printed book replacing the manuscript as the main vehicle in the dissemination of knowledge (see e.g. McKitterick 2003).

The earliest English version of the text dates from the early phases of this transition period. The text survives in a single fifteenth-century manuscript copy, British Library, Sloane 6, dating from the heyday of scholasticism and the first phases in the vernacularisation of learned medicine (see Getz 1991). The second English text, a printed version by Thomas Gale, published in 1566, dates from a time when Galen's texts were rediscovered in the original Greek. New, accurate translations of Galen were made available in Latin and used in university teaching, while vernacular medical texts were in general becoming increasingly common among contemporary reading audiences and non-Latinate practitioners (see e.g. Slack 1979; Wear 2000). The third vernacular version is a printed text by Peter English, published in 1656. It represents a period when Galen's ancient medical theory was criticised and eventually challenged in its entirety, empirical methods were gaining ground, and the English language was already replacing Latin in the communication of original scientific discoveries (see e.g. Wear 1995; Taavitsainen *et al.* in press).

As the texts go back to different intervening versions of Galen's Greek text that have not been conclusively identified, they will be studied here as parallel versions of the same text rather than translations. Each version presents an opportunity for examining the linguistic and textual choices adopted in the communication of Galen's medical knowledge to English audiences of its time. In a comparative frame, the texts provide evidence of diachronic changes in English medical communication. The study illustrates some of the salient diachronic trends by comparing a set of linguistic and textual features observed in the three versions. For a broader perspective, the phenomena are also examined in relation to more general trends observed in contemporary medical language, with the corpora of *Middle English Medical Texts* (MEMT) and *Early Modern English Medical Texts* (EMEMT) as reference material.[2] The features selected for scrutiny are text structure, the use of reporting verbs and special terminology. Through the analysis and comparison of these features in Book 3 of *Methodus medendi*, discussing ulcers, the study

---

[2] For MEMT and EMEMT, see e.g. Taavitsainen *et al.* (2006), Taavitsainen *et al.* (in press) or www.helsinki.fi/varieng/CoRD/index.html.

illuminates the communication of ancient medical knowledge in Middle and Early Modern English and changes taking place in it in relation to changing sociocultural and domain-specific contexts of communication over time.

2. Textual tradition and the three English versions of Galen's *Methodus medendi*

The transmission of Galen's *Methodus medendi* into medieval Europe is complicated. The Greek text was first translated into Middle-Eastern languages, including Arabic, and later into Latin (Nutton 1991: 1; Weisser 1991). The Latin manuscript tradition of the work has not been extensively studied, but it is known to survive in a multitude of copies, representing at least three different Latin versions. The earliest one is an eleventh-century paraphrase from Arabic by Constantinus Africanus (d. 1087), known as *Megategni*. A second translation from Arabic, *De ingenio sanitatis*, was made in the twelfth century by Gerard of Cremona (d. 1187). A third translation, *Therapeutica*, consists of Books 7–14 translated directly from Greek in the twelfth century by Burgundio of Pisa (c. 1110–93) and Books 1–6, also from Greek, by Niccolò da Reggio in the early fourteenth century (Kibre 1991; McVaugh 2002, 2006).

The first complete translation directly from Greek into Latin was made in the early sixteenth century by Thomas Linacre (c. 1460–1524), the founder and first president of the Royal College of Physicians. Linacre's translation was printed in 1519; the several successive reprints made it widely accessible in Renaissance Europe and gave it an authoritative status (Durling 1977: 85–9).

The three English texts analysed in this study are ultimately versions of the same source text, but their textual histories vary from one another a great deal. The texts were translated in different centuries from different source versions with different intervening transmission histories and under different sociocultural settings, reflected in the language of each version. As the earliest version is a part of a manuscript while the two later ones come from printed books, it is necessary to examine the production context of each version individually before the texts can be meaningfully compared to each other.

2.1 British Library, MS Sloane 6

The unique manuscript copy of the Middle English translation of *Methodus medendi* is contained on ff. 183v–203v of British Library, MS Sloane 6, a sizeable paper volume of 203 folios.[3] The text contains only a fragment

---

[3] A faithful diplomatic transcription of this unedited manuscript text was produced by Ville Marttila, Päivi Pahta and Carla Suhr for this study. The orthography and word division follow the manuscript, with scribal additions and corrections incorporated into the text and abbreviations expanded.

of Galen's original work, comprising Book 3 and the first three and a half chapters of Book 4, focusing on the nature and treatment of ulcers. The choice of this section of Galen's work for inclusion in Sloane 6 is in line with the general character of the codex, which is a surgical compendium, composed of booklets copied by different scribes and compiled into a single volume in the fifteenth century (Getz 1991: 156). Most texts are translations from Latin. In addition to the Galen fragment, the manuscript includes translated extracts from several authors of the medieval medical canon and well-known surgeons (see Getz 1991: 154–5; and eVK). In this collection of a wide variety of contemporary knowledge on prognosis and treatment, *Methodus medendi* specifically supplies the theoretical basis of surgical treatment and the healing of wounds.

The Middle English text belongs to the first phase of the gradual process of vernacularisation of learned medicine that began in late medieval Europe (see Voigts 1989; Crossgrove 1998; Pahta and Taavitsainen 2004). In the course of the fourteenth and fifteenth centuries, sophisticated medical treatises, which had previously circulated exclusively in Latin, became available in English for the first time, most of them translated from Latin source texts. In this body of writing, the Galen fragment in Sloane 6 is unique, as it is the first and only substantial medieval translation of Galen's authentic writings into English. The translation dates from *c.* 1400 (Getz 1991: 147). It is apparently based on the twelfth-century Latin translation made from Arabic by Gerard of Cremona; this identification rests on the title of Gerard's version, *De ingenio sanitatis*, occurring in the explicit of Book 3 of the Middle English text (*Here endeth þe þrid boke of galiene de ingenio sanitatis*, f. 198v). The organisation of the subchapters in the English text follows that of the Latin text (Getz 1991).

Nothing is known about the actual production circumstances of the Middle English text, but codicological and paleographical evidence indicates that it was intended as a workaday copy, possibly a surgeon's handbook, not a display object. The text is written in a Secretary hand using dark brown ink, varying in darkness. The writing space is framed, but the *mise-en-page* is not very carefully executed. There are frequent scribal corrections, some of them on the line in the running text, others interlinear. Interlinear glosses are also frequent, consisting of synonyms of lexical items or rewording of phrases occurring in the text. There are no decorations. At the beginning of chapters, space has been left for large initials, indicated in the margin, but these have not been added. There are only few annotations in the margins.

2.2 *Thomas Gale's* Certaine vvorkes of Galens, called Methodvs medendi *(1566 and 1586)*

The first Renaissance version of *Methodus medendi* was produced by Thomas Gale (*c.* 1507–67), one of the foremost surgeons of the sixteenth century. He was an active member of the Company of Barber-Surgeons after its formation in 1540, and succeeded Thomas Vicary as master of the Company in 1561.

As a surgeon, Gale received his training in apprenticeship rather than at a university, and although he himself was literate in Latin, he was acutely aware that this was not the case within the profession at large. This shows in his preface to *Methodus medendi*, defining the target audience as 'Prentises and young men, which haue not beene trained vp in schooles, neither yet can vnderstand the Greeke or Latine tongue' (Gale 1586: A3v). Lack of Latin literacy effectively precluded most surgeons from reading the highest strata of medical literature, a fact that contributed to the widely held view of surgeons as second-class medicos with skills gained through experience and practice but without true scientific understanding (see Furdell 2002: 20). Gale shared this concern: 'MY friendlie and welbeloued brethren, when I did consider with my selfe the great defect and imbecilitie which doth remain amongst our Companie, for lacke of learning in the speculatiue part, of this worthie art of Chirurgerie, which chieflie doth appertaine vnto the same' (1586: 39v). Although Gale advocated vernacularisation of medicine, his concern was to promote the dissemination of knowledge only among proper students of surgery and not to disclose the secrets of the art more widely (Furdell 2002: 83). Gale's intended audience can thus be defined quite precisely as non-Latinate students of surgery and 'physick'. As Wear (2000: 220) points out, Gale's rhetoric is typical for a contemporary surgical reformer, arguing heavily against charlatans and empirics at least partly in a deliberate effort to ingratiate the surgical profession with university medicine. Along with several other leading surgeons, Gale took action to remedy the poor availability of surgical works in English (Payne 2002: 71). His surgical masterpiece, *Certaine workes of chirurgerie*, was published in 1563, along with a separate treatise on gunshot wounds. In the next four years, Gale translated two works by Galen and initiated work on several other books that were never published due to his untimely death (ODNB, s.v. Thomas Gale).

Certaine vvorkes of Galens, called Methodus medendi was completed in 1566 and printed in quarto by Thomas East. It was sold bound with texts by contemporary surgeons François Valleriola and Jean Tagault. Although Gale is usually accredited as the translator, Furdell (2002: 20) suggests that Gale rather 'sponsored the translation of Galen's *Methodus medendi* into English'. Gale himself notes in the prefatory address that 'I with the help of my friends have set forth these bokes in English' (A¹5v). Regardless of who the translator was, the source text for the translation was most probably Thomas Linacre's groundbreaking Latin translation published in 1519.[4] A second edition of *Certaine vvorkes of Galens* was printed in 1586, also by East, without the

---

[4] Gale makes a direct reference to Linacre's translation in the 'Office of a Chirurgion', a prefatory text to the collection *Certaine workes of Galens* (p. 11).

accompanying texts. Both the prefatory sections and the translations appear identical to the first edition.

2.3   Galen's Method of Physick *by Peter English (1656)*

The 1656 *Method of Physick* was compiled from an unknown source text by Peter English and printed in Edinburgh by A. A. [Andrew Anderson] for the stationers George Suinton and James Glen. A duodecimo of 344 pages, this version was the last early modern vernacular edition of Galen. Peter English, possibly a pseudonym, is styled on the front page as a 'st[udent] of physick'. Although many contemporary medical works are written by authors styled as students – most notably perhaps the famous Nicholas Culpeper, another translator and editor of Galen's works – such a title clearly identifies the writer as someone without the full credentials of a university-trained physician.

Although recognisable as deriving from *Methodus medendi*, the text is much more extensively edited than Sloane 6 or Gale (see section 3). The extent to which it differs from the two earlier versions, and from Galen's text, begs the question whether the term 'translation' can reasonably be applied to it at all.[5] English's intention seems to have been to take the essence of Galenic knowledge and transmit it, appended with his own views, to readers on lower rungs of the profession. In doing this, English treats Galen at once reverently and critically. While respectful of Galen, he does not shy away from omitting significant parts of Galen's argumentation, such as references to Galen's contemporaries and to complicated methodological discussions. In their stead, he adds 'succinct and plain' commentary sections between the books for further discussion of Galenic theory. Thus, for example, in the commentary to Book 1, English writes: 'Yet give me leave to say the Author [Galen] is a little mistaken in calling mortall and immortall, rationall and irrationall, meek and fierce, proper differences of a living creature: for it is known among Philosophs, that some of them are very common and accidentall' (p. 15). Comments like this, not least by someone identifying himself as a student, are a striking reflection of the changing landscape of medicine and academic writing (see French 2003: 196).

3. Analysis

Although the specific source texts of the vernacular versions are not known, all three unambiguously derive from Galen's *Methodus medendi*. Using Book 3 from each text and treating them as parallel versions, this section presents a micro-level analysis of how the same underlying text was communicated to English readers over a period of some two hundred years. First, the structural

---

[5] The electronic English Short Title Catalogue gives Galen and not English as the author of the *Method of Physick*.

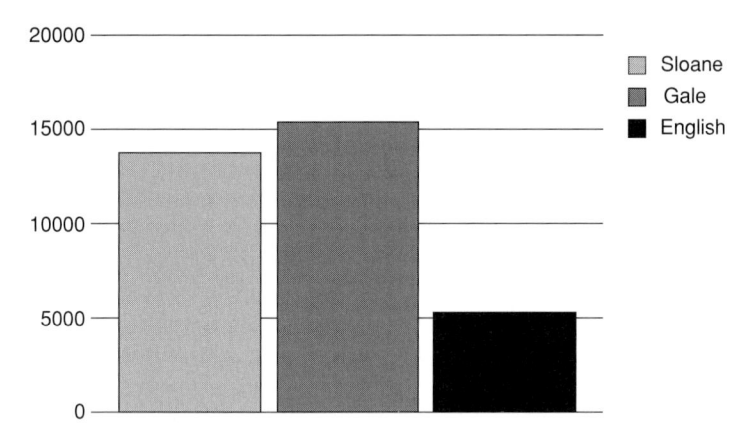

Figure 13.1 Total word counts of the three English versions of *Methodus medendi*, Book 3

composition of the sample will be examined by quantitative means. Then, reporting verbs are used as an example of change in discoursive style and, finally, medical terminology will be examined in some detail as an example of domain-specific developments.

3.1 Text structure

The simplest quantitative measure for comparing the textual structure of parallel texts is the word count. Although a comprehensive definition of what constitutes a 'word' in the text-analytical sense is not easy to achieve – particularly when it comes to medieval palaeography – sufficient uniformity can be achieved for analytical purposes. In printed texts, a word was defined as a distinct orthographic unit, while with Sloane 6 the editing process produced a transcript with distinct word units (see footnote 3).

A comparison of word counts of Book 3 shows that while Sloane 6 and Gale are similar in length, the version by English is considerably shorter (see figure 13.1). It is noteworthy that the authors of the two older versions would, despite going back to different intervening source texts, produce texts of practically the same length, especially since Gale is unlikely to have had access to the Middle English version.

The length of Book 3 in the 1558 edition of Thomas Linacre's Latin translation is around 12,000 words,[6] i.e. closer to the word count of Sloane 6 and Gale than English. This suggests that while the two earlier versions follow the original text more or less faithfully, English has a much more liberal attitude to the transmission of Galen's knowledge. At a total length of

---

[6] The word count quoted here was extrapolated from the first full page; although approximate, the figure is likely to be fairly reliable thanks to the tight and consistent layout of the Linacre edition.

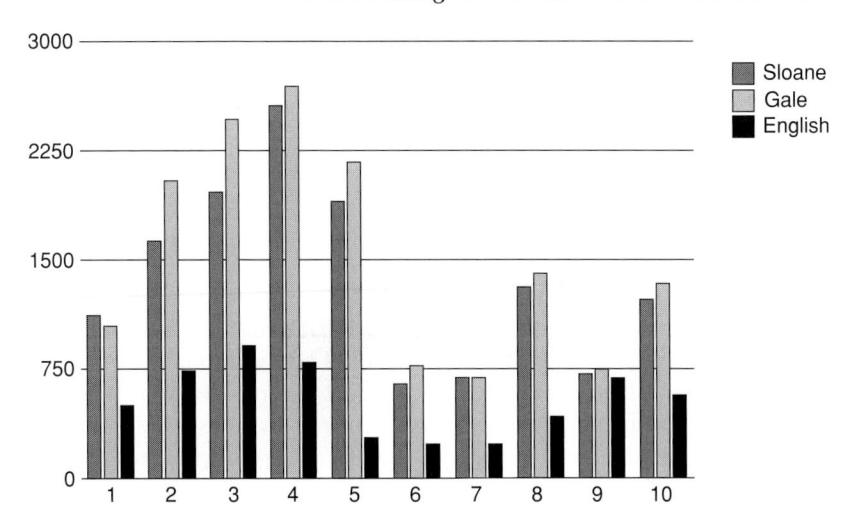

Figure 13.2 Word counts for the ten chapter equivalents in the three English versions of *Methodus medendi*, Book 3

only a third of Sloane 6 or Gale, English's version is much more dense than the previous two and omits significant amounts of content. It must be noted, however, that the word count for English does not include the commentary of approximately 1,500 words, which covers some of the content that the earlier texts include in the main body of the book.

Examining text structure beyond the overall word count requires that the texts first be aligned. The original division of Book 3 into ten chapters, observed in Sloane 6 and Gale, could be used as a rough guideline here, but because English does not divide the book into distinct chapters the only option is to analyse the texts down to the sentence level and then perform the aligning. Gale's and English's versions are predictably straightforward in this regard, as both exhibit standardised punctuation in marking sentence breaks overtly. Sloane 6, on the other hand, is far more complicated. Although many sentences in the manuscript begin with a *littera notabilior*, not all do, and so instead of formally marked sentences one has to rely on what might be called 'sentence equivalents', that is, word sequences that could reasonably be considered as corresponding with ideational sentence breaks. These were identified by a combination of orthographic clues, where available, by overt devices of grammatical cohesion, such as sentence initial conjunctive adverbs, and by close comparative reading with the two parallel texts. Only a few sentences could be aligned exactly between all three texts, although in general the order of presentation remained largely the same from one to another.

After the sentence segmentation and alignment, 'chapter equivalents' in English's version could be identified and the text analysed further. Figure 13.2 gives the word counts of the ten chapters.

While all three texts follow a roughly analogous pattern of chapter-by-chapter word count, the similarity between Sloane 6 and Gale is particularly striking. Here, too, English departs from the pattern. When it comes to the actual content of the versions, the most significant difference is seen in the weight given in each text to issues of language, on the one hand, and to Galen's views on differing schools of medicine and the finer points of theoretical arguments, on the other. This observation is by no means unique to the texts at hand. Nutton (1997: 17) notes that by the end of the sixteenth century the emphasis of Galenic scholarship had shifted away from issues to do with translation and the correct definition of individual terms, and toward 'wider discussion of the medical principles involved'. Thus, while Gale emphasises in the epilogue that his main purpose in producing vernacular translations is to make the 'principles of their Arte, with their true divisions and definitions' (1586: A4r) accessible to monolingual surgeons, English appears to consider much of this irrelevant or uninteresting to his audience, omitting references to ancient schools of thought and theoretical principles, and retaining only the points most pertinent to practical methodology. Conversely, English's commentaries suggest great interest in issues of natural philosophy and concern that these be properly understood.

The number and length of sentences in a text can be used as rough indicators of its complexity (see Hiltunen 2001). The three versions show considerable differences in sentence length. At an average of nearly sixty-eight words per sentence, Gale is the most verbose of the three, with Sloane 6 and English reaching averages of fifty and thirty-six, respectively. All the texts exhibit average sentence lengths in excess of what would be characteristic for written texts today (see e.g. Peters 2002).[7] In the case of Gale and English, contemporary reference data specific to medical writing is available in the corpus of *Early Modern English Medical Texts* (EMEMT).[8] Compared to EMEMT, Gale's sentences are more than twice the average length found in sixteenth-century medical texts. English, on the other hand, produces sentences of exactly the average length for the seventeenth century (see figure 13.3).

Variation in sentence length can be used as an indicator of stylistic consistency. Comparing the average length of each chapter – or, in the case of English, the length of the treatment of the corresponding content – reveals that while Sloane 6 and Gale show considerable variation, English consistently holds to almost exactly the same average length (see figure 13.4).

The difference between English and the two earlier texts can be understood in light of the developing standards of academic writing. Unlike Gale, a

---

[7] The standard figure to quote is twenty-two words per sentence, given by Francis and Kučera (1992: 552), based on the *Brown Corpus*.

[8] For this approximation, only full-length samples from three out of six EMEMT categories were used, i.e. the 'comprehensive treatises', 'specialized treatises' and 'surgical texts'. Sentence length was determined by punctuation, ignoring abbreviations and ordinal numbers.

Communicating Galen's *Methodus medendi* 187

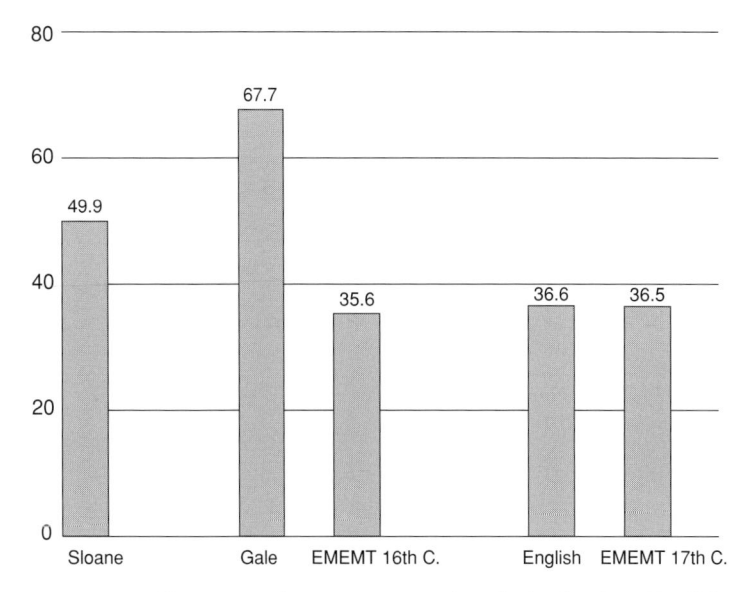

Figure 13.3 Average sentence lengths in the three English versions of *Methodus medendi*, Book 3, and reference corpora

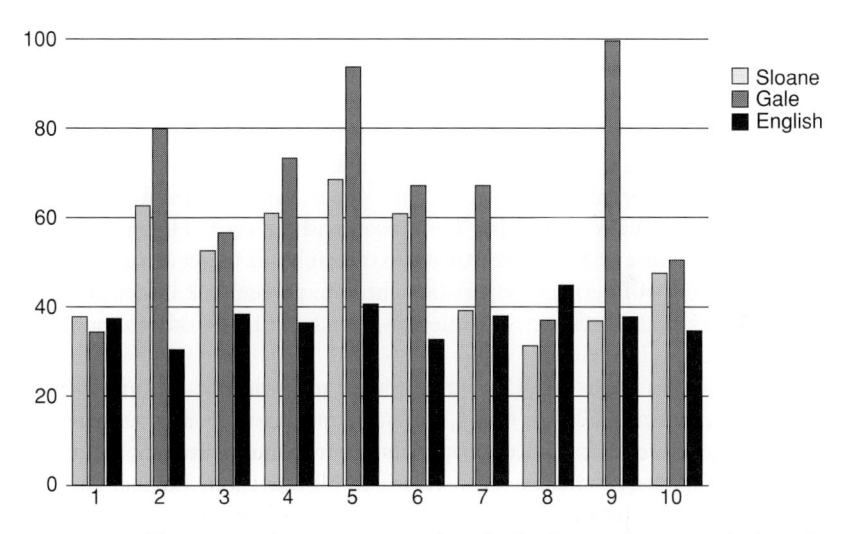

Figure 13.4 Average sentence lengths for the ten chapter equivalents in the three English versions of *Methodus medendi*, Book 3

front-runner in vernacular writing with fewer earlier models to follow, English, a 'st[udent] of physick', could and probably did copy an established style. The stylometric parameters can thus be taken to support the hypothesis that the communicative choices in the three versions were

Table 13.1 *The most common reporting verbs in the three English versions of* Methodus medendi, *Book 3 (spellings standardised)*

Sloane 6 (207 tokens)	Gale (153 tokens)	English (6 tokens)
say (119)	speak (35)	speak (3)
show (25)	say (26)	say (1)
dispute (10)	show (13)	plead (1)
deem (8)	declare (11)	profess (1)
treat (7)	write (6)	
write (5)	affirm (5)	
	answer (5)	
	teach (5)	

influenced not only by a desire to transmit Galenic knowledge faithfully, but also by changes in the target audience and the style of scientific writing.

3.2 Use of reporting verbs

Reporting verbs (RVs) are understood here broadly as speech-act verbs or verbs of communication that are used to report speech, thought and attitudes. Writers may use such verbs either to make a claim of their own or to make an explicit reference to another text. In the former situation, the source of the proposition is the writer, whereas in the latter the proposition is attributed to someone else. The use of RVs is intricately linked to evaluation and the expression of stance, and thus, by manipulating the RV, the writer may express different levels of certainty about, and commitment to, the proposition (see Valle 1999; also Thompson and Ye 1991; Hunston 2000). Comparing the use of RVs in the three texts enables us to get an insight into how the authors of vernacular versions chose to present the information of Galen's work to their respective audiences, which in turn is indicative of how they assessed its information value.

Differences in the use of RVs between the three versions are summarised in table 13.1. First, Sloane 6 has the most instances of RVs and Gale's translation has somewhat fewer. English's version differs markedly from the other two, containing merely six instances of RVs; this reflects the fact that Galen's views on various schools of medicine have been omitted from this version (see section 3.1). Second, Sloane 6 shows a strong preference for the verb *say*, while there is more variation in the choice of RV in Gale's translation.

Almost half of the RVs in Sloane 6 (48%) and in Gale (43%) have a first-person subject. Of these, the first-person singular *I* is more frequent in Sloane 6 than in Gale, which is partially explained by the frequent usage of *therefore I say* in Sloane 6 for emphasis. Meanwhile, the frequency of first-person plural pronouns is higher in Gale's version, partly as a result of the frequent use of the so-called 'authorial we' (see Wales 1996: 65).

RVs with a second-person pronoun as subject are very infrequent in all three versions. The few instances are found in a short passage at the beginning of the second chapter containing a hypothetical dialogue between Galen and Thessalus of Tralles, an adherent of the Methodic school of medicine; in Gale's version, Thessalus has been replaced by his follower, possibly in an attempt to update the text. In the dialogue, Galen invites his opponent to explain the Methodic approach by answering his questions, only to show the flaws in it. This dialogue has been omitted altogether from the version by English.

By contrast, RVs are often used following a subject that is either a third-person pronoun or a noun phrase denoting a person other than the writer of the text, or a group of people that does not include the writer of the text. The latter type is almost without exception a school of medicine, such as the Methodic or Empiric school, with whom Galen was at odds. The opinions of these schools are alluded to so that they can be dismissed as misguided, thus receiving the same treatment as the hypothetical dialogue. These instances of RVs therefore serve a definite purpose in the text: the assertions made in the text are conveniently construed as responses to claims attributed to these schools of medicine.

RVs of this kind are somewhat more frequent in Sloane 6 than in Gale's translation, but Gale's version makes use of a larger variety of RVs (Sloane 6 employs twenty-two and Gale thirty-two different verbs). It seems, thus, that in Gale's translation more attention is paid to how the claim that is being reported is phrased in terms of its truth value.

In example (1a), the Sloane translator uses the verb *say* to report a statement by a follower of the Methodic school regarding the better efficacy of treatment when the physician visits the patient rather than when he prescribes medicines blindly. In the corresponding passage from Gale's version (1b), the same statement is introduced with the non-entailing factive verb *confess*, which already implies the erroneousness of the Methodic claim of one common cure working for all patients regardless of age, sex or individual humoural makeup. Note also that the claim is attributed to the Methodic school in Sloane 6 and to the Empiric school in Gale's version.

(1a) Methoycenes also. þair studie yputte in knowyng of custome *saiþ* þat leche knoweþ bettre þe medicynes of þat sekeman. which he haþe ofte sene. þat he þat biheld hym neuer (Sloane f. 194r, emphasis added in italics in all examples)

(1b) Those with the rest, the Empericks receiue, and also do *confesse*, that the Phisition which visiteth the pacient, shall better cure him, than he who hath not seene the sicke. (Gale 1586: 55r)

There is only one passage where all three versions use the RV in a parallel manner. This passage is interesting, as it also shows how different RVs are used to give an account of the same content. Sloane 6 has two instances of the verb *say* (see example (2a)), whereas the other two versions both use verbs that are more argumentative. The first instance of *say* corresponds to the verb *contend* in Gale's translation (2b) and *plead* in English's (2c), and the second has been replaced with *affirm* in (2b), but in (2c) the reporting verb has been left out altogether.

(2a) Metoycenes forsoþe *seiþ* þat all þings ar to be treted with experimente or experience We forsoþe *sey*. þat som þings bene knowen with experiment. and som þings with reson ffor why all þings ar nower knowen ne perceyued with experience al one ne with reson all one. (Sloane f. 183r)

(2b) And the Emperikes do boldlie *contend*, that all things are to be found out by experience, but we trulie doe *affirme*, that they are found out partlie by experience, and partlie by reason, seeing that neither experience onelie, neither yet reason, can finde out all thinges. (Gale 1586: 42r)

(2c) Empyricks do *plead* that all things may be found out by experience: But we partly by experience and partly by reason, seeing neither experience only nor reason only can find out all things. (English 1656: 36)

As a rule, it is difficult to determine the precise rhetorical function of passages that refer to the claims of others without providing any more documentation on the source text. However, the frequent substitution of the neutral verb *say* with more evaluative verbs in later versions seems to suggest a growing awareness of the potential rhetorical impact of formulating citations to other texts in a particular way.

3.3 Specialised terminology

The translation of Latin learned medicine into English also entailed the establishment of specialised professional English vocabulary (see McConchie 1997; Norri 2004). In this light, it is interesting to examine the choices made in the vernacular versions for rendering some key medical concepts into English. Since Book 3 deals with the treatment of wounds, the terms used to describe wounds and the methods for curing them fall into focus. Table 13.2 summarises the terms used in the three texts for various aspects, complications and issues connected with wounds and other injuries of the flesh.

There seems to be an arching movement in the types of wound terms used in the three texts. Sloane 6 uses a large proportion and variety of native words of Germanic origin (e.g. *wound, brekyng, brissyng, crampe, ake*), but also some direct classical loans (*aposteme, erisipilla, sclirosis*), reflecting the inchoate

Table 13.2 *Summary of terms used for describing and characterising wounds in the three English versions of* Methodus medendi, *Book 3*

Type of injury	Sloane 6	Gale	English
Wound	cuttyng, fychynge, wound	wound, vlcer *exulcerate*	wound, vlcer, vulneration, *exulcerated*
Infection in wound	aposteme, ille humour, putrefaccion/ putrefiyng, gnawyng, rotynnes / rotyngnes, ruste, erisipilla, corrupcion *bolned, cancrous, erisipilarous, filthi, putred, roten*	cachochimia, corrosion, corruption, erisipelas, filthinesse, gangrena/gangrene, inflamation, intemperatenesse, putrefaction, rumes, *cancerous, corrosiue, deuouring, filthy, infected, rotten, stinking*	defluctions, distemper, Gangrene, moisture, rot, inflammation, Phlegmon, putrefaction, Rose, sickned, *corrhoding, corrupt, filthy, inflaming, naughty, stinking*
Hardened wound	sclirosis, (hardeneþ þe lippes)	oxthothe, swollen lips	
Fracture	brekyng(e)	catagma, fracture	fracture
Sprain	brissyng	regma, ruption	rupture
Tear in tendon		conuulsion, spasma,	convulsion
Dislocation	separacion	luxation, *dislocated*	Luxation
Loss of unity	dissolucion, disseueryng or separacion of ivnyng, lowsyng, separacion(e) of þe innyng or iuncture, *cutted/ycutte, tuynned*	diuision, solution of continuitie, solution of vnitie, *diuided*	dissolution of unity, *clefted, disunited, gaped, loosed*
Loss of flesh	loste, parted fro the body, taken away	lost, perished	*corrupted*
Cramp	crampe, spasme	conuulsion	convulsion
Pain	ake, akyng	dolour, pain(e), *tormenting*	hurt, pain
Superfluous flesh	ouermyche flesch, superflue flesche	hyposarcosin, supercrescent flesh, superfluous fleshe	excrescency of flesh, *sticking out*

Note: All terms in Table 13.2 have been converted into the singular. Adjective forms used together with some generic noun (part, flesh, wound, etc.) to describe the specific type of wound are given separately in italics.

state of professionalisation and the less systematic translation strategies preceding the sixteenth century 'style wars'. Gale, on the other hand, prefers Latinate terms, both old medieval ones (e.g. *vlcer, ruption, paine/dolour*) and sixteenth-century neologisms (e.g. *luxation, fracture, conuulsion, gangrene*) instead of their native alternatives. In addition, he frequently uses Greek terms in describing wounds or their symptoms (e.g. *cachochimia, catagma, regma, spasma, oxthothe, hyposarcosin*), but almost as often explains them in

English. This tendency reflects Gale's educational aspirations (section 2.2), as introducing and explaining classical terminology to readers was a common way of educating them in the language of learned medicine (Wear 2000: 84). English uses largely the same Latinate terms as Gale (e.g. *vlcer*, *rupture*, *pain*, *luxation*, *fracture*, *convulsion*, *gangrene*), but no Greek, which might require glossing.

Gale is aware of the difficulties in translating and creating terminology, a fact that is not in accordance with later commentators accusing him of being an inept translator (ODNB, s.v. Thomas Gale):

> There is also another thing to be noted, that Galen doth not make such diuisions betwixt *wounds* and *vlcers*, as wee commonlie doe, for hee doth name all those that commeth with solution, or separation of the skinne. elkos in Greeke, that is to saie, an *vlcer*. (Gale 1586: Epistle to the Reader, f. 40r)

Although this distinction between *wound* and *ulcer* is found in other contemporary surgical texts included in the MEMT corpus, Sloane 6 does not apply it but uses *wound* for all references to solution of unity in the skin, qualifying it with adjectives to describe varieties of wounds. Thus Gale's introduction of this distinction can be seen as a way of updating or enhancing Galen's text based on contemporary surgical knowledge. Both the distinction and Gale's formulation of it (1586: 42v–43r) are in line with other contemporary surgical texts, as all sixteenth-century surgical texts included in the EMEMT corpus that mention both wounds and ulcers (six out of fifteen) make a clear distinction between the two.

The tendency to adapt and enhance Galen's text can be seen to indicate an increased sense of liberty with regard to Galen's original, even if his authority is never directly questioned. The contrast to Sloane 6 is, in this regard, especially striking, since the focus of Book 3 on various kinds of hollow wounds, or ulcers, results in the instances of *ulcer* in Gale's version outnumbering those of *wound* with a ratio of more than ten to one.

While English also uses both *wound* and *ulcer* in roughly the same proportion as Gale, there does not seem to be a semantic distinction: *ulcer* is used as the default term for a 'solution of unity' in the skin, often in cases where a simple wound is intended. This loss of distinction between the two terms does not seem to be a unique trait of this text, as it is also seen in some of the seventeenth-century surgical texts included in EMEMT.[9]

In addition to terms denoting wounds, the terms for healing them are equally prominent. One of the most frequent terms of this type in Sloane 6 is the verb *souden*[10] ('to heal by promoting cicatrization or knitting', MED).

[9] Thirteen of the twenty-two seventeenth-century surgical texts in EMEMT use both terms *ulcer* and *wound*, eleven of which make a distinction between them.
[10] Including the variant form *consouden*, which is used synonymously (one instance in Sloane 6, ten instances in MEMT, which are all in Lanfranc's *Chirurgia magna*).

This verb with its derivative participial form *soudyng(e)* seems to have fallen from use in the transition period from Late Middle to Early Modern English, its functions taken over by other terms. A search of MEMT indicates that *souden* was not a common verb even in Late Middle English. It only occurs fifty-five times in the half-a-million-word corpus, including its participial and nominal forms; thirty instances are found in surgical texts (0.11 occurrences per 1,000 words). In contrast, the term is considerably more frequent in Book 3 of the Middle English *Methodus medendi*, where *souden* occurs thirty times, including three participial and two nominal occurrences (2.17 instances per 1,000 words).

Although the verb *souden* itself does not occur in the two later versions, the majority of the occurrences in Sloane 6 (twenty-four) have a parallel expression in Gale and English. The occurrences of *souden/soudynge* in Sloane 6 and their parallel expressions in Gale and English are summarised in table 13.3. Some of the verbs used in these parallel expressions also occur elsewhere in Sloane 6, such as *cicatrise* in its various forms, used instead of *souden* on five occasions in Gale and on two in English. In Sloane 6, *cicatrise* occurs ten times; Gale uses the same verb in all ten corresponding instances and English in six. Interestingly, *cicatrise* seems to have been considered an unfamiliar word by the author of Sloane 6, as on three occasions it has been glossed with the synonymous expression *makyng erres*. As *cicatrise* has not only been retained in the later versions but is also used to replace *souden*, it appears to be one of the terms taking over the functions of *souden*.[11]

The terms *souded* and *soudyng(e)* are also used in Sloane 6 in binomial constructions with their synonyms, including *cicatrise*, as shown in example (3a) below.

(3a) þe flesch of it no3t beyng after þe nature of hym self. on þe same wise it schal no3t mow be *souded* ne *cicatriced*. (Sloane f. 194v)
(3b) ... or **adglutination** to be made, or to **ciccatrize** well, except the fleshe subiect be according to nature, ... (Gale 1586: 56r)
(3c) ... or its **agglutination**, or the **Cicatrization** thereof can be arightly performed unlesse the flesh it self be in a good temper. (English 1656: 50)

Examples (3b) and (3c) indicate that while *cicatrise* is preserved, *souded* is replaced by *(ag)glutination* in both Gale and English (see also section 2 in table 13.3). Interestingly, *(a)glutinative* is also used in both of the later texts for *soudyng(e)* (section 9 in table 13.3); this suggests that each author perceived the term very consistently. This new term, found neither in Sloane 6 nor the MEMT corpus, is in fact the most frequent parallel

---

[11] This does not seem to indicate an increase in the frequency of *cicatrise* on a larger scale, however, since the term remains marginal in both MEMT and EMEMT, with only 0.05 and 0.03 instances per 1,000 words, respectively.

Table 13.3 Souded *and* soudyng(e) *in MS Sloane 6 with parallels in Gale's and English's versions of* Methodus medendi, *Book 3*

	Sloane 6	Gale	English
1	souded	bring it to a cicatrise	the scare may be introduced
	souded	inducing a ciccatrize	–
	souded & heled	cicatrised	–
	souded & helede	cicatrised	maybe brought to ascare
2	souded and cycatrized	adglutinated or cicatrised	–
	schal noȝt mow be souded ne cicatriced	adglutination to be made, or to ciccatrize well	agglutination, or the cicatrization
	souded with	adconglutinated with	
3	make flesch and soude	engendring flesh, and adglutination	glutination and restitution of the flesh
4	souded and ioyned	close	conjoin
	souded	close together	conjoined
	souded	–	enclosing
	souded	close	closed
5	souded	vnition	uniting
	sowded	vnition	uniting
	sowded	made vnion	reuniting
6	souded	grow together	grow up and gather together
	souded	grow together	bound together
7	souded	cured	–
8	soudyng	vnited	–
	soudyng	ioyning & closing	
9	solidatiues or soudynge	Aglutinatiue	glutinative
	solidatiues or sowdyngs	glutinatiues	–
	soudynge	a glutinatiue medicine	aglutinative medicament
10	sowdynge & flesch genderynge	cicatrise [...] incarnate and glutinate	aglutinative medicament [...] cicatrising

for *souded* and *soudyng(e)* in both Gale (nine instances) and English (five). In Gale, there is significant variation in the form of this term, occurring as *(ad)glutinate, adglutinated, adglutination, (a)glutinatiue, conglutinate*, as well as the fusion form *adconglutinated*. This variation could be taken to suggest that Gale is either struggling with terminology or perhaps being hypercorrect. There is less variation in English, who uses the forms *(a)glutinative* and *(ag)glutination* as parallels to *souden*.

Many parallel expressions for *souded* and *soudyng(e)* in Gale and English utilise terms not specifically medical (see sections 4–6, 8 in table 13.3). The most common terms are *unite* and *close* in both texts.

As can be seen in table 13.3, the terms *souded* and *soudyng(e)* are paralleled in Gale and English with a variety of different expressions, six in Gale and nine in English. The two most frequent terms, *agglutinate* and *cicatrise*, represent specialised terminology, the first coming into use only in the early modern period. The variation in form and spelling of the new term *agglutinate* that is evident in Gale and also attested in EMEMT is to be expected, considering the changing linguistic situation in the sixteenth century and the abundance of Latin-based neologisms. The other term, *cicatrise*, established itself already in Middle English and is one of the variant terms contributing to the decline of *souden* and *consouden*. In comparison to Gale, English is clearly less bound to the original text, which can be seen in the lack of parallels for many passages recorded in table 13.3. Latinate loans, such as *cicatrise*, are less frequent in English's version than in Gale's, perhaps because of a wider intended audience.

4. Conclusion

The study of three early English versions of Galen's *Methodus medendi* illustrates variation in the communication of the same ancient medical information to vernacular readers over a period of two hundred years. This period is characterised by major sociocultural and domain-specific changes affecting the construction and transmission of medical knowledge. The shifting position of Galen of Pergamon as a medical authority is reflected in the degree of liberty with which the vernacular translators treated his text.

The examination of text structure in the three texts suggests that the versions dating from the heyday of Galenism – the anonymous translation in the fifteenth-century MS Sloane 6 and the sixteenth-century printed version by Thomas Gale, one of the leading surgeons of his time – aimed at unqualified transmission of Galen's knowledge to a vernacular audience, although Gale's edition already shows some signs of a perceived need to update or modernise the text. In contrast, in the seventeenth century, Peter English, calling himself a student of medicine, presents a very different version of the text: a selection of Galen's knowledge that apparently English himself deemed useful and worthy of transmission and comment, with an information structure that differed radically from the original text.

The use of reporting verbs suggests that editorial intervention in transmitting Galen's knowledge became more possible over time. It also illustrates the emergence of more nuanced rhetorical devices for developing the argument and indicating the author's stance. The analysis of medical terminology illustrates fluctuations in the special language of medicine, where some terms are seen to hold ground from one century to another, while others become obsolete and are replaced by new ones, coined from native lexical resources or adopted from the traditional languages of medical science, Latin and Greek. Taken together, these changes reflect epistemological shifts and the advance of vernacularisation in medicine, as well as the gradual shift of Galenic thinking away from the core of medical science and towards the realm of medical history.

While revealing considerable differences in the communication of Galen's *Methodus medendi* to medieval and Renaissance audiences in English, the analysis also shows great similarity between the two earliest versions of the text. In view of the vernacularisation of medicine, it is striking that the Middle English version of Galen's text in Sloane 6 in fact attempts to record accurately the complex disputes of the medical schools of thought in Galen's times without simplifying or omitting any of the theoretical content. Like several other vernacular texts in Sloane 6 and a multitude of other manuscripts, the Middle English *Methodus medendi* serves as an example of the keen interest of the time in making texts by the best medical authors also accessible in the vernacular, often, though not always, for the benefit of non-Latinate practitioners. With its unique manuscript copy, the Middle English *Methodus medendi* bears witness to the fact that some of the best medical knowledge of the time was also available in vernacular writing. In this respect, the knowledge communicated in Gale's Early Modern English translation was not entirely new in the vernacular. However, because of the manuscript medium, medicine in Middle English was usually only accessible to a few random readers, and only with the shift in the medium of communication from manuscript to print did the dissemination of Galen's medical knowledge to larger vernacular audiences become possible.

14 Prepositional modifiers in early English medical prose

A study *on* their historical development *in* noun phrases

DOUGLAS BIBER, BETHANY GRAY, ALPO
HONKAPOHJA AND PÄIVI PAHTA

1. Introduction

The fourteenth and fifteenth centuries represent the first phase in the gradual vernacularisation of science that began in England and elsewhere in Europe in the later Middle Ages (see e.g. Crossgrove *et al.* 1998). Most scientific medical treatises in manuscripts from this period are translations or adaptations of texts originally composed in Latin or Greek in ancient or medieval scholastic centres of learning; some English versions are based on intervening French translations. The treatises represent relatively few, but complicated, textual traditions, reflecting a multilayered and multilingual transmission of medicine across cultural and linguistic borders, involving successive stages of copying, translating, paraphrasing, excerpting and conflating, by scribes and translators over several centuries (see Pahta and Taavitsainen 2004). As a result, most texts within one subject area in fact recycle the same information, ultimately going back to a few prestigious Latin and Greek medical works, often using the exact same words.

Detailed consideration of these medieval manuscript-based treatises highlights the challenges that the first English translators of medical texts faced in their attempt to vernacularise medical science. English had yet to develop the lexical resources and syntactic conventions to address learned topics rich in technical and theoretical details for which the Greco-Roman learned tradition had developed its own means of expression over a millennium. Latin was the logical place to look for a model, and many texts in this category are characterised by heavy reliance on the source language. The difficulties of expressing abstract concepts and complicated causal and spatial relations in English have been pointed out in earlier studies (Taavitsainen *et al.* 2005, 2006). However, it is also likely that this rapidly changing communicative setting proved to be important in the evolution of new grammatical constructions.

Corpus studies over the past two decades have explored the distinctive grammar of written (versus spoken) registers (see e.g. Biber 1988; Biber *et al.* 1999). One important finding documented by these studies is that the discourse of academic prose is characterised by an extremely heavy reliance on nouns and non-clausal noun phrase modification, in contrast to the clausal embedding common in spoken registers (and popular written registers like fiction).

For example, the following sentence is typical of modern-day academic prose:

(1) Specifically, we were interested in the qualitative ecological difference in emphasis between changes in composition vs. changes in relative abundance.

In this example, the authors attempt to adopt a friendly style of presentation, using the first-person pronoun *we* rather than a passive voice construction. However, the structure of this sentence is almost entirely phrasal rather than clausal. That is, there is only one verb in the sentence (*were*) but numerous nouns (*difference, emphasis, changes, composition, changes, abundance*), attributive adjectives (*qualitative, ecological, relative*) and prepositional phrases functioning as noun modifiers (*difference in emphasis between changes in composition vs. changes in relative abundance*).

This grammatical discourse style is unlike the discourse of most other present-day registers – both spoken and popular writing – which rely on clausal structures rather than non-clausal modification. For example, the following turn from a conversation illustrates the dense use of verbs and dependent clauses that is typical in spoken language.

(2) Well they, they had a party. I forget what it was. They had it at a friend's house. I can't remember why it wasn't at their house anyway. And they had bought a bottle of Bailey's because they knew I liked Bailey's.

Written fiction similarly relies mostly on clausal discourse, such as:

(3) Rambo stared at the square of wood until it seemed to enlarge and drift toward him, filling his vision. He no longer heard the wind chimes, no longer smelled the incense, no longer felt the blow.

Historical studies have documented many grammatical changes within academic writing over the last several centuries. For example, Biber and Finegan (1997) use MultiDimensional Analysis to show how academic writing has steadily evolved over the past three centuries towards an increasing use of noun phrase structures.

One of the most important grammatical devices employed in this historical development is the prepositional phrase (PP), especially functioning as a post-nominal modifier. Biber and Clark (2002) analysed the patterns of use for post-nominal modifiers in medical research writing from the ARCHER

On and *in* in early English medical prose 199

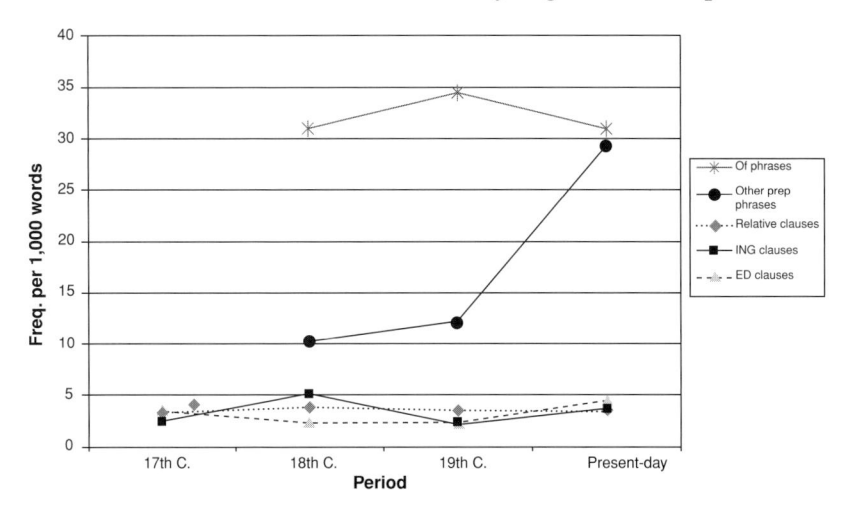

Figure 14.1 Noun post-modifier types in medical prose, across periods

corpus, extending over the period 1650–1990. Figure 14.1 (adapted from that study) shows that many types of noun post-modification have been stable in medical prose across the past four centuries. For example, *of*-phrases were frequent in academic writing across all periods. In contrast, the other prepositions (e.g. *in, on, between, for, with*) have increased dramatically as noun modifiers, and this change accounts for much of the distinctiveness of modern academic prose (see example (1) above).

One possible explanation for these historical developments is the unique communicative circumstances of writing, which permit extensive planning and revision, in contrast to the real-time communicative circumstances of speech (see Biber 2009; Biber and Conrad 2009). That is, writers can take as much time as they want to plan exactly what they want to write, and if they write something unintended, they can delete/add/revise/edit the language of the text. Thus, the final written text that an external reader sees might bear little resemblance to the initial words that the author produced, and readers usually have no overt indication of the extent to which the author has revised the original draft. Nearly all written registers offer the opportunity for extensive planning and revising during production, even if the author does not avail him/her-self of this opportunity. Other communicative factors, especially relevant in academic writing, are also influential here, such as the 'information explosion', the associated need for economy as there is more information to be communicated, and the increasing specialisation of the audience.

The historical changes documented to date represent a fundamental shift in the discourse style of academic writing. However, we know little about the origins of these developments. In particular, we know little about the early history of prepositions other than *of*: when did these prepositions first come to be used as noun modifiers (versus adverbials and other clausal functions)? Further, is it possible to track the evolution in the kinds of meanings that these prepositions express?

The fourteenth and fifteenth centuries are likely to be important in this development, given the rise of vernacularised scientific medical writing during that period. The present study describes the early history of the prepositions *in* and *on* as noun modifiers. The study is based on analysis of medical manuscripts from the period 1375–1500, and the use of these prepositions is compared to that in medical treatises from the early years of printing (1500–1700).

2. Corpus and methods

The texts analysed for the study come from the corpora *Middle English Medical Texts* (MEMT, 1375–1500) and *Early Modern English Medical Texts* (EMEMT, 1500–1700) – the first two components of the *Corpus of Early English Medical Writing*, a three-part domain-specific corpus containing a wide range of medical texts from the period 1375–1800 (see Taavitsainen and Pahta 1997; Taavitsainen *et al.* 2006; Taavitsainen and Pahta in press). For this study we have analysed the category of 'specialized treatises' in MEMT and its equivalent, 'treatises on specific topics', in EMEMT.

The MEMT data (99,059 words, twenty-five texts) consist of medical treatises that circulated in manuscripts written in the period 1375–1500, with the exception of one text, i.e. William Caxton's *Ars moriendi*, a popular handbook providing spiritual and practical guidance for people who are dying, one of the earliest printed English texts containing medical information, printed in 1491. As noted above, these treatises represent the early emergence of scientific medical writing in English rather than Latin. They include learned theoretical treatises on physiology and natural philosophy, as well as tracts focusing on a specific illness or field of specialisation, or a particular method of prognosis or treatment. A wide range of specific topics are treated, such as ophthalmology, reproduction, gynaecology and obstetrics, urinoscopy, phlebotomy, epilepsy, syphilis and the plague.

The 'treatises on specific topics' in EMEMT (514,132 words, sixty texts) are samples of printed texts, representing the bulk of early English printed books on medicine from the period 1500–1700. In the early part of the period, original publications in medical science were mostly written in Latin and translated into vernacular languages, and thus many of the early texts in this dataset are also based on Latin originals. Translations from other languages became more common in this period as well, which is also reflected in the data. It is also worth noting that some of the early printed texts had earlier circulated in manuscript form. However, during the 200-year period, the functional range of languages changed, and towards the end of the period it is increasingly common to find theoretical cutting-edge science published originally in English; the most notable witness to this development is the *Philosophical Transactions of the Royal Society of London*, which began to appear in 1665 (see e.g. Atkinson 1999; see also Gray *et al.* in press).

The EMEMT samples also cover a wide range of topics in a wide variety of styles, the common denominator being a focus on an individual disease, method or therapeutic substance. The category has been divided into five subcategories based on the focus of the text:

(a) texts on specific diseases (e.g. struma, ague, fevers, pox)
(b) texts on specific methods of diagnosis or treatment (e.g. urinoscopy, astrology, phlebotomy)
(c) texts on specific therapeutic substances (e.g. nitre, gold, mithridatum)
(d) texts on midwifery and children's diseases
(e) texts on plague

The target audiences range from academic specialists to the widest popular readership, e.g. included in category (d) along with treatises for top experts in obstetrics is the most popular sex guide for centuries, *Aristotle's Masterpiece* (Taavitsainen and Pahta in press; Taavitsainen *et al.* in press).

For the quantitative analyses, we divided the MEMT and EMEMT texts into four major historical periods: 1375–1449, 1450–1499, 1500–1599 and 1600–1700. All occurrences of *on* were coded in the analysis. However, because the preposition *in* occurred more frequently, we coded a 10 per cent sample of tokens for the 1500–1599 and 1600–1700 periods, considering every tenth token from all texts.

In order to make further register and time-period comparisons, we also analysed the use of these prepositions in seventeenth-century dialogues, present-day conversation and present-day academic research writing. The seventeenth-century dialogues are taken from *A Corpus of English Dialogues* (CED), considering the court transcripts and depositions in that corpus (458,600 words, 60 texts). Present-day conversations were taken from the *Longman Spoken and Written English Corpus* (see Biber *et al.* 1999: 29); the data analysed here consist of a 25 per cent sample of the prepositions from fifty randomly selected texts (340,199 words). We constructed our own corpus of twentieth-century academic research articles, sampling from science (biology, medicine, ecology, physiology), education, psychology and history in the years 1965, 1985 and 2005. For the purposes of the present study, we again analysed a 25 per cent sample of the prepositions for a subset of forty-two academic research articles (316,420 words) from 1965 and 2005.

The first step in the analysis was to code each token of the prepositions *in/on* for their syntactic function. The primary distinction here was between noun modifiers and other functions, although, when possible, we also attempted to identify the specific function of clausal uses (e.g. as an adverbial or adjective complement). For example:

(4) *in*
 noun modifier: Circulus with grauell betokoneth <u>ache in the backe nyghe vnto the fundyment</u>
 adverbial: And this colour apere <u>in Haruest or in winter</u>
 adjective complement: This vryne yf it be thycke <u>in sustau[n]ce</u>
(5) *on*
 noun modifier: This colour betokeneth a Feuer throughe chafynge of the lyuer/ a Feuer quartayne/ & a postume <u>on the longes</u>
 adverbial: Also make a playster of Dywte & of wyne yf it be ye Flowres and lay it <u>on the nauell</u>
 adjective complement: The nose somwhat heary <u>on the end</u>... declareth that manne to be of a good condicion in all thynges

The subsequent detailed analyses of meaning focused on uses that were clearly noun modifiers. Some occurrences were indeterminate because they could be interpreted as either noun modifiers or adverbials, as in:

(6) And yf thou se two small graynes <u>in the seconde regyon</u> or mo or lesse knytte to a small sky / than it betokeneth peyne in the brest of rewme

These uses are counted in the 'other' functions and not included in the detailed analyses of noun modifiers.

For the quantitative analysis of meanings, we coded a two-way distinction: concrete/locative meanings versus abstract meanings. Our rubric for this distinction was simple: if the head noun referred to a tangible, physical entity and the prepositional phrase identified a concrete location or a tangible object, the occurrence was coded as a concrete/locative meaning. All other uses were coded as 'abstract'. The hypothesis for this part of the analysis was that the initial meanings associated with *in/on* as noun modifiers were concrete/locative, reflecting the stereotypical uses of these prepositions to identify the physical location of an object. The extension to other uses was hypothesised to be a later historical development, associated with the more abstract concepts and relationships described in later medical prose.

3. Frequency of use

Figure 14.2 plots the frequency of use for prepositional phrases with *in*, distinguishing between noun modifiers and other functions. This figure shows that the use of *in* PPs was quite stable in medical writing across the centuries covered by MEMT and EMEMT: *in* as a noun modifier was already well established by 1375, but rare in comparison to other functions, and essentially this same pattern of use continues across all four centuries.

For the sake of comparison, we also report the patterns of use in seventeenth-century dialogues, present-day conversation and present-day

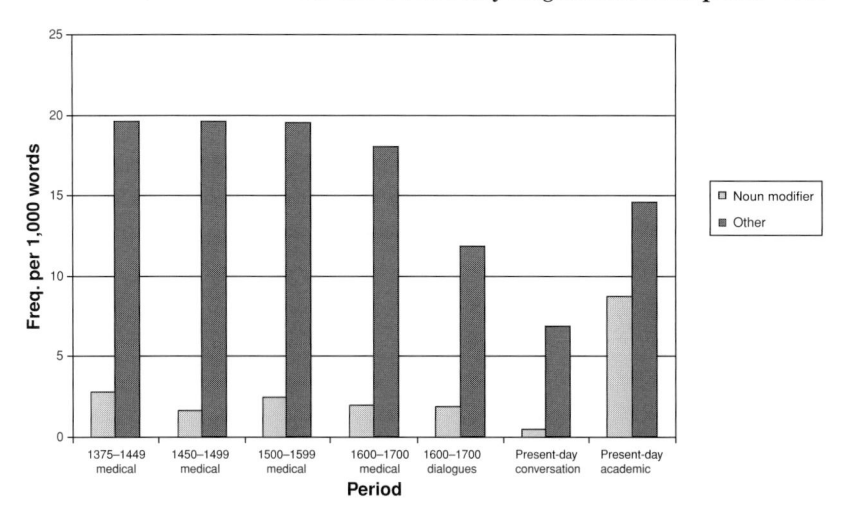

Figure 14.2 *In* as noun modifier versus other functions, across periods

academic research writing. In the seventeenth century, there was little register variation in the use of *in* PPs: figure 14.2 shows that the overall frequency of *in* was somewhat lower in seventeenth-century dialogues, but the low proportional use of noun modifiers is essentially the same as in medical writing. There are even fewer occurrences of *in* PPs as noun modifiers in modern conversation, although the overall frequency of *in* is also lower. In contrast, the only dramatic pattern of change shown in figure 14.2 is for present-day academic prose, where *in* PPs as noun modifiers account for almost 40 per cent of all occurrences of *in*. Thus, the patterns of grammatical use for *in* PPs remained relatively constant across registers for several centuries, followed by recent strong change focused on academic writing.

Figure 14.3 shows that the overall trends are similar for *on* PPs. Although the overall frequencies of use are considerably lower than for *in* PPs, the patterns are stable across the entire period 1375–1700: *on* PPs as noun modifiers are attested already in the period 1375–1450, but they are quite rare in comparison to other functions in all of these periods. Seventeenth-century dialogues show essentially the same pattern, indicating that there was little register variation in the use of *on* PPs during these periods. In this case, modern conversation shows a much higher overall use of *on* (in large part due to the increase in phrasal verbs), but the use of *on* PPs as noun modifiers remains rare. However, here again the dramatic historical change has occurred in academic writing over the past two centuries, so that 40 per cent of all *on* PPs in present-day academic writing are functioning as noun modifiers.

Thus, considering only the quantitative frequency of use, we would conclude that little change occurred during the period 1375–1700: both *in* and

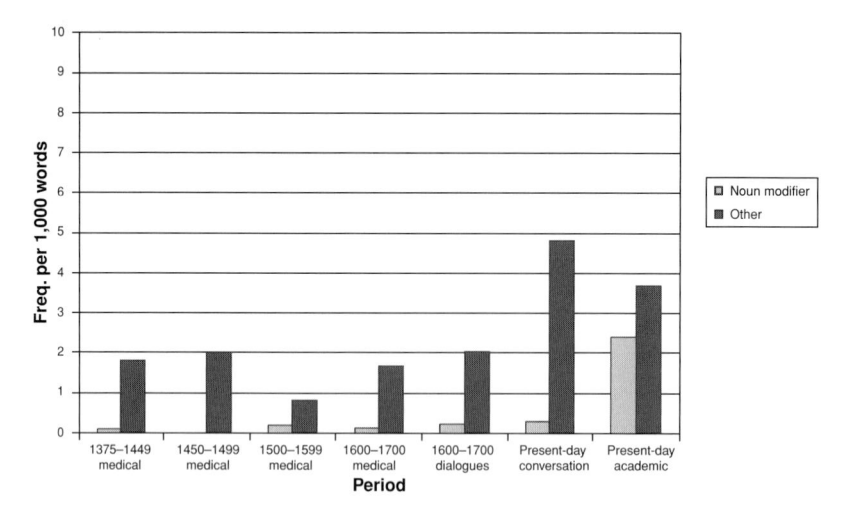

Figure 14.3 *On* as noun modifier versus other functions, across periods

on were used as noun modifiers in all historical periods, apparently in both academic writing and in speech (at least since 1600), but that use was quite rare in comparison to other grammatical functions. However, when we turn to a detailed consideration of the meanings expressed by *in* PPs and *on* PPs, we can begin to observe the early stages of the dramatic historical changes that occurred in later centuries.

4. Extension of meanings

While the overall frequency of use for *in* and *on* as nominal modifiers has been relatively stable across the period 1375–1700, the meanings expressed by these structures have undergone change and extension from concrete/locative meanings to more abstract meanings. In the fourteenth and fifteenth centuries, the large majority of noun-modifying *in* PPs expressed concrete/locative meanings, while abstract meanings became more prevalent in the sixteenth and seventeenth centuries (see figure 14.4). The development of noun-modifying *on* PPs lags behind *in* PPs, so that the first abstract uses begin to emerge in the sixteenth century and become somewhat better established by the seventeenth century (see figure 14.5).

Thus, both *in* and *on* are used mostly for concrete/locative meanings in the fourteenth and fifteenth centuries. For example,

(7) Glaucus a posteme in the right side, a bledder on the lunge Circulus

On PPs are used consistently to express the meaning of physical location, usually on the surface of some object. This is the primary meaning of *on* PPs up through the seventeenth century; for example, see (8):

On and *in* in early English medical prose   205

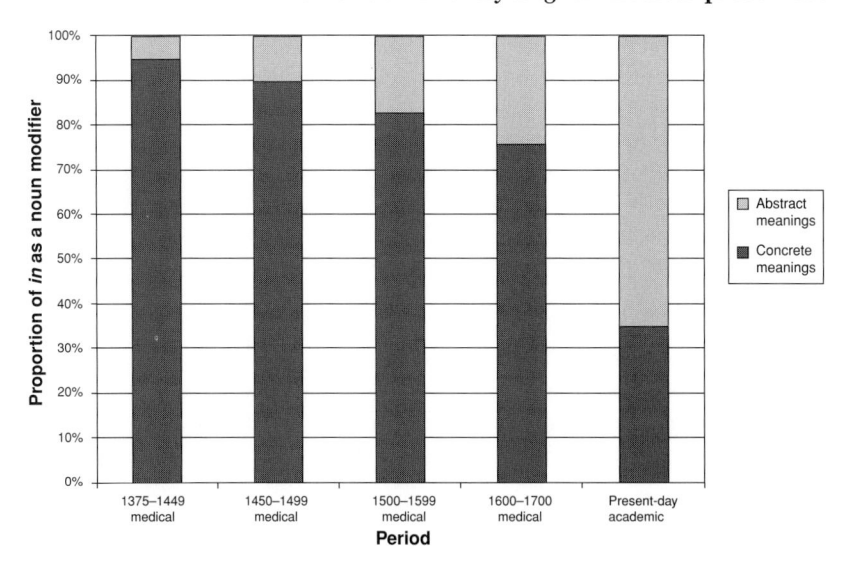

Figure 14.4 *In* as noun modifier: concrete versus abstract meanings

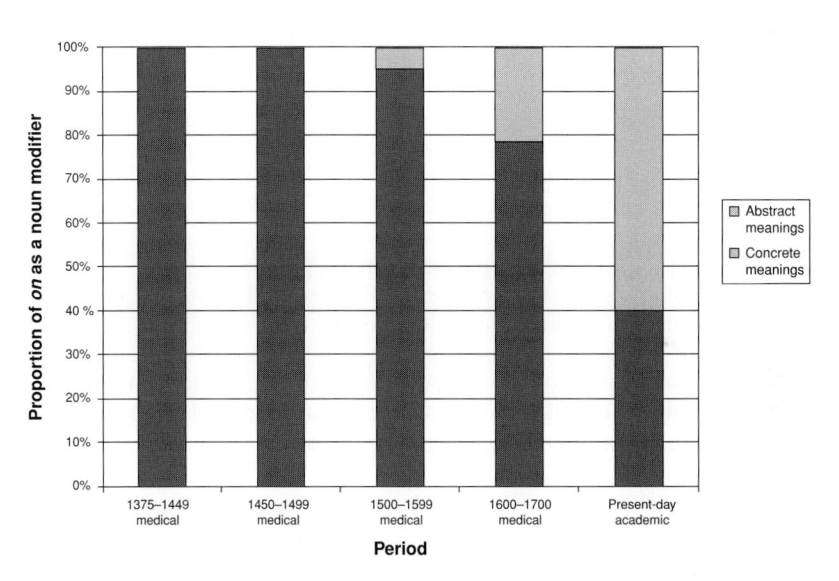

Figure 14.5 *On* as noun modifier: concrete versus abstract meanings

(8) a postume on the longes
    blisters and hackes on the lips
    two on each side

In contrast, *in* PPs express a range of specific meanings that can be considered concrete/locative. These include:

(9) *location inside a body part*
     a wynde in the heed
     ache in the backye
     pain in his knee
(10) *location inside an object or substance*
     the oil in the thermometer
     kernels in your meat
     quantity of opium in it [*i.e. Theriacle*]
(11) *geographic location*
     our apothecaries in England
     John Bissite in St. Peters Parish
(12) *textual location*
     the foregoing chapters in the first part
     his judgement and candor in his writings

In addition, *in* PPs were used to express concrete meanings other than physical location. These were coded as 'concrete', but they express intermediate meanings that can be considered as extensions to the core locative meanings. Two major uses are attested here: time expressions and generic reference. The time references can be seen as an extension of physical location to the temporal domain, as in:

(13) each day in the weeke
     seaven of the clocke in the morning
     his own experience in the same time
     experience in his time

On PPs were also occasionally used with this meaning:

(14) the first houre of the sunne-rising on every day

With the generic uses, both the head noun and the 'location' noun have concrete/tangible meanings, but the whole construction refers to a general entity rather than a specific object or person, as in:

(15) mercury in medicines

Interestingly, this use was especially prevalent in the fifteenth century; for example:

(16) And þare is anoþer maner of blak in uryn þat is causyd of adustyoun complet

   Citryn color in uryn sais þat colre & fleume regnys in þe body, bod mare colre þan fleume.

   þai are þe vaynys in þe wrestys & are callyd þe vayn powcys or þe pows vaynes

Alsa rubeus or subrubeus with a body thyk & drubly says roringe & disturblynge of humours in þe body.

The prevalence of this use in the fourteenth- and fifteenth-century manuscripts reflects the communicative purposes of those texts: to document general medical conditions and the recommended treatments for those conditions. In contrast, the more recent texts include descriptions of specific case studies, and as a result we find a mix of both specific and generic uses of *in* PPs. Most occurrences with this meaning in the sixteenth and seventeenth centuries use generic reference to identify a condition that is characteristic of humans generally, as in:

(17)   helthe in a sanguyne man
       rot . . . in dead men
       privy parts in women
       the cause of rheume in children
       a companion in the whole generation

There are few genuinely abstract uses of these prepositional constructions in these texts and, for the most part, those uses begin to emerge in the sixteenth century. One of the uses for *on* PPs is to refer to a logical rather than a physical position, as in:

(18)   probabilitie on both sides
       one principall reason on their side

On is also used in the idiomatic expression *travel on foot* to refer to the physical entity used to accomplish movement; according to the *Oxford English Dictionary*, this use can be traced back to Old English.

The most common abstract meaning for *on* PPs in the sixteenth and seventeenth centuries is to identify the topical domain that is associated with the head noun:

(19)   a poem on the virtue of a laurel leaf
       some remarks on the late debate about X
       occasional notes on dr. George Thompsons
       a learned author on this subject

Using the OED as a searchable corpus (available at corpus.byu.edu) indicates that this use emerged in the early fifteenth century, as shown in the following example from a legal will:

(20)   iiij quayres of Doctours on Mathewe (1422)[1]
       'Four quires of commentaries on the Gospel of Matthew'

In PPs commonly occur with a similar meaning, identifying the general research domain (rather than a specific topic). For example:

---

[1] We are grateful to Dr Matti Kilpiö for his help with this translation.

(21) my studie in ciuile and humane learnynge
that Axiome in philosophie
his learning in all sciences
our work in the Astrological or chymical way of physic
the masterly heroes in medicine
new discoveries in medicine
writers in medicine
my sentiments in these matters

Figures 14.4 and 14.5 show that the uses in academic writing of both *in* PPs and *on* PPs as noun modifiers have changed dramatically from the seventeenth century to the present day: in present-day academic prose, the majority of these constructions are used to express abstract meanings rather than concrete/locative meanings. Those abstract uses include the identification of topical domain, as in seventeenth-century medical prose. However, there are also other abstract uses that were only beginning to emerge in the seventeenth century.

For *on* PPs, three abstract uses are especially important in modern academic writing:

(i) *a nominalisation* + on *PP, corresponding to a prepositional verb construction; for example*:
a biological dependence on physical conditions
(*compare*: it depends on physical conditions)

his reliance on the evolutionary thesis
(*compare*: he relied on the evolutionary thesis)

a focus on measures of student outcomes
(*compare*: someone focused on measures of student outcomes)

(ii) *a process noun* + on *PP, corresponding to a transitive verb with a direct object that is the 'patient' of the verb; for example*:
a significant influence on the tragic developments that followed
(*compare*: something influenced the tragic developments)

two factors have the greatest impact on college grades
(*compare*: two factors impact college grades)

a greater emphasis on intellectual behaviours
(*compare*: someone emphasises intellectual behaviours)

(iii) *constructions with an -ing non-finite clause following the preposition* on; *for example*:
an effect on determining choice
emphasis on providing support
any restriction on publishing it
research on promoting science learning

While the meaning of 'topical domain' still occurs in present-day academic prose, these other three uses are actually much more common. However, only one of these three is attested in our corpus of early medical texts: a conversion of the prepositional verb *operate on* to the corresponding nominalised equivalent:

(22) neither heat nor cold can obstruct its influential operation on the Body (1699)

This example comes from the very end of the historical period considered in our study (1699), while the other two 'abstract' uses that are common in modern academic writing are unattested in our Early Modern English medical corpus. Thus, it appears that the prevalent 'abstract' uses of *on* PPs in modern academic writing mostly began to emerge after the historical period in focus here.

In contrast, the prevalent abstract meanings of present-day *in* PPs are beginning to emerge in the seventeenth-century medical texts in our corpus. Two abstract uses are especially common in modern academic writing:

(i) *a process noun* + in *PP, corresponding to an intransitive verb with a subject that is the 'patient' of the verb; for example*:
the chief reason for Britain's decline in exports
(*compare*: Britain's exports declined)

a rapid increase in the size of the egg
(*compare*: the size of the egg increased)

variation in frequency
(*compare*: the frequency varied)

(ii) *constructions with an -ing non-finite clause following the preposition* in; *for example*:
invaluable assistance in recording electrocardiographs from canaries

difficulty in separating the sarcoplasmic proteins from the myofibrils

errors in rounding the total score

Both of these innovations are attested in the seventeenth-century texts from our corpus. The earliest and best established noun to occur with the first meaning is *difference*:

(23) whereupon riseth this difference in norishment (1576–1600)
there are found manifest differences in the male (1601–1625)
and female
And there is no more difference in the nature (1626–1650)
of essence
and besides her difference in Longitude (1651–1675)
and Latitude

Beyond that, only one other process noun, *change*, occurs with an *in* PP in EMEMT:

(24) Poyson is either taken unawares, or given by subtility and stealth by wicked men. And this is a common sign, it presently makes a great change in the body, by which it differs from those that are bred from humors in the body by putrefaction. (1651–1675)

The second innovation (N + *in* + V-*ing*) first occurs in 1575–1600, but it appears to have become relatively well established during the seventeenth century; for example:

(25) the vertues and worth of this Medicine in helping and curing many diseases

pains in making water

the difficulty in searching out the causes of them

the truth of the marchaunt in transporting the same

5. Conclusion

In sum, if we focus only on frequency of use, our corpus investigation shows little historical change for the period 1375–1700: both *in* and *on* were used as noun modifiers in all historical periods, apparently in both academic writing and in speech (at least since 1600), but that use was quite rare in comparison to other grammatical functions. In contrast, dramatic changes in frequency of use occurred in academic writing after the period in focus here, i.e. in the last two centuries.

When we turn to a detailed consideration of the meanings expressed by *in* PPs and *on* PPs as noun modifiers, we can begin to observe the early stages of these dramatic historical changes of later centuries. That is, there were marked extensions in the range of meanings expressed by *in* PPs (and to a lesser extent *on* PPs), especially in the period 1600–1700. In particular, *in* PPs, and to a lesser extent *on* PPs, came to be used to express abstract meaning relationships, as opposed to the concrete/locative meanings expressed in earlier periods.

The earliest abstract use, for both *in* and *on*, is to identify a topical domain. Other abstract uses for *in* begin to emerge in the seventeenth century (e.g. to identify the semantic patient of a process). *On* PPs lag behind *in* PPs in the development of abstract uses: some of the abstract uses for *on* PPs have not yet emerged in the seventeenth century, even though those uses come to be prevalent by the twentieth century.

Considering the influence of Latin can help explain why *in* PPs change more rapidly than *on* PPs in taking on abstract uses: *in* is a common preposition with a noun head in Latin, while there is no direct equivalent for *on*.

The Latin phrases incorporated into Middle English medical texts seem to be nearly direct equivalents to the *in* PPs described above, mostly expressing concrete/locative meanings.[2] For example:

(26) location inside a body part: *in stomacho* ('in the stomach/gullet')
in a sickness: *in tussi & asmate* ('in a cough and asthma')
in a substance: *in vino* ('in wine')
in a work cited: *in historijs antiquo[rum]* ('in histories of the Ancients')
time of the year: *in autu[m]pno & i[n] uento boriali* ('in Autumn and in a Northern wind')

However, generic uses of *in* PPs also have parallel usages in Latin, as in:

(27) *roringe & disturblynge of humours in þe body (venae in carpis)*
compare: *Hec aqua renouat corpus humanu[m] & augmentat o[mn]ia naturalia i[n] cor[por]e humano* (This water refreshes human body and increases everything natural in the human body)

While the abstract meanings of *in* PPs, and to a lesser extent *on* PPs, become increasingly common in the early printed medical texts, in medieval medical treatises of the manuscript period abstract uses are rare. One explanation for these historical developments is the shifting communicative purposes found in medical treatises after the transition from manuscript to print. English medical treatises of the medieval period, circulating in manuscripts, typically communicated medical knowledge as generally accepted truths, derived from few authoritative sources, some of them originally written over a thousand years earlier. Despite their complex transmission histories, all texts within the same topic area said pretty much the same things. This began to change in the sixteenth and seventeenth centuries when gradual changes took place in the epistemology of science and medical knowledge became something that could be constructed here and now. Medical treatises of this period, disseminated in print, are characterised, for example, by more direct observation, attention to physical details and their physical or logical relationship, description of specific case studies and a wider range of information about particular treatments. Processes – in the natural world and in the research endeavour itself – started to become the object of description, resulting in medical communication characterised by greater use of nominalisations and, accompanying this, greater use of 'abstract' meanings for *in/on* PPs as noun modifiers.

---

2 Latin examples are taken from Alpo Honkapohja's on-going PhD research, a digital edition of the late medieval medical manuscript O.1.77. located at Trinity College Cambridge. The manuscript is dated to *c.* 1460. It is previously unedited.

15 The pragmatics of punctuation in Older Scots

JEREMY SMITH AND CHRISTIAN KAY

1. Introduction

Any text can be viewed as a conversational partnership between transmitter and receiver. In face-to-face conversation, communication is assisted by extra-linguistic features such as tone of voice or facial expression; problems of interpretation are often solved by context. For written texts, a greater range of factors may render communication problematic, not least the key role of a third participant in the conversation: the scribe or editor who mediates between the creator and the reader of the text. The further back in time the reader goes, the more problematic this role becomes. When a text has been copied or edited over hundreds of years, repeated opportunities are available to modify or reinterpret not only its language but pragmatic features such as layout, punctuation or capitalisation, all of which affect reception. As the edition grows more remote from its source, the importance of recognising the significance of such features increases. Punctuation is a case in point, since its absence can be as significant as its presence. In the sixteenth century, for example, when the system we now know was in its infancy, a range of other devices, both visual and linguistic, was used to indicate structure or to signal important meanings.

This chapter examines such issues in the context of the complex editorial history of a short Older Scots poem, William Dunbar's *Discretioun in Taking*, as witnessed in three early modern manuscripts: the sixteenth-century Bannatyne and Maitland Folio Manuscripts, and the early seventeenth-century Reidpath Manuscript.[1] Comparison is then made with the assumptions in eighteenth-century and modern editions of the text.

2. The problematisation of editing

Editing has always been central to literary study. If the object of study is texts, however defined, then the scholarly conversation constituting academic life

---

[1] The poem is generally regarded as one of a set of three, linked by stanza form and the key word *Discretioun*, hence *Discretioun Poems* is sometimes used as a short title for the group. The others deal with asking and giving. They are numbered 44–6 in Bawcutt's edition (Bawcutt 1998: 21, 142–8, 378).

demands comparatively easy access to those texts. But, as is well-known by those who engage in it, editing is by no means a clear-cut activity, and a good deal of recent scholarship has problematised editorial practices. Such problematisation is, of course, in principle a good thing, and is a commonplace of good practice in all disciplines with any theoretical pretensions. As the philosopher of science Rom Harré puts it: 'The explicit identification of the structure and components of one's conceptual system releases one from bondage to it' (Harré 1972: 17). More simply, the linguist Roger Lass states: 'The most important thing... is to know at all times exactly what we are doing' (Lass 1976: 220).

The outcome of this increasing attention to the editorial process has been a greater awareness that the editorial task can never be truly finished. The ultimate edition of a text, implying that no further edition will ever be needed, is neither a theoretical nor a practical possibility. Editorial practices are the product of contemporary intellectual assumptions, and because these assumptions are subject to change, so are the practices. Editing, traditionally referred to as 'textual criticism', is never neutral: it is an act of interpretation, mediating between the creator of the text and the reader. Since fashions in interpretation change, examination of editorial practice allows a special insight into the intellectual history and linguistic assumptions of particular periods. Thus, an examination of how eighteenth-century and later editors approach Older Scots texts reflects contemporary views about well-formed literary expression and the presentation of the vernacular.

3. Critical, diplomatic and conservative editions

Traditionally, editorial practice has been governed by two axioms, as enunciated by Reynolds and Wilson:

> The business of textual criticism is... to follow back the threads of transmission and try to restore the texts as closely as possible to the form which they originally had. (1974: 186)

> [T]he basic essential equipment is taste, judgement, common sense, and the capacity to distinguish what is wrong in a given context: and these remain the perquisite of human wit. (1974: 213)

These axioms inform the construction of a 'critical edition'. Since the nineteenth century, the critical edition has been the result of the following processes, known collectively as 'recension': the comparison of the surviving versions (witnesses) of the text in question (collation); the construction of a 'family tree' (a stemma) of witnesses on the basis of the detection of presumed substantive errors (more properly: non-original readings) shared or not shared between them; the reconstruction of a presumed common ancestor (archetype) of all witnesses; and the emendation of that common ancestor to produce what is presumed to be the author's original conception of the work. This original conception is then presented to the reader as a critical edition of the work.

3.1 The critical edition

For Anglicists, especially those working in the earliest periods of English literature, perhaps the most significant twentieth-century theorists of the critical edition have been George Kane and Talbot Donaldson. For them, the critical edition is 'a theoretical structure, a complex hypothesis designed to account for a body of phenomena in the light of knowledge about the circumstances which generate them' (Kane and Donaldson 1974: 212). They developed their ideas in the creation of the great, if controversial, Athlone edition of a complex, long and textually challenging English poem from the end of the fourteenth century: William Langland's *Piers Plowman*. The Athlone edition was a major intellectual achievement, providing scholars with three radically different versions of Langland's poem (the A-, B- and C-texts); it was designed to reflect, as nearly as possible, the poet's original conception of each stage in his creation of the work. As well as providing a substantial apparatus recording substantive variants from the fifty or so surviving medieval manuscripts of the poem, Kane and Donaldson presented what they believed to be authoritative texts, purged of the errors they considered to have been introduced by scribes, and in a form of language that they believed corresponded most closely to Langland's own. They included in their edition lengthy introductions setting out their editorial principles, principles that they also pursued in supporting publications (e.g. Donaldson 1970).

Kane and Donaldson were impressively willing to be methodologically explicit and intellectually courageous in correlating theory and practice. Not all scholars have been so daring, and they were criticised by some reviewers for exercising what was termed, by an early commentator on their B-text edition, 'editorial free choice' in a 'radical, if not revolutionary' way (Hudson 1977: 44, 42); 'radical' is here not necessarily a term of commendation. However, they felt they had to be radical, since Langland's poem was so very challenging; not only did Langland himself seem to have carried out a species of rolling revision of his work, but also many copyists seem to have regarded *Piers Plowman* as a living text, open to quite extensive interpretative intervention. Kane and Donaldson therefore felt at liberty to draw much more freely on the witnesses available, setting aside the construction of a comprehensive stemma in favour of an interventionist style of editing, governed in their decisions much more overtly than had hitherto been the case by their own conception of the various stages of the poem, and drawing repeatedly on all the variants presented to them by their witnesses.

Even Kane and Donaldson's choice of the variety of English in which to present the poem is arguably problematic. Whereas Langland's 'own' language was almost certainly a South-West Midland form of Middle English, the variety of English in which Kane and Donaldson presented the B-text, for instance, is largely a London usage, so-called 'Type III' language of a kind also found in the Ellesmere and Hengwrt Manuscripts of the *Canterbury Tales*. Recent scholarship has shown that the Ellesmere and Hengwrt Manuscripts were both written by the scribe who was also responsible for the Trinity College Cambridge *Piers Plowman*, the manuscript that supplied Kane and Donaldson with the linguistic forms ('accidentals') for their B-text. (See Samuels 1963; also Smith 1988; Horobin and Mooney 2004.)

3.2 The conservative critical edition

A safer, less radical option, the 'conservative critical edition', now seems dominant in medieval English studies, even though such editions have been seen as, in Patterson's phrase, 'undermin[ing] both the rigor and the inclusiveness of the interpretive activity that is at the heart of textual criticism' (1987: 112). Conservative critical editors use the techniques of collation, stemma-construction and reconstruction of the archetype discussed above, but are much less interventionist than were Kane and Donaldson, keeping close to the one witness that has been determined, through recension, as providing the 'best text' of the work in question.

The outcome of such timidity might be exemplified by the editing of a little poem by Geoffrey Chaucer, *Adam Scriveyn*, given here as presented in the Riverside Chaucer edition:

> Adam scriveyn, if ever it thee bifalle
> Boece or Troylus for to wryten newe,
> Under thy long lokkes thou most have the scalle,
> But after my makyng thow wryte more trewe;
> So ofte adaye I mot thy werk renewe,
> It to correcte and eke to rubbe and scrape,
> And al is thorugh thy negligence and rape.
> (Benson 1988: 650)

Adam Scriveyn survives in only one manuscript, MS Cambridge, Trinity College R.3.20, copied in the middle of the fifteenth century by a scribe and literary enthusiast called John Shirley. The Riverside editors, juggling to cater for a range of different audiences, print their inheritance from Shirley, though discreetly introducing unhistorical punctuation. They have kept apparently disyllabic *thorugh* rather than imposing a monosyllabic form such as Ellesmere's *thurgh*, as required by the metre. The editors have not modified the phrase *thy long lokkes* to *thy longe lokkes*, which would have marked plurality in the adjective in accordance with established Chaucerian grammar and removed what Chaucer's contemporary London circle would have considered, if reflected in pronunciation, a prosodic irregularity associated with either the vulgar or with Northern incomers. They may be *trewe* to Shirley, therefore, but are they *trewe* to Chaucer? Are they not rather, like Adam in Chaucer's formulation, perpetuators of *negligence and rape*? They have not been in any way radical; they are conservative critical editors. Of course, given that they had only one manuscript to choose from, and that the function of their edition was to present the text for a modern, largely student, audience while attempting to avoid 'over-interpreting' the poem, it is hard to see that they could have behaved very differently.

It was probably practices such as these in the Riverside Chaucer that Patterson had in mind when he issued his theoretical challenge. Patterson's peroration – a survey of the state of medieval studies in 1987 – still resonates as a statement of a distinct critical position: he is concerned that there is a 'dismaying... refusal to edit – which is part of the larger refusal to interpret... an all too tenacious tradition within medieval studies' (1987: 112).

3.3 The diplomatic edition

Amongst these exercises in 'not editing', Patterson places another kind of edition: 'a diplomatic printing that candidly offers little more than the transcription of a single manuscript' (1987: 112); this assertion is perhaps rather unfair, since it does not take account of the very different goals of the other kind of editorial activity, the creation of the 'diplomatic edition'. For Anglicists, the apogee of the art of diplomatic editing is the set of editions of various manuscripts of *Ancrene Riwle*, published by the Early English Text Society (EETS), and culminating in Zettersten and Diensberg's edition of the Vernon text, published in 2000. These *Ancrene Riwle* editions continue a great EETS tradition, going back at least to Richard Morris's superbly accurate parallel-text edition of the texts of *Cursor Mundi*, and relating to the part played by EETS in the creation of what became the *Oxford English Dictionary*. For the Scottish Text Society (STS), this tradition is reflected in the splendid diplomatic editions of the great poetic miscellanies – Ritchie's text of the Bannatyne Manuscript (B), or Craigie's texts of the Maitland Folio Manuscript (MF) and the Asloan Manuscript – which appeared during the decade after 1919 and clearly relate to the beginnings of the *Dictionary of the Older Scottish Tongue*.

Although such editions may now be considered old-fashioned by many, the arguments for them were well made in what is arguably the most impressive, and certainly the most ambitious, of the EETS *Ancrene Riwle* editions, that of MS London, British Library Cotton Cleopatra C.vi, published by Eric Dobson in 1972. Dobson's discussion of the diplomatic editor's task deserves quoting in full:

> To publish a photographic facsimile is not the way out. It is true that photographs present the facts (or some of them, and not always truthfully), but they do nothing to interpret them; the interpretation is left to the individual reader . . . it is no answer to the editorial problem simply to put a photographic facsimile in the hands of postgraduate students or even of their teachers. What is necessary is that a single editor should spend the time necessary to solve the problems of the manuscript, even those that are themselves trivial and unimportant, and should find a means of presenting his [*sic*] results so that others may benefit from his [*sic*] pains; the job should be done thoroughly once, not superficially by each individual user of a facsimile.[2] (Dobson 1972: xii–xiii)

Diplomatic editions demand high-level hermeneutic (paleographical, codicological, linguistic) skills, and it was therefore somewhat unfair of Patterson to take a reductive view of the activity. It should rather be seen as editing of a kind very different from that undertaken by, for example, Kane and Donaldson, but arguably still worthwhile – if, of course, undertaken in a methodologically explicit way – alongside the production of critical editions. In the remainder of this chapter, a survey of textual criticism in the editing of the Middle Scots poet William Dunbar, and the issues involved in the making of critical and diplomatic editions, will be further explored.

4. Editing Dunbar

William Dunbar's *Discretioun in Taking* is witnessed in three early modern manuscripts: the well-known sixteenth-century Bannatyne and Maitland Folio Manuscripts, and the Reidpath Manuscript, an early seventeenth-century transcript of part of MF that contains material that has since disappeared from the earlier text. Like Chaucer, Dunbar 'showed a concern for textual integrity, and was sensitive to the way poetry might be "mangellit", or mutilated, once it passed from the author's possession' (Bawcutt 1998: 11). It is therefore interesting to see how Dunbar's editors have served him.

Modern readers have comparatively easy access to texts of this poem, but its editorial history has been complex. Passages from six editions are presented here:

---

[2] Facsimiles, especially when presented in digitised form to a high specification, as in the British Library's *Beowulf* facsimile or the Bodleian's forthcoming facsimile of the fourteenth-century Vernon Manuscript, have many virtues; not only do they have an obvious conservation role, but they also allow, through image-enhancement, for new discoveries to be made about the text. One useful way of engaging with issues raised in this chapter is to study Dunbar alongside a facsimile, so that editorial interventions can be noted and readers can engage with such areas as book history, which sees textual production as the result of the intervention of a series of agents or actors: poet, scribe, printer, editor, reader.

218 Smith and Kay

(a) from W. Tod Ritchie's transcript of the Bannatyne Manuscript (1928)
(b) from Sir William Craigie's transcript of the Maitland Folio Manuscript (1919)
(c) from Allan Ramsay's version in *The Ever Green* (1724)
(d) from Lord Hailes's version in *Ancient Scottish Poems* (1770)
(e) from W. Mackay Mackenzie's edition (1932)
(f) from Priscilla Bawcutt's edition (1998).

The texts as they appear in the above editions are given in the Appendix to this chapter.

4.1 Texts (a) and (b)

Our analysis begins with an examination of texts (a) and (b). There is no punctuation as we would understand it in either the Bannatyne or Maitland Folio texts. B uses punctuation elsewhere in the manuscript, notably the *virgula suspensiva* (or slash) to indicate a pause, or the double *virgula suspensiva*, which appears sporadically for a final pause (in some poems used fairly frequently). The *virgula suspensiva* appears elsewhere in MF, but somewhat sparingly. In both texts, other strategies are used to indicate the structure of verse and argument. In B, features of layout are used, such as an initial rubric to mark the poem's beginning, and *litterae notabiliores* (capitals) to mark sense divisions in lines 4 and 8. Capitals are used interestingly at the beginning of lines; we might compare their presence and absence at the beginning of lines 4 and 14. In MF too, features of layout are used. However, there is no title marking off the poem from that which precedes it. Capitals are not used in the same way in mid-line; they occur initially, though note their absence in lines 8 and 14. MF introduces a further communicative strategy by using features of discourse grammar to flag steps in the argument, notably the deictic *Thir* in lines 6 and 11. Such demonstratives are usually glossed 'these', which is generally adequate in etymological terms although the semantics of demonstratives in Older Scots and Middle English is subtly distinct from that in Present-day English. MF emphasises the strategy by adding an extra stanza beginning *Thir merchandis*, thus completing the three estates into which society was divided (cf. *Thir clarkis... Thir baronis*) and adding a new theme to the poem.

To modern eyes, the absence of titles may seem a strange communicative lapse; we are accustomed to these features, or at least some kind of numbering sequence, as a convenient shorthand for identifying a text. In Dunbar's case, however, many were invented by eighteenth- and nineteenth-century editors (Bawcutt 1998: 17–21).[3]

---

[3] Titles are increasingly the object of textual critical attention; for an interesting discussion of the topic, see work by Victoria Gibbons of Cardiff University (Gibbons 2008). For the role of the title page in later centuries, see Sher (2006) and references cited therein.

Some spelling differences between B and MF are interesting to philologists, though not recorded by modern editors because they are regarded as 'accidental' rather than 'substantive', e.g. line 1 *geving* (B), *giffing* (MF); line 2 *gud* (B), *gude* (MF); line 5 *sowld* (B), *suld* (MF). In Older Scots manuscripts the letters <þ> and <y> were generally written identically, as *y*, though, interestingly, Craigie and Ritchie both use <þ> (alongside <th>) to represent a presumed dental fricative and reserve <y> to represent a vowel. MF uses <þ> a little more consistently than B, e.g. line 9 *yair* (MF: Craigie gives *þair*), *thair* (B), but cf. *yat* in line 4 (B: Ritchie gives *þat*). Obvious errors are not corrected; thus Ritchie does not supply <be> in line 10, though clearly required by the context.

4.2 Texts (c) and (d)

Let us now compare the transcripts of B and MF with the eighteenth-century versions, (c) and (d). Ramsay's text in *The Ever Green* derives overtly from B; his title-page states that the texts come from a work 'wrote by the ingenious before 1600'. Despite this acknowledgement, *Of Discretioun in Taking* is presented according to eighteenth-century practices. Semicolons are introduced at line endings, and in place of B's capitals marking a sense change, Ramsay has introduced mid-line commas. He capitalises according to incipient early eighteenth-century conventions, whereby key words in discourse, usually nouns, appear with capitals: *Giving, Taking, Gude, Autoritie, Discration*. Ramsay intervened too in the text's discourse grammar, highlighting the contrast with the previous poem in the series by adding *Now* at the outset, as well as adopting, in modified form, B's connecting rubric as the italicised title for the poem (though, interestingly, but understandably, *Follows* is dropped in the running head). Layout of the text has been changed to create a more interesting appearance on the page and emphasise the refrain.

Spellings are partially modernised, e.g. *Giving*, but other interventions have been made to accord the text with Ramsay's own version of Scots, e.g. *Deil* 'devil' in line 9, for B's *diuill*. Ramsay's form is a hyper-Scotticism; *v*-deletion, i.e. the dropping of [v] with compensatory lengthening of the vowel, is common in Scots after *c.* 1450, but is clearly not reflected in B's or MF's spellings. Inflections that are syllabic in Older Scots are removed, e.g. *taks* in line 3 for B's *takkis*. Further, Ramsay generally drops the characteristically Scots and Northern Middle English present plural verb inflection in -*s* (e.g. *The Clerks tak* for B's *The clerkis takis* in line 6), save in line 14 (*gars*) where it is possible that he has failed to note concord between the verb and the subject (i.e. *Barons*, cf. B's *Barronis*).

When Lord Hailes (formerly Sir David Dalrymple) re-edited the texts some fifty years later, he commented critically on Ramsay's practice, though patronising him as a man of 'singular native genius', writing:

> This is the MS. which the editor of the *Evergreen* used: but he has omitted some stanzas, and added others; has modernized the versification, and varied the ancient manner of spelling. Hence, they who look in the *Evergreen* for the state of language and poetry among us during the fifteenth century [*sic*], will be missed, or disappointed.
>
> The many and obvious inaccuracies of *the Evergreen*, suggested the idea of this new collection. In it the MS. has been fairly copied; no liberties in amending or interpolating have been taken. The reader will find the language, versification, and spelling, in the same state as they were in 1568. (Hailes 1770: preface)

Hailes's preface illustrates well some practices of punctuation that are distinct from those favoured in educated/prestigious Present-day English, notably with regard to the semicolon and comma. He was clearly influenced in his choice of prose punctuation by contemporary Elocutionist views. In the eighteenth century, 'rhetorical' and 'grammatical' punctuation are used side-by-side; commas and semicolons are introduced to indicate 'elocutionary' units, 'where the speaker or reader is expected to pause for effect' (Parkes 1992: 91).

Despite what he says, or perhaps because he did not think that punctuation and capitalisation had a significant communicative function, in editing *Discretion in Taking*, Hailes modified his original's usage, introducing punctuation like Ramsay's, and removing B's capital letters. His capitalisation was more restrained than Ramsay's, and indeed much like Present-day English practice, except for *Discretioun*, which he evidently chose to capitalise for thematic reasons. Although he did not hyper-Scotticise by introducing *v*-deletion in *divill*, he replaced the graph <u> with <v>, and <þ> has gone. Hailes 'modernised' word division, e.g. *ouir hé* for B's *ouirhie* in line 13, treating *ouir* as an intensifying adverb rather than a prefixed bound morpheme, and adding a diacritic accent to distinguish adjective 'high' from pronoun 'he'; B deals with this potential ambiguity by distinctive spellings <hie> and <he>. There are also other spelling variants, such as *sould/sowld* (line 10) and *fruitt/fruct* (line 12). These modifications interestingly problematise Hailes's claim (above) that 'The reader will find the language, versification, and spelling, in the same state as they were in 1568.'

4.3 Texts (e) and (f)

The final pair of editions examined here are Mackenzie's of 1932 and Bawcutt's of 1998. Both editors employ, essentially, grammatical punctuation, but there are some interesting differences. Mackenzie uses colons before the refrain, which he plainly sees as summative, presumably requiring a special intonation; in this sense, he is continuing the Elocutionist tradition. It is possibly significant that both colon and semicolon are preceded by a space, whereas comma and full stop are not (although this might well be the decision of a publisher, a covert fourth player in the communicative situation). Bawcutt uses punctuation as parsing, emphasising grammatical structure to help readers understand constructions; for example, by using a full stop to detach the refrain. Both editors use capitals in the same way as Hailes, but do not capitalise *discretioun*. Both stick closely to B's spellings, though both drop <þ>; Bawcutt explains that, because <þ> and <y> are written identically, she replaces the former with <th> when it 'represents modern *th*' (1998: 21). Only Bawcutt keeps <u> for <v>. Elsewhere she praises MF, but she does not introduce deictic *Thir* in line 6. Mackenzie does not adopt it there either, though scathing of another contemporary editor, Schipper, who dropped *Thir* in his reproduction of a stanza unique to MF, where Mackenzie keeps it. Mackenzie offers emended editions of the extra MF stanzas, placing them in square brackets. Bawcutt rather likes the additional stanzas, describing them as possessing 'a pithy, proverbial character not untypical of Dunbar' (1998: 382), but thinks they 'fit awkwardly into the poem', relegating them to footnotes, where they appear in diplomatic form, except that, as in her main text, she transliterates <þ> as <th>.

5. Conclusion

This survey of the various versions of the poem shows that editors have all brought their own time- and taste-driven interpretations of the poem to bear on their task. Ramsay, while claiming authenticity as part of a recuperative agenda, imposed his own notions of taste, as did Lord Hailes. Mackenzie offered the first edition of Dunbar ever to become widely available – for many years his was the only student edition – and had to balance authenticity against accessibility. Bawcutt's scholarly text, accompanied by a comprehensive critical apparatus, is a fine example of a conservative critical edition, with limited emendation and interpretative punctuation designed to offer a grammar-driven interpretation of the poem. Even the diplomatic editions of Ritchie and Craigie supply interpretation of the original manuscripts, distinguishing <þ> from <y> not in accordance with the *figura* (written manifestation) used by the scribe, who did not distinguish between the forms, but in accordance with the two *potestates* (sound equivalents) onto which the symbol mapped.

Although some editors were more methodologically explicit than others, they all had one very worthy goal in mind: they wanted to improve the accessibility of Dunbar for their contemporaries. But to achieve that goal, even when claiming authenticity, they had to make compromises, and in compromising they transformed what they were editing. Thus, when we use these editions our interpretation is filtered through Ramsay's reading, or Hailes's reading, or Mackenzie's reading, or Bawcutt's reading – or, for that matter, the B or MF readings presented by Ritchie or Craigie. All of these editions were valuable in their own time and achieved what they set out to do, but all of them represented different conceptions – sometimes radically different conceptions – of the editorial task. It is hard to see what the editors concerned might otherwise have done, given their disparate aims in their editing, but it is worth recalling not only Rom Harré's advice about methodological explicitness but also what Michael Warren said of the punctuation of Shakespeare: 'I cannot but believe that the Folio versions... are infinitely superior in authority and potential for interpretation to the modernized, regularized, even eccentric re-punctuated versions of these modern editions. Despite their many virtues in bringing Shakespeare's work to us, these editions continue to erect invisible barriers between us and the plays' (Warren 1987: 469).

In sum, we need to be aware that the editorial process is unavoidably a transformative process, and one that can impede as well as aid communication. This issue matters because, though we are used to engaging with, and challenging, interpretative criticism and encourage our students to do the same, we are perhaps less used to encouraging them explicitly to challenge textual criticism and to be aware of editorial intervention. Now that hypertext versions are increasingly available, it is possible to harness the multiplicity of available versions of a text. Not only does such an approach help us to be alert to issues of intellectual history and editorial intervention, but it also invites us to reflect on our own practices in a way that allows us to engage more accurately with the cultural alterity of Dunbar and other writers from the past.

Appendix: Versions of the poem

(a)　Ritchie (1928): *The Bannatyne Manuscript*

ffollowis discretioun in taking

Eftir geving I speik of taking
Bot littill of ony gud forsaiking
Sum takkis our littill awtoritie
And sum our mekle And þat is glaiking
In taking sowld discretioun be   5

The clerkis takis beneficis w^t brawlis
Sum of sanct petir and sum of sanct pawlis
Tak he the rentis No cair hes he
Suppois the diuill tak all thair sawlis
In taking sowld discretioun   10

Barronis takis fra the tenne*n*tis peure
all fruct þat growis on þe feure
In mailis and gersomes rasit ouirhie
and garris thame beg fra dur to dure
In taking sowld discretioun be   15

(b) Craigie (1919): *The Maitland Folio Manuscript*

>Eftir giffing we will speik of taking
>Not litle of na gude giftis forsaiking
>Sum takis o*ur* litle authorite
>And sum o*ur* mekle and þat is glaiking
>In taiking suld discretioun be   5
>
>Thir clarkis takkis benefices w*ith* bralis
>Sum of sanct Petir and sum of S. paulis
>sett he þe rent na cure giffis he
>Suppois þe dewill tak all þair saulis
>In taking etc   10
>
>Thir baronis takis frome þair tenne*n*tis pure
>All fructis þat growis in þe fure
>Males and gressowmes ar raisit so hie
>and garris þame beg fra dur to dure
>In taking etc   15
>
>Thir merchandis takis vnlesum win
>Qu*hi*lk makis þair pakkis oftymes full thin
>Be þair successioun ʒe may see
>That ill won geir Riches not þe kin
>In taking etc   20

(c) Ramsay (1724): *The Ever Green, being a Collection of Scots Poems, Wrote by the Ingenious before 1600*

>*Follows Discration in Taking.*
>I
>NOw after Giving I speik of Taking,
>But litill of ony Gude forsaiking;
>Sum taks owre scrimp Autoritie,
>And sum owre-mekle, and that is glaiking;
>In Taking suld Discration be.
>II
>THE Clerks tak Benifices with Brawls,
>Sum of Saint *Peter*, sum of Saint *Pauls*,
>Take he the Rents, nae Cair hes he,
>Abeit the Deil tak all thair Sauls;
>In Taking suld Discration be.
>III
>BARONS tak frae thair Tenans pure
>All fruit that grows upon the Feure,
>In Mails and Fersomes raist owre hie,

        And gars them beg frae Dore to Dore;
        In Taking suld Discration be.

(d)   Hailes (1770): *Ancient Scottish Poems*

        I
        Eftir geving I speik of taking,
        Bot littill of ony gud forsaiking;
        Sum takkis our littill autoritie,
        And sum oure-mekle, and that is glaiking;
        In taking sould Discretioun be.
        II
        The clerkis takis beneficis with brawlis,
        Sum of Sanct Peter, and sum of Sanct Paulis;
        Tak he the rentis, no cair hes he,
        Suppois the divill tak all thair sawlis;
        In taking sould Discretioun be.
        III
        Barronis takis fra the tennentis peure,
        All fruitt that growis on the feure,
        In mailis and gersomes raisit ouir hé,
        And garris thame beg fra dure to dure;
        In taking sould Discretioun be.

(e)   Mackenzie (1932): *The Poems of William Dunbar*

        EFTIR GEVING I speik of taking,
        Bot littill of ony gud forsaiking.
        Sum takkis our littill awtoritie,
        And sum our mekle, and that is glaiking :
        In taking sowld discretioun be.   5

        The clerkis takis beneficis with brawlis,
        Sum of Sanct Petir, and sum of Sanct Pawlis;
        Tak he the rentis, no cair hes he,
        Suppois the divill tak all thair sawlis :
        In taking sowld discretioun be   10

        Barronis takis fra the tennentis peure
        All fruct that growis on the feure,
        In mailis and gersomes rasit ouirhie,
        And garris thame beg fra dur to dure :
        In taking sowld discretioun be.   15

        [Thir marchandis takis unlesum win,
        Quhilk makis thair pakkis oftymes full thin;
        Be thair successioun ye may see

            That ill won geir riches not the kin :
            In taking suld discretioun be.]   20

(f)   Bawcutt (1998): *The Poems of William Dunbar*

            1
            Eftir geving I speik of taking,
            Bot littill of ony gud forsaiking.
            Sum takkis our littill awtoritie,
            And sum our mekle, and that is glaiking.
            In taking sowld discretioun be.   5
            2
            The clerkis takis beneficis with brawlis,
            Sum of Sanct Petir and sum of Sanct Pawlis.
            Tak he the rentis, no cair hes he,
            Suppois the diuill tak all thair sawlis.
            In taking sowld discretioun be.   10
            3
            Barronis takis fra the tennentis peure
            All fruct that growis on the feure,
            In malis and gersomes raisit ouirhie,
            And garris thame beg fra dur to dure.
            In taking sowld discretioun be.[4]   15

[4] MF has a stanza not in B:

            Thir merchandis takis vnlesum win
            Quhilk makis thair pakkis oftymes full thin
            Be thair successioun ȝe may see
            That ill won geir riches not the kin
            In taking &c. (Bawcutt 1998: 147)

Part IV

Manuscripts and their communicating characters

16 Greetings and farewells in Chaucer's *Canterbury Tales*

ANDREAS H. JUCKER

1. Introduction

In this chapter, I want to provide a case study of two largely phatic speech acts in Chaucer's *Canterbury Tales*: greetings and farewells. They function as openings and closings of interactions between speakers, and they also serve to establish and re-establish the speakers' relationship with each other in terms of their respective places in the social hierarchy, their familiarity and their respective power.

Literary language may, of course, differ considerably from the spoken language of the day. This study, therefore, does not make any claims about how greetings and farewells were used in Middle English in general. It merely focuses on the use of these speech acts in the fictional world of Chaucer's *Canterbury Tales*. It is tempting to perceive the *Canterbury Tales* as a magnificent, unified whole with a well-balanced variety of diverse genres, 'as a wonderfully complex linked set of short stories, wholly conceived as such in all its details' (Meyer-Lee 2008: 1). But, as Meyer-Lee is quick to point out, such a view is an 'utter fiction'. It is a fiction that is based on the monumental editorial undertaking of the early editors of Chaucer's work going back to the fifteenth century and which still lives on in such outstanding editions as *The Riverside Chaucer*.

In the historical medieval reality there is no such unity (see also Matthews 1999: 162–86). There are over eighty extant manuscripts, which contain part or all of what today is considered to be the *Canterbury Tales*, some containing only a single tale or mere fragments (Benson 1987: 1,118; but see also Robinson 2003: 126). In addition there are six early prints that may go back to additional manuscripts that have not survived. The two most important manuscripts are the Hengwrt 154 (National Library of Wales, Aberystwyth) and the Ellesmere 26 C 9 (Henry E. Huntingdon Library, San Marino, California). Literary interpretations of the tales often depend on the order of specific editions (see, for instance, Phillips 2000: 14–16, who lists some relevant examples of such interpretations). From a pragmatic point of view, we may also be interested to know more about Chaucer's audience. Did he write for a highly educated, middle-class audience or for princes and courtiers (Pearsall 1992a: 178–85)? The complexity of the historical manuscript reality, however, defies easy answers to such questions, and the unity and coherence of modern editions should not be taken as a source for speculation on the answers to such questions.

However, whether in their fictional unity or in fragments, the *Canterbury Tales* is a collection of tales with a frame narrative and numerous narratives within narratives, i.e. stories told not only by the characters in the frame but also by the characters in the individual tales and even by characters that occur in such embedded stories. As such, they offer a rich world for pragmatic studies, even if it is a world that has been mediated from Chaucer's manuscript reality to our modern scholarly editions of the *Tales*.

Recent research in the history of specific speech acts has revealed a number of theoretical and methodological problems. One of the most obvious problems is the comparability of a particular speech act across time. On what level is a medieval insult the same as a modern insult (Jucker and Taavitsainen 2000)? Is a compliment of introduction in the eighteenth century really comparable to a compliment on the delicious food at a present-day dinner invitation (Taavitsainen and Jucker 2008)? Such questions have been discussed as the problem of a *tertium comparationis* (e.g. Krzeszowski 1984). Can we trace specific illocutions or perlocutions across different stages in the development of a language? Does the use of a specific speech-act verb, such as 'insult' or 'compliment' or their earlier cognates guarantee a constant illocution across time so that a comparison really compares comparable entities? On a first approximation, greetings and farewells seem particularly well suited for a historical comparison because they can be easily located as the speech acts that open or close a conversation, and thus their *tertium comparationis* seems to be fairly solid. But the analysis will show that the realities are more complex. What appear to be greetings and farewells in the fictional world of Chaucer's *Canterbury Tales* differ not only in their realisation from present-day greetings and farewells but also in their basic function.

2. Greetings and farewells

The speech acts of greetings and farewells have received a considerable amount of attention in the relevant literature. Searle (1969: 67) described greetings as devoid of propositional content and lacking in sincerity conditions. The only condition for a successful greeting was, according to him, the extra-linguistic context in which the speaker and the addressee have just met each other. Eisenstein *et al.* (1996: 92) point out that, in their data of native speakers of American English, greetings often convey feelings and thus are not the empty formulas suggested by Searle. Feelings and emotions can even be explicitly formulated ('Oh, it's nice to see you') or they can be expressed in a warm tone of voice. Eisenstein *et al.* (1996: 93–6) distinguish between different types of greetings. In the 'greeting on the run', acquaintances see each other and exchange nothing more than perhaps a smile and a brief phatic statement or a formulaic question that does not require a response. In a 'speedy greeting', some information is exchanged, but it begins and ends abruptly. 'The chat' is a somewhat longer version of a speedy greeting involving a short discussion. 'The long greeting' is used to re-establish bonds between the speakers after longer periods of separation. It is characterised by several individual greetings that are separated by narrative sequences. 'The intimate greeting' is used by people who know each other well and can leave almost everything either implied or unsaid, or it may consist almost entirely of non-verbal gestures. 'The all-business greeting' is typical for situations in which the interlocutors, e.g. an agent and a client who do not have a social relationship, start an interaction without any phatic talk. In 'the introductory greeting', two people who have not previously met start an interaction. Further types are 'service encounter greetings' or 're-greetings'. On the basis of this classification and their data, Eisenstein *et al.* show that greetings can be very simple, consisting of a single speech act, or they can be complex and extended. They can be merely phatic and formulaic or they can be meaningful and creative.

Duranti (1997), who investigated greetings in Western Samoa, also makes the point that greeting sequences need not be devoid of propositional content. He proposed the following six features for identifying greeting sequences (Duranti 1997: 67):

(i) near-boundary occurrence;
(ii) establishment of a shared perceptual field;
(iii) adjacency pair format;
(iv) relative predictability of form and content;
(v) implicit establishment of a spatio-temporal unit of interaction; and
(vi) identification of the interlocutor as a distinct being worth recognising.

Even without a detailed discussion of these features, it is clear that Duranti focuses on a somewhat more restricted set of speech events than Eisenstein *et al.* (1996). In several Samoan greetings, form and content are entirely creative and not predictable, and in many cases the adjacency pair format is extended to an interaction between two or more interlocutors over several turns. But, even so, Samoans use greeting sequences to accomplish a variety of social acts. They may, for instance, search for new information, compliment the addressee or sanction social behaviour.

Rash (2004), on the other hand, stresses the formulaic nature of greetings in Swiss German. She also distinguishes between 'passing greetings' and 'conversation openings' (2004: 51), where passing greetings are used when passing people in the street (especially in rural areas), on mountain paths or in shops. In her interviews with native speakers of Swiss German, she found a great concern for greetings, which are seen as politeness rituals that are important as signs of respect and as devices strengthening social cohesion.

Thus it appears that not only in Present-day English but also in other languages greeting sequences can be brief and formulaic but they can also be extended and creative. They can be largely phatic and devoid of propositional content but they can also be multifunctional with other meaningful social activities. And they can be short adjacency pairs or longer sequences extending over several turns.

This general picture is further reinforced by diachronic studies of greetings and farewells. Such historical studies include Stroebe (1911) on Old Germanic greetings; Lebsanft (1988) on greetings in Old French; Hauser (1998) on greetings and farewells in Swiss German from the fifteenth century to the present day; Grzega (2008) on greetings in English; and Arnovick (1999: ch. 6) on *goodbye* in English. Lebsanft (1988) and Grzega (2008) both use a lexical approach and provide large inventories of greetings. Grzega draws his greetings from the entire history of the English language, and Lebsanft provides a full inventory of lexical elements in Old French that are used to talk about greetings and that are used to actually greet.

Lebsanft (1988: 18) discusses the degree of formulaicity or phraseological fixity of the greetings in his data. He distinguishes between syntactic fixity ('*materielle Fixiertheit*') (choice and order of elements) and semantic fixity ('*inhaltliche Fixiertheit*') (meaning of the phrase derivable directly from the meanings of its parts). It appears that Old French greetings are only marginally formulaic. In Old French, speakers choose and combine the individual elements freely, and the greetings can be interpreted on the basis of their individual elements. Typical examples are *Dieus vos saut* or *Dieus vos gart de aucune rien*.

Lebsanft (1988) distinguishes carefully between verbal greetings and non-verbal greetings in order to describe the different lexical means in Old French to talk about them, and he distinguishes between address greetings (*Begrüßung*) and leave-taking (*Abschied*), for which German offers *Grüßen* 'greet' as a superordinate expression. In the third part of his book, Lebsanft describes the pragmatics of Old French greetings. He discusses in detail who greets whom, the number and sequence of turns in greeting exchanges, the return greeting and the question of who greets first (Lebsanft 1988: 245).

Hauser (1998) traces greeting rituals in Swiss German from the fifteenth century to the present day. He particularly focuses on the interaction between greetings and face work, and he discerns a decline of politeness in the twentieth century, which he ascribes to the increased demographic mobility and the influence of the mass media. He distinguishes a great range of different greetings, especially for Present-day Swiss German, including greetings that are accompanied by special gestures and variations of handshakes, such as the Zurich greeting, the skateboarder's greeting, the techno greeting, the pot-smoker's greeting, the snowboarder's greeting and the hip-hopper greeting (Hauser 1998: 164).

Stroebe (1911) observes that in Old English *wes hal* with syntactic variants, together with *wilcuman* or *þu art wilcuma*, were the most common greeting forms. Christian greetings, such as *Deo gratias*, on the other hand seem to have been rare in Old English. They only emerged in the fourteenth and fifteenth centuries. Grzega (2008: 191) notes that Middle English displays a greater range of greetings, but they do not seem to be fossilised. Many phrases occur only once or a few times. The more formulaic greetings in Old and Middle English fall into four different classes. In Old English, there are attention getters and wishes for well-being. And in Middle English, there are wishes for a good time and enquiries about the addressee's health. Various speech acts that implicitly also served as greetings turned into pure greetings.

Arnovick (1999: ch. 6) provides a detailed diachronic study of one specific leave-taking formula, Present-day English *goodbye*. On the basis of her data culled from the Chadwyck-Healey electronic corpus, she dates the first occurrences back to the late fifteenth century and thus antedates the *Oxford English Dictonary*'s earliest attested examples from the mid to late sixteenth century (Arnovick 1999: 98). She shows that in Early Modern English the phrase *God be with you* was an explicit blessing and an implicit greeting, which in the course of time turned into the strictly secular greeting that it is today with the main purpose of structuring the conversation in a polite way.

On the basis of the research summarised above, we should expect greetings and farewells in Chaucer's Middle English to show considerable variability. All these studies have shown both the diversity and creativity of greetings and farewells and at the same time the tendency for certain forms to become formulaic and ritualistic. In earlier periods, religious invocations at the beginning and at the end of conversations were common and it can be expected that this tendency will also surface in Chaucer's use of greetings and farewells in his *Canterbury Tales*.

3. Analysis

In this section, I will analyse the constitutive elements of greetings and farewells in Chaucer's *Canterbury Tales*. For the purpose of this chapter, all greeting and farewell sequences were manually located in fragments 1 to 9 of the *Canterbury Tales*, excluding only fragment number 10 with the Parson's Prologue and Tale, and Chaucer's Retraction.[1] The search included

---

[1] The search was based on *The Riverside Chaucer* (Benson 1987). The following quotations are also taken from *The Riverside Chaucer*. References are given in the format fragment number in Roman numerals and line numbers in Arabic numerals. The abbreviations for individual tales follow *The Riverside Chaucer* (Benson 1987: 779). My thanks go to Lucien Palser for considerable help with the data and to Daniela Landert and Päivi Pahta for valuable comments on a draft version of this chapter. The usual disclaimers apply.

Table 16.1 *Recurring elements in greetings and farewells in Chaucer's* Canterbury Tales *(individual speech acts may contain several or none of these elements)*

	Greetings (total n = 67)	Farewells (total n = 73)
Well-wishing	8	23
Identification	47	15
Blessing	8	14
Interjection	19	3
Leave-taking		7
Dismissal		14

direct speech exchanged at the opening or closing of an encounter between characters in the narration and the descriptions of such openings and closings. Speech acts in narratives can occur in direct speech ascribed to individual characters, they can be reported indirectly or they can be merely described by the narrator. Conversations often start *in medias res* without any speech act that we would want to label as a greeting even if it is obvious that the characters have only just met; or the conversation breaks off without any concluding words even if it is clear that the characters are parting. Often, the narrator records only the greeting or leave-taking sequence of one participant and does not give the addressee's response.

There are a total of sixty-seven greetings and seventy-three farewells in the data, of which fifteen and eighteen cases, respectively, are indirect descriptions without any direct speech. The remaining sequences record the words of at least one of the characters greeting or bidding farewell. They reveal a large range of different formulations and thus confirm Grzega's (2008: 191) claim that Middle English greetings show very little fossilisation. Many greetings and farewells are creative, some of them are relatively long, extending over many lines, but there are also very brief ones consisting of one or two words only. The main elements that regularly occur both in greetings and in farewells are the following: well-wishing, identification of the addressee, blessings and interjections. Farewells also often include leave-takings and dismissals (see table 16.1). The categories will be described in the following.

The figures show that some kind of identification of the addressee is the most important element in the greetings. It occurs in forty-seven out of sixty-seven cases. In farewells, this category is less important with only fifteen occurrences in seventy-three farewells. The categories well-wishing and blessing occur only occasionally in greetings and slightly more often in farewells. Interjections occur more frequently in greetings and only very rarely in farewells. The last two categories, leave-taking and dismissal, are obviously restricted to farewells.

3.1 Well-wishing

The well-wishing sequences in greetings may consist of an enquiry after the addressee's health or a formulaic wish for a good time of the day (Grzega 2008: 185, 184). Thomas's wife addresses friar John with 'Ey, maister, welcome be ye, by Seint John!/ . . . how fare ye, hertely?' (SumT III 1800–1). And Aleyn greets the miller with the words 'Al hayl, Symond, y-fayth!/ Hou fares thy faire doghter and thy wyf?' (RvT I 4022–3).

In the farewell sequences, the well-wishing often consists of the formulaic *farewell*, or the equally formulaic *have good day*. Aleyn – after having spent the night in her bed – bids the miller's daughter farewell with the words: 'Fare weel, Malyne, sweete wight!/ The day is come; I may no lenger byde;/ But everemo, wher so I go or ryde,/ I is thyn awen clerk, swa have I seel!' (RvT I 4236–9). Don John in the Shipman's Tale bids farewell with the words: 'Farewel, have good day!' (ShipT VII 320).

The *farewell* formula appears to be the most formulaic element that occurs either in greetings or in farewells, and indeed it still gives the entire speech act its name. It is still a 'common English parting salutation' (Arnovick 1999: 96) with a form that has been used since Middle English. In the *Canterbury Tales*, it is to some extent still creative. It is sometimes broken up as in 'fareth now weel' or 'fare now wel' (e.g. MLT II 1159; MerT IV 1688; ShipT VII 279) or in 'Lat hym fare wel' (WBPro III 501), in which the two elements still function as a verb and an adverb. The full form has not undergone lexicalisation yet, but it also appears in the merged form, as in 'Farewel, cosyn' (ShipT VII 264). It is also used to describe prototypical situations of parting, as, for instance, in the Knight's Tale: 'And hoom wente every man the righte way./ Ther was namoore but "Fare wel, have good day!"' (KnT I 2739–40). After the tournament in which Arcite is mortally wounded, Theseus decrees an end to all hostility and the crowds that have gathered for the tournament and the festivities can now disperse with the routine farewell wishes. The *farewell* formula appears in twenty-one out of seventy-three farewells in the *Canterbury Tales*.

3.2 Identification

The characters very often use nominal terms of address when they greet each other and sometimes also when parting. Chaucer's use of forms of address has often been analysed in connection with politeness or impoliteness (see, for instance, Mazzon 2000; Stévanovitch 2003; and Jucker 2006). Horobin (2007a: 151) draws attention to the way in which the Host, Harry Bailly, addresses his fellow pilgrims with nominal terms of address. For a range of pilgrims he uses the polite *Sir* plus professional name, such as *Sire Knyght, Sire Clerk, Sire Man of Lawe* or *Sir Parisshe Prest*. But on certain occasions, he drops the polite *Sir* and addresses a pilgrim by his/her professional name only, such as the Franklin, whom he addresses as 'Frankeleyn' (SqT V 696) when, at the end of the Squire's Tale, he rebukes him for his ramblings. But the Host also uses this form of address in less confrontational situations to characters of lesser social standing, e.g. to the Squire, the Merchant or the Manciple (Horobin 2007a: 151).

In greetings and farewells, I distinguish between several subtypes of nominal terms of address; honorifics, occupations, names, terms of family relation, terms of endearment and terms of abuse. Honorifics comprise forms such as 'sire' (e.g. ShipT VII 215), 'goode sire' (e.g. CYT VIII 1295), 'My righte lady' (FranT V 1311) or 'Madame' (MLT II 732). Occupational terms of address do not occur very often in greetings and farewells, even though they occur elsewhere. Those that do occur are mostly terms designating the noble or clerical rank of the addressee rather than a middle-class profession. Relevant examples are 'Sire knyght' (WBT III 1001), 'my sovereyn lady queene' (WBT III 1048) and 'frere John' (SumT III 2171). These nominal terms of address in greetings, therefore, also serve the purpose of establishing or re-establishing the social relationship between the speaker and the addressee.

Names on their own occur fairly often in greetings and occasionally in farewells. When Absolon visits the blacksmith in order to borrow a ploughshare, he greets him with: 'Undo, Gerveys, and that anon' and – after he has identified himself – he is greeted by: 'What, Absolon! for Cristes sweete tree,/ Why rise ye so rathe?' (MilT I 3765–8). The few instances of terms of occupations mostly occur together with an honorific. Names are sometimes combined with an honorific, as in 'maister Nicholay' (MilT I 3579).

Terms of family relationship are also used in greetings and in farewells, but often they do not denote actual family relations but are expressions of respect or of close friendship. In the Wife of Bath's Tale, for instance, the knight addresses the old hag on their first encounter with the very polite 'My leeve mooder' (WBT III 1005) and, in the Shipman's Tale, the merchant's wife addresses the monk with the words: 'O deere cosyn myn, daun John' (ShipT VII 98).

Terms of endearment and terms of abuse are both creative categories, but their overall frequency is rather low. Absolon, the village dandy in the Miller's Tale, greets Alisoun with the following words: 'What do ye, honycomb, sweete Alisoun,/ My faire bryd, my sweete cynamome?/ Awaketh, lemman myn, and speketh to me!' (MilT I 3698–700). In the Reeve's Tale, Malyne bids farewell to Aleyn with: 'And, goode lemman, God thee save and kepe!' (RvT I 4247). In the beast fable of the Nun's Priest's Tale, Pertelote, the farmyard hen, addresses her husband, Chauntecleer, as 'Herte deere' (NPT VII 2889) and in the Merchant's Tale, January greets May, his wife, with the words: 'Rys up, my wyf, my love, my lady free!' (MerT IV 2138).

Table 16.2 gives an overview of the frequency of nominal terms of address in Chaucer's *Canterbury Tales*.

Table 16.2 *Nominal terms of address in greetings and farewells in Chaucer's* Canterbury Tales

	Greetings	Farewells
Honorifics	20	7
Occupation (with honorific)	4 (3)	1 (1)
Names (with honorific)	18 (4)	3 (0)
Family relation	7	4
Terms of endearment	5	2
Terms of abuse	5	0

3.3 Blessings

Taavitsainen (1997a) has drawn attention to the co-occurrence of blessings or pious wishes with greetings and other opening phrases in Middle English. She stresses the influence of genre on the choice of formulaic uses. In my data, blessings in greetings and farewells are not as frequent as might have been expected, but they do occur occasionally. The old man in the Pardoner's Tale provides a typical example when he greets the three rioters with the words: 'Now, lordes, God yow see!' (PardT VI 715) or the wife in the Friar's Tale, who greets the summoner with the words: 'benedicitee!/ God save you, sire, what is youre sweete wille?' (FrT III 1584–5). It is perhaps significant that the blessings in both these cases are directed at addressees of very dubious character.

The more elaborate blessings take forms such as 'Fareth now wel. God have yow in his grace' (MerT IV 1688); 'And God be with yow, where ye go or ryde!' (PardT VI 748); or 'God save yow, that boghte agayn mankynde' (PardT VI 766). Several blessings appear at the end of individual tales in which the narrator ends his or her narration with good wishes to the audience. These are not really farewells in the strict sense, as the speaker and addressees do not part, but the formulations suggest a great similarity to actual farewells. The Miller, for instance, finishes with 'This tale is doon, and God save al the rowte!' (MilT I 3854) or, in a more elaborate version, the Man of Law: 'And fareth now weel! my tale is at an ende./ Now Jhesu Crist, that of his myght may sende/ Joye after wo, governe us in his grace,/ And kepe us alle that been in this place! Amen' (MLT II 1159–62).

3.4 Interjections

Many greetings and a few farewells are accompanied by interjections, such as *now*, *o*, *what* or *benedicitee*. As in the case of blessings, the choice and meaning of specific interjections also depends to some extent on the genre in which they occur (Taavitsainen 1995b, 1998: 199). In romances of the *Canterbury Tales*, for instance, they are used to convey feelings of despair, sorrow and regret, but they are also used as foregrounding devices and markers of episode boundaries. In saints' lives, they are used in invocations and prayers. And in the fabliaux, they are mainly used as stereotypical reactions in specific situations. As features of personal affect, they also help to describe the different characters of the *Canterbury Tales* (Taavitsainen 1999). In connection with greetings and farewells, the following are relevant examples. The old man greets the rioters with the words: 'Now, lordes, God yow see!' (PardT VI 715). The merchant's wife greets the monk: 'O deere cosyn myn, daun John' (ShipT VII 98). And the carpenter tries to address Nicholas, who is pretending to be in a stupor and reading the stars: 'What! Nicholay! What, how! What, looke adoun!' (MilT I 3477). These may serve a number of different functions. They can be attention getters or expressions of surprise or they can be what might best be described as discourse-structuring elements, as in the case of *now*.

In some cases there might even be an overlap between the category of blessing and interjection, as in the case of a pious oath (see Taavitsainen 1995a: 448). The old wife in the Friar's Tale greets the summoner with 'benedicitee!/ God save you, sire, what is youre sweete wille?' (FrT III 1584–5), in which the *benedicitee* serves both as an interjection and a pious oath. In the Summoner's Tale, the lord greets the friar with 'Benedicitee!/ What, frere John, what maner world is this?' (SumT III 2170–1).

In farewells, interjections are rare. But Malyne bids farewell to Aleyn with the words: 'Now, deere lemman... go, far weel!' (RvT I 4240) or, similarly, the priest to the Canon in the Canon's Yeoman's Tale: 'Now, goode sire, go forth thy wey and hy the' (CYT VIII 1295). In both cases, *now* functions as a discourse marker in the sense of Schiffrin (1987: 228–66). The third farewell that is accompanied by an interjection occurs in the Miller's Tale, where Alison sends away her husband to prepare everything for the impending flood predicted by her lover Nicholas: 'Allas! Go forth thy wey anon,/ Help us to scape, or we been dede echon!' (MilT I 3607–8).

The elements outlined above can occur both in greetings and in farewells. Two further elements, by their very nature, can only occur in farewells. These are the categories of leave-taking and dismissal.

3.5 *Leave-taking and dismissal*

In farewells, speakers often explicitly take their leave or ask for permission to withdraw. Grisildis, for instance, takes her leave from her husband with the words: 'And heer take I my leeve/ Of yow, myn owene lord, lest I yow greve' (ClT IV 888–9). Sometimes the leave-taking is described without direct speech, as in the Franklin's Tale, 'He taketh his leve' (FranT V 1339) and 'They take hir leve, and on hir wey they gon' (FranT V 1490); or in the Squire's Tale, 'For of hir fader hadde she take leve/ To goon to reste soone after it was eve' (SqT V 363–4).

The last category describes cases in which one of the characters dismisses his or her addressee. In the Shipman's Tale, for instance, the lecherous monk dismisses the merchant's wife with the words: 'Gooth now youre wey, . . . al stille and softe,/ And lat us dyne as soone as that ye may;/ For by my chilyndre it is pryme of day./ Gooth now, and beeth as trewe as I shal be' (ShipT VII 204–7). And in the Miller's Tale, Nicholas dismisses the foolish carpenter: 'Go now thy wey, and speed thee heer-aboute' (MilT I 3562).

On the basis of all these examples from Chaucer's *Canterbury Tales*, it can be concluded that the same general situation obtains as described for other languages and for other varieties of English by the scholars reviewed in the previous section. Greetings and farewells can be brief and formulaic but they can also be creative and they can extend over several turns. I have identified a small range of elements that tend to co-occur with greetings and farewells. These elements can reinforce the phatic nature of the speech act or they can provide additional functions, such as the establishment or re-establishment of social relationships through the use of appropriate terms of address, the structuring of the discourse through the use of discourse markers, or the invocation of pious wishes through the use of blessings.

4. Conclusion

In the frame story of the *Canterbury Tales* virtually all social classes (estates) are represented: the clergy with a prioress, a monk, a summoner, a friar, a pardoner and a parson; the aristocracy with a knight and a squire; and the commons with a miller, a reeve, a cook, a shipman and so on. The diversity of characters in the tales themselves is even richer, with characters both from realistic settings in fourteenth-century England and in fictional settings, such as the court of King Arthur, or even a farmyard with talking and philosophising animals. It is, therefore, not surprising that greetings and farewells also show a great diversity. By and large, they are less routinised and less conventionalised than in Present-day English. Speakers make use of a range of elements that frequently occur both in greetings and in farewells, but none of which seem to be obligatory. The most important elements of greetings and farewells are the formulaic wishes for the addressee and the identification of the addressee through an address term, an honorific or a term of endearment. A blessing is also often used and an enquiry into the addressee's health or his or her family's health. In farewells, the speakers often ask for permission to take their leave or they dismiss their addressee, depending on the situation and the social ranks of the interactants.

The *Canterbury Tales* are a rich source for fictional interactions and conversations, even if 'a single form for the *Tales* will necessarily remain an editorial fiction, and hence the ground of formalist treatments of its text always, to greater and lesser degrees, shaky' (Meyer-Lee 2008: 13; see also Pearsall 1992b). To use these conversations as data for analysis of different forms of greeting and farewells does not depend on any claims for the unity of this work. Not even the frequency figures provided in tables 16.1 and 16.2 should be interpreted as a claim that the *Canterbury Tales* are somehow a unified and finished set of data. Nevertheless, a pragmatic analysis, like any other linguistic or literary analysis of the *Canterbury Tales*, is deeply indebted to the editors of the modern editions because it relies on their mediating efforts to let Chaucer's work communicate with present-day readers and scholars.

17 Attitudes of the accused in the Salem Witchcraft Trials

LEENA KAHLAS-TARKKA
AND MATTI RISSANEN

1. Introduction

In recent years, courtroom examinations have been amply studied from the discoursal point of view. Both present-day trials and records dating from earlier centuries have been in focus. A number of articles are based on transcripts of the Salem trials published in three volumes by Paul Boyer and Stephen Nissenbaum in 1977. More recently, studies have also made use of a project for transcribing the Salem witchcraft records anew and adding until now unknown documents to the material, which has resulted in a 1,000-page volume, *Records of the Salem Witch-Hunt* (Rosenthal *et al.* 2009). The new edition presents the documents in chronological order to give a better idea of the whole chain of events, and it includes substantial introductory essays that contribute to the understanding of the legal procedures, the historical and social context of the events as well as the language of the period. This chapter is based on the material in this new volume.[1]

In studies from the past dozen or so years, attention has been focused on various aspects of trial discourse. Hiltunen (1996) discusses questions in cases that record trials in direct-speech form. These include questions both from the examiners, often presupposing guilt, and from the defendants who either resort to rhetorical questions or even to counter-questioning strategies. Archer (2002) also focuses on questioning, but adds an analysis of responses in terms of Grice's Cooperative Principle. One of her main arguments is that 'the Salem magistrates adopted a "guilty but unwilling to confess" paradigm that led them to assume that defendants who maintained their innocence were lying' (2002: 1). A pragmatic analysis of the question and answer patterns from the point of view of both the examiners and the accused is also presented by Doty and Hiltunen (2002), whose study includes an analysis of narrative patterns based on Labov's work on oral narratives. Cooperativeness and the lack of it are illustrated by Kahlas-Tarkka and Rissanen (2007). Types of questions, responses and discourse markers as well

---

[1] Important information is also available in the Documentary Archive of the Salem Witch Trials at www2.iath.virginia.edu/salem/home.html.

as the notion of impoliteness in Early Modern English court trial records are thoroughly investigated by Kryk-Kastovsky (2000, 2006a).

In many of the above studies, the theoretical framework involves politeness theory (Brown and Levinson 1987). Most recently, Chaemsaithong (2009) studied response strategies within the framework of politeness, more explicitly of self-politeness and self-face. He argues, particularly, that the aim of politeness should not be understood only as being polite to and saving the face of the listener – the judges in the case of the Salem trials – but that speakers use politeness to save their own face, too. In this he follows and expands on Chen's proposal on self-face (2001). In a very detailed study, Chaemsaithong examines the accused individuals' response strategies in the Salem trials and argues convincingly that 'the accused's responses were also driven by "what they thought others thought of them", which is part of their "face"' (2009: 56), and can thus define self-politeness as 'strategies or expressions that a person develops to mitigate self-face threats, in accordance with his or her calculation of what others may think of him or her' (2009: 63).

In this chapter we will, however, distance ourselves from the above-mentioned theories, even though we are well aware of their importance and relevance for all analyses of courtroom dialogues between the examiner and the defendant. We feel that, for historical material like the Salem documents, a more 'intuitive' approach is preferable, as each individual and his/her sociocultural background plays a very important role, which has to be kept in mind throughout a study like this one. Our main purpose is to analyse the types of defendants' replies from the point of view of the various ways of convincing the court that the accused is not a witch. Special attention is paid to the length of the responses and to the ways adopted of reacting and responding. Strategies of showing cooperation, when the accused admits his/her involvement in witchcraft, will also be touched upon. By our survey of original manuscripts we wish to get as close to late seventeenth-century communication as possible.

2. Data and the role of recorders

As mentioned above, the records discussed in this article are taken from Rosenthal *et al.* (2009), which consists of some one thousand documents from the Salem Witchcraft Trials. We analysed all the records that include the first-person direct-speech utterances of the defendants, with the exception of a few cases in which only one or two replies are recorded. We also omitted the so-called Andover Examination Copies because they do not represent the original manuscripts of the recorders present on the examination occasion (documents 425 and 428).[2] Furthermore, the examinations with an unknown recorder were not analysed because their scribal history is unclear (77, 78,

---

[2] The numbers of the documents refer to the numbers in Rosenthal *et al.* (2009).

144). The Examination of Daniel Eames (509) was omitted because John Higginson's recording does not clearly indicate the division between the defendant's utterances and other text.

A list of the defences analysed here is shown in table 17.1. The records are listed in chronological order, as was adopted in the new edition to give a more accessible account of the whole chain of events. The characteristics of the utterances discussed in more detail in section 3, below, are marked in the columns on the right.

Four recorders were occupied in writing down the examinations discussed in this article: Ezekiel Cheever, Samuel Parris, Jonathan Corwin and Simon Willard. Some examinations were recorded by two recorders, most notably those of Tituba (Cheever and Corwin: 3, 6), Bridget Bishop (Cheever and Parris: 63, 64) and Mary Warren (Parris and Corwin: 75, 145). For some, two versions by the same scribe exist: Susannah Martin and John Willard by Parris (104 and 105, 173 and 174). The second versions are clean copies of the first ones and there are no essential differences in the contents. Abigail Hobbs, Mary Warren and Deliverance Hobbs were examined for a second time in prison (77, 78, 116). These records are not included because the discourse setting was different from that of the other examination occasions.

The role of the recorders is vital and should not be underestimated in the analysis of the defences. Rev. Samuel Parris, Minister of Salem Village, was the recorder of no less than sixteen examinations included in table 17.1. Ezekiel Cheever, farmer and tailor, recorded four examinations; Simon Willard, a weaver and clothier, and brother to Rev. Samuel Willard, three; and Jonathan Corwin, merchant and (later) judge, two. The educational background of the recorders probably influenced the wording and even content of the examinations (see Grund 2007; Hiltunen and Peikola 2007). As noted by Doty (2007), Parris, in particular, and also Cheever seem to have preferred to record the proceedings as direct discourse. We can assume, however, that substantial differences in the length and means of expression of the utterances in different documents produced by the same recorder represent real variation in the strategies of defence. It is also worth noting that although the recordings of two recorders of the same examination differ from each other in length and details, the overall contents and the tone of the utterances remain the same. This is true of Cheever's and Corwin's records of Tituba's examinations (3 and 6) and Cheever's and Parris's records of Bridget Bishop's examinations (63 and 64). There are remarkable similarities even in the wording of the recordings; cf. the passages in example (1) on page 245:[3]

---

[3] All examples are quoted in exactly the same form as in the new edition, editorial markings included. (H) = John Hathorne, the examiner; (T) = Tituba. Emphases in bold (in examples below) have been added.

Table 17.1 *Examination records including direct speech of the defendants in the Salem Witchcraft Trials*

	Deny guilt	Admit guilt	Survived	No neg. attitude	Mild neg. attitude	Strong neg. attitude	Number of utterances	Number of long utterances	Figurative language	Appeals to God and Christ	Address examiner/audience	Imperatives	Questions to examiner	Questioning accusation	Sarcasm	Aggressiveness	Laughter
February–March 1692																	
No. 3 Sarah Good (Cheever)	x	–	–	–	–	x	18	5	–	–	x	–	x	x	–	x	–
No. 3 Sarah Osburn (Cheever)	x	–	–	x	–	–	14	3	–	–	–	–	–	–	–	–	–
No. 3 Tituba (Cheever)	–	x	x	x	–	–	39	8	–	–	–	–	–	–	–	–	–
No. 6 Tituba (Corwin)	–	x	x	x	–	–	47	20	–	–	–	–	–	–	–	–	–
No. 16 Martha Cory (Parris)	x	–	–	–	–	x	66	11	–	x	x	x	x	x	x	–	x
No. 28 Rebecca Nurse (Parris)	x	–	–	–	x	–	24	3	x	x	x	–	x	–	–	–	–
April 1692																	
No. 63 Bridget Bishop (Cheever)	x	–	–	–	x	–	12	3	x	–	–	–	–	–	–	–	–
No. 64 Bridget Bishop (Parris)	x	–	–	–	x	–	13	2	–	x	x	–	–	x	–	–	–
No. 67 Abigail Hobbs (Parris)	–	x	x	x	–	–	61	7	–	x	–	–	–	–	–	–	–
No. 75 Mary Warren (Parris)	–	x	x	x	–	–	8	2	–	x	–	–	–	–	–	–	–
No. 84 Mary Black (Parris)	x	–	x	x	–	–	7	–	–	–	–	–	–	–	–	–	–
No. 86 Mary Esty (Parris)	x	–	–	–	x	–	12	3	–	x	x	–	x	–	–	–	–
No. 89 Deliverance Hobbs (Parris)	–	x	x	x	–	–	42	1	–	x	–	–	–	–	–	–	–
No. 90 Sarah Wilds (Parris)	x	–	–	x	–	–	4	–	–	x	–	–	–	–	–	–	–
No. 90 William Hobbs (Parris)	x	–	x	–	x	–	33	2	x	x	x	–	–	–	–	–	–
May 1692																	
No. 102 Dorcas Hoar (Parris)	x	–	x	–	–	x	24	1	–	x	x	–	x	–	–	x	–
No. 104 Susannah Martin (Parris)	x	–	–	–	–	x	26	5	–	–	x	x	x	–	x	–	x
No. 133 George Jacobs, Sr (Parris)	x	–	–	–	–	x	23	8	x	x	x	x	x	x	–	–	x
No. 145 Mary Warren (Corwin)	–	x	x	x	–	–	15	9	–	–	–	–	–	–	–	–	–
No. 173 John Willard (Parris)	x	–	–	–	–	x	23	7	x	x	x	x	–	x	–	–	x

Salem Witchcraft Trials: attitudes of the accused 245

Table 17.1 (cont.)

	Deny guilt	Admit guilt	Survived	No neg. attitude	Mild neg. attitude	Strong neg. attitude	Number of utterances	Number of long utterances	Figurative language	Appeals to God and Christ	Address examiner/audience	Imperatives	Questions to examiner	Questioning accusation	Sarcasm	Aggressiveness	Laughter
No. 235 Martha Carrier (Parris)	x	–	–	–	–	x	7	1	–	–	x	–	x	–	–	–	–
No. 241 Elizabeth How (Parris)	x	–	–	–	x	–	11	1	–	x	x	–	–	–	–	–	–
July 1692																	
No. 399 Ann Pudeator (Willard)	x	–	–	x	–	–	4	1	–	–	–	–	–	–	–	–	–
No. 429 Richard Carrier (Willard)	–	x	x	x	–	–	21	–	–	–	–	–	–	–	–	–	–
August 1692																	
No. 511 Rebecca Eames (Willard)	–	x	x	x	–	–	16	2	–	–	–	–	–	–	–	–	–

(1) (H) Titibe what ~~sp~~ evil spirit have you familiarity with (T) none (H) why doe you hurt these children, (T) I doe not hurt them (H) who is it then ~~the de~~ (T) the devil for ought I ~~ken~~ know (3. Examinations of Sarah Good, Sarah Osburn and Tituba, recorder Cheever)

Q. Whatt ffamilliarity have you wth ye devill, or w^t is itt y^t you Converse wthall? Tell ye Truth, Whoe itt is y^t hurts y^m? A. the Devill for ought I know. (6. Two examinations of Tituba, recorder Corwin)

Thus, although scribal interference is a factor to be constantly kept in mind in the analysis of the records, it seems justifiable to draw conclusions on the basis of the vastly different impressions we get, for instance, from Cheever's records of the examinations of Sarah Good and Tituba, and from Parris's records of the examinations of Mary Black, Mary Warren, Susannah Martin and George Jacobs, Sr. These recorders would have had no motivation to add such expressions as, for instance, 'I scorn it', 'You tax me for a Wizard, you may as well tax me for a Buzard', 'Amen. Amen. A false tongue will never make a guilty person' or 'no, sweet heart' in the text unless they had heard the defendant say so in the examination occasion. Also, reading the records, one gets the impression that the recorders regarded it as highly important to give the correct overall impression of the examination event and that they made an effort to reproduce the crucial statements as accurately as possible.

The references to the defendants' laughter may be taken as one indication of this effort.

As can be seen in table 17.1, the number of defendants' utterances in the records varies considerably, from sixty-six (16. Examination of Martha Cory) to four (90. Examination of Sarah Wilds and 399. Examination of Ann Pudeator). Some defendants tend to give long answers to the examiners' questions while others resort to short responses of only one or two finite clauses. Table 17.1 shows the number of each defendant's utterances as well as the number of utterances consisting of more than two finite clauses. Interestingly, all the examinations with a reasonable number of direct-speech utterances date from the first eight months of the year 1692. The low number of original recordings from the summer months, from June to August, after the establishment of a special court, The Court of Oyer and Terminer, is also significant.

It seems that from July 1692 onwards the role played by examinations changes and summarising rather than word-for-word recording was regarded as sufficient. As also noted by Doty and Hiltunen (2002: 332), 'there is a historical progression from records presented in direct discourse during the early months of 1692 to those presented in reported discourse in the late summer and early autumn'.[4]

3. Strategies of defence

The defendants of the Salem courtroom examinations can be divided into two groups: those who deny being witches and those who admit it. The first group is more interesting than the second because the strategies claiming innocence vary and show a scale from simple and neutral negative statements and short narrative passages to eloquent and emphatic declarations of innocence. Some of the replies can be regarded as showing negative attitudes or are even aggressive or face-threatening.

In the present analysis, attention is called to the following discourse features appearing in the responses of the defendants (see also the right-hand columns of table 17.1):

(i) Use of figurative language
(ii) Appeals to God and/or Christ
(iii) Addressing the examiners/audience
- using imperatives
- asking questions
- questioning the justification of the accusations

(iv) Sarcasm
(v) Expressions of aggressiveness
(vi) Laughter

---

[4] Illustrative tables of the timing of different phases of individual cases are presented in Norton (2002: 315–17).

The mildest form of emphasising innocence is to use a figurative expression comparing the innocence of the defendant to that of an unborn or newborn baby. Appeals to God or Christ to confirm innocence are also common. One dividing line between simple, neutral denials and more emphatically negative ones seems to be the examinee's tendency to address the examiners and the audience. This strategy creates an argumentative discourse situation instead of a one-sided question–answer sequence. Asking questions is an efficient discoursal device for the defendant to take the initiative; using imperatives is another. More obvious and aggressive ways of defence are questioning the justification of the accusations, outright statements that the accusers are lying, sarcastic comments, threatening or contemptuous remarks and, finally, laughter.

Those defendants denying any connection with witchcraft can be divided into three groups on the basis of their strategies to respond to the accusations (see table 17.1): those just giving simple and neutral answers to the examiners' questions and showing no negative attitudes (Osburn, Black, Wilds, Pudeator); those emphasising their innocence, with some replies that can be interpreted as showing slightly negative attitudes (Nurse, Bishop, Esty, W. Hobbs, How); and those showing strongly negative attitudes, even including features that can be interpreted as aggressive or face-threatening (Good, Cory, Hoar, Martin, Jacobs Sr, Willard, M. Carrier). Defendants admitting a connection to witchcraft can be divided into those who give simple and neutral answers (R. Carrier, D. Hobbs, Eames) and those who wish to show cooperation by including ample narrative details in their replies or emphasising remorse by emotional outbursts (Tituba, A. Hobbs, Warren).

These groupings are partly based on intuitive interpretations of the contents of the responses but they are, at least to some extent, supported by the number of the above-listed discoursal features appearing in the utterances.[5]

3.1 Strategies of the defendants denying guilt

3.1.1 Simple answers, no negative attitudes

The examination of Sarah Osburn, which took place on the first day of the trials (1 March 1692), can be quoted as a typical example of a defence consisting of simple and neutral replies, with a minimum of narrative or argumentative elements. Osburn does not address the examiners or other people in the courtroom. She does not use figurative expressions, nor does she question the wisdom of the examiners or the truthfulness of the witnesses. Most of her replies are short: only one or two finite clauses. The narrative element is very scarce. One explanation for her short and simple replies may have been that she was ill: she died in prison two months after the

---

[5] See also, e.g., Rissanen (2003); Kahlas-Tarkka and Rissanen (2007).

examination. Her last comment in the examination record is 'alas I have been sike and not able to goe' (example (2)).

(2)   Sarah Osburn her examination
(H) what evil spirit have you familiarity with (O) **none**. (H) have you made no contract with the devill (O) **I no I never saw the devill in my life** (H) why doe you hurt these children (O) **I doe not hurt them** (H) who doe you imploy then to hurt them (O) **I imploy no body**. (H) what familiarity have you with Sarah good (O) **none I have not seen her these 2 years**. (H) where did you see her then (O) **one day agoing to Town**, (H) what communications had y<ou> with her, (O) **I had none, only how do you doe or so I d<i>d not know her by name**

. . .

(H) Sarah good saith that it was you that hurt the children, (O) **I doe not know that the devil goes about in my likenes to doe any hurt**

. . .

(H) did you never see anything else (O) **no**.

. . .

(O) **alas I have been sike and not able to goe**
(3. Examinations of Sarah Good, Sarah Osburn and Tituba, recorder Cheever)

As can be seen from table 17.1, Mary Black, Sarah Wilds and Ann Pudeator follow the same strategy of short replies with no negative attitudes expressed. This policy was not, however, successful: only Mary Black saved her life. She was a negro slave and perhaps regarded as less responsible for her activities – in the eyes of the examiners.

3.1.2   Answers emphasising innocence, slightly negative attitudes
There are two main ways in which the five defendants belonging to this group emphasise their innocence: appealing to God or Christ as witness and using the figurative expression 'as innocent as a child unborn' in various forms (examples (3) to (5)). Again, this strategy did not help the defendants: only William Hobbs saved his life.

(3)   Goody Nurse, here are two An: Putman the child & Abigail Williams complains of your hurting them What do you say to it
N. **I can say before my Eternal father I am innocent, & God will clear my innocency**

. . .

You would do well if you are guilty to confess & give Glory to God
I am as clear as the child unborn
(28. Examination of Rebecca Nurse, recorder Parris)

(4) What do you say, are you guilty?
I can say before Christ Jesus, I am free.
(86. Examination of Mary Esty, recorder Parris)

(5) [Lost]at [= What] say you, are you guilty or not?
[Lost] [= I] can speak in the presence of God safely, as <I> must look to give account another day, I that I am as clear as a newborn babe.
(90. Examination of William Hobbs, recorder Parris)

All the five defendants in this group address the examiner(s), but not in an aggressive way. They point out that they cannot confess something they have not done even though they are urged to do so (examples (6) and (7)). This is a natural way of objecting to the examiners' starting point of 'guilty but unwilling to confess' (see also Archer 2002):

(6) Those that have confessed, they tell us they used images & pins, now tell <us> what you have used.
You would not have me confess that which I know not
(241. Examination of Elizabeth How, recorder Parris)

(7) Can you act Witchcraft here, & by casting your eyes turn folks into fits?
You may judge your pleasure, my soul is clear.
. . .
What do you call that way of looking upon persons, & striking them downe?
You may judge your pleasure.
(90. Examinations of Sarah Wilds and William Hobbs, recorder Parris)

Addressing the examiners may, however, be a dangerous strategy because it is easily regarded as face-threatening and is likely to create negative attitudes in the examiners. The responses quoted above can be regarded as slightly aggressive, particularly William Hobbs's 'You may judge your pleasure' (example (7)) with the implication 'but you are wrong'. The same is true of the responses formulated as questions to the examiner (examples (8) and (9)):[6]

(8) How can you say you know nothing, when you see these tormented, & accuse you that you know nothing?
Would you have me accuse my self?
Yes if you be guilty.
How far have you complyed wth Sa<ta>n, whereby he takes this advantage ag^t you?

---

[6] See also Hiltunen (1996: 28–30).

> Sir, I never complyed but prayed against him all my dayes. I have no complyance with Satan, in this. What would you have me do?
> Confess if you be guilty.
> ...
> It is marvailous to me that ~~she~~ you should somtimes think they are bewitcht, & sometimes not, when severall confess that they have been guilty of bewitching them.
> **Well Sir would you have me confess that that I never knew?**
> (86. Examination of Mary Esty, recorder Parris)

(9) why should not you also be guilty, for your apparition doth hurt also. **Would you have me bely [= belie] {my} ~~your~~ self**
 (28. Examination of Rebecca Nurse, recorder Parris)

As to other negatively coloured responses, attention can be called to Bridget Bishop's emphatic way of answering the examiner's question (10):

(10) (m^r Har) tell us the truth in this matter how comes these persons to be thus tormented and to charge you with doing (Bish) **I am not come here to say I am a witch to take away my life**
 (63. Examination of Bridget Bishop, recorder Cheever)

3.1.3 *Answers including strong negative and even aggressive attitudes*

The responses of the seven defendants belonging to this group are more elaborately and eloquently formulated and include openly aggressive and critical addresses to the examiners and other people present at the examination occasion. Only Dorcas Hoar saved her life, thanks to her later confession of being a witch.

Even these defendants appeal to God or Christ to confirm their innocence, but in a more rhetorical way (examples (11) and (12)):

(11) we require you to confess the truth in this matter. **I shall, as I hope, I shall be assisted by the Lord of Heaven, & for my ~~flying away I~~ going away I was affrighted & I thought by my withdrawing it might be better, I fear not but the Lord in his due time will make me as white as snow.**
 (173. Examination of John Willard, recorder Parris)

The recorder, Parris, also notes that Willard 'offered large talk' and the examiner retorts, 'we do not send for you to preach'.

(12) **Christ hath suffered.3. times for me.**
 ...
 He suffered the Crosse & gall
 ...

Well! burn me, or hang me, I will stand in the truth of Christ, I know nothing of it
(133. Examination of George Jacobs, Sr, recorder Parris)

Martha Cory, an esteemed member of the village church, emphasises her religious conviction. She asks to be allowed to 'go to prayer' and points out she is 'a Gospel Woman' (13):

(13) Pray give me leave to goe ['goe' written over 'give'] to prayer
This request was made sundry times
We do not send for you to go to prayer
But tell me why you hurt these?
I am an innocent person: I never had to do with Witchcraft since I was born. I am a Gosple Woman
(16. Examination of Martha Cory, recorder Parris)

She not only appeals to God to confirm her innocence but also to correct the false accusations made by the examiners. The fact that this was no doubt regarded as insulting by the examiners certainly did not help her in the trial (14):

(14) Do not you see these complain of you
The Lord open the eyes of the Magistrates & Ministers: the Lord show his power to discover the guilty.
(16. Examination of Martha Cory, recorder Parris)

There are two men in this group, John Willard and George Jacobs, Sr. Willard is less eloquent than Jacobs, although his replies contain many features regarded as showing a negative attitude: he accuses the accusers of lying and gives advice to the examiner (example (17) below), he is mildly sarcastic (example (18) below) and even laughs. George Jacobs, Sr, an old farmer and, according to his own statement, illiterate, shows remarkable argumentative skill and an ability to take the initiative in the examination situation.[7] It is perhaps not unfair to say that he is the best informant of the richness and variability of early American English amongst the accused whose utterances are recorded in the first person (15).

(15) Here are them that accuse you of acts of witchcraft.
Well, let vs hear who are they, & what are they.
Abigail Williams
        Jacobs laught
Because I am falsly accused – Your worships all of you do you think this is true?
Nay: what do you think?
I never did it.

---

[7] See also Rissanen (2003); Kahlas-Tarkka and Rissanen (2007).

> Who did it?
> Don't ask me.
>
> ...
>
> **Pray do not accuse me, I am as clear as your Worships; You must do right judgment**
>
> ...
>
> You had as good confesse (said Sarah Churchwell) if you are guilty.
> **Have you heard that I have any Witchcraft?**
> I know you lived a wicked life.
> **Let her make it out.**
> (133. Examination of George Jacobs, Sr, recorder Parris)

In the passage quoted above, Jacobs uses the imperative form four times and gives advice to the examiners: 'You must do right judgment'. This activity no doubt increased the negative attitudes of the examiners. He also uses clever wordplay in his sarcastic remark (16):

(16) **You tax me for a Wizard, you may as well tax me for a Buzard. I have done no harm.**
(133. Examination of George Jacobs, Sr, recorder Parris)

John Willard advises the examiners as to how to carry out the examination (17):

(17) Benj^a Wilkins gave in evidence of his unnaturall usage to his wife.
You had much need to boast of your affections
There are a great many lyes told, I would desire my wife might be called
Peter Prescot testifyed that he with his own mouth told him of his beating of his wife

...

Let some person go to him
Ann Putman said she would go.
He said let not that person but another come
(173. Examination of John Willard, recorder Parris)

There is hidden sarcasm in his retort to the examiners (18):

(18) Open your mouth, don't bite your lips
I will stand with my mouth open, or I will keep it shut, I will stand any how, if you will tell me how
(173. Examination of John Willard, recorder Parris)

The female defendants, too, are ready to question the truthfulness of the accusations, mainly those presented by the young girls and other members of the audience (examples (19) and (20)):

(19) Mary Walcot, Susan Sheldon, & Abigail Williams said they saw a black man whispering in her ears.
Oh! you are liars, & God will stop the mouth of liars
(102. Examination of Dorcas Hoar, recorder Parris)

(20) You see you look upon them & they fall down.
It is false the Devil is a liar.
I lookt upon none since I came into the room but you.
. . .
You do see them, said the accusers.
You lye, I am wronged.
(235. Examination of Martha Carrier, recorder Parris)

Sarah Good tells the examiner in plain words that the accusations are false (21):

(21) (H) what creature doe you imploy then, (g) **no creature but I am falsely accused**
(3. Examinations of Sarah Good, Sarah Osburn and Tituba, recorder Cheever)

Susannah Martin, a 67-year-old widow, points out that the accusers in the audience are just pretending (22):

(22) What is the reason these [some of the accusers] cannot come near you
I do not know but they can if they will <or> else if you please, I will come to them
(104. Examination of Susannah Martin, recorder Parris)

She also uses sarcasm in a masterly way to underline the unreliable quality of the young girls' accusations (23):

(23) The examinant laught.
What do you laugh at it?
Well I may at such folly.
. . .
Pray God discover you, if you be guilty.
Amen. Amen. A false tongue w<ill> never make a guilty person.
You have been a long time coming to the Court to day, you can come fast enough in the night. Said Mercy Lewes
No, sweet heart, said the Examinant
. . .
D<o> no<t> y<ou> s<ee> h<ow> God <evi>dently [Lost] you?
No, not a bit for that.
All the congregation think so.

> Let them think w^t they will.
> (104. Examination of Susannah Martin, recorder Parris)

It is also possible to trace hidden sarcasm in Martha Carrier's reply to the examiner (24):

(24) What black man did you see?
I saw no black man but your own presence.
(235. Examination of Martha Carrier, recorder Parris)

Aggressive emotion is obvious in Sarah Good's utterances, which, although short, reflect her strong antagonism (25). The recorder, Cheever, notes that her answers were 'in {a} very wicked, spitfull manner reflecting and retorting against the authority with base and abuseive words and many lies':

(25) (H) why doe you hurt these children (g) **I doe not hurt them I scorn it**.
...
H<?> who doe you imploy then (g) **I imploy no body I scorn it**
...
(H) what is it that you say when you goe muttering away from persons houses ^{(g)} **if I must tell I will tell** (H) doe tell us then (g) **if I must tell I will tell it is the commandments I may say my commandments I hope** (H) what commandment is it (g) **if I must tell you I will tell it is a psalm**
(3. Examinations of Sarah Good, Sarah Osburn and Tituba, recorder Cheever)[8]

The examiners regard Dorcas Hoar's half-serious retort as threatening (26):

(26) Oh said some of the afflicted there is one whispering in her ears. **There is some body will rub your ears shortly**, said the Examinant Immediately they were afflicted, & among others Mercy Lewes. Why do you threaten they should be Rubb'd?
I did not speak a word of Rubbing.
Many testifyed she did.
(102. Examination of Dorcas Hoar, recorder Parris)

Finally, laughter was a natural way to indicate the defendants' attitude to false accusations (27), but it was regarded as an insulting and contemptuous expression of emotion by the examiners. Perhaps for this reason the recorders marked it conscientiously; see also the quotations from George Jacobs, Sr (example (15) above) and Susannah Martin (example (23) above):

---

[8] (g)=Good, here rendered as in the original document according to the editorial principles.

Salem Witchcraft Trials: attitudes of the accused 255

(27) Now tell me y^e truth will you, why did you say that the Magistrates & Ministers eyes were blinded you would open them
She laught & denyed it.

...

Is it a laughing matter to see these afflicted persons
She denyed it

...

She laught
The Children cryed there was a yellow bird with her
When Mr Hathorn askt her about it she laught
When her hands were at liberty the afflicted persons were pincht
Why do not you tell how the Devil comes in your shapes & hurts these, you said you would
How can I know how
Why did you say you would show us
She laught again
(16. Examination of Martha Cory, recorder Parris)

3.2 Strategies of the defendants admitting guilt

The defendants admitting connections with witchcraft do not use any expressions that could be interpreted as indications of negative attitude, not to speak of aggressiveness or face-threatening. They do not even address the examiners. It is in their interest to be cooperative, and, indeed, all of them saved their lives.

3.2.1 Simple answers, with only a few short narrative comments

As can be seen in table 17.1, there are three defendants admitting guilt in simple utterances and avoiding narrative details of emotive expressions. Richard Carrier's examination (28) closely resembles that of Sarah Osburn quoted in example (2) above. There are several one-word affirmative replies, and not a single response consists of more than two finite clauses. The only somewhat personal comment refers to the quarrel between Bradbury and Swan.

(28) {Q} have you bin in ye devils s<n>are A: yes.
{Q} is yor bro: Andrew: ensnared by ye devils snare: A: **Yes** how long: has yor brother bin a wich: A: **Near a monthe** how long: have you bin a witch: A: **not long**: Q have you Joined in aflicting: ye aflicted persons: A: **Yes**: Q you help<t> to hurt: Timo Swan: did you A: **yes**: Q how long: have yo^u bin a wich: A **abo^t five weeks**: who was in company when you Covnanted with ye devill: A **Mrs Bradbery** did she help {yo^u aflict **yes:**} what was ye ocasion: Mrs Bradbery: would

have to aflict Timo Swan: A **becaus: her husband & Timo Swan fell out about a scyth: I think**:
(429. Examination of Richard Carrier, recorder Willard)[9]

Only one of Deliverance Hobbs's forty-two utterances is fairly long (29). She describes her 'sights':

(29)   **I have seen sundry sights.**
What sights.
Last Lords day in ~~the~~ ^{this} meeting hours & out of the door, I saw a great many ^{birds} cats & dogs, & heard a voice say come away.
(89. Examination of Deliverance Hobbs, recorder Parris)

Rebecca Eames's examination follows the same pattern. Fourteen utterances are short and only two somewhat longer. The first (30):

(30)   Q who came w^t ye devil when he made you a witch A: **a ragged girl: they came togethe^r and they perswaded me to afflict: & I afflicte Mary Warin & an other fayr face: it is abo^t a quarter of a year agoe: I did it by sticking of pins.**
(511. Examination of Rebecca Eames, recorder Willard)

The second utterance of more than two finite clauses is simple in structure and content: 'I do not know he [her son Daniel] is a wich but I am afrayd he is'.

3.2.2 *Answers including ample narrative details or expressions of repentance*

Of the three defendants including ample narrative details or emotive expressions of repentance in their utterances, Tituba is the most efficient in showing her willingness to cooperate. She clearly indicates that it is the Devil who makes her hurt the children, so she cannot be held responsible. Her replies include narrative details exciting the audience's imagination (31):

(31)   (H) Titibe what ~~sp~~ evil spirit have you familiarity with (T) **none** (H) why doe you hurt these children, (T) **I doe not hurt them** (H) who is it then ~~the de~~ (T) **the devil for ought I ~~ken~~ know**

. . .

(H) what is this appearance you see (T) **sometimes it is like a hog and some times like a great dog** this appearnce shee saith shee did see 4 times (H) what {did} it say to you (T) ~~it s~~ **the black dog said serve me but I said I am afraid he** ^{said} **if I did not he would doe worse to me** (H) what did you say to it (T) **I will serve you no longer then he said he would hurt me and then he lookes like**

---
[9] The seeming discrepancy in indicating questions (Q) and answers (A) goes back to the original document.

a man and threatens to hurt me. shee said that **this man had a yellow bird that keept with him and he told me he had more pretty things that he would give me if I would sere him.**
(3. Examinations of Sarah Good, Sarah Osburn and Tituba, recorder Cheever)

Mary Warren's verbosity describes her own miserable and sinful state. She, too, emphasises that she has been possessed by the devil; if she is regarded as a witch, it is not her own choice (32):

(32) Mary Warren continued a good space in a fit, ~~the~~ ^{that} she did neither see, nor hear, nor speak. Afterwards she started up, & said **I will speak & cryed out, Oh! I am sorry for it, I am sorry for it,** & wringed her hands, & fell a little while into a fit again: & then came to speak, but immediately her Teeth were set, & then she fell into a violent fit, & cryed out, **Oh Lord help me, Oh good Lord save me!** And then afterwards cryed again, **I will tell, I will tell,** & then fell into a dead fit againe. And afterwards cryed, **I will tell, they did, they did, they did,** & then fell into a violent fit again. After a little recovery she cryed **I will tell, I will tell, they brought me me to it**; & then fell into a fit again: which fits continuing, she was ordered to be had out, & the next to be brought in, viz: Bridget Byshop

. . .

Mary Warren called in, afterwards in private, before Magistrates & Ministers. She said, **I shall not speak a word: but I will,** ~~speak~~ **I will speak satan** – she saith **she will kill me. Oh!** she saith, **she owes me a spite, & will claw me off Avoid Satan, for the name of God avoid.** And then fell into fits again: & cryed **will ye; I will prevent ye, in the Name of God**
(75. Examination of Mary Warren, recorder Parris)

Remorse is also indicated in Abigail Hobbs's utterances, albeit in a less eloquent or elaborate way (33):

(33) Are you guilty, or not? Speak the truth
I will speak the truth, I have seen sights, & been scared: I have been very wicked, I hope I shall be better: <&> God will keep me.
(67. Examination of Abigail Hobbs, recorder Parris)

4. Final remarks

We hope that this survey of the types of utterances made by the defendants accused of witchcraft in Salem in 1692 will give some additional illustration to the study of discourse strategies in extreme situations, here the outcome of the discourse being either life, or death by hanging. The value of the recorded examination dialogues is increased by the fact that they survive in original manuscripts created in authentic courtroom situations. Aspects of politeness strategies, face-threatening or self-face-saving acts were certainly important even in this discourse environment, but there were other, perhaps more relevant issues for the defendants, which need to be taken into consideration. Paradoxically, some of the defendants were no doubt aware that admitting guilt and showing cooperation was the best – if not the only – way to save their lives. The attitudes of the defendants denying guilt, on the other hand, may have been motivated partly by the wish to save self-face, even at the cost of death, partly by the hope that 'justice would win' if they were able to prove that the examiners and other accusers were wrong, and partly by religious conviction: martyrdom and heaven versus admitting witchcraft and hell.

The defendants denying witchcraft as well as those admitting it show how different the strategies to reach the goals outlined above may be. The background and the character – including verbosity, and not forgetting gender – of the defendant no doubt played a role in choosing the strategy. Some defendants resorted to as simple and factual responses as possible; some were outwardly neutral but showed occasional negative attitudes; some were openly unsociable and aggressive; and some self-confident, intelligent and verbally talented, with a tendency for sarcasm and laughter. We hope that the recently published *Records of the Salem Witch-Hunt* will open new doors for the study of the life, language and mind of the late seventeenth-century New Englander.

Bibliography

A Corpus of English Dialogues 1560–1760. (**CED**) 2006. Compiled under the supervision of Merja Kytö (Uppsala University) and Jonathan Culpeper (Lancaster University). See www.helsinki.fi/varieng/CoRD/corpora/CED/index.html.

A Representative Corpus of Historical English Registers (**ARCHER**). 1992. ARCHER1 Compiled by Douglas Biber (Northern Arizona University) and Edward Finegan (University of Southern California). See www.llc.manchester.ac.uk/research/projects/archer/.

Adams, Joseph Q. (ed.) 1924. *Chief Pre-Shakespearean Dramas*. Cambridge: The Riverside Press.

Agha, Asif 2007. *Language and Social Relations*. Cambridge: Cambridge University Press.

Allerton, David J. 1996. 'Proper names and definite descriptions with the same reference: A pragmatic choice for language users', *Journal of Pragmatics* 25: 621–33.

Anon. 1827. 'Original letters, illustrative of English history; including numerous royal letters: from autographs in the British Museum, and one or two other collections. By Henry Ellis, F. R. S. Sec. S. A. Keeper of the MSS. In the British Museum. Second series', *The Edinburgh Review, or Critical Journal* XLVI: 195–217.

Archer, Dawn 2002. 'Can innocent people be guilty? A sociopragmatic analysis of examination transcripts from the Salem witchcraft trials', *Journal of Historical Pragmatics* 3: 1–30.

   2007. 'Developing a more detailed picture of the English courtroom (1640–1760): Data and methodological issues facing historical pragmatics', in **Susan Fitzmaurice** and **Irma Taavitsainen** (eds.), pp. 185–217.

Archer, Dawn, McEnery, Tony, Rayson, Paul and **Hardie, Andrew** 2003. 'Developing an automated semantic analysis system for Early Modern English', in *Proceedings of the Corpus Linguistics 2003 Conference*. UCREL, Lancaster University, UK, pp. 22–31. Online at http://ucrel.lancs.ac.uk/tech_papers.html.

Armstrong, Charles A. J. 1960. 'An Italian astrologer at the court of Henry VII', in E. F. **Jacob** (ed.), *Italian Renaissance Studies: A Tribute to the Late C. M. Ady*. New York: Barnes and Noble, pp. 432–54.

Arn, Mary-Jo 1990. 'The Bute manuscript of "The Privity of the Passion" (Yale University, Beinecke MS 660)', *Manuscripta* 34: 177–89.

260 Bibliography

Arnold, John H. and Lewis, Katherine J. (eds.) 2004. *A Companion to the Book of Margery Kempe*. Cambridge: D. S. Brewer.

Arnovick, Leslie K. 1999. *Diachronic Pragmatics: Seven Case Studies in English Illocutionary Development*. Amsterdam/Philadelphia: John Benjamins.

Atkinson, Dwight 1999. *Scientific Discourse in Sociohistorical Context: The Philosophical Transactions of the Royal Society of London, 1675–1975*. Mahwah, NJ: Lawrence Erlbaum.

Austin, J. L. 1962. *How to Do Things with Words*. Oxford: Clarendon.

Bailey, Richard 1996. *Nineteenth-century English*. Ann Arbor: The University of Michigan Press.

Baker, Donald C. 1989. 'When is a text a play? Reflections upon what certain late medieval dramatic texts can tell us', in Marianne G. Briscoe and John C. Coldewey (eds.), *Context for Early English Drama*. Bloomington: Indiana University Press, pp. 20–40.

Baker, Donald C. and Murphy, John L. 1967. 'The late medieval plays of MS Digby 133: Scribes, dates and early history', *Research Opportunities in Renaissance Drama* 10: 153–66.

(eds.) 1976. *The Digby Plays: Facsimiles of the Plays of Bodley MSS Digby 133 and e Museo 160*. Leeds: University of Leeds.

Baker, Donald C., Murphy, John L. and Hall, Luis B. Jr. (eds.) 1982. *The Late Medieval Religious Plays of Bodleian MSS Digby 133 and e Museo 160*. Oxford: Oxford University Press.

Baron, Alistair and Rayson, Paul 2008. '*VARD* 2: A tool for dealing with the spelling variation in historical corpora', in *Proceedings of the Postgraduate Conference in Corpus Linguistics*, Aston University, Birmingham, UK, 22 May 2008. Online at www.comp.lancs.ac.uk/~barona/vard2/ (accessed 10 August 2009).

Baron, Naomi S. 2000. *Alphabet to Email: How Written English Evolved and Where it's Heading*. London/New York: Routledge.

Bawcutt, Priscilla (ed.) 1998. *The Poems of William Dunbar*. Glasgow: Association for Scottish Literary Studies.

Beadle, Richard 1991. 'Prolegomena to a literary geography of later medieval Norfolk', in Felicity Riddy (ed.), pp. 89–108.

Beal, Peter and Edwards, A. S. G. (eds.) 2005. *Scribes and Transmission in English Manuscripts 1400–1700*. London: British Library.

Bennett, Jacob 1978. 'The Mary Magdalene of Bishop's Lynn', *Studies in Philology* 75: 1–9.

Benson, Larry (ed.) 1987. *The Riverside Chaucer*. 3rd edn. Boston: Houghton Mifflin. Online at www.courses.fas.harvard.edu/~chaucer/teachslf/tr-index.htm. Reprinted 1988. Oxford: Oxford University Press.

Berger, Peter L. 1999. *Homo Ridens: La dimensione comica dell'esperienza umana*. Bologna: Il Mulino.

Bevan, Bryan 1994. *Henry IV*. Basingstoke: Palgrave Macmillan.

Bevington, David (ed.) 1975. *Medieval Drama*. Boston: Houghton Mifflin.

Biber, Douglas 1988. *Variation across Speech and Writing*. Cambridge: Cambridge University Press.

2004. 'Historical patterns for the grammatical marking of stance: A cross-register comparison', *Journal of Historical Pragmatics* 5: 107–36.

Bibliography 261

2006. *University Language: A Corpus-based Study of Spoken and Written Registers*. Amsterdam/Philadelphia: John Benjamins.

2009. 'Are there linguistic consequences of literacy? Comparing the potentials of language use in speech and writing', in **David R. Olson** and **Nancy Torrance** (eds.), *Cambridge Handbook of Literacy*. Cambridge: Cambridge University Press, pp. 75–91.

Biber, Douglas and Clark, Victoria 2002. 'Historical shifts in modification patterns with complex noun phrase structures: How long can you go without a verb?', in **Teresa Fanego**, **María José López-Couso** and **Javier Pérez-Guerra** (eds.), *English Historical Syntax and Morphology*. Amsterdam/Philadelphia: John Benjamins, pp. 43–66.

Biber, Douglas and Conrad, Susan 2009. *Register, Genre, and Style*. Cambridge: Cambridge University Press.

Biber, Douglas and Finegan, Edward 1989. 'Drift and the evolution of English style: A history of three genres', *Language* **65**: 487–517.

1997. 'Diachronic relations among speech-based and written registers in English', in **Terttu Nevalainen** and **Leena Kahlas-Tarkka** (eds.), *To Explain the Present: Studies in the Changing English Language in Honour of Matti Rissanen*. Helsinki: Société Néophilologique, pp. 253–75.

Biber, Douglas, Johansson, Stig, Leech, Geoffrey, Conrad, Susan and Finegan, Edward 1999. *Longman Grammar of Spoken and Written English*. London: Longman.

Birrell, T. A. 1987. *English Monarchs and their Books: From Henry VII to Charles II*. London: British Library.

Black, Merja 1998. 'Lollardy, language contact and the Great Vowel Shift: Spellings in the defence papers of William Swinderby', *Neuphilologische Mitteilungen* **99**: 53–69.

Blake, Norman F. 1979. *The English Language in Medieval Literature*. London: Methuen.

1989. 'Manuscript to print', in **Jeremy Griffiths** and **Derek Pearsall** (eds.), pp. 403–8.

(ed.) 1992. *The Cambridge History of the English Language, 1066–1470*. Cambridge: Cambridge University Press.

Blodgett, James E. 1979. 'Some printer's copy for William Thynne's 1532 edition of Chaucer', *The Library* **6**: 97–113.

Boffey, Julia and Edwards, Anthony S. G. 2005. *A New Index of Middle English Verse*. London: British Library.

Bowers, Robert, H. 1965. 'The tavern scene in the Middle English Digby play of *Mary Magdalene*', in **Robert A. Bryan**, **Alton C. Malton**, **A. A. Murphree** and **Audrey L. Williams** (eds.), *All These to Teach: Essays in Honour of C. A. Robertson*. Gainesville: University of Florida, pp. 15–32.

Boyer, Paul and Nissenbaum, Stephen (eds.) 1977. *The Salem Witchcraft Papers*. 3 vols. New York: Da Capo Press.

Bradley, Arthur G. 1902. *Owen Glyndwr and the Last Struggle for Welsh Independence*. New York/London: G. P. Putnam's Sons.

Brewer, John 1977. *The Pleasures of the Imagination: English Culture in the Eighteenth Century*. London: Harper-Collins.

Briquet, Charles M. 1968. *Les Filigranes: The New Briquet, Jubilee Edition*. Amsterdam: Allan Stevenson.
Britnell, Richard 2006. 'Town life', in **Rosemary Horrox** and **W. Mark Ormrod** (eds.), pp. 134–78.
Brook, George L. 1963. *English Dialects*. London: André Deutsch.
Brown, Penelope and Levinson, Stephen C. 1987. *Politeness: Some Universals in Language Use*. Cambridge: Cambridge University Press.
Brunner, Karl 1970. *An Outline of Middle English*. Oxford: Basil Blackwell.
Bryson, Anna 1998. *From Courtesy to Civility: Changing Codes of Conduct in Early Modern England*. Oxford: Clarendon.
Burnett, Charles, Yamamoto, Keiji and Yano, Michio (eds.) 2004. *Al-Qabīṣī (Alcabitius): The Introduction to Astrology*. London: Warburg Institute.
Burnley, David 2003. 'The T/V pronouns in later Middle English literature', in **Irma Taavitsainen** and **Andreas H. Jucker** (eds.), pp. 27–45.
Burrow, John A. 1986. *The Ages of Man: A Study in Medieval Writing and Thought*. Oxford: Clarendon Press.
Bush, Jerome 1989. 'The resources of *Locus* and *Platea* staging: The Digby *Mary Magdalene*', *Studies in Philology* 86: 139–65.
Busse, Beatrix 2006. *Vocative Constructions in the Language of Shakespeare*. Amsterdam/Philadelphia: John Benjamins.
Busse, Ulrich 2002. *Linguistic Variation in the Shakespeare Corpus*. Amsterdam/Philadelphia: John Benjamins.
Bylebyl, Jerome J. 1991. 'Teaching *Methodus medendi* in the Renaissance', in **Fridolf Kudlien** and **Richard Durling** (eds.), pp. 157–89.
Caie, Graham D. 2006. A digitised edition of *The Middle English Romaunt of the Rose*. Online at www.memss.arts.gla.ac.uk (accessed 23 October 2009).
Camille, Michael 1992. *Image on the Edge: The Margins of Medieval Art*. London: Reaktion Books.
Carey, Hilary M. 1992. *Courting Disaster: Astrology at the English Court and University in the Later Middle Ages*. New York: St Martin's.
Carter, Philip 2005. 'Kit-Cat Club (*act*. 1696–1720)', in *Oxford Dictionary of National Biography*, Oxford University Press. Online at www.oxforddnb.com/view/theme/73609 (accessed 9 September 2009).
Catalogue 562: Rare Books and Manuscripts 1994. Zurich: Hellmut Schumann.
Chaemsaithong, Krisda 2009. 'Re-visiting Salem: Self-face and self-politeness in the Salem witchcraft trials', *Journal of Historical Pragmatics* 10: 56–83.
Chartier, Roger 1995. *Forms and Meanings: Texts, Performances, and Audiences from Codex to Computer*. Philadelphia: University of Pennsylvania Press.
Chauvin, Sister Mary John of Carmel 1951. *The Role of Mary Magdalene in Medieval Drama*. (Diss.) Washington: The Catholic University of America Press.
Chen, Rong 2001. 'Self-politeness: A proposal', *Journal of Pragmatics* 33: 87–106.
Clanchy, Michael T. 1979. *From Memory to Written Record: England 1066–1307*. London: Edward Arnold.
Clark, Herbert H. and Bangerter, Adrian 2004. 'Changing ideas about reference', in **Ira A. Noveck** and **Dan Sperber** (eds.), *Experimental Pragmatics*. Basingstoke: Palgrave Macmillan, pp. 25–49.

Coldewey, John C. 1975. 'The Digby plays and the Chelmsford records', *Research Opportunities in Renaissance Drama* 18: 103–21.
Coleman, Joyce 1996. *Public Reading and the Reading Public in Late Medieval England and France*. Cambridge: Cambridge University Press.
Coletti, Teresa 1979. 'The design of the Digby play of *Mary Magdalene*', *Studies in Philology* 76: 313–33.
Cornelius, Roberta D. 1930. 'The figurative castle: A study in the medieval allegory of the edifice with especial reference to religious writings'. PhD thesis, Bryn Mawr.
Corpus of Early English Correspondence 1998. Compiled by Terttu Nevalainen, Helena, Raumolin-Brunberg, Jukka, Keränen, Minna Nevala, Arja, Nurmi and Minna Palander-Collin at the Department of English, University of Helsinki. See www.helsinki.fi/varieng/CoRD/corpora/CEEC/index.html.
Corpus of Early English Medical Writing (CEEM) In progress. Compiled under the supervision of Irma Taavitsainen and Päivi Pahta. See www.helsinki.fi/varieng/CoRD/corpora/CEEM/index.html.
Craigie, William (ed.) 1919. *The Maitland Folio Manuscript*. Edinburgh/London: Scottish Text Society.
  (ed.) 1923–1925. *The Asloan Manuscript*. Edinburgh/London: Scottish Text Society.
Crismore, Avon 1989. *Talking with Readers: Metadiscourse as Rhetorical Act*. Bern: Peter Lang.
Crombie, Alistair Cameron 1994. *Styles of Scientific Thinking in the European Tradition: The History of Argument and Explanation Especially in the Mathematical and Biomedical Sciences and Arts*. 3 vols. London: Duckworth.
Crossgrove, William 1998. 'Introduction', in **William Crossgrove** *et al*. (eds.), pp. 81–7.
Crossgrove, William, Schleissner, Margaret and Voigts, Linda Ehrsam (eds.) 1998. *The Vernacularization of Science, Medicine, and Technology in Late Medieval Europe*. Special issue, *Early Science and Medicine* 3. 2.
Culpeper, Jonathan and Kádár, Daniel Z. (eds.) 2010. *Historical (Im)politeness*. Bern: Peter Lang.
Culpeper, Jonathan and Kytö, Merja 2000. 'Data in historical pragmatics: Spoken interaction (re)cast as writing', *Journal of Historical Pragmatics* 1: 175–99.
Culpeper, Jonathan, Short, Mick and Verdonk, Peter (eds.) 1998. *Exploring the Language of Drama: From Text to Context*. London/New York: Routledge.
Dahlberg, Charles (ed.) 1999. *The Romaunt of the Rose*. The Variorum Edition of the Works of Geoffrey Chaucer, vol. 7. Norman: University of Oklahoma Press.
Dalrymple, Roger 2000. *Language and Piety in Middle English Romance*. Cambridge: D. S. Brewer.
David, Alfred 1987. 'Textual notes', in **Larry Benson** (ed.), pp. 1103–16 and 1198–210.
Davidson, Clifford 1972. 'The Digby *Mary Magdalene* and the Magdalene cult of the Middle Ages', *Annuale Medievale* 13: 70–87.
Davies, Rees R. 1995. *The Revolt of Owain Glyn Dwr*. Oxford: Oxford University Press.

(ed.) 1971. *Paston Family: Paston Letters and Papers of the Fifteenth Century, Part I, A Machine-Readable Transcription.* Online at http://etext.lib.virginia.edu/toc/modeng/public/PasLett.html, University of Virginia Library (accessed 8 April 2009).

Davis, Norman 1965. 'The litera Troili and English letters', *The Review of English Studies*, New Series **16**: 233–44.

De Haas, Nynke 2008. 'The origins of the Northern Subject Rule', in **Marina Dossena** *et al.* (eds.), vol. 3, pp. 111–30.

Del Lungo Camiciotti, Gabriella 2005. 'Metanarrative frame and evaluation in late medieval saints' lives', in **Anne Betten** and **Monika Dannerer** (eds.), *Dialogue in Literature and the Media*. Tübingen: Max Niemeyer, pp. 269–78.

2006. '"Conduct yourself towards all persons on every occasion with civility and in a wise and prudent manner; this will render you esteemed": Stance features in nineteenth-century business letters', in **Marina Dossena** and **Susan Fitzmaurice** (eds.), pp. 153–74.

2007a. 'Discoursal aspects of the *Legends of Holy Women*', in **Susan Fitzmaurice** and **Irma Taavitsainen** (eds.), pp. 285–305.

2007b. 'A pragma-linguistic approach to medieval narrative: The case of saints' lives', in **Gabriella Mazzon** (ed.), *Studies in Middle English Forms and Meanings*. Bern: Peter Lang, pp. 101–15.

2008. 'Self-disclosure as co-constructed discursive activity in the *Book of Margery Kempe*', in **John Douthwaite** and **Domenico Pezzini** (eds.), *Words in Action: Diachronic and Synchronic Approaches to English Discourse. Studies in Honor of Ermanno Barisone*. Genova: Ecig, pp. 18–29.

DeLatte, Louis (ed.) 1942. *Textes latins et vieux français relatifs aux Cyranides: La traduction latine du XIIe siècle. Le Compendium aureum. Le De XV stellis d'Herme. Le livre des secrez de la nature.* Liège: Faculté de Philosophie et Lettres, fasc. 93.

Demaitre, Luke 1980. *Doctor Bernard de Gordon: Professor and Practitioner.* Toronto: Pontifical Institute of Mediaeval Studies

Devlin, Vianney M. (ed.) 1966. 'An edition of the Digby Plays (Bodleian 133), with Introduction, Notes and Glossary'. PhD thesis, University College London.

Dickey, Eleanor 1997. 'Forms of address and terms of reference', *Journal of Linguistics* **33**: 255–74.

Dinshaw, Carolyn and Wallace, David (eds.) 2003. *The Cambridge Companion to Medieval Women's Writings.* Cambridge: Cambridge University Press.

Dobrée, Bonamy 1959. *English Literature in the Early Eighteenth Century 1700–1740.* Oxford: Clarendon.

Dobson, Eric J. 1968. *English Pronunciation, 1500-1700.* London: Oxford University Press.

1972. *The English Text of the Ancrene Riwle: The Cleopatra Text.* London: Oxford University Press.

Donaldson, E. Talbot 1970. *Speaking of Chaucer.* London: Athlone Press.

Donovan, Robert B. (ed.) 1977. 'The MS Digby 133 Mary Magdalene: A critical edition'. PhD thesis, Arizona State University. Published on demand by University Microfilms, Ann Arbor, Michigan.

Dossena, Marina 2004. 'Towards a Corpus of Nineteenth-century Scottish Correspondence', *Linguistica e Filologia* 18: 195–214.
    2006. 'Forms of self-representation in nineteenth-century business letters', in **Marina Dossena** and **Irma Taavitsainen** (eds.), *Diachronic Perspectives on Domain-Specific English*. Bern: Peter Lang, pp.173–90.
    2008. '"Many strange and peculiar affairs": Description, narration and evaluation in Scottish emigrants' letters of the nineteenth century', *Scottish Language* 27: 1–18.
    2010. 'Building trust through (self-)appraisal in nineteenth-century business correspondence', in **Päivi Pahta, Minna Nevala, Arja Nurmi** and **Minna Palander-Collin** (eds.), *Social Roles and Language Practices in Late Modern English*. Amsterdam/Philadelphia: John Benjamins.
    In press. '"I write you these few lines": Metacommunication and pragmatics in nineteenth-century Scottish emigrants' letters', in **Axel Hübler** and **Ulrich Busse** (eds.), *From the Metacommunicative Lexicon to Historical Pragmatics*.
Dossena, Marina, Dury, Richard and Gotti, Maurizio (eds.) 2008. *English Historical Linguistics 2006: Selected Papers from the Fourteenth International Conference on English Historical Linguistics (ICEHL 14), Bergamo, 21–25 August 2006*. 3 vols. Amsterdam/Philadelphia: John Benjamins.
Dossena, Marina and Fitzmaurice, Susan (eds.) 2006. *Business and Official Correspondence: Historical Investigations*. Bern: Peter Lang.
Dossena, Marina and Tieken-Boon van Ostade, Ingrid (eds.) 2008. *Studies in Late Modern English Correspondence: Methodology and Data*. Bern: Peter Lang.
Doty, Kathleen L. 2007. 'Telling tales: The role of scribes in constructing the discourse of the Salem witchcraft trials', *Journal of Historical Pragmatics* 8: 25–41.
Doty, Kathleen L. and Hiltunen, Risto 2002. '"I will tell, I will tell": Confessional patterns in the Salem Witchcraft Trials, 1692', *Journal of Historical Pragmatics* 3: 299–335.
Duffy, Eamon 1992. *The Stripping of the Altars: Traditional Religion in England 1400–1580*. New Haven: Yale University Press.
    2006. 'Religious belief', in **Rosemary Horrox** and **W. Mark Ormrod** (eds.), pp. 293–339.
Duranti, Alessandro 1997. 'Universal and culture-specific properties of greetings', *Journal of Linguistic Anthropology* 7: 63–97.
Durling, Richard J. 1977. 'Linacre and medical humanism', in **Francis Maddison, Margaret Pelling** and **Charles Webster** (eds.), *Essays on the Life and Work of Thomas Linacre*. Oxford: Clarendon, pp. 78–103.
Dury, Richard 2006. 'A Corpus of Nineteenth-century Business Correspondence: Methodology of transcription', in **Marina Dossena** and **Susan Fitzmaurice** (eds.), pp. 193–205.
    2008. 'Handwriting and the linguistic study of letters', in **Marina Dossena** and **Ingrid Tieken-Boon van Ostade** (eds.), pp. 113–35.
Dyboski, Roman (ed.) 1908. *Songs, Carols, and other Miscellaneous Poems from the Balliol MS 354, Richard Hill's Commonplace-Book*. London: Kegan Paul.
Eagleton, Catherine and Spencer, Matthew 2006. 'Copying and conflation in Geoffrey Chaucer's *Treatise on the Astrolabe*: A stemmatic analysis using

phylogenetic software', *Studies in History and Philosophy of Science*, Part A **37**: 237–68.

Early Modern English Medical Texts **(EMEMT)** Forthcoming. Compiled by Irma Taavitsainen, Päivi Pahta, Turo Hiltunen, Ville Marttila, Martti Mäkinen, Maura Ratia, Carla Suhr and Jukka Tyrkkö with the assistance of Anu Lehto and Alpo Honkapohja. CD-ROM with EMEMT Presenter Software by Raymond Hickey. Amsterdam/Philadelphia: John Benjamins. See www.helsinki.fi/varieng/CoRD/corpora/CEEM/EMEMTindex.html.

Edwards, Anthony S. G. and **Takamiya, Toshiyuki** 2001. 'A new fragment of Gower's "Confessio Amantis"', *Modern Language Review* **96**: 931–6.

Eisenstein Ebsworth, Miriam, Bodman, Jean W. and **Carpenter, Mary** 1996. 'Cross-cultural realization of greetings in American English', in **Susan M. Gass.** and **Joyce Neu** (eds.), *Speech Acts across Cultures: Challenges to Communication in a Second Language*. Berlin/New York: Mouton de Gruyter, pp. 89–107.

Eisner, Sigmund (ed.) 2002. *A Treatise on the Astrolabe*. A Variorum Edition of the Works of Geoffrey Chaucer, vol. VI, The Prose Treatises, part 1. Norman: University of Oklahoma Press.

Ellis, Henry 1827. *Original Letters, Illustrative of English History; Including Numerous Royal Letters: From Autographs in the British Museum, and One or Two Other Collections*. 2nd series. 4 vols, vol. 1. London: Harding and Lepard.

Elton, William 1948. '*Paradise Lost* and the Digby *Mary Magdalene*', *Modern Language Quarterly* **9**: 412–14.

Emden, Alfred Brotherston 1957–9. *A Biographical Register of the University of Oxford to A.D. 1500*. Oxford: Clarendon.

Enfield, N. J. and **Stivers, Tanya** (eds.) 2007. *Person Reference in Interaction: Linguistic, Cultural and Social Perspectives*. Cambridge: Cambridge University Press.

English, Peter 1656 = **Galenos, Claudius** 1656. *Galen's Method of Physick: or, his great master-peece; being the very marrow and quintessence of all his writings.... Whereto is annexed a succinct and plain commentary for explaining the difficulties thereof, / by its translatour, Peter English, st. of physick*. Edinburgh.

eTK = **(electronic Thorndike-Kibre)** 1963. An expanded and updated digital version of **Lynn Thorndike** and **Pearl Kibre**, *A Catalogue of Incipits of Mediaeval Scientific Writings in Latin*, rev. edn with two supplements. Cambridge, MA.: Medieval Academy of America. Online at www.medievalacademy.org.

Eves, Charles Kenneth 1939. *Matthew Prior, Poet and Diplomatist*. New York: Columbia University Press.

eVK = **Voigts, Linda E.** and **Kurtz, Patricia D.** 2000. *Scientific and Medical Writings in Old and Middle English: An Electronic Reference*. CD. Ann Arbor: University of Michigan Press.

eVK2 = A revision of **Voigts, Linda E.** and **Kurtz, Patricia D.** 2001. *Scientific and Medical Writings in Old and Middle English: An Electronic Reference*. Ann Arbor: University of Michigan Press. Online at www.medievalacademy.org.

Fairman, Tony 2003. 'Letters of the English labouring classes 1800–34 and the English language', in **Marina Dossena** and **Charles Jones** (eds.), *Insights into Late Modern English*. Bern: Peter Lang, pp. 265–82.

2007. '"Lower-order" letters, schooling and the English language, 1795 to 1834', in **Stephan Elspaß, Nils Langer, Joachim Scharloth** and **Wim Vandenbussche** (eds.), *Germanic Language Histories from Below (1700–2000)*. Berlin/New York: Mouton de Gruyter, pp. 31–43.

Fanger, Claire and **Láng, Benedek** 2002. 'John of Morigny's *Liber visionum* and a Royal Prayer Book from Poland', *Societas Magica Newsletter* 9: 1-4.

Feuillerat, Albert 1908. *Documents Relating to the Office of the Revels in the Time of Queen Elizabeth*. Louvain: A. Uystpruyst.

Filppula, Markku 2008. 'The Celtic hypothesis hasn't gone away: New perspectives on old debates', in **Marina Dossena** *et al.* (eds.), vol. 3, pp. 153–70.

Fisiak, Jacek (ed.) 1984. *Contrastive Linguistics: Prospects and Problems*. Berlin/New York: Mouton de Gruyter.

Fitzmaurice, Susan 2000. 'Coalitions and the investigation of social influence in linguistic history', *European Journal of English Studies* 4: 265–76.

2002. *The Familiar Letter in Early Modern English: A Pragmatic Approach*. Amsterdam/Philadelphia: John Benjamins.

2006. 'Diplomatic business: Information, power, and persuasion in Late Modern English diplomatic correspondence', in **Marina Dossena** and **Susan Fitzmaurice** (eds.), pp. 77–106.

2007. 'Questions of standardization and representativeness in the development of social networks-based corpora: The story of the Network of Eighteenth-century English Texts', in **Joan C. Beal, Karen P. Corrigan** and **Hermann L. Moisl** (eds.), *Creating and Digitizing Language Corpora. Volume II: Diachronic Databases*. Basingstoke: Palgrave Macmillan, pp. 49–81.

2008. 'Epistolary identity: Convention and idiosyncrasy in Late Modern English letters', in **Marina Dossena** and **Ingrid Tieken-Boon van Ostade** (eds.), pp. 77–112.

2010a. 'Changes in the meaning of *politeness* in eighteenth-century England: Discourse analysis and historical evidence', in **Jonathan Culpeper** and **Daniel Z. Kádár** (eds.), pp. 87–115.

2010b. 'Coalitions, networks, and discourse communities in Augustan England: The Spectator and the early eighteenth-century essay', in **Raymond Hickey** (ed.), *Eighteenth-century English*. Cambridge: Cambridge University Press, pp. 106–32.

In press. 'Sociability: Conversation and the performance of friendship in early eighteenth-century letters', in **Alex Hübler** and **Ulrich Buste** (eds.), *From the Metacommunicative Lexicon to Historical Pragmatics*.

Fitzmaurice, Susan and **Taavitsainen, Irma** (eds.) 2007. *Methods in Historical Pragmatics*. Berlin/New York: Mouton de Gruyter.

Fludernik, Monica 2000. 'Genres, text types, or discourse modes? Narrative modalities and generic categorizations', *Style* 34: 274–92.

Francis, Nelson W. and **Kučera, Henry** 1992. *Frequency Analysis of English Usage: Lexicon and Grammar*. Boston: Houghton Mifflin.

French, Roger 2003. *Medicine before Science: The Business of Medicine from the Middle Ages to the Enlightenment*. Cambridge: Cambridge University Press.

Furdell, Elizabeth Lane 2002. *Publishing and Medicine in Early Modern England*. Rochester, NY: University of Rochester Press.

268 Bibliography

Furnivall, Frederick J. (ed.) 1882. *The Digby Mysteries*. London: Bungay.
Gale, Thomas 1566 = Galenos, Claudius 1566. *Methodi medendi, vel de morbis curandis libri XIIII: postrema hac editione ad cujuscumque varietatis exemplarium fidem collati & restituti*. Translatus per Thomam Linacrum. Lugdvni.
  1586 = Galenos, Claudius 1586. *Certaine vvorkes of Galens, called Methodus medendi, with a briefe Declaration of the worthie Art of Medicine, the Office of a Chirurgion, and an Epitome of the third booke of Galen, of Naturall Faculties: all translated into English, by Thomas Gale Maister in Chirurgerie*. London.
Garth, Elizabeth M. 1950. 'Saint Mary Magdalene in medieval literature', *Johns Hopkins University Studies in Historical and Political Science* **67**: 366–97.
Genette, Gérard 1987. *Seuils*. Paris: Editions du Seuil.
Gernsbacher, Morton Ann and Shroyer, Suzanne 1989. 'The cataphoric use of the indefinite *this* in spoken narratives', *Memory and Cognition* **17**: 536–40.
Getz, Faye Marie 1990. 'Medical practitioners in medieval England', *Social History of Medicine* **13**: 245–83.
  1991. 'The *Method of Healing* in Middle English', in Fridolf Kudlien and Richard J. Durling (eds.), pp. 147–56.
Gibbons, Victoria 2008. 'Reading premodern titles: Bridging the premodern gap in modern titology'. Cardiff Humanities Research Institute. Online at www.cardiff.ac.uk/chri/researchpapers/pgconference/Papers%201%20-%207/1.Gibbons.html (accessed 7 September 2009).
Görlach, Manfred 1999. *English in Nineteenth-century England: An Introduction*. Cambridge: Cambridge University Press.
Grantley, Darryll R. (ed.) 1983. 'A critical edition of the play of *Mary Magdalene*'. PhD thesis, University of London.
Gray, Bethany, Biber, Douglas and Hiltunen, Turo In press. 'The expression of stance in early (1665–1712) publications of the *Philosophical Transactions* and other contemporary medical prose: Innovations in a pioneering discourse', in Irma Taavitsainen and Päivi Pahta (eds.).
Greene, Robert 1594. *The historie of Orlando Furioso, one of the twelue pieres of France As it was plaid before the Queenes Maiestie*. London: Printed by Iohn Danter for Cuthbert Burbie, and are to be sold at his shop nere the Royall Exchange, 1594. Copy from Henry E. Huntington Library and Art Gallery.
Griffiths, Jeremy and Pearsall, Derek (eds.) 1989. *Book Production and Publishing in Britain 1375–1475*. Cambridge: Cambridge University Press.
Grund, Peter 2007. 'From tongue to text: The transmission of the Salem Witchcraft Examination Records', *American Speech* **82**: 119–50.
Grzega, Joachim 2008. '*Hāl, Hail, Hello, Hi*: Greetings in English language history', in Andreas H. Jucker and Irma Taavitsainen (eds.), pp. 165–93.
Gunn, Steven J. 2008. 'Henry VII (1457–1509)', *Oxford Dictionary of National Biography*. Oxford: Oxford University Press. Online at www.oxforddnb.com/view/article/12954 (accessed 27 July 2009).
Gurr, Andrew 1992. *The Shakespearean Stage 1574–1642*. 3rd edn. Cambridge: Cambridge University Press.
Hailes, Lord (Sir David Dalrymple) 1770. *Ancient Scottish Poems*. Edinburgh: Balfour.
Halliday, Michael A. K. and Hasan, Ruqaiya 1976. *Cohesion in English*. London: Longman.

Hammond, Eleanor P. 1927. *English Verse between Chaucer and Surrey*. Durham, NC: Duke University Publications.

Hanks, William F. 1992. 'The indexical ground of deictic reference', in **Alessandro Duranti** and **Charles Goodwin** (eds.), *Rethinking Context: Language as an Interactive Phenomenon*. Cambridge: Cambridge University Press, pp. 43–76.

Hardman, Philippa 1997. 'Windows into the text: Unfilled spaces in some fifteenth-century English manuscripts', in **John Scattergood** and **Julia Boffey** (eds.), *Texts and their Context: Papers from the Early Book Society*. Dublin: Four Courts Press, pp. 44–70.

Harré, Rom 1972. *The Philosophies of Science: An Introductory Survey*. London: Oxford: Oxford University Press.

Hassell Smith, A. [2004] 2005. 'Bacon, Sir Nathaniel (1546?–1622)', in *Oxford Dictionary of National Biography*. Oxford: Oxford University Press. Online at www.oxforddnb.com/view/article/998 (accessed 29 March 2007).

Hassell Smith, A. and **Baker, Gillian M.** (eds.). 1987–1988. *The Papers of Nathaniel Bacon of Stiffkey*. 3 vols. Norwich: Norfolk Record Society.

Hauser, Albert 1998. Grüezi *und* adieu: *Gruss- und Umgangsformen vom 17. Jahrhundert bis zur Gegenwart*. Zürich: Verlag Neue Zürcher Zeitung.

Hellinga, Lotte and **Trapp, J. B.** (eds.) 1999. *The Cambridge History of the Book in Britain, Volume III: 1400–1557*. Cambridge: Cambridge University Press.

Herman, Vimala 1995. *Dramatic Discourse: Dialogue as Interaction in Plays*. London/New York: Routledge.

Hesse, Carla 1996. 'Books in time', in **Geoffrey Nunberg** (ed.), *The Future of the Book*. Tournout: Brepols, pp. 21–33.

Hiltunen, Risto 1996. '"Tell me, be you a witch?": Questions in the Salem Witchcraft Trials of 1692', *International Journal of the Semiotics of Law* **25**: 17–37.

2001. 'Some syntactic properties of English law language: Twenty-five years after Gustafsson (1975)', in **Risto Hiltunen, Keith Battarbee, Matti Peikola** and **Sanna-Kaisa Tanskanen** (eds.), *English in Zigs and Zags: A Festschrift for Marita Gustafsson*. Turku: Pallosalama, pp. 53–66.

Hiltunen, Risto and **Peikola, Matti** 2007. 'Trial discourse and manuscript context: Scribal profiles in the Salem witchcraft records', *Journal of Historical Pragmatics* **8**: 43–68.

Hingeston, Francis C. (ed.) 1860. *Royal and Historical Letters During the Reign of Henry the Fourth, King of England and of France, and Lord of Ireland*, vol. 1. London: Longman, Green, Longman, and Roberts.

Hirsch, John C. 1975. 'Author and scribe in *The Book of Margery Kempe*', *Medium Aevum* **44**: 145–50.

Hoey, Michael 1991. *Patterns of Lexis in Text*. Oxford: Oxford University Press.

Holland, Peter 2006. 'Introduction: Printing performance', in **Peter Holland** and **Stephen Orgel** (eds.), *From Performance to Print in Shakespeare's England*. Basingstoke: Palgrave Macmillan, pp. 1–12.

Holmes, Geoffrey 1993. *The Making of a Great Power: Late Stuart and Early Georgian Britain 1660–1722*. London: Longman.

Honourable Society of Cymmrodorion 1828. *Transactions of the Cymmrodorion, or, Metropolitan Cambrian Institution*, vol 2. London: Metropolitan Cambrian Institution.

Bibliography

Horobin, Simon 2006. 'A new fragment of the Romaunt of the Rose', *Studies in the Age of Chaucer* **28**: 205–15.
  2007a. *Chaucer's Language*. Basingstoke: Palgrave Macmillan.
  2007b. 'A manuscript found in the library of Abbotsford House and the lost legendary of Osbern Bokenham', *English Manuscript Studies* **14**: 132–64.
Horobin, Simon and Mooney, Linne 2004. 'A *Piers Plowman* manuscript by the Hengwrt/Ellesmere scribe and its implications for London Standard English', *Studies in the Age of Chaucer* **26**: 65–112.
Horowitz, Mark R. 2009. 'Who was Henry VII? The 500th anniversary of the death of the first Tudor king (1509–2009)', *Historical Research* **82**: 375–592.
Horrox, Rosemary 2008. 'Arthur, Prince of Wales (1486–1502)', *Oxford Dictionary of National Biography*. Oxford: Oxford University Press. Online at www.oxforddnb.com/view/article/705 (accessed 27 July 2009).
Horrox, Rosemary and Ormrod, W. Mark (eds.) 2006. *A Social History of England 1200–1500*. Cambridge: Cambridge University Press.
Huber, Magnus 2007. '*The Old Bailey Proceedings, 1674–1834*: Evaluating and annotating a corpus of eighteenth- and nineteenth-century spoken English', in Anneli Meurman-Solin and Arja Nurmi (eds.), *Annotating Variation and Change*. Research Unit for Variation, Contacts and Change in English, University of Helsinki. Online at www.helsinki.fi/varieng/journal/volumes/01.
Hudson, Anne 1977. 'Middle English', in A. G. Rigg (ed.), *Editing Medieval Texts*. New York: Garland, pp. 34–57.
Huebert, Ronald 1997. 'Privacy: The early social history of a word', *The Sewanee Review* **105**: 591–609.
Hunston, Susan 2000. 'Evaluation and the planes of discourse: Status and value in persuasive texts', in Susan Hunston and Geoff Thompson (eds.), *Evaluation in Text: Authorial Stance and the Construction of Discourse*. Oxford: Oxford University Press, pp. 176–207.
Jacobs, Andreas and Jucker, Andreas H. 1995. 'The historical perspective in pragmatics', in Andreas H. Jucker (ed.), pp. 3–33.
James, Montague Rhodes 1901. *The Western Manuscripts of Trinity College Cambridge: A Descriptive Catalogue*, vol. 2. Cambridge: Cambridge University Press. Online at http://rabbit.trin.cam.ac.uk/James/R.15.18.html.
Jefferson, Judith 2005. 'The distribution of infinitives in *-e* and *-en* in some Middle English alliterative poems', *Medium Aevum* **74**: 221–47.
Jeffrey, David L. 1973. 'English saints' plays', in Denny Neville (ed.), *Medieval Drama*: Stratford-upon-Avon Studies **16** New York: Crane Russak, pp. 69–89.
Johnson, Ian 1994. 'Tales of a true translator: Medieval literary theory, anecdote and autobiography in Osbern Bokenham's *Legendys of Hooly Wummen*', in Roger Ellis and Ruth Evans (eds.), *The Medieval Translator*, vol. 4. Exeter: University of Exeter Press, pp. 104–24.
Jones, Mary L. 1978. 'How the seven deadly sins "dewoyde from þe woman" in the Digby *Mary Magdalene*', *American Notes and Queries* **16**: 118–19.
Jones, Michael K. and Underwood, Malcolm G. 1992. *The King's Mother*. Cambridge: Cambridge University Press.

Jones, Peter Murray 2004. 'Argentine, John (*c.* 1443–1508)', *Oxford Dictionary of National Biography*. Oxford: Oxford University Press. Online at www.oxforddnb.com/view/article/642 (accessed 29 September 2009).
Jucker, Andreas H. (ed.) 1995. *Historical Pragmatics: Pragmatic Developments in the History of English*. Amsterdam/Philadelphia: John Benjamins.
   2000 'Slanders, slurs and insults on the road to Canterbury: Forms of verbal aggression in Chaucer's *Canterbury Tales*', in **Irma Taavitsainen, Terttu Nevalainen, Päivi Pahta** and **Matti Rissanen** (eds.), *Placing Middle English in Context*. Berlin/New York: Mouton de Gruyter, pp. 369–90.
   2006. '"Thou art so loothly and so oold also": The use of *ye* and *thou* in Chaucer's *Canterbury Tales*', *Anglistik* 17: 57–72.
   2008a. 'Historical pragmatics', *Language and Linguistics Compass* 2: 894–906.
   2008b. 'Politeness in the history of English', in **Marina Dossena** *et al*. (eds.), vol. 2, pp. 3–29.
Jucker, Andreas H. and Smith, Sara W. 2003. 'Reference assignment as a communicative task: Differences between native speakers, ESL- and EFL-speakers', in **Ewald Mengel, Hans-Jörg Schmid** and **Michael Steppat**, (eds.), *Anglistentag 2002 Bayreuth Proceedings*. Trier: Wissenschaftlicher Verlag Trier, pp. 401–10.
Jucker, Andreas H. and Taavitsainen, Irma 2000. 'Diachronic speech act analysis: Insults from flyting to flaming', *Journal of Historical Pragmatics* 1.1: 67–95.
   2003. 'Introduction', in **Irma Taavitsainen** and **Andreas H. Jucker** (eds.), pp. 1–25.
   (eds.) 2008. *Speech Act History of English*. Amsterdam/Philadelphia: John Benjamins.
   (eds.) 2010. *Handbook of Historical Pragmatics*. Berlin: Mouton de Gruyter.
Kahlas-Tarkka, Leena and Rissanen, Matti 2007. 'The sullen and the talkative: Discourse strategies in the Salem examinations', *Journal of Historical Pragmatics* 8: 1–24.
Kane, George and Donaldson, E. Talbot (eds.) 1974. *Piers Plowman: The B-Text*. London: Athlone Press.
Ker, Neil Ripley 1969. *Medieval Manuscripts in British Libraries*, vol. 1. Oxford: Clarendon.
Kibre, Pearl 1991. 'A list of Latin manuscripts containing medieval versions of the *Methodus medendi*', in **Fridolf Kudlien** and **Richard J. Durling** (eds.), pp. 117–22.
Knighton, C. S. 2004. 'Busby, Richard (1606–1695)', in *Oxford Dictionary of National Biography*. Oxford: Oxford University Press. Online at www.oxforddnb.com/view/article/4157 (accessed 30 May 2009).
Knowles, Richard Brinsley 1872. *Third Report of the Royal Commission on Historical Manuscripts*, Appendix. London: Her Majesty's Stationery Office.
Koch, Peter 1999. 'Court records and cartoons: Reflections of spontaneous dialogue in early Romance texts', in **Andreas H. Jucker, Gerd Fritz** and **Franz Lebsanft** (eds.), *Historical Dialogue Analysis*. Amsterdam/Philadelphia: John Benjamins, pp. 399–429.
Kopytko, Roman 1995. 'Linguistic politeness strategies in Shakespeare's plays', in **Andreas H. Jucker** (ed.), pp. 517–40.

272 Bibliography

Kraus, H. P. 1988. 'Typescript catalogue of manuscripts', unpublished.
Kroch, Anthony 1989. 'Reflexes of grammar in patterns of language change', *Language Variation and Change* 1: 199–244.
Kryk-Kastovsky, Barbara 2000. 'Representations of orality in Early Modern English trial records', *Journal of Historical Pragmatics* 1: 201–30.
    2006a. 'Impoliteness in Early Modern English courtroom discourse', *Journal of Historical Pragmatics* 7: 213–43.
    (ed.) 2006b. *Historical Courtroom Discourse*. Special issue of *Journal of Historical Pragmatics* 7.
    (ed.) 2007. *Historical Courtroom Discourse*. Special issue of *Journal of Historical Pragmatics* 8.
Krzeszowski, Tomasz P. 1984. 'Tertium comparationis', in Jacek Fisiak (ed.), pp. 301–12.
Kudlien, Fridolf and Durling, Richard J. (eds.) 1991. 'Galen's Method of Healing': *Proceedings of the 1982 Galen Symposium*. Leiden: E. J. Brill.
Kühn, C. G. (ed.) 1825. *Claudius Galenus: Opera omnia, Graece et Latinae*, vol. 10. Lipsiae.
Kytö, Merja (comp.) 1996. *Manual to the Diachronic Part of the Helsinki Corpus of English Texts: Coding Conventions and Lists of Source Texts*. 3rd edn. Department of English, University of Helsinki.
Kytö, Merja and Walker, Terry 2006. *Guide to A Corpus of English Dialogues 1560–1760*. Uppsala: Acta Universitatis Upsaliensis.
Laing, Margaret 1991. 'Anchor texts and literary manuscripts in Early Middle English', in Felicity Riddy (ed.), pp. 27–52.
    1999. 'Confusion *wrs* confounded', *Neuphilologische Mitteilungen* 100: 251–70.
    2008. 'The early Middle English scribe: *Sprach er wie er schrieb?*', in Marina Dossena et al. (eds.), vol. 3, pp. 1–44.
Laing, Margaret and Lass, Roger 2003. 'Tales of 1001 nists: The phonological implications of litteral substitution sets in some thirteenth-century South-West Midland texts', *English Language and Linguistics* 7: 257–78.
    (eds.) 2007. *A Linguistic Atlas of Early Middle English, 1150–1325* (LAEME). The University of Edinburgh. Online at www.lel.ed.ac.uk/ihd/laeme1/laeme1.html (accessed 8 April 2009).
Laird, Edgar 1990. 'Astrology in the court of Charles V of France, as reflected in Oxford, St John's College, MS 164', *Manuscripta* 34: 167–76.
Laird, Edgar and Fischer, Robert (eds.) 1995. *Pèlerin de Prusse on the Astrolabe*. Binghamton: CMERS, State University of New York.
Láng, Benedek n.d. 'Angels around the Crystal: The prayer book of King Wladislas and the treasure hunts of Henry the Bohemian', *Średniowiecze*. Online at. http://staropolska.pl/sredniowiecze/opracowania/Lang.html and /Lang_01.html (accessed 29 December 2009).
Langbein, John H. 1978. 'The criminal trial before the lawyers', *University of Chicago Law Review* 263: 278–9.
Lass, Roger 1976. *English Phonology and Phonological Theory*. Cambridge: Cambridge University Press.
Layder, Derek [1997] 2003. *Modern Social Theory: Key Debates and New Directions*. London/New York: Routledge.

Lebsanft, Franz 1988. *Studien zu einer Linguistik des Grusses: Sprache und Funktion der altfranzösischen Grußformeln*. Tübingen: Max Niemeyer.
Lerner, Gene H. 1996. 'On the place of linguistic resources in the organization of talk-in-interaction: "Second person" reference in multi-party conversation', *Pragmatics* 6: 281–94.
Levinson, Stephen C. 2007. 'Optimizing person reference – perspectives from usage on Rossel Island', in **N. J. Enfield** and **Tanya Stivers** (eds.), pp. 29–72.
Locher, Miriam 2004. *Power and Politeness in Action: Disagreements in Oral Communication*. Berlin/New York: Mouton de Gruyter.
Lochrie, Karma 1991. *Margery Kempe and Translations of the Flesh*. Philadelphia: University of Pennsylvania Press.
Longman Spoken and Written English Corpus. See Biber *et al*. 1999.
Louis, Cameron (ed.) 1980. *The Commonplace Book of Robert Reynes of Acle: An Edition of Tanner MS 407*. New York: Garland Publishing.
Machan, Tim William 1994. *Textual Criticism and Middle English Texts*. Charlottesville/London: University Press of Virginia.
Maci, Stefania Maria 2008. *The Linguistic Design of Mary Magdalene*. Bergamo: CELSB.
Mackenzie, W. Mackay (ed.) 1932. *The Poems of William Dunbar*. London: Faber.
Maltman, Sister Nicholas 1979. 'Light in and on the Digby *Mary Magdalene*', in **Margot H. King** and **Wesley M. Stevens** (eds.), *Saints, Scholars and Heroes: Studies in Medieval Culture in Honour of Charles W. Jones*. Ann Arbor: University Microfilm International, pp. 257–80.
Malvern, Marjorie M. 1969. 'The Magdalene: An exploration of the shaping of myths around the Mary Magdalene of the New Testament canonical Gospels and an examination of the effects of the myths on the literary figure, particularly on the heroine of the 15th century Digby play *Mary Magdalene*'. Ph.D thesis, Michigan State University. Published on demand by University Microfilm, Ann Arbor, Michigan.
Manuscript of Geoffrey Chaucer's 'Astrolabe' and Other Middle English Documents: (c. 1460–1487). 1995. Nara: Asahata Barman Lace Co.
Matheson, Lister and Shannon, Ann (eds.) 1994. 'A treatise on the elections of times', in **Lister Matheson** (ed.), *Popular and Practical Science of Medieval England*. East Lansing, MI: Colleagues Press, pp. 23–59.
Matthews, David 1999. *The Making of Middle English, 1765–1910*. Minneapolis: University of Minnesota Press.
Mazzon, Gabriella 2000. 'Social relations and form of address in the *Canterbury Tales*', in **Dieter Kastovsky** and **Arthur Mettinger** (eds.), *The History of English in a Social Context: A Contribution to Historical Sociolinguistics*. Berlin/New York: Mouton de Gruyter, pp. 135–68.
McAvoy, Liz Herbert (ed.) 2008. *A Companion to Julian of Norwich*. Cambridge: D. S. Brewer.
McConchie, R. W. 1997. *Lexicography and Physicke: The Record of Sixteenth-century English Medical Terminology*. Oxford: Clarendon.
McIntosh, Angus 1983. 'Present indicative plural forms in the later Middle English of the North Midlands', in **Douglas Gray** and **Eric G. Stanley** (eds.), *Middle*

English Studies Presented to Norman Davis in Honour of His Seventieth Birthday. Oxford: Clarendon, pp. 235–44.

McIntosh, Angus, Samuels, M. L. and Benskin, Michael (eds.) 1986. *A Linguistic Atlas of Late Medieval English* (LALME). 4 vols. Aberdeen University Press.

McKinnel, John 1984. 'Staging the Digby *Mary Magdalene*', *Medieval English Theatre* 6: 127–52.

McKitterick, David 2003. *Print, Manuscript and the Search for Order 1450–1830*. Cambridge: Cambridge University Press.

McVaugh, Michael R. 2002. 'The lost Latin Galen', in Vivian Nutton (ed.), *The Unknown Galen: Galen Beyond Kühn, Bulletin of the Institute of Classical Studies, Supplement* 71: 153–62.

2006. 'Niccolò da Reggio's translations of Galen and their reception in France', *Early Science and Medicine* 11: 275–301.

MED = *Middle English Dictionary*. University of Michigan Press. Online at quod.lib.umich.edu/m/med/.

Meyer-Lee, Robert J. 2008. 'Manuscript studies, literary value, and the object of Chaucer studies', *Studies in the Age of Chaucer* 30: 1–37.

Middle English Compendium. University of Michigan. Online at quod.lib.umich.edu/m/mec (accessed June 2009).

Middle English Medical Texts (MEMT) 2005. Compiled by Irma Taavitsainen, Päivi Pahta and Martti Mäkinen. CD-ROM with MEMT Presenter Software by Raymond Hickey. Amsterdam/Philadelphia: John Benjamins. See www.helsinki.fi/varieng/CoRD/corpora/CEEM/MEMTindex.html.

Minnis, A. J. and Brewer, Charlotte (eds.) 1992. *Crux and Controversy in Middle English Textual Criticism*. Cambridge: D. S. Brewer.

Misrahi, Jean 1943. 'A *Vita Sanctae Mariae Magdalena (BHL 5456)* in an eleventh century manuscript', *Speculum* 18: 335–9.

Mooney, Linne R. 1995. *The Index of Middle English Prose, Handlist XI: Manuscripts in the Library of Trinity College, Cambridge*. Cambridge: D. S. Brewer.

Morris, Richard (ed.) 1874–1893. *Cursor Mundi*. London: Early English Text Society.

Mossé, Ferdinand 1958. *A Handbook of Middle English*. Baltimore/London: The Johns Hopkins University Press.

Mühlhäusler, Peter and Harré, Rom 1990. *Pronouns and People: The Linguistic Construction of Social and Personal Identity*. Oxford: Basil Blackwell.

Nevala, Minna 2004a. *Address in Early English Correspondence: Its Forms and Sociopragmatic Functions*. Helsinki: Société Néophilologique.

2004b. 'Accessing politeness axes: Forms of address and terms of reference in early English correspondence', *Journal of Pragmatics* 36: 125–60.

2010. 'Keeping up appearances: Facework in self- and addressee-oriented person reference', in Jonathan Culpeper and Daniel Z. Kádár (eds.), pp. 147–73.

Norri, Juhani 2004. 'Entrances and exits in English medical vocabulary, 1400–1550', in Irma Taavitsainen and Päivi Pahta (eds.), pp. 100–43.

North, John David 1977. 'The Alfonsine tables in England', in Yasukatsu Maeyama and Walter Saltzer (eds.), *Prismata: Naturwissenschaftsgeschichtliche Studien*. Wiesbaden: Steiner, pp. 269–301. Reprinted in John David North (1989). *Stars, Minds and Fate*. London: Hambledon, pp. 325–59.

Norton, Mary Beth 2002. *In the Devil's Snare: The Salem Witchcraft Crisis of 1692.* New York: Alfred Knopf.
Nurmi, Arja 1999. *A Social History of Periphrastic* Do. Helsinki: Société Néophilologique.
Nutton, Vivian 1991. 'Style and context in the *Method of Healing*', in **Fridolf Kudlien** and **Richard J. Durling** (eds.), pp. 1–25.
  1997. 'Greek science in the sixteenth-century Renaissance', in **Judith Veronica Field** and **Frank A. J. L. James.** (eds.), *Renaissance and Revolution: Humanists, Scholars, Craftsmen and Natural Philosophers in Early Modern Europe.* Cambridge: Cambridge University Press, pp. 15–29.
Old Bailey Trials 1674–1834. Subpart of **Clive Emsley, Tim Hitchcock** and **Robert Shoemaker** (eds.), *The Old Bailey Proceedings Online.* Online at www.oldbaileyonline.org.
Orme, Nicholas 1973. *English Schools in the Middle Ages.* London: Methuen.
Oxford Dictionary of National Biography (ODNB). Online at www.oxforddnb.com.
Oxford English Dictionary Online. Oxford: Oxford University Press. Online at www.oed.com. Also available as a searchable corpus at http://corpus.byu.edu.
Pächt, Otto and Alexander, Jonathan J. G. 1966–70. *Illuminated Manuscripts in the Bodleian Library, Oxford.* 2 vols. Oxford: Clarendon Press.
Pahta, Päivi and Taavitsainen, Irma 2004. 'Vernacularisation of scientific and medical writing in its sociohistorical context', in **Irma Taavitsainen** and **Päivi Pahta** (eds.), pp. 1–18.
Palander-Collin, Minna 2006. '(Re)constructing style and language as social interaction through first- and second-person pronouns in Early Modern English letters', in **Irma Taavitsainen, Juhani Härmä** and **Jarmo Korhonen** (eds.), *Dialogic Language Use.* Helsinki: Modern Language Society, pp. 339–62.
  2009. 'Patterns of interaction: Self-mention and addressee inclusion in letters of Nathaniel Bacon and his correspondents' in **Arja Nurmi, Minna Nevala** and **Minna Palander-Collin** (eds.), *The Language of Daily Life in England 1400–1800.* Amsterdam/Philadelphia: John Benjamins, pp. 53–74.
Palfrey, Simon and Stern, Tiffany 2007. *Shakespeare in Parts.* Oxford: Oxford University Press.
Parkes, Malcolm B. 1976. 'The influence of the concept of *ordinatio* and *compilatio* on the development of the book', in **Jonathan J. G. Alexander** and **Margaret T. Gibson** (eds.), *Medieval Learning and Literature: Essays Presented to Richard William Hunt.* Oxford: Clarendon, pp. 115–45.
  1991. *Scribes, Scripts and Readers: Studies in the Communication, Presentation and Dissemination of Medieval Texts.* London: Hambledon Press.
  1992. *Pause and Effect.* London: Scolar.
Patterson, Lee 1987. *Negotiating the Past: The Historical Understanding of Medieval Literature.* Madison: University of Wisconsin Press.
Payne, Linda 2002. '"A Spedie Reformacion": Barber-Surgeons, anatomization, and the reformation of medicine in Tudor London', in **Gerhild Scholz Williams** and **Charles D. Gunnoe** (eds.), *Paracelsian Moments: Science, Medicine, and Astrology in Early Modern Europe.* Kirksville: Truman State University Press, pp. 71–93.

Pearsall, Derek 1984. 'Thomas Speght (c. 1550–?)', in Paul G. Ruggiers (ed.) *Editing Chaucer: The Great Tradition*. Norman: University of Oklahoma Press, pp. 71–92.
  1992a. *The Life of Geoffrey Chaucer*. Oxford: Blackwell.
  1992b. 'Authorial revision in some Late-Medieval English texts', in A. J. Minnis and Charlotte Brewer (eds.), pp. 39–48.
Peters, Pam 2002. 'Textual morphology from Gutenberg to the e-book', in Andreas Fischer, Gunnel Tottie and Hans Martin Lehmann (eds.), *Text Types and Corpora: Studies in Honour of Udo Fries*. Tübingen: Gunter Narr, pp. 77–91.
Phillips, Helen 2000. *An Introduction to the Canterbury Tales: Reading, Fiction, Context*. London: Longman.
Pingree, David 2008. 'Al-Qabīsī, Abū Al-Saqr 'Abd Al-'Azīz Ibn 'Uthmān Ibn 'Alī', in Charles Gillispie (ed.), *Complete Dictionary of Scientific Biography*, vol. XI. New York: Cengage Learning, pp. 226. Gale virtual reference library. Online at find.galegroup.com (accessed 9 June 2009).
Plomer, Henry Robert 1913. 'Bibliographical notes from the Privy Purse expenses of King Henry the Seventh', *The Library* 3rd Series 4: 291–305.
Pollard, Alfred W. (ed.) 1890. *English Miracle Plays, Moralities and Interludes*. Oxford: Clarendon.
Postles, Dave 2005. 'The politics of address in Early-Modern England', *Journal of Historical Sociology* 18: 99–121.
Powys, John Cowper [1940] 2002. *Owen Glendower*. Charlbury, Oxford: Walcot Books.
Prior, Matthew 1692. *AN ODE, In Imitation of the Second Ode of the Third Book of Horace*. Written in the Year 1692. London: Printed for Jacob Tonson. Copy from Henry E. Huntington Library and Art Gallery. Early English Books Online (EEBO) at gateway.proquest.com/openurl?ctx_ver=Z39.88-2003&res_id=xri:eebo&rft_id=xri:eebo:citation:11981491 (accessed 29 June 2009).
  1695. *An ODE. Presented to the KING, on his Majesty's Arrival in Holland, AFTER The QUEEN's Death. 1695*. London: Printed for Jacob Tonson. Copy from Harvard University Library. Early English Books Online (EEBO) at gateway.proquest.com/openurl?ctx_ver=Z39.88-2003&res_id=xri:eebo&rft_id=xri:eebo:citation:12360197 (accessed 29 June 2009).
Ramsay, Allan 1724. *The Ever Green, being a Collection of Scots Poems, Wrote by the Ingenious before 1600*. Edinburgh: Ruddiman.
Rash, Felicity 2004. 'Linguistic politeness and greeting rituals in German-speaking Switzerland', *Linguistik online* 20: 47–72. Online at www.linguistik-online.de/20_04/rash.html.
Raumolin-Brunberg, Helena 1996. 'Forms of address in Early English correspondence', in Terttu Nevalainen and Helena Raumolin-Brunberg (eds.), *Sociolinguistics and Language History: Studies based on the Corpus of Early English Correspondence*. Amsterdam: Rodopi, pp. 167–81.
Rayson, Paul, Archer, Dawn, Baron, Alistair, Culpeper, Jonathan and Smith, Nick 2007. 'Tagging the Bard: Evaluating the accuracy of a modern POS tagger on Early Modern English corpora', in *Proceedings of Corpus Linguistics 2007, July 27–30, Birmingham University, UK*.

See also ucrel.lancs.ac.uk/VariantSpelling/ and www.comp.lancs.ac.uk/~barona/*VARD2* (accessed 10 August 2009).
Rayson, Paul, Archer, Dawn and Smith, Nick 2005. '*VARD* versus WORD: A comparison of the UCREL variant detector and modern spellcheckers on English historical corpora', in *Proceedings of Corpus Linguistics 2005, July 14–17*, Birmingham University, UK; Proceedings from the Corpus Linguistics Conference Series 1. Online at eprints.comp.lancs.ac.uk/1157/
Rees, William (ed.) 1953. *A Survey of the Duchy of Lancaster Lordships in Wales, 1609–1613: Public Record Office, Duchy of Lancaster Miscellaneous Books, nos. 120–123*. Cardiff: University of Wales Press.
Renevey, Denis and Caie, Graham D. (eds.) 2008. *Medieval Texts in Context*. London/New York: Routledge.
Reynolds, L. D. and Wilson, N. G. 1974. *Scribes and Scholars*. Oxford University Press.
Riddy, Felicity (ed.) 1991. *Regionalism in Late Medieval Manuscripts and Texts*. University of York, Centre for Medieval Studies.
  2000. *Prestige, Authority and Power in Late Medieval Manuscripts and Texts*. York: York Medieval Press, in association with Boydell & Brewer and The Centre for Medieval Studies, University of York.
Rigg, A. G. 1968. *A Glastonbury Miscellany of the Fifteenth Century*. Oxford: Oxford University Press.
Rissanen, Matti 2003. 'Salem witchcraft papers as evidence of early American English' *English Linguistics* (English Linguistics Society of Japan) **20**: 84–114.
Ritchie, Harry M. 1963. 'A suggested location for the Digby *Mary Magdalene*', *Theatre Survey* **4**: 51–8.
Ritchie, W. Tod (ed.) 1928. *The Bannatyne Manuscript*. Edinburgh/London: Scottish Text Society.
Robbins, Rossell Hope (ed.) 1955. *Secular Lyrics of the XIVth and XVth Centuries*. 2nd edn. Oxford: Clarendon.
Roberts, Ian 1985. 'Agreement parameters and the development of English modal auxiliaries', *Natural Language and Linguistic Theory* **3**: 21–58.
Robinson, F. N. (ed.) 1957. *The Works of Geoffrey Chaucer*. Oxford: Oxford University Press.
Robinson, Peter 2003. 'The history, discoveries, and aims of the *Canterbury Tales* project', *The Chaucer Review* **38**: 126–39.
Rosen, Edward 2008. 'Schöner, Johannes', in **Charles Gillispie** (ed.), *Complete Dictionary of Scientific Biography*. New York: Cengage Learning, pp. 199–200. Gale virtual reference library. Online at find.galegroup.com (accessed 29 July 2009).
Rosenthal, Bernard (general ed.), Adams, Gretchen A., Burns, Margo, Grund, Peter, Hiltunen, Risto, Kahlas-Tarkka, Leena, Kytö, Merja, Peikola, Matti, Ray, Benjamin C., Rissanen, Matti, Roach, Marilyn K. and Trask, Richard B. (eds.) 2009. *Records of the Salem Witch-Hunt*. Cambridge: Cambridge University Press.
Sacks, Harvey and Schegloff, Emanuel A. 2007. 'Two preferences in the organization of reference to persons in conversation and their interaction', in **N. J. Enfield** and **Tanya Stivers** (eds.), pp. 23–8.

Saenger, Paul 1982. 'Silent reading: Its impact on late medieval script and society', *Viator* **13**: 367–414.
Samuels, Michael L. 1963. 'Some applications of Middle English dialectology', *English Studies* **44**: 81–94.
Schegloff, Emanuel A. 1996. 'Some practices for referring to persons in talk-in-interaction: A partial sketch of a systematics', in **Barbara Fox** (ed.), *Studies in Anaphora*. Amsterdam/Philadelphia: John Benjamins, pp. 437–85.
  2007. 'Conveying who you are: The presentation of self, strictly speaking', in **N. J. Enfield** and **Tanya Stivers** (eds.), pp. 123–48.
Schiffrin, Deborah 1987. *Discourse Markers*. Cambridge: Cambridge University Press.
Schmidt, Karl 1885. 'Die Digby Spiele', *Anglia* **8**: 371–93.
Scott, Kathleen L. 1996. *Later Gothic Manuscripts 1390–1490*, Survey of Manuscripts Illuminated in the British Isles, vol. 4, parts 1 and 2. London: Harvey Miller.
Scott, Mike 1996–2009. *WordSmith Tools Manual Version 5*. Oxford: Oxford University Press. See www.lexically.net/downloads/version5/HTML/index.html (accessed 10 August 2009).
  2007. *WordSmith Tools 4*. Oxford University Press. Online at www.lexically.net/wordsmith/index.html (accessed 08 April 2009).
SDBM = Schoenberg Database of Manuscripts. Online at http://dla.library.upenn.edu/dla/schoenberg.
Searle, John R. 1969. *Speech Acts: An Essay in the Philosophy of Language*. Cambridge: Cambridge University Press.
  1976. 'A classification of illocutionary acts', *Language in Society* **5**: 1–24.
  1979. *Expression and Meaning: Studies in the Theory of Speech Acts*. Cambridge: Cambridge University Press.
Serjeantson, Mary S. [1938] 1971. *Legendys of Hooly Wummen by Osbern Bokenham*. Oxford: Oxford University Press.
Seymour, Michael C. 1995. *A Catalogue of Chaucer Manuscripts, vol. I: Works before the* Canterbury Tales. Aldershot: Scolar.
Shank, Michael 2008. 'Regiomontanus, Johannes', in **Charles Gillispie** (ed.), *Complete Dictionary of Scientific Biography*. New York: Cengage Learning, pp. 216–19. Gale virtual reference library. Online at find.galegroup.com (accessed 9 June 2009).
Sher, Richard 2006. *The Enlightenment and the Book*. Chicago: University of Chicago Press.
Shoemaker, Robert B. 2008. '*The Old Bailey Proceedings* and the representation of crime and criminal justice in eighteenth-century London', *Journal of British Studies* **47**: 559–80.
Siewierska, Anna 2004. *Person*. Cambridge: Cambridge University Press.
Skeat, Walter William (ed.) 1899. *The Complete Works of Geoffrey Chaucer*, vol. 1. 2nd edn. Oxford: Clarendon.
  (ed.) 1926. *The Complete Works of Geoffrey Chaucer*, vol. 3. Oxford: Clarendon.
Slack, Paul 1979. 'Mirrors of health and treasures of poor men: The uses of the vernacular medical literature of Tudor England', in **Charles Webster** (ed.), *Health, Medicine, and Mortality in the Sixteenth Century*. Cambridge: Cambridge University Press, pp. 237–73.

Smith, J. Beverley 1967. 'The last phase of the Glyndwr rebellion', *The Bulletin of the Board of Celtic Studies* **22**: 250–60.
Smith, Jeremy J. (ed.) 1988. *The English of Chaucer and his Contemporaries: Essays by M. L. Samuels and J. J. Smith*. Aberdeen: Aberdeen University Press.
  1996. *An Historical Study of English: Function, Form and Change*. London/New York: Routledge.
Smith, Sara W. and Jucker, Andreas H. 1998. 'Interactive aspects of reference assignment in conversations', *Pragmatics and Cognition* **6**: 153–87.
Sotheby's. *Catalogue of the Bute Collection*, 13 June 1983, lot 32, pp. 113–15.
Spens, Susan 1997. *George Stepney 1663–1707: Diplomat and Poet*. Cambridge: James Clarke & Co.
Staley, Lynn 1994. *Margery Kempe's Dissenting Fictions*. University Park: Pennsylvania State University Press.
Stamp, Gavin 2004. 'Stuart, John Crichton-, sixth Marquess of Bute (1933–1993)', *Oxford Dictionary of National Biography*. Oxford: Oxford University Press. Online at www.oxforddnb.com/view/article/51532 (accessed 28 May 2009).
Stern, Tiffany 2000. *Rehearsal from Shakespeare to Sheridan*. Oxford: Oxford University Press.
  2004. 'Re-patching the play', in **Peter Holland** and **Stephen Orgel** (eds.), *From Script to Stage in Early Modern England*. Basingstoke: Palgrave Macmillan, pp. 151–80.
Stévanovitch, Colette 2003. 'Tutoiement et violence verbale dans les Contes de Canterbéry', *Cercles* **6**: 62–73. Online at www.cercles.com.
Stivers, Tanya 2007. 'Alternative recognitionals in person reference', in **N. J. Enfield** and **Tanya Stivers** (eds.), pp. 73–96.
Stone, Walter Beryl 1953. 'The prediction of Regiomontanus: A study in the eschatology of Elizabethan England'. PhD thesis, Harvard University.
Stroebe, Klara 1911. *Altgermanische Grussformen*. Heidelberg: Winter.
Sutherland, James 1969. *English Literature of the Late Seventeenth Century*. Oxford: Clarendon.
Sutherland, Ronald (ed.) 1968. *The Romaunt of the Rose and Le Roman de la Rose, A Parallel-Text Edition*. Oxford: Blackwell.
Swedenburg Jr., H. T. 1946. 'George Stepney, my Lord Dorset's boy', *Huntington Library Quarterly* **10**: 1–33.
Taavitsainen, Irma 1995a. 'Interjections in Early Modern English: From imitation of spoken to conventions of written language', in **Andreas H. Jucker** (ed.), pp. 439–65.
  1995b. 'Narrative patterns of affect in four genres of the *Canterbury Tales*', *Chaucer Review* **30**: 191–210.
  1997a. '*By Saint Tanne*: Pious oaths or swearing in Middle English? An assessment of genres', in **Raymond Hickey** and **Stanisław Puppel** (eds.), *Language History and Linguistics Modelling: A Festschrift for Jacek Fisiak on his 60th Birthday*. Berlin/New York: Mouton de Gruyter, pp. 815–26.
  1997b. 'Genres and text types in Medieval and Renaissance English', *Poetica* **47**: 49–62.
  1998. 'Emphatic language and Romantic prose: Changing functions of interjections in a sociocultural perspective', *European Journal of English Studies* **2**: 195–214.

280 Bibliography

1999. 'Personality and styles of affect in the *Canterbury Tales*', in **Geoffrey Lester** (ed.), *Chaucer in Perspective: Middle English Essays in Honour of Norman Blake*. Sheffield: Academic Press, pp. 218–34.

2001. 'Middle English recipes: Genre characteristics, text type features and underlying traditions of writing', *Journal of Historical Pragmatics* **2**: 85–113.

2002. 'Historical discourse analysis: Scientific language and changing thought-styles', in **Teresa Fanego, Belen Méndez-Naya** and **Elena Seoane** (eds.), *Sounds, Words, Texts and Change*. Amsterdam/Philadelphia: John Benjamins, pp. 201–26.

2009. 'The pragmatics of knowledge and meaning: Corpus linguistic approaches to changing thought-styles in early modern medical discourse', in **Andreas H. Jucker, Daniel Schreier** and **Marianne Hundt** (eds.), *Corpora: Pragmatics and Discourse*. Amsterdam: Rodopi, pp. 37–62.

Taavitsainen, Irma and **Fitzmaurice, Susan** 2007. 'Historical pragmatics: What it is and how to do it', in **Susan Fitzmaurice** and **Irma Taavitsainen** (eds.), pp. 11–36.

Taavitsainen, Irma, Jones, Peter, Pahta, Päivi, Hiltunen, Turo, Marttila, Ville, Ratia, Maura, Suhr, Carla and **Tyrkkö, Jukka** In press. 'English medical texts in 1500–1700 and the corpus of *Early Modern English Medical Texts*', in **Irma Taavitsainen** and **Päivi Pahta** (eds.).

Taavitsainen, Irma and **Jucker, Andreas H.** 2007. 'Speech act verbs and speech acts in the history of English', in **Susan Fitzmaurice** and **Irma Taavitsainen** (eds.), pp. 107–38.

2008. '"Methinks you seem more beautiful than ever": Compliments and gender in the history of English', in **Andreas H. Jucker** and **Irma Taavitsainen** (eds.), pp. 195–228.

2010. 'Trends and developments in historical pragmatics', in **Andreas H. Jucker** and **Irma Taavitsainen** (eds.).

(eds.) 2003. *Diachronic Perspectives on Address Term Systems*. Amsterdam/Philadelphia: John Benjamins.

Taavitsainen, Irma and **Pahta, Päivi** 1995. 'Scientific thought-styles in discourse structure: Changing patterns in a historical perspective', in **Sanna-Kaisa Tanskanen, Brita Wårvik** and **Risto Hiltunen** (eds.), *Organization in Discourse*. English Department, University of Turku, pp. 519–29.

1997. 'The Corpus of Early English Medical Writing', *ICAME Journal* **21**: 71–8.

(eds.) 2004. *Medical and Scientific Writing in Late Medieval English*. Cambridge: Cambridge University Press.

(eds.) In press. *Medical Writing in Early Modern English*. Cambridge: Cambridge University Press.

Taavitsainen, Irma, Pahta, Päivi and **Mäkinen, Martti** 2005. 'Introduction', in *Middle English Medical Texts* (MEMT).

2006. 'Towards a corpus-based history of specialized languages: *Middle English Medical Texts*', in **Roberta Facchinetti** and **Matti Rissanen** (eds.), *Corpus-based Studies in Diachronic English*. Bern: Peter Lang, pp. 79–94.

Talbot, Charles H. and **Hammond, Eugene A.** 1965. *The Medical Practitioners in Medieval England: A Biographical Register*. London: Wellcome Library.

Thompson, Geoff and **Ye, Yiyun** 1991. 'Evaluation in the reporting verbs used in academic papers', *Applied Linguistics* **12**.4: 365–82.

Thompson, John J. 2000. 'A poet's contact with the great and the good: Further considerations of Thomas Hoccleve's texts and manuscripts', in **Felicity Riddy** (ed.), *Prestige, Authority and Power in Late-Medieval Manuscripts and Texts*. Woodbridge, Suffolk: Boydell and Brewer, pp. 77–101.
Thomson, Peter 1997. 'Rogues and rhetoricians: Acting styles in early English drama', in **John D. Cox** and **David Scott Kastan** (eds.), *A New History of Early English Drama*. New York: Columbia University Press, pp. 321–35.
Thorndike, Lynn 1934–41. *A History of Magic and Experimental Science: The Fourteenth and Fifteenth Centuries; The Sixteenth Century* vols. III–V. New York: Columbia University Press.
Tompson, Richard S. 2000. *Islands of Law: A Legal History of the British Isles*. Bern: Peter Lang.
Tuckerman, Bryant 1964. *Planetary, Lunar, and Solar Positions A.D. 2 to A.D. 1649 at Five-day and Ten-day Intervals*. Philadelphia: American Philosophical Society.
Tyler, James E. 1838. *Henry of Monmouth: or, Memoirs of the Life and Character of Henry the Fifth as Prince of Wales and King of England*. vol. 1 of 2 vols. London: Richard Bentley.
Valle, Ellen 1999. *A Collective Intelligence: The Life Sciences in the Royal Society as a Scientific Discourse Community, 1665–1965*. University of Turku.
Velz, John W. 1968. 'Sovereignty in the Digby *Mary Magdalene*', *Comparative Drama* 2: 32–43.
Voigts, Linda Ehrsam 1986. 'The Latin verse and Middle English prose texts on the Sphere of Life and Death in Harley 3719', *Chaucer Review* 21: 291–305.
   1989. 'Scientific and medical books', in **Jeremy Griffiths** and **Derek Pearsall** (eds.), pp. 345–402.
   1994. 'The golden table of Pythagoras', in **Lister Matheson** (ed.), *Popular and Practical Science of Medieval England*. East Lansing, MI: Colleagues Press, pp. 123–39.
   1996. 'What's the word? Bilingualism in late-medieval England', *Speculum* 71: 813–26.
Wales, Katie 1996. *Personal Pronouns in Present-day English*. Cambridge: Cambridge University Press.
Walker, Terry 2007. Thou *and* You *in Early Modern English Dialogues, Trials, Depositions, and Drama Comedy*. Amsterdam/Philadelphia: John Benjamins.
Warren, Michael 1987. 'Repunctuation as interpretation in editions of Shakespeare', in **Vivian Salmon** and **Edwina Burgess** (eds.), *A Reader in the Language of Shakespearean Drama*. Amsterdam/Philadelphia: John Benjamins, pp. 455–69.
Wear, Andrew 1995. 'Medicine in Early Modern Europe, 1500–1700', in **Laurence Conrad, Michael Neve, Vivian Nutton, Roy Porter** and **Andrew Wear** (eds.), *The Western Medical Tradition 800 BC to AD 1800*. Cambridge: Cambridge University Press, pp. 215–363.
   2000. *Knowledge and Practice in English Medicine, 1550–1680*. Cambridge: Cambridge University Press.
Weisser, Ursula 1991. 'Zur Rezeption der *Methodus medendi* in *Continens* des Rhazes', in **Fridolf Kudlien** and **Richard J. Durling** (eds.), pp. 123–46.

Werlich, Egon 1976. *A Text Grammar of English*. Heidelberg: Quelle und Meyer.
White, P. R. R. 2003. 'Beyond modality and hedging: A dialogic view of the language of intersubjective stance', *Text* **23**: 259–84.
Wickham, Glynne 1972. 'The staging of saint plays in England', in **Sandro Sticca** (ed.), *Medieval Drama*. Albany: State University of New York Press, pp. 99–119.
Wilson, Andrew J. and Zeitlyn, David 1995. 'The distribution of person-referring expressions in natural conversation', *Research on Language and Social Interaction* **28**: 61–92.
Windeatt, Barry 2000. *The Book of Margery Kempe*. Harlow: Longman.
Winn, James Anderson 1987. *John Dryden and his World*. New Haven/London: Yale University Press.
Wogan-Browne, Jocelyn, Watson, Nicholas, Taylor, Andrew and Evans, Ruth 1999. *The Idea of the Vernacular: An Anthology of Middle English Literary Theory, 1280–1520*. Exeter: University of Exeter Press.
Wolfe, Don M. (ed.) 1953. *Complete Prose Works of John Milton*, vol. 1. New Haven: Yale University Press.
Wright, Joseph and Wright, Elizabeth Mary 1928. *An Elementary Middle English Grammar*. Oxford: Oxford University Press.
Wright, Thomas 1852. *The History of Ludlow and its Neighbourhood: Forming a Popular Sketch of the History of the Welsh Border*. London: Longman.
Wrightson, Keith [1982] 2003. *English Society 1580–1680*. London/New York: Routledge.
Zettersten, Arne and Diensberg, Bernhard (eds.) 2000. *The English Text of the Ancrene Riwle: The Vernon Text*. Oxford: Oxford University Press.
Zinner, Ernst 1990. *Regiomontanus: His Life and Work*, trans. Ezra Brown. Amsterdam: North-Holland.
Zum Brunn, Emilie and Epiney-Burgard, Georgette (eds.) 1989. *Women Mystics in Medieval Europe*. New York: Paragon House.

Index of manuscripts

Aberystwyth, National Library of Wales,
    Peniarth 392 D (*olim* Hengwrt 154)
    215, 229

Bank of Scotland letter book no.
    NRAS945/1/146/44   138
Bute, Library of the Marquess of Bute
    Bute 13   6, 38
    Bute 85   39
    Bute F.16 (*now* Yale University, Beinecke
        Library 660)   141

Cambridge University Library, Reidpath
    MS   212, 217
Cambridge, Magdalene College (Pepys
    Library), Maitland Folio   212, 216,
    217, 218
    O.5.26   41
    O.7.2   41
    R.15.18   47, 49, 53
Cambridge, Trinity College
    R.3.20   215

Edinburgh, Advocates' Library, Bannatyne
    MS   212, 216, 217, 218, 222

Glasgow University Library, Hunter
    409

London, British Library
    Arundel 66   51
    Cotton Cleopatra C.vi   216
    Cotton Cleopatra F.iii   85
    Harley 1612   43

Harley 2320   xxi
Royal 12.B.vi   51
Sloane 6   9, 179, 180, 181, 183, 184, 185,
    186, 188, 189, 190, 191, 192, 193, 194,
    195, 196
Sloane 636   42, 43, 52, 53
London, Royal College of Physicians 384
    47, 49, 52, 53
London, Wellcome Library 510   52, 53

Nara, Japan, Asahata Collection, Asahata
    MS   39

Oxford, Bodleian Library
    Digby 133   55
    Rawlinson liturg. d. 6   49
    Selden supra 77   51
    Tanner 407   6
    Vernon MS (Eng. poet.a.1)   216, 217
Oxford, St John's College 164   41

Paris, Bibliothèque nationale, lat   51
Philadelphia, University of Pennsylvania,
    Schoenberg Center for Electronic Text
    and Image (SCETI)
    ljs 188   39, 40, 45, 47
    ljs 191   39, 47, 48

San Marino, Huntington Library, Ellesmere
    MS (EL 26.C.9)   215, 229

Yale University, Beinecke Library 660 (*olim*
    Bute F.16)   39
York Minster Library, XVI N. 2   51

Index

A Representative Corpus of Historical English Registers (ARCHER), 198
abbreviation, 119, 136, 141
academic writing, 9, 183, 186, 198, 199, 203, 204, 208, 209, 210
Adam Scriveyn, 215
Addison, Joseph, 120
address, 70, 97, 103, 107, 137, 142
  direct, 73–6, 120
  formula, 94
  indirect, 70, 76–8
  pronoun of, 93, 94
  terms of, 9, 23, 93, 97, 98, 163, 168
Agha, Asif, 105
Aleyn/Alleyn/Allen, James, 38, 39
Alkindi, 42
allegory, 55
Allen, Thomas, 57
alliteration, 62, 64, 67
Al-Qabiṣi (Alcabitius), 40
amanuensis, 30, 62, 91, 134, 139
American English, 230, 251
anapaest, 64
Ancrene Riwle, 216
Anglicana. *See* script
annotation, 27, 29, 35, 175, 181
apocryphal gospel, 56
Arabic, 53, 180, 181
archetype, 213, 215
Argentine, John, 50
argumentative, 190, 247, 251
artefact, 5, 35
Arthur. *See* Prince of Wales
Asahata, Shozo, 39
Assize of Bread and Ale, 16, 20, 22
astrolabe, 54
astrologer, 50, 54
astrological
  book, 51
  calculation, 6, 38, 43, 54
  manuscript, 38–54
  prognostication, 44, 53, 54
  reckoning, 42, 43, 47
  table, 45
  treatise, 6, 42, 50, 53, 57
astronomer, 50, 51, 54
astronomical
  calculation, 54
  manuscript, 38–54
  prognostication, 54
  table, 45, 51, 54
  treatise, 6, 38, 50, 54
audience
  author relationship, 6, 25, 27, 28, 29, 30, 33, 34, 35, 36, 62, 67
  construction of, 7, 69–80
  involvement, 6, 34
Austin, J. L., 21
autograph, 118

Bacon, Anne, 111, 112
Bacon, Anne, Lady, 111
Bacon, Nathaniel, 7, 57, 102–17
Bacon, Nicholas, Sir, 104, 108, 109, 110, 111, 113, 115
Bacon, Roger, 56
Bawcutt, Priscilla, 217, 218, 220, 221
Beaufort, Margaret, Lady, Countess of Richmond, 50
Beowulf, 217
Bernard of Gordon, 43
Bible, 67
Bishop of Asaph, 100
blessing, 233, 234, 237, 238, 239
Blomefylde, Myles, 57, 58
Boerio, John Baptist, M.D, 50
Bokenham, Osbern, 6, 27, 32, 33, 34, 35, 36
Bonatus de Foralivio, Guido, 51
Book of Margery Kempe, The, 6, 27, 28–32, 35, 36
Book of the Duchess, The, 150
booklet, 38, 39, 51, 53, 181
Brizdle, Barbara, 38, 39
Brown, Penelope, 92, 93, 94, 95, 242
Burgundio of Pisa, 180
business communication, 8, 140

284

Caie, Graham, 5, 8
calligraphy, 145
Cambre, Piers, 87, 100
Canterbury Tales, The, 4, 10, 150, 215, 229–40
Captain Rock's notice, 88
captatio benevolentiae, 94, 97
Carrier, Martha, 254
Cecil, William, 111, 112, 113, 115
CED. See *Corpus of English Dialogues*
Certaine workes of chirurgerie, 182
change
  diachronic, 162, 199, 203, 204, 210
  discourse, 184
  genre, 24, 134, 203
  spelling, 160, 170
  text function, 21–3
Chaucer, Geoffrey, 4, 8, 10, 53, 54, 149–61, 215, 216, 217, 229–40
Chelmsford, 55
Chelmsford records, 55
Chirkesland, 85, 99, 100
codex, 6, 38–54, 151, 181
codicology, 5
cohesion, 158, 167, 172
  grammatical, 185
  lexical, 167
  social, 231
collation, 213, 215
colophon, 41, 49, 54
communicative
  act, 3, 26, 120
  event, 4
  situation, 4, 5, 9, 106, 221
Company of Barber-Surgeons, 182
conduct book, 103, 106
Congreve, William, 121, 130
Constantinus Africanus, 180
conversation, 4, 5, 10, 26, 29, 30, 31, 34, 69, 74, 75, 76, 80, 107, 123, 146, 167, 171, 198, 201, 202, 203, 212, 230, 231, 233, 234, 239
Cooperative Principle, 140, 145, 241
cooperativeness, 241
corpus linguistics
  historical, 14, 23, 24
Corpus of 19th-century Scottish Correspondence, 133
Corpus of Early English Correspondence, 103
Corpus of Early English Medical Writing, 200
Corpus of English Dialogues (CED), 168, 169, 201
Court of Oyer and Terminer, The, 246
court record, 4, 5
courtroom examination, 241, 246
Craigie, William, Sir, 216, 218, 219, 221, 223

Crichton-Stuart, John, 38
critical edition. *See* edition
Culpeper, Nicholas, 183

da Reggio, Niccolò, 180
Dahlberg, Charles, 151, 152, 158, 159, 160
Dalrymple, David, Sir. *See* Hailes, Lord
David, Alfred, 159, 160
Deykus Vaghan, 90
dialect, 60, 61, 64, 67, 84, 89–91
  continuum, 91
  Early Modern English, 106
  East-Midland, 59
  Kentish, 58
  Middle English, 155
  Midland, 64, 66
  Norfolk, 58
  Northern, 61
  Northumbrian, 60
dialogue, 9, 28, 34, 35, 36, 162, 163, 165, 167, 168, 176, 189, 201, 202, 203, 242, 258
diary, 4
Digby, Kenelm, Sir, 57, 66
diplomatic edition. *See* edition
direct speech, 168, 234, 238, 244
discourse, 5, 16, 23, 25, 27, 30, 64, 66, 68, 72, 73, 102, 103, 109, 163, 177, 198, 219, 238, 239, 243, 246, 258
  devotional, 27
  marker, 238, 239, 241
  religious, 35, 36
  reported, 246
  setting, 243
  situation, 247
  strategies, 10, 257
  studies, 5
  trial, 241
discourse analysis
  historical, 69
discourse grammar, 218, 219
Discretioun in Taking, 9, 212, 217, 220
Dobson, Eric J, 61, 216, 217
domain theory, 102
Donaldson, E. Talbot, 214, 215, 217
drama, 168, 171, 173, 174, 177
  corpus, 168
drama comedy, 168
Dryden, John, 119, 121, 122, 124, 125, 129
Dunbar, William, 9, 212, 217–21, 222, 224, 225
Duranti, Alessandro, 231

Earl of Richmond, 50
Early English Books Online, 129, 166
Early Modern English Medical Texts (EMEMT), 9, 179, 186, 192, 195, 200, 201, 202, 210

286 Index

editing, 10, 184, 212–13, 214, 215, 217, 220, 221, 222
  diplomatic, 216
  text, 5, 9
edition, 5, 8, 10, 15, 41, 50, 56, 88, 136, 149, 150, 151, 152, 155, 157, 158, 159, 161, 182, 183, 184, 195, 211, 212, 213, 214, 215, 216, 218, 221, 241, 243
  critical, 149, 213, 214, 215
  digital, 141, 151
  diplomatic, 216
Education Act of 1870, 162
Edward IV, 50
Edward V, 50
Elizabeth I, 104
Elizabeth, wife of Henry VII, 50
EMEMT. See *Early Modern English Medical Texts*
emendation, 56, 119, 150, 157, 213, 221
English, Peter, 179, 183, 195
Ephemerides, 45, 47, 48, 53, 54

face, 8, 92, 98, 122, 242
  enhancing, 145
  negative, 93, 94, 96, 97, 137, 143
  positive, 94, 95, 96, 121, 135, 137, 140
  self-face, 242, 258
face-threatening act (FTA), 84, 93, 95, 142, 246, 247, 249, 255, 258
facework, 232
facsimile, 39, 149, 150, 217
farewell, 10, 229–40
fiction, 3, 4, 10, 83, 89, 198, 229, 230, 239
figurative expression, 247, 248
flyleaf, 38, 39, 41, 52, 160
foliation, 41, 85
font, 144, 145, 146
form of address. *See* address, terms of

Gale, Thomas, 178–96
Galen of Pergamon, 9, 178–96
Galenism, 195
Galilei, Galileo, 56, 57
gender, 7, 103, 106, 126, 258
genre, 5, 6, 8, 14, 16, 24, 26, 27, 32, 35, 36, 84, 102, 103, 104
  analysis, 5
  change, 24
  conventions, 6, 92
geomancy, 52, 53, 57
Gerard of Cremona, 180, 181
Germanic, 190, 232
gloss, 28, 31, 181, 193, 218
Glyndŵr, Owain, 84, 85, 87, 88, 100
Gothic. *See* script
Greek, 179, 180, 191, 192, 196, 197
Green, Robert, 165
greeting, 4, 10, 94, 134, 229–40
Gresham, Anne, Lady, 111

Gresham, Thomas, Sir, 109, 110, 111, 114
Grey, Reginald
  third Lord of Ruthin, 83–101
Grice's Cooperative Principle. *See* Cooperative Principle
Gruffuth ap Dauid ap Gruffuth, 83–101
guilds, 15, 16, 21, 59

hand, 3, 51, 52, 55, 57, 58, 91, 133, 136, 137, 139, 143, 150, 151, 155, 157, 159, 161, 181
handwriting, 3, 4, 8, 119, 133, 140, 143, 149
handwritten, 4, 5, 7, 8, 9, 13, 133, 135, 136, 139, 143, 144, 145, 146, 149, 161
Hanks, William, 106
Harré, Rom, 102, 105, 106, 213, 222
Hauser, Albert, 232
Helsinki Corpus of English Texts 24
Henry IV, 85, 89
Henry V, 85, 86
Henry VII, 49, 50, 51, 54
Henry VIII, 51
heroic couplet, 124
historical pragmatics, 4, 5, 10, 13, 14, 15, 23
historical sociolinguistics, 5
Historie of Orlando Furioso, The, 165
historiography, 83, 87
holograph, 134, 139
honorifics, 236, 239
Horace, 126, 129
Horobin, Simon, 155, 157, 215, 235, 236
Huber, Magnus, 70, 71, 72, 79
Hunter, William, 161

idiolect, 3, 62
illocution, 92, 230
imperative, 22, 23, 75, 129, 246, 247, 252
incipit, 41, 42, 43, 44, 45, 49, 52
indexical framework, 106
indexicality, 105
inflection, 61, 64, 219
insults, 78, 84, 91, 92, 94, 95, 96, 97, 98, 101, 123, 230, 251, 254
  ad hoc, 92
  creative, 94, 96
  ritual, 92
  rule-governed, 92
  typified, 92
interactant, 4, 105, 106, 107, 109, 115, 139, 167, 239
interaction, 6, 10, 16, 23, 26, 28, 36, 75, 77, 102, 104, 105, 106, 107, 108, 115, 116, 229, 231, 239
  communicative, 62
  courtroom, 5
  polite, 75
  spoken, 10

interjection, 10, 31, 33, 234, 237, 238
interpersonality, 6
intersubjectivity, 70
Introduction to the Art of Astrology, 40

Jucker, Andreas H., 4, 23, 74, 84, 92, 93, 94, 96, 107, 230, 235
Julian of Norwich, 29

Kane, George, 214, 215, 217
Kempe, Margery, 6, 28–32
keyshat, 85, 99
Killingworth, John, 51
Kit Cat Club, 118
Kraus, H. P., 39

Langland, William, 214, 215
Lass, Roger, 56, 61, 213
Latin, 6, 16, 20, 21, 32, 33, 38, 42, 43, 44, 45, 47, 48, 52, 53, 54, 55, 59, 126, 179, 180, 181, 182, 184, 190, 192, 196, 197, 200, 210, 211
Layder, Derek, 102, 115, 117
layout, 3, 8, 27, 163, 212, 218, 219
leave-taking, 232, 233, 234, 238
Lebsanft, Franz, 232
Legenda Aurea, 6, 32
Legends of Holy Women, 27, 32, 36
Lerner, Gene H, 107
letters, 4, 6, 7, 8, 14, 78, 83, 84, 85, 86, 87, 88, 89, 91, 92, 95, 97, 98, 101, 102, 103, 104, 105, 106, 108, 109, 110, 111, 113, 114, 115, 116, 117, 119, 120, 122, 130, 131, 132, 133, 134, 135, 136, 139, 140, 141, 143, 146
  business, 5, 135, 140
  holograph, 139
  personal, 103, 115, 135
  private, 5, 143
Levinson, Stephen C, 92, 93, 94, 95, 105, 107, 242
Lewis of Caerleon, M.D, 50
lexical richness, 9, 167, 168, 171, 172, 177
Liber introductorius ad judicia stellarum, 51
Life of St Anne, 16, 21
Linacre, Thomas, 180, 182, 184
Linguistic Atlas of Late Mediaeval English (LALME), 90
literacy, 3, 6, 14, 24, 25, 27, 35, 36, 100, 182
literary collaborator, 8
literary production, 8, 120
literary text, 5, 8, 26, 163
littera
  cursiva, 58
  notabilior, 185, 218
Longman Spoken and Written English Corpus, 201
Lord Hailes, 218, 219, 220, 221, 224

Mackay Mackenzie, W., 218
manual
  letter-writing, 103, 137, 145
marginalia, 160, 161
Mariensüss, Barholomaeus, 47, 53, 54
Marquess of Bute, 38
Mary II, 118, 120, 122, 126, 127
Mary Magdalene, 6, 55, 56, 57, 58, 59, 60, 61, 62, 63, 64, 65, 67, 68
medical recipe, 6, 14, 16, 44
medical treatise, 181, 197, 200, 211
Medieval Welsh, 91
Megategni, 180
MEMT. See *Middle English Medical Texts*
Messahala, 42
Methodus medendi, 9, 178–96
metre, 65, 126, 158, 215
  iambic, 124
Meyer-Lee, Robert, 229, 239
Middle English, 6, 8, 38, 39, 41, 44, 53, 55, 59, 93, 149, 155, 157, 180, 181, 184, 193, 195, 196, 211, 215, 218, 219, 229, 233, 234, 235, 237
  correspondence, 92
Middle English Compendium, 87
Middle English Dictionary, 61
Middle English Medical Texts (MEMT), 9, 179, 192, 193, 200, 201, 202
Midlands, 90, 91
mise-en-page, 3, 28, 181
mixed-language manuscript, 6, 38–54
modality, 142
Montagu, Charles, 119, 120, 121, 130, 131
morality, 75, 76
Morris, Richard, 216
Mühlhäusler, Peter, 102, 105, 106

name-calling, 92
narrative, 27, 28, 30, 32, 34, 35, 36, 71, 77, 79, 80, 85, 100, 230, 234, 241, 246, 247, 255, 256
  devices, 34
  past tense, 33
  patterns, 241
  sequences, 231
National Library of Scotland, The, 155–7
neologism, 191, 195
New Index of Middle English Verse, 87
nominalisation, 208, 211
Norman Conquest, 59, 61
noun phrase, 189, 198
  modification, 9, 198

Ode in Imitation of Horace, 129
Of Discretioun in Taking, 219
Old Bailey Corpus, 7, 69, 71
Old English, 60, 207, 233

Old French, 59, 232
Older Scots, 9, 212–22
orthography, 60, 61, 91, 180
Oswestry, 85, 100
Oxford English Dictionary, 61, 106, 207, 216

paleography, 181, 217
Palfrey, Simon, 164, 165, 167
parallel versions, 179, 183
paratext, 27, 30, 33, 36
parchment, 3, 32, 38
Park of Brinkiffe, 90, 97
parody, 67
Parron, William, M.D, 50, 51
Paston Letters, 64
Patterson, Lee, 215, 216, 217
Pèlerin de Prusse, 41
penmanship, 145
perlocution, 84, 92, 230
person reference, 7, 102–17
  kinship term, 107, 112
  personal name, 106, 107
  pronoun, 22, 75
personalisation, 134–45
Philosophical Transactions of the Royal Society of London, 201
physical appearance, 8, 135
Piers Plowman, 214, 215
play, 6, 7, 9, 55, 56, 57, 58, 60, 62, 63, 65, 66, 67, 68, 162, 168, 169, 170, 171, 175, 176, 177, 242
  actor, 163, 164, 165, 166, 176, 177
  comedy, 177
  early modern, 164, 167, 168, 169, 170, 171, 175, 176, 177
  performance, 163, 164
  play-text, 5, 9, 162–77
  playwright, 67, 164, 167, 168, 171, 176, 177
  present-day, 167, 168, 176
poem, 8, 9, 10, 14, 16, 18, 21, 22, 43, 118, 119, 120–2, 123, 125, 126, 127, 128, 129, 130, 131, 155, 161, 163, 212, 214, 215, 216, 217, 218, 219, 221, 222, 223, 224, 225
poetry, 5, 126, 130, 217, 220
politeness, 7, 8, 70, 75, 80, 102, 141, 142, 143, 145, 232, 233, 235, 236, 242
  impoliteness, 7, 146, 235, 242
  rituals, 231
  strategies, 91–101, 134, 258
  theory, 84, 242
Powys, John Cowper, 89
pragmatic space, 92
prayer, 6, 14, 238, 251
prepositional phrase, 9, 198, 202, 207, 208, 209, 210
Present-day English, 93, 218, 220, 232, 233, 239

Prince of Wales, Arthur, 7, 50, 84, 85, 86, 87, 99
Prior, Matthew, 8, 118–32
Proceedings of the Old Bailey, 60, 70, 71, 72, 73, 74, 75, 76, 78, 79
prognostication, 14, 16, 18, 22, 42, 44, 53, 54
Promptorium Parvolorum, 58
pronoun, 23, 33, 64, 65, 93, 105, 107, 115
  first person, 103, 108, 109, 189, 198
  personal, 23, 64, 141, 189, 198
  possessive, 116
  second person, 22, 94, 103, 107, 108, 109, 115, 141, 189
  third person, 189, 220
prose, 5, 220
  medical, 197–211
proverb, 6, 14, 221
punctuation, 185, 212–22
Pynson, Richard, 150

question, 66, 74, 103, 166, 189, 231, 241, 246, 247, 249, 250, 252

Radix Mundi, 56, 57
Ramsay, Allan, 218, 219, 220, 221, 223
Rash, Felicity, 231
reader. *See* audience
recipe. *See* medical recipe
reconstruction, 6, 39, 163, 213, 215
Records of the Salem Witch-Hunt, 241, 258
reference
  generic, 206, 207
  person, 7, 102–17
  pronominal, 22, 75
  time, 206
Regiomontanus (Johann Müller), 45, 47, 48, 53, 54
register, 56, 59, 103, 105, 109, 201, 203
  analysis, 5
  formal, 5
  speech related, 109
  spoken, 198
  variation, 203
  written, 109, 198, 199
religious
  discourse, 35, 36
  plays, 59, 62
  writing, 5, 34
Renaissance, 25, 178, 180, 181, 196
Reynes, Robert, 6, 13–24
rhetoric, 27, 35, 108, 110, 115, 119, 120, 171, 182, 190, 220, 250
  stycomythia, 171
rhetorical question, 241
rhetorical resources, 36, 196
rhetorical strategies, 6, 33, 34
rhyme, 61, 89, 125, 152, 158

Index

rhythm, 60, 64, 124
Ritchie, W. Tod, 216, 218, 219, 221, 222
Robinson, F. N., 151
Roman de la Rose, 151, 152, 157
Romaunt of the Rose, 8, 149, 150, 151, 155, 157
Royal College of Physicians, 47, 52, 53, 54, 180
rubric, 41, 42, 44, 45, 48, 202, 218, 219
Ruthin, 85, 89, 90, 91

Sacks, Harvey, 105
Salem Village, 243, 257
Salem Witchcraft Trials, 10, 79, 255–8
salutatio, 94, 97
salutation, 133, 145, 235
sarcasm, 246, 252, 253, 254, 258
Schegloff, Emanuel A., 105, 107
Schipper, Jakob, 221
Schoenberg, Lawrence J., 38, 39, 40, 45, 47
Schöner, Johannes, 40, 45, 47, 53
science, 6, 179, 196, 197, 200, 201, 211, 213
  scholastic, 178
scientific
  knowledge, 6, 9
  manuscript, 38–54
  thought-style, 178
  treatises, 5, 197
  writing, 188, 200
scribal, 7
  error, 56, 62, 63, 155, 161, 181
  inconsistency, 7, 55, 56, 59, 67
  interference, 23, 245
  intervention, 3
  practice, 51, 56–8, 59–62, 91
scribe, 3, 5, 6, 9, 15, 17, 18, 25, 27, 28, 29, 30, 31, 32, 53, 56, 57, 58, 59, 60, 61, 62, 64, 67, 68, 70, 72, 139, 145, 150, 152, 155, 157, 158, 159, 160, 161, 164, 181, 197, 212, 214, 215, 221, 243
script, 35, 36, 41, 42, 43, 44, 47, 51, 174. *See also* hand
  Anglicana, 58, 150
  Gothic, 58
  Secretary, 58
Searle, John, 22, 230
Secretary, *See* script
Shakespeare, William, 9, 163, 171, 222
Shirley, John, 215, 216
Shoemaker, Robert, 69, 72
signature, 38, 39, 97, 145
slander, 92, 95, 96
social
  attitudes, 7
  class, 239
  distance, 94
  hierarchy, 108, 229
  identity, 7, 68
  inferior, 94, 97, 101, 108, 116

network, 8, 13, 15, 131
rank, 7, 103, 104, 113, 236, 239
relations, 102, 177
relationship, 106, 108, 231, 236, 239
role, 105, 133, 134, 143
status, 56, 61, 84, 89, 98, 99, 100, 106, 116, 168, 236
superior, 94, 104
theory, 102
sociopragmatics, 103
South English Legendary, 56
space
  authorial, 28, 31, 35
  discursive, 28, 29, 35, 36
  pragmatic, 92
  textual, 27, 28
speech act, 10, 22, 92, 96, 97, 229, 230, 231, 233, 234, 235, 239
  commissive, 95
  directive, 22
  illocutionary force, 92
  perlocutionary effect, 84
  phatic, 229
spelling, 60, 61, 219, 220, 221
  inconsistent, 61
  innovative, 59, 60, 160, 219
  mistake, 58
  Norfolk, 60
  Northern, 59
  Northumbrian, 60
  Old English, 60
  VARD2, 170
  variation, 60, 65, 119, 169, 195, 219, 220
  Welsh, 90
spoken language, 134. *See also* conversation, dialogue, oral communication
St Anne's Guild, 15, 16, 21, 59
stance, 109, 110, 115, 121, 122, 128, 188, 196
standard, 61, 65, 141, 144, 146
status. *See* social, status
stemma, 213, 214, 215
Stepney, George, 8, 118–32
Stern, Tiffany, 163, 164, 165, 166, 167
Stivers, Tanya, 107, 108, 116
Storia lune, xxi
Stroebe, Klara, 232, 233
style, 57, 98, 108, 114, 122, 168, 187, 188, 191, 201
  discursive, 184, 198, 199
  formal, 30
  friendly, 115, 198
  humiliate, 108
  in medias res, 94
  of drama, 177
  poetical, 62
subjectification, 109
subjectivity, 70

290 Index

surgical texts, 181, 182, 192, 193
Sutherland, Roland, 151, 152
'Swing' letter, 88
Swiss German, 231, 232

Taavitsainen, Irma, 4, 24, 69, 73, 74, 84, 92, 94, 109, 179, 181, 197, 200, 201, 230, 237, 238
tag. *See* annotation
terminology
  medical, 178, 179, 184, 190–5, 196
terms of abuse, 236
terms of endearment, 236, 239
tertium comparationis, 230
text
  composer, 17
  copyist, 17, 61, 137, 139, 140, 214
  functions, 13–24
  structure, 179, 184–8, 195
text(ual) culture, 6, 26, 30, 36
textual history, 5, 55, 163, 180
The Ever Green, 218, 219, 223
Therapeutica, 180
thou, 75, 94, 106
Thynne, Thomas, 161
Thynne, William, 8, 149–61
title
  deferential, 106, 108, 115
  Your Honour, 106
  Your Ladyship, 106
  Your Lordship, 106, 108, 115
  Your Worship, 106
Tonson, Jacob, 8, 118–32
translation, 9, 20, 39, 45, 47, 53, 60, 151, 158, 179, 180, 181, 182, 183, 184, 186, 188, 189, 190, 191, 195, 196, 197, 200
Treatise on the Astrolabe, 42, 53
trial, 10, 110
  Old Bailey, 7, 69–80. See also *Proceedings of Old Bailey*

records, 5
Salem Witchcraft. *See* Salem Witchcraft Trials
turn-taking, 167, 170, 171, 176

VARD2, 170
variation. *See also* dialect, genre, register
  diastratic, 55–68
  diatopic, 55–68
verbal aggression, 92, 98
vernacular texts, 6, 25, 38, 179, 196
vernacularisation, 6, 179
  of medicine, 179, 181, 182, 196, 197
  of science, 197, 200
Vernon, James, 121, 130
Vicary, Thomas, 182
vocative form, 140

Wales, 83, 90, 98, 100, 101
Warren, Michael, 222
watermark, 47, 57, 58
Wele, John, 85, 87, 94, 95, 99, 100
well-wishing, 10, 234, 235
Welsh Uprising (1400–14), 7, 83, 84, 85
Western Samoa, 231
William III, 118, 127, 131
Wilson, Andrew J, 107
Wisdom, 57, 66
witchcraft. *See* Salem Witchcraft Trials
witness
  depositions, 4
  manuscript, 47, 149, 155, 161, 212, 213, 217
wordplay, 252

you, 33, 75, 102, 103, 105, 106, 107, 108, 110, 115

Zeitlyn, David, 107